Baseball's
TOP 100

The Best Individual Seasons of All Time

by
John Benson and Tony Blengino

**DIAMOND
LIBRARY**

Senior Editors: Marc Bowman, Mary Alice Benson, and Larry Michaels
Associate Editors: Bill Gray, Fred Matos, Bill Gilbert, and Lary Bump
Layout and Design: Stephen Wade Lunsford and Brian Weaver

Cover design by Stephen Wade Lunsford
Production layout and concepts by Brian Weaver
Photographic Consultant - Mark Rucker, Transcendental Graphics
Artistic Consultant - John Todd Waterman
Historical Consultant, 19th Century - James Benson
Historical Consultant, Negro Leagues - Lary Bump
Historical Consultant, Joe Wood - Robert K. Wood
Editorial Consultant - Alice Virginia Burgess
Managing Editor - John Benson
Baseball card images - Courtesy the Topps Company, Inc.

Library of Congress Cataloging-in-Publication Data:
Benson, John
Baseball's Top 100 - The Best Individual Season's of All Time
1. Baseball -- United States -- History
2. Baseball -- United States -- Records
I. Title

ISBN 1-880876-01-9

For information address: Diamond Library.

Published by Diamond Library, a division of Diamond Analytics Corporation
with offices at 196 Danbury Road, Wilton, Connecticut, 06897.
Telephone: 203-834-1231.

PRINTED IN THE UNITED STATES OF AMERICA

Dedication

To the living memory of Mickey Mantle
1931 - 1995

WRITERS

David W. Alvarez
John Benson
Tony Blengino
Alan Boodman
Marc Bowman
Lary Bump
Richard Burnham
Greg Gajus
Bill Gilbert
Peter Golenbock
David Gordon
Bill Gray
Bill James
Joey Kusnick
David Luciani
Fred Matos
Joe Nunziata III
Fr. Jerome C. Romanowski
Steven Rubio
David Smith
Brian Weaver
David Wetter
Robert O. Wood

Acknowledgments

From John Benson:

The 23 names on the facing page tell you clearly: this book was a team effort, like so many projects that end up with my name on the cover. This is their book, not mine. Each and every name is so vital, I can't find words to praise their gifts by singling out any of them. My appreciation for all is deep and sincere.

Some of the writers accepted additional roles for which they get extra mention below, and of course there were others who didn't write but were nonetheless indispensable. First and foremost, Tony Blengino's role soared beyond the limits of any attempt to describe it. He was there at the projects's inception, infused energy and insight at every point, accepted writing assignments with gargantuan enthusiasm, and spread his vigor to others.

Brian Weaver was indispensable in a range of duties that encompassed roles from assignments editor in the beginning, to production supervisor at the end. Brian was the most versatile member of the our team. Without him the book could not have been finished.

Marc Bowman made numerous editorial suggestions to maintain a uniformity of dialect while leaving the writers their own distinct voices. This task is longer and more difficult than it sounds when described so briefly. Marc's contribution is the least visible in relation to its magnitude, because his hundreds of little successes all result in something the reader will never notice. Marc also contributed numerous factual improvements and creative direction.

Lary Bump demonstrated his usual editorial expertise and multifaceted capacity to fill gaps deftly and quickly. He was especially valuable in the pinch and had a magical quality of appearing at the most crucial times and delivering the goods with a consistency that can only be described as professional excellence.

Bill Gray personifies the answer to the question that he raised himself in one of the best essays in this volume, describing performance that goes beyond measurement. Bill knows what I mean, and so will you after seeing what he has to say. It's deep.

Stephen Wade Lunsford just keeps getting better and better as Diamond Library's cover designer and layout artist. He's been with us for years, and I honestly don't know what we would do without him, and where I would be now, if Steve hadn't been there for me, so many times. He has the amazing knack of surpassing himself with every project, always glowing with creativity and good-natured enthusiasm that gets me through many of the roughest deadlines, time and time again. Every team should be so lucky as we are to have Steve.

Lawr Michaels was as instrumental as any relief specialist ever brought into a tight game in the ninth inning. His were among the last eyes to see the text proofs before they went to press, and he was a valuable contributor in this vital role, delivering sharp, on-target work in the face of real time pressure.

For photographs, we got immense help from Transcendental Graphics. Mark Rucker went above and beyond the call of duty on numerous occasions as we made repeated demands on his time. In baseball publishing, Mark has a well-deserved and unequaled reputation. His work ethic, joy in excellence, and genius at linking text and photography in a unified art form, must all be experienced first hand to be fully appreciated, yet it's also true that the photographs in this volume speak for themselves.

Some day I would like to write a whole book telling about the many gifts of the people with whom I have come into contact in this wonderful world of baseball writing and analysis. Not having a whole book for that purpose, I can offer only the above brief expressions of appreciation, and conclude with a word of heartfelt thanks to ... James Benson for intellectual curiosity and passionate belief that specters from the past can come alive to delight the minds of youthful fans, and for reminding me of truths like Roger Maris being just as distant as Nap Lajoie for many fans (and the good news that all such cases can be glorified and appreciated no matter how distant); Mary Alice Benson for boundless patience and tireless proofreading; John Todd Waterman for the inspiration that can come only through the eye of a darned smart artist; Dave Smith of Retrosheet for shedding light into dark recesses of the past, restoring life to lost corners from which it had long since departed, and offering historical perspective rarely available in the baseball community today; Dave Gordon for enthusiasm that he spread willingly to others who came into the project; Glen Waggoner for giving valuable counsel that pointed the way toward that light at the end of the tunnel; Pete DeCoursey for contributing his sense of cultural perspective; the Total Baseball organization collectively and individually -- Mike Gershman, Pete Palmer, and John Thorn -- for their unparalleled wisdom, enthusiasm, and generosity in pursuit of truth; and last but not least, Bill James for lighting the way down so many roads in baseball research that it's becoming nearly impossible to find any place he hasn't already probed and left a clear map for the next explorer.

And finally, thanks to my beloved wife Carmelita for standing by me for better or worse, as both came and went through the course of this project.

From Tony Blengino:

First and foremost, I'd like to thank John Benson for giving me the opportunity to co-author this book. The idea came from a discussion about all-time great individual seasons between myself, John and his son James, at the Ballpark in Arlington in June 1994. I really thought I knew a good bit about baseball until I started to work on this book; it has given me a new appreciation for the players, and for the game itself.

I'd like to thank our dedicated crew of writers, especially the group that formed the "Pittsburgh Consensus" -- our final ranking of the top individual seasons. That group consisted of myself, John Benson, Bill Gray, Lary Bump, Bill Gilbert and Fred Matos. Each writer brought a passion for the game that shows in his work. Personally, it is a dream come true to appear in the same book as Bill James, the person whose work transformed me from a baseball fan into a baseball fanatic. I'd like to thank the fine people at the Diamond Library who contributed their typesetting, proofreading and layout design skills; we couldn't have done it without you. I'd like to thank the Society for American Baseball Research, both for improving the general understanding of the game and its nuances, and for providing the appropriate intellectual context in which we could bring this project to its conclusion, at their 1995 national convention in Pittsburgh.

On a personal level, I'd like to thank several people. My mother, Jessie, who seemed to buy me just the right baseball book for each of my birthdays from age five on; my father, Franco, for the complete set of the "Fireside Books of Baseball", which exposed me to the full spectrum of the game at a very young age; my Uncle Elmer, for taking me to virtually all of Steve Carlton's home starts in 1972, when I was nine; my sister Lisa, for showing me the meaning of inner strength; my wife, Kathy, for giving me the latitude to explore this silly little "hobby" of mine; and my children, Jessica and Anthony, for the inspiration always to keep moving forward. And Father Jerome Romanowski, for this amazing trifecta: teaching me to hit the curveball, marrying me and my wife, and agreeing to contribute some essays on his beloved Philadelphia A's.

And for those late, lonely evenings when I found myself at work, I'd like to thank various individuals for their efforts in keeping me awake, people like Pearl Jam, Matthew Sweet, Stone Roses, Jane's Addiction, the Sports Center anchors, and even Beavis and Butthead.

Finally, thanks to baseball: the only sport that can simultaneously be simple enough for small children to understand and enjoy, and complex enough to challenge even the most active minds.

Introduction: Who's the Greatest?
by *John Benson*

People often ask me if a certain player belongs in the Hall of Fame. I have surprisingly little to say about this question -- especially for someone who makes a living doing baseball player evaluations. The problem with any Hall debate is that it's a Hall of Fame, not a hall of skill or a hall of milestones. My simple answer is: if a player was famous, he should get in. The criteria for ''fame'' are soft and elusive, and subject to change. I much prefer to do my thinking (and contending) within a clearly defined context, using objective measures. And having said that fame should be the criterion for the Hall, who am I to debate whether a player was famous? I study performance, not fame. Yet the question keeps arising.

Americans are driven by a relentless desire to classify and rank every person, place and thing imaginable. Every day brings us more lists: the most active stocks, the biggest movers on the NYSE, the best-dressed men and women, the most popular films, places to visit, top colleges, the best small towns, the top 40 recordings, and for sports fans: today's stats and standings and (eventually) this year's batting titles and MVP awards. This endless pursuit of ratings leads, inevitably, to longer lists and lengthier time frames for the classification processes.

Baseball of course has many lists and rankings along the road to the Hall of Fame, and much scholarly literature that lies beyond it. Many books have already been written about the greatest players, the toughest pitchers, the most powerful home run hitters, the strongest teams, and even the smartest managers. Baseball writers and analysts gladly feed the demand for ratings, and they freely offer advice to handle ongoing arguments about their accuracy.

Amazingly, no one has ever before focused an entire book on player greatness defined solely in terms of the single season. I say it's amazing to find this field so largely unexplored, because so many

intelligent observers have glanced at the possibilities (sometimes even proposing lists) and yet moved on to broader, more elusive definitions of greatness, like who really belongs in the Hall of Fame, for their meaty, book-length works.

There is one other big reason to be surprised at the absence of books addressing the question of single-season excellence: The single season is the universal language of baseball performance measurement. The official major league accounting period has created a long trail of meticulously-documented and neatly-packaged feats which are widely accepted as the building blocks in any assessment of player greatness. Talk about a player hitting .400, or reaching 50 homers, and everyone knows you mean one full season, no more, no less. Look up any player in any reference book, and what you get is a series of lines, each line concisely summarizing the results of a single season's effort.

Individual players and single seasons have long been linked in fans' minds. Say ''Roger Maris'' and the astute fan will think immediately of 1961. Say ''1927'' and Babe Ruth (or Lou Gehrig) will come to mind. The year 1968 has become a synonym for pitching dominance -- as reflected in performances of Bob Gibson and Denny McLain and others so effective that the mound had to be lowered. The year 1930 will always be known as the season when the National League tried a more tightly-wound ball and hit a composite .303 (even with the pitchers' at bats included) thus moderating excitement about Hack Wilson's 190 RBI and Bill Terry's .401 average. With these details I am beginning to get ahead of myself, but the point is: it's fitting and natural to think about player greatness in terms of single season marks, because so many of these marks have already been embedded in our memories.

One final benefit of the single-season focus is

that the World Series suddenly becomes an integral part (and the natural climax) of each season, not just a statistical appendage or historical footnote. Not every player in this book made it to the Hall of Fame; some didn't even make it to a World Series, but many did, and their postseason accomplishments are often necessary to complete the definition of what they achieved in their finest years. Mickey Mantle's 18 home runs in the World Series really did count (one of them gave Don Larsen a memorable victory) although such numbers are not included in "official" career statistics. Bringing all these accomplishments into focus, along with all the events leading up to October, is a big part of Baseball's Top 100.

So you may ask me about the Hall of Fame and get a mere shrug; but ask me about which players achieved the highest excellence in their greatest season, and you will get an earful.

This book is about the best individual seasons ever played. It is a salute to excellence: great players in their finest years when they surpassed everyone, including even themselves. In telling about their exploits, we have two goals:

(1) Focusing on the single season links each individual player to his own unique pennant race, team and personal rivalries, pursuit of batting titles, 20-win and 40-homer marks, and all the annual rites that give each season its own unique story line, complete with a clear outcome. These hundred individual stories, delivered in chronological order, present a detailed sketch of baseball history in a highly readable format, more digestible than a collection of career biographies spanning diverse time frames, and with more clarity than any epic history where central come and go repeatedly.

(2) Cutting through the numbers to consider each player within the context of his own time, we rediscover and elevate the stature of some top hitters from years dominated by pitchers, and vice versa. Carl Yastrzemski, Dick Allen, Joe Jackson and Nap Lajoie, for example, all gain luster for offensive stardom through times of pitcher dominance; also gaining appreciation are the likes of Dazzy Vance and Greg Maddux, for pitching shutouts while their peers were serving up hitters' feasts. Other players necessarily faded from view. Bill Terry (the last man before Ted Williams to reach .400) didn't make our top hundred.

Neither did Dutch Leonard, the pitcher with the lowest ERA in the 20th century, nor did the pitcher who (good trivia question) like Bob Gibson, had an ERA under two in the National League in 1968.

A book such as this one could easily have fallen in line with the many "greatest player" volumes that recite the glittering ERA's of the dead ball ERA and the massive batting exploits of the 1930's (and then repeat the same pattern for years like 1968 and 1994). Baseball's Top 100 adds to the reader's knowledge by telling how to get away from the parade of superficial stats and focus more on the reality that each player faced in his finest year.

In telling these hundred stories (I wrote some and edited others) it was inevitable that I would learn a few things. We have new insights from exclusive interviews with some of the players, previously unpublished statistical facts such as what kind of numbers earned Stan Musial his nickname "The Man" while playing against Brooklyn at Ebbets Field in 1948 (and the exact date the name took hold).

Many specific discoveries appear in the player essays, but I can cite a few general themes from personal experience. First and foremost, I was humbled to learn just how much I didn't know about baseball history (thank God for the 23 writers in this volume). It gives me pleasure to think that many readers of this book may have an experience parallel to my own: graduating from self-assurance about what we know, to the higher level of awareness that we don't really know so much, after all. That step was the central hump in my own learning curve in this field where knowledge can come before wisdom. Biting off a hundred years of history all at once can bring a measure of enlightenment to anyone accustomed to digesting baseball one year at a time.

Secondly, this work has added immensely to my appreciation for baseball journalists, especially those of the past. Scrutinizing what was once the standard in this profession, and comparing it to the vastly different genre that often passes for sports journalism in the 1990's, I cannot avoid a sense of regret that the golden era is long gone. Reading game stories over 50 years old and visualizing the plays as clearly as if I had been there just yesterday, I pause and wonder how these virtuoso writers of the past can now be subjected to revisionist criticism for not asking the "tough" questions about salaries and alcohol, etc. They were simply watching the game, reporting what they saw, with beauty in their craft.

As baseball fans, we are both uniquely blessed, and in many ways encumbered, with a mass of data built on the long tradition of detailed record-keeping. For no other team sport would fans routinely attempt, much less enjoy, writing down what every athlete does, play by play, and preserving their notations.

The scoresheet culture has given more than a century to creating daily box scores and building them into annual statistics which are both precise and comprehensive. The record is so complete, and offers so much in the way of pleasure and enlightenment (especially when viewed through discerning eyes like those of Bill James or Pete Palmer) that any observer might be seduced into believing that baseball records and baseball history are somehow synonymous.

The commonest illusions arise in the field of player comparisons and rankings, with which this book is very much concerned. Numbers don't lie, but they can mislead. Any analyst with an agenda can work wonders (proving, for example, that a .275 batting average is actually higher than a .300 average, because of ballpark effects and the strength of opposition pitching) and often as not, such analysts are perfectly correct.

Now guess who comes to the aid of fans who get confused by statistics that aren't what they appear to be? Right: more statisticians! In the baseball analysis business today, there is a growing and regrettable tendency to propose thoroughly quantitative answers for every question, or at least to suggest that a quantitative answer can always be found by collecting more data. Such thinking is akin to believing that improved technology must eventually solve all the world's problems. The human element is forever missing.

All the number-crunching in the world could never create a universal context for comparing all players from all times and places. The more the subject is pursued by fine minds with powerful tools, the more unlikely it seems that anyone will ever come up with a precise catch-all measure for player value. With over a hundred years of history and so many changes, there are just too many unknowns.

Much of what happens on a baseball field cannot be recorded on a scoresheet. How could we even attempt to factor the circumstances of Jackie Robinson's first season into a mathematical formula? We cannot recreate, with any objective measures, the conditions under which Robinson played in. That case is extreme, but the problem is general. We can never know what any athlete was trying to do: slap the ball to get on base, or hit a home run; steal a base, or just tease a pitcher while waiting. Rarely do we know what the manager asked him to do. If a player executes his manager's instructions perfectly, how can say that is a failure, just because the manager had the wrong idea? Lacking any certain knowledge of what each player was trying to do, how can we compare their relative success?

The best analysts understand these limitations and go beyond the numbers, looking into the question of circumstance and into the hearts and minds of the players. James for example is a master explainer and a story-teller who understands that people who buy books are (surprise, surprise) generally people who read books; and these readers tend to be well-informed about their chosen subject matter, and they tend to appreciate good writing. Pete Palmer, likewise, is articulate about the most refined numbers being "just one way of looking at it," and his work benefits immensely from the grandmaster prose of John Thorn. Meanwhile many of James' and Thorn/Palmer's would-be competitors crank out ever-fancier statistics with so-so writing and little or no story-telling; and then they wonder why their books don't sell well, muttering that James isn't such a terrific statistician, never understanding that he is simply one of the great English language writers of the 20th century, and that is why people buy his books.

Having labored extensively at both writing and statistics in the field of baseball, I can tell you that the numbers work is a lot easier than the writing. To all who have written about this wonderful game, I owe heartfelt thanks and gratitude. The profession as a whole has done nobly.

What if all we had was numbers?

On Saturday, September 23, 1995 in the press box at Yankee Stadium, a writer who has seen me there many times, writing about today's newest players, voiced surprise to see me reading a page titled "Duke Snider - 1955." It was the blue line proof for this book. This day featured a rare double header (in which John Wetteland would save both ends, blowing away the Tigers). On the whole it would prove to be a productive day for me as well the Yankees, because I ended up fielding a rather difficult question about this book, got some useful feedback from other writers concerning my personal choices for the best individual seasons ever, and got this sage advice from David Cone between games: "The worst that can happen is that I give my best shot and fail, and that's not so bad," which gave me the final push of confidence to let go of this book, finally.

The difficult question was this: Why don't you just pick up Total Baseball, turn to page 2314, and use the list of all-time single season leaders in Total Player Rating? Or what about using the Bill James Runs Values and Win-Loss percentages for each player for each season and make a list of greatest seasons using that? If Palmer and James both give you "best season" measures, why make another one? The answer is going to take a little working-through, but it builds toward an idea for the future of numbers-based answers about player value, so I'm going to let the answer run a bit long. First, as background, you must understand that I do use the Palmer and James methods. The essays in this book are jammed full of concepts and measures from their work.

There are five reasons why I don't go all the way to that final step of using a numbers-based list of player value, and why I would try to use a different method from what James and Palmer have done, even if my final rankings had to be entirely numbers-based.

(1) The number-crunching without a story-line context is inescapably boring. You can't have a good argument, using just numbers, without first getting into a rather small, esoteric arena where few readers would want to go.

(2) James and Palmer both use runs as the currency of value when looking at players. It is natural to do so, because runs can be converted into wins, and winning is the final answer, as James and Palmer and others have long ago proven.

The problem is simply that not all runs have the same value. James and Palmer both have minor reservations about using runs, and James in particular

verbalizes a concern about his distilled essence of value measurement, the player's offensive winning percentage: that it "artificially constrains the impact" of Babe Ruth's runs on team victories. James chose (perhaps not coincidentally) as an example for this point, the one season of the one player that we chose as the clear best in this book: Ruth in 1920.

Anyone who followed the 1960 World Series can tell you that the linkage of runs to victories isn't 100% direct and isn't 100% reliable. Rather than measure player performance in terms of runs, I would prefer getting directly at player impacts on the probability of winning each game, if I had to use a numbers-based rating system. But first let's examine the best work based on player performance in terms of runs, i.e. James' and Palmer's.

The math necessary to break down various baseball events into pieces of runs can be confusing, but it's got to be done if we are later going to add up the pieces and see what each player was worth in terms of runs created, to use James' term for the value measure. Palmer and James have already explained their work, far above my ability to add or clarify. Anyone interested in this subject has, I hope, already studied their books: The Hidden Game and Total Baseball, by John Thorn and Pete Palmer, and the series of annual Abstracts and the Historical Abstract, by Bill James. Anyone who's read this far and doesn't have those books, take my advice and get them.

The Palmer work moves along lines that end up close to an area that I will explore. He uses two different methods to measure the fractional run value of various offensive and defensive events, and he gets essentially the same answers using both methods. The second of his methods is the one that intrigues me for offering a bright future in value measurement, but I will recap the first method first, because it is the more widely known: linear weights.

For anyone who remembers their calculus, there is a wonderful practical application, using partial derivatives to fit a line by the least squares method in pursuit of the relationship between two or more variables. I am talking, of course, about regression analysis, where you have a list of some independent variables and one suspected dependent variable, and by collecting a large enough sample of cases where you know the values of all these variables, you can detect the average impact of each independent variable on the resulting dependent variable. Gosh that was a mouthful.

Here are two illustrations, one from the business world and then the one from baseball. In business, you may have a factory that manufactures, say, four types of widgets, A, B, C and D, in a labor intensive environment with many workers involved every day in the production of all the widget types, and little or no information about how much time each worker spends on each type of widget. And although you are too cheap to hire a cost accountant who would devise a way to keep track of such things, you do at least generally know your total factory payroll cost each day. The problem, obviously, is that you don't have a clear idea how much it costs to produce each kind of widget. You might want this information for purposes such as knowing what's a good price to charge for type A and type B, etc., and you may want to project your spending budget for next month or next year if customer orders show a coming shift in demand, say a surge in orders for types A and C and with an offsetting drop in B and D. If your factory has been around long enough producing all four types of widgets, and if your records have enough data showing quantities produced for each type of widget and how much you spent in total each week or each month, you can probably get good estimates of the actual individual costs for widget types A, B, C and D by using regression analysis. It works. I've done it. And it beats the heck out of following your workers around all day with a stop watch and a clipboard.

In baseball, regression analysis can be used to calculate the impact of numerous independent variables (walks, singles, doubles, triples, home runs etc.) on the resulting totals of runs scored in all games. And that's exactly what Pete Palmer did and published with John Thorn in The Hidden Game. And they recapped their findings in the latest version of Total Baseball: 0.47 runs for a single, 0.78 runs for a double, 0.30 runs for a stolen base, and so on. Palmer and Thorn call these run values ''linear weights'' which I find a much easier and more descriptive term than the alternative phrase ''regression coefficient'' which I was taught years ago.

Even in the most successful and reliable results, however, there is always a problem in any regression analysis, and the problem is always the data. In business applications such as tracking the total labor costs shared by products A, B, C and D in the same factory, there will be time periods when the factory ceased producing widget type B for a week or a month because of a raw material shortage; and another odd period when everyone worked on type C for a week to fill a vital government contract, and there will be other unsettling events like a strike, or a shutdown for repairs, or even gaps in the labor data when the time clock broke. Through such events, it is nonetheless possible to keep a regression equation running smoothly (remember, we must be working with a long enough time frame, or the results wouldn't be useful anyway, so we want a period when ''everything'' happened, especially if we are going to use our regressions to project future outcomes).

Part of this subject that doesn't get much emphasis in college classes, is the extent to which judgment plays a role in numbers-based problem-solving. For regressions to work, the analyst must make critical decisions about what time frame to use, which data to reject, and where to interpolate. In the real world outside the classroom, the emphasis on intuitive discretion becomes paramount. One key ingredient that separates the master statisticians (and best-paid consultants) from the baby-faced MBA's fresh out of Harvard or Wharton, is the seasoned experts' lengthy experience that allows them to maintain an illusion of authoritative 100% fact-based conclusions, when the reality may be more like a 70/30 mixture of data and judgment. It's not uncommon in elite consulting circles for the few who understand technically what's going on, to get a chuckle about the amazing similarity between the senior guru's statistical answers and the completely intuitive gut-feel guesses of the corporate president who is paying for those answers.

In baseball's pursuit of linear weight values for all offensive events, the usual regression problem rears its head: data with gaps and inconsistencies. The types of events that got recorded in different eras of the game are not all the same. Here and there, from the old days, we may or may not have data concerning sacrifice flies, sacrifice bunts, caught stealing, grounded into double plays, and so on. Other subjective decisions must go into choosing the time frame for the equation.

Finally, in addition to nitpicking gaps in data and calling attention to the much-overlooked significance of judgment, I have another concern: defense. Defensive data collection is not well developed when compared to offense. Ask sabermetric pioneer Pete DeCoursey, who has spent several years on the frontier of knowledge in this field, and he will likely tell you that explorers in this area have only begun to scratch the surface. The information that we have about defense is useful but still less than adequate for a concept like Total Player Rating. And the relative importance of defense in total performance measurement is not at equal among the various field positions, as any baseball man will tell you. For example, a catcher's defense, which includes pitcher handling and game-calling, is more important than defense from an outfielder. It is difficult for me to embrace a Fielding Runs measure suggesting that Duke Snider's mediocre outfield defense was ever more valuable than Roy Campanella's or Yogi Berra's contributions behind the plate.

This discussion of regression analysis is here for two purposes. First, I want readers to see one more reason why this book doesn't rely solely on numbers for catch-all measures of single season performance. Second, I wanted to pay that first method the attention it deserves based on its tradition of usage, before proceeding to the second quantitative method, which in my opinion offers much more in the way of satisfactory statistical measures of player value: the lesser-known but equally important work using base/out situations.

This second method that Palmer and Thorn published, and the one that intrigues me so much for its future possibilities, is the so-called table of base/out situations and the inherent run potential in each situation. There are only 24 base/out situations: no outs with no one on, no outs with a runner on first, etc. These 24 situations have all arisen so many times over the years, that statisticians can say with much precision, both theoretically and practically, how many runs a team can be expected to score in each situation. For example with the bases loaded and no one out, the average outcome is 2.254 runs.

Each time a batter comes to the plate, his performance will in some way change the base/out situation, for better or worse. When he gets done, there may be another out, or there may be another baserunner.

Whatever happens, the change in the inherent run potential can be seen precisely. Add up all these changes resulting from all the plate appearances of any player from one full season or from an entire career, and you get a precise measurement of the player's offensive value. Palmer used the base/out run potential tables to test and validate his results from the linear weights measurement. The results match nicely. And Bill James likes the modeling of before-and-after run potential, using these base/out situation tables, to evaluate offensive performance. He said the method offers great potential, calling it "unquestionably, a major signpost for the future of sabermetrics."

Since everybody likes the method and sees the validity of base/out run potential studies, what's problem? The problem, like I said several paragraphs ago, is that not all runs are the same. When Bobby Thomson hit his home run off Ralph Branca, scoring Clint Hartung and Whitey Lockman ahead of him, those three runs instantly changed the score from a 4-2 ninth-inning deficit to a 5-4 triumph.

We all know, intuitively, that offensive events have different values at different times. A single in the second inning, for a team trailing by five runs, doesn't carry the same offensive weight as a single with the bases loaded and two out in the bottom of the eighth inning for a team down by one run. You may assume that, over the course of a year, or during a player's whole career, these events will average out, but my gut feeling is that they don't all average out. They may average out for some players but not for others, or for some players in some years but not for the same players in other years or for their whole careers.

The individual seasons featured in this book include a preponderance of cases where run-causing events did not average out, and that is part of the reason why they are great seasons.

I wouldn't dwell on this "runs are not all equal" theme unless I was building up to a constructive suggestion. My suggestion is to employ the "tables" method as it was used for run potential in each base/out situation, and look instead at WIN probability in each base/out, run/inning situation. Much evidence is lying right there, waiting to be examined. In fact, Palmer has already created a table showing a team's probability of winning, in every base/out situation in every inning, with run counts ranging from a seven-run lead to a seven-run deficit. [Pete, modest as always, tells me others may have created their own similar tables.]

Since I studied these subjects years ago, either the textbook terminology has improved, or writers like John Thorn have been coming up with better terms than my professors had available to them. We used to call these lovely tables by the somewhat daunting name "Markov chains" or (even more tongue-tying) "Markovian switching matrices."

Whatever you call them, the arithmetic is the same, and I remember being taught something about the use of Markov chains for solving real-world problems: don't make tables of "interim" outcome measures, when you can go after the final answer from the outset. In business, for example, it's a relatively common pitfall to set up tables measuring expected sales revenue outcomes, when what you really want to know is the change in probable profit that results from each change in circumstance. That pitfall is easy to stumble into, because revenue (price times quantity) information is often readily available and highly precise, while profit calculations may be cumbersome and elusive. Also, revenue leads to profit, so it's not a silly surrogate. But they taught me: go after the answer you really want, before building those lengthy Markov chains.

To get an answer to the question of baseball player value, why not use those tables expressing the probability of a win, rather than the expected value of runs to be scored, in each game situation? I asked the one man best qualified to handle such a question [and he really deserves much longer thanks and praise in the acknowledgments of this book]: Pete Palmer. Not only did he know the answer, but he was able to listen to my convoluted statement of the question, grasp it immediately, and give a quick, direct answer: "because we do not have enough data." Pete was not at all negative about using Markov chains to measure directly a player's contribution to the probability of victory, and even walked me through a few examples. Bobby Thomson's Shot Heard 'Round the World lifted his team from 0.30 probability of winning, to

1.00 probability, a gain of 0.70 wins on one swing of the bat -- and in a big game, too (imagine the player value measure if we set up a Markov table for the probability of winning of pennant, as opposed to winning one game; Thomson's swing could be mathematically proven as the biggest hit in history).

The most extreme examples naturally occur in the final inning. A ground slam home run with the bases loaded and two outs in the bottom of the ninth, with a three-run deficit, would lift a team from 0.09 probability of winning to 1.00. An ace reliever getting three outs with bases loaded and none out in the bottom of the ninth with a one-run lead would lift his team from 0.25 probability to 1.00; achieving this 0.75 win improvement with a triple play would be the pitcher's equivalent of that bases-loaded grand slam.

The problem of data being in short supply for such studies of player value is really just a "practical proof" concern for validating the theoretical measures of player contribution to the probability of winning, not a bar to using the theoretical tables now, especially in today's scoresheet culture which gives us more than a decade of baseball history play-by-play, with another 2,268 games of new data coming along each year through the efforts of groups like STATS, Inc. There is no reason why this method of player evaluation couldn't be undertaken right now, if you want another way of looking at players' numbers to assess their value.

Oh, I almost forgot. I promised you five reasons for not using totally mathematical answers to rate the top players. The first two took a long time.

(3) Defense was number three. I mentioned it above but didn't count it yet. I'll quote Bill James, because he stated the case as eloquently as I could ever hope to: defensive evaluations based on sketchy linear weight formulas are not nearly adequate to the difficult task of assessing defensive performance.

(4) I really think postseason play, especially the World Series, needs to be included in the factors worthy of consideration when choosing a player's greatest year.

(5) Using just numbers would have made this book too short, and much less entertaining.

Nap Lajoie - 1901

by David Gordon

G	AB	R	H	2B	3B	HR	RBI	BB	AVG	OBP	SLG	SB
131	544	145	232	48	14	14	125	24	.426	.462	.643	27

There have been many great players in the history of baseball, but very few have ever had a major league team named after them. Cleveland's franchise in the American League has not always been known as the Indians. For a time, they were the Cleveland Naps, named after you-know-who. This rare honor was bestowed upon the player who can rightfully be considered the American League's first superstar.

Lajoie (also known as Larry) was born in 1874 in Woonsocket, Rhode Island. After some semi-pro ball, he made his professional debut in 1896 with Fall River of the New England League. He was leading the league with an impressive .429 batting average when the Philadelphia Phillies bought him. He made his major league debut on August 12, 1896 and immediately began establishing himself as one of the premier players of the era. He batted over .300 every one of his five years in the National League, including marks of .361 in 1897 and .378 in an injury- shortened 1899 season. Lajoie was instrumental in lifting the Phillies from a second division club to a first division club.

In 1901, Ban Johnson converted the American League (formerly the Western League) into a full-fledged competitor in the major league market, with every intention to field a show equal to the National League's product offering. National League teams were raided for players, with Connie Mack luring Lajoie from away the Phillies to join the newly formed cross-town Philadelphia Athletics. The Phillies sued to have Lajoie returned, but a Philadelphia court turned them down in May, 1901, and Lajoie stayed with the Athletics for the 1901 season while the Phillies pressed an appeal through the court system.

Lajoie inaugurated the new league with a remarkable year. His average of .426 tops Hornsby's .424 for the best in the 20th century. He won the Triple Crown by adding 14 homers and 125 RBI. He also led the league in hits, slugging average, total bases, doubles, and runs scored.

Despite this remarkable season, the A's could finish no better than fourth, nine games behind the White Sox. It was the pitching that let them down, as their 4.00 team ERA was well off the pace established by the other teams in the pennant race. Lajoie's great season was slightly tarnished by the notion that the American League in 1901 (and, to some degree in 1902 also) was only nominally a major league. This point remains arguable, but it's a standout fact that no other star lured by the upstart American League did nearly as well as Lajoie did (the next best batting average, for instance, was .347, and Lajoie's 227 hits were 37 more that the runner-up). If Lajoie wasn't facing real major league pitching, everyone else in the American League surely was!

After only one game had been played in the 1902 season, the courts of Pennsylvania ruled that Lajoie should be returned to the Phillies. Rather than return to the Phillies, however, Lajoie stayed away from Philadelphia for six weeks, until manager Connie Mack, realizing how valuable Napoleon was to the fledgling American League, and looking for a way to keep Lajoie in the new league, sold him to the Cleveland Indians. For the remainder of the season, when the Indians traveled to Pennsylvania, Lajoie stayed behind, thus avoiding arrest. The Phillies dropped the matter late in 1902 and Nap was again able to play in Pennsylvania.

Lajoie was such a hit in his shortened season in Cleveland that the team name was changed to the Naps before Opening Day, 1903. Napoleon responded with two more league-leading performances, a .355 average in 1903 and .381 in 1904. In 1904 he also led the league in hits (211), doubles (50), and RBI (102). It was his last season with 100+ RBI. In September, 1904, Manager Bill Armour resigned and Lajoie was named interim manager. The subtitle "interim" was later removed, and for the next five years Lajoie was the player-manager of the team named for him.

On July 1, 1905, Lajoie suffered a spike wound which became badly infected, effectively ending his season as a player. He produced only a .329 average in his 249 at bats, but then rebounded in 1906 with a .355 average, second in the league to George Stone's .358 (it was an all-around career year for Stone). After that, the pressure of managing took its toll, and for two years Lajoie's average dipped below .300. In the second of those two years, 1908, Cleveland was involved in a wild pennant race.

The year 1908 was truly a great one for baseball. In the National League, the Giants lost the pennant when Merkle neglected to touch second base (although there is a lot more to that story). In the American League, four teams battled it out for most of the year, although it came down to Detroit, Cleveland, and Chicago for the final week. On the second to last day of the season, the Naps were eliminated when they lost a heartbreaker to the St. Louis Browns. This was the closest Lajoie got to a pennant, and it was a source of great disappointment to him.

Lajoie rejoined the ranks of the .300 hitters in 1909 with a .324 mark, but that was also the year he resigned as manager. It was not a role in which he was comfortable. He had taken it reluctantly and was glad to be rid of it. Free to concentrate on his playing, he

zoomed to a .384 average in 1910. That was the year that the Chalmers Automobile Company offered a car to the leading batter in each league, and Lajoie and Cobb battled to the end. The race was filled with "official" and "unofficial" averages being reported daily, and many newspapers were in conflict about the facts. At the end of the batting race, the St. Louis Browns somehow let Lajoie bunt his way on seven times in a doubleheader, while the third baseman played way back. Lajoie also tripled once, making an 8-for-8 day. This apparent generosity was attributed to Cobb being so universally disliked and Lajoie so generally well regarded. The hits stood, although the Browns' manager and a coach were both dismissed as a result, at the insistence of league president Ban Johnson. The "official" records eventually showed Cobb the winner by .385 to .384, but cars were awarded to both players as Chalmers was embarrassed to have contributed to such a controversy.

Lajoie had excellent years in 1911 to 1913 (.365, .368, .335), although his 1911 season was shortened to 90 games by a torn leg muscle. He also missed some time in 1912 due to the death of his mother. The Naps were in the pennant race in 1913 until late season injuries did them in.

By 1914, the 39-year-old Lajoie dipped under .300 for only the third time in his career. However, late in the season, he became the third player to reach 3,000 hits (Cap Anson was the first, followed by Honus Wagner just a bit earlier in 1914). In 1915, Lajoie returned to the Philadelphia Athletics after a 12-year absence. It did not take long for the Cleveland team to be renamed (the Blues).

The Athletics had won pennants four of the five previous seasons, but Connie Mack had just sold all his best players rather than enter a bidding war with the new Federal League. The remaining players, with modest salaries, stumbled to a 43-109 last place finish. Lajoie's .280 season was not much help. The next year was even worse, 36-117, the lowest winning percentage of the 20th century (yes, even lower than the 1962 Mets!) -- 54 1/2 games out of first. It was Lajoie's last season in the majors, and he batted a mere .246. However, one season like that didn't detract much from his career. Lajoie finished with a lifetime batting average of .338, 17th all-time.

Lajoie spent 1917 managing and playing for Toronto of the Class AAA International League. His .380 average led the league, and Nap won a long-awaited pennant. A playoff was arranged with Indianapolis of the American Association, and Toronto lost. Lajoie then went over to Indianapolis in 1918 to be their player-manager. That team, renamed the Indianaps in his honor, struggled to field a team, as many players were being enlisted in the army. In late July, baseball was deemed non-essential to the war effort, and most minor leagues, including the American Association, shut down. This abruptly ended the season, and also Lajoie's career.

After retiring as a player, Lajoie went into the tire and rubber business, settling down in Cleveland, Ohio. Later he moved to Florida and lived there until his death in 1959. He was elected to the Hall of Fame in 1937, the second year of voting. When the Hall of Fame building was completed in 1939, Lajoie was formally inducted, and was part of the famous picture of the first inductees.

In addition to his winning skills on the field, Lajoie also had a winning personality. He was always popular with fans, teammates, and writers. His kindly disposition was part of his legacy to the game, gone but not forgotten. During a game in June 1993, when Eddie Murray surpassed Lajoie on the all-time RBI leaders' list, writers in the press box at Shea Stadium began wondering if the tight-lipped Murray might be willing to make a post-game comment. The oldest writer present, one who rarely spoke himself, quipped, "More likely we could get a quote from Lajoie!" The eager-to-please friendliness of a bygone era still hadn't been forgotten.

Cy Young - 1901

by David Gordon

W	L	PCT	G	GS	CG	SV	IP	SO	BB	B/I	ERA
33	10	.767	43	41	38	0	371	158	37	0.97	1.62

Does this man deserve to be the only player to have an award named for him? Well, the mark of 500 wins (511 actually) says a lot. But, you may say, he pitched in the last century, for crying out loud. Didn't a guy named Radbourn win 60 games in one season in the 1800's? Weren't there some strange rules back then? Couldn't anybody in the right situation have won 500 games under those conditions?

First of all, half of Young's playing career was in the 20th century. Secondly, when Radbourn won 60 games (some say 59), he pitched from 50 feet away and had to throw seven balls in order to walk a batter, while Young pitched under today's pitching rules his entire career (except for two and a half seasons where the only difference was in the pitching distance, 55 feet, 6 inches instead of 60 feet, 6 inches). Finally, perhaps anybody could have won 500 in those days, but only one man did. The closest anyone came was 361 wins, even including those hurlers who had advantages similar to Radbourn's. What separated Young from his contemporaries was his longevity. In his day, it was common to work on little rest, but that method took its toll. Most pitchers from 1910 and earlier were effective for 10 or 12 years at the most. Young was effective for more than 20.

Cy (real name Denton True Young) was born in Gilmore, Ohio in 1867. He had pitched a little semi-pro ball when he was invited to spring training in 1890 with Canton of the Tri-State League. He made the squad and posted a modest 15-15 record, but one victory was an 18 strikeout no-hit masterpiece. In early August, the Cleveland Spiders (then of the National League) purchased his contract for a mere $300. It was in Cleveland that he picked up his nickname "Cy." Some sources say it was because of his fastball (or "Cyclone"), others say the name meant a raw farmboy, which he was; they were derisively called "Cyrus" in those days, later, "Rube." At any rate, he posted a 9-7 record for the rest of 1890, and it would be two decades before he failed to win more than 10 games.

The Spiders' first season was 1889, the year before Young arrived. However, with Young on the staff, they finished second three times and third once, in the five years from 1892 to 1896. The closest the Spiders came to a pennant was in 1895 when they finished three games behind the mighty Baltimore Orioles, who had three pennants and two second place finishes in five years.

With the Spiders, Young was piling up the victories. Over a six year span (1891 to 1896), he won 186 (an average of 31 per year) while losing 96 (an average of 16 per year). In five of those six seasons, he pitched over 400 innings, yet never once led the league in innings! In each of the next two seasons (1897 and 1898), Young won 20 games (composite 46-32), but the Spiders finished fifth both years (in a 12 team league). What happened next defies imagination.

After the 1898 season, the owner of the St. Louis Cardinals (Chris Van der Ahe, the Bill Veeck of his time) was forced to sell his team due to financial difficulties. The buyer was Frank Robison, who already owned the Cleveland Spiders. Robison moved all the best Spiders, including Young, to the Cardinals. The Spiders stumbled to a 20-134 finish, the worst record ever. Unfortunately, Robison was unable to build a contender in St. Louis. The Cardinals finished fifth in each of the next two seasons. Young contributed with seasons of 26-16 and 19-19. The latter (1900) was the only year he was held to under 20 wins from 1891 to 1904. By this time, Young had established himself as a premier control artist. In six different seasons, he allowed less than one walk per nine innings, culminating in 1904 when he allowed only 29 walks in 380 innings (0.69 per 9 innings).

In 1901, Ban Johnson declared his American League to be a major league and stocked the teams with players from the established National League. Cy Young, who had been paid the salary cap limit of $2,400, jumped leagues for a $600 raise and landed up in Boston. A new stadium (Huntington Avenue Grounds) greeted the new team, and the inaugural year was a special one for Cy.

Young won the mythical pitching triple crown in 1901, leading the league in wins (33), ERA (1.62), and strikeouts (158). Only 14 pitchers this century have led in all three categories in one year. It was the third of five seasons that Young would lead the league in wins, and the fourth of five seasons in which he would win 30 or more games.

In typical fashion, Young completed 38 of the 41 games he started and walked only 37 in 371 innings (0.897 per 9 innings). Boston was in the thick of the pennant race until late August, when they hit a 5-12 skid and watched the White Sox pull away. Boston finished strong in late September, but it was too little too late, and they ended up four games behind.

Young, now in his mid 30's, continued to excel for the next three years. His composite record for 1902 to 1904 was 86-36, with an ERA slightly over 2.00. In 1903, Boston won the pennant handily, by 15 games over the A's. The two leagues agreed to the first modern World Series, and Boston helped establish the American League by beating the Pirates 5-3 (for four years the series was best 5-of-9 games). In the eight games played, only three relief pitchers were used. Young pitched three complete games (winning two) and relieved in another.

In 1904, the American League saw the first of many great pennant races. It was New York and Boston down to the wire (a classic Yankees and Red Sox chase, although they were known as the Highlanders and the Pilgrims then). The season ended with the two teams squaring off against each other for two doubleheaders in three days, with a day off in between. Young pitched three shutouts down the stretch, including the second game in the first doubleheader. That increased Boston's lead to 1 1/2 games, which meant that New York needed to sweep the final doubleheader. In the first game that day, New York's 41-game winner Jack Chesbro unleashed an infamous wild pitch, leading to the Highlanders ultimate defeat. Thus, Boston and Young won their second pennant in two years. It was to be Cy Young's last pennant-winning season. There would be no World Series that year as the National League champion Giants refused to play the upstart league.

Young pitched four more seasons for Boston. In 1905, the team dropped from first place to mediocrity while Young fell below 20 wins for only the second time since 1890. However, it was the second consecutive season he had 200 or more strikeouts, the only two times in his career. In 1906 the Pilgrims finished last, and it was another disappointing season for Young (13 wins). However, in 1907, he rebounded with a 21-15 mark and was briefly the manager of the team, one of the few pitcher-managers of all time. In 1908, he was 21-11 with a career low ERA of 1.26, all at the age of 41! He is still the only pitcher to win 20 games twice while in his 40's. Also in 1908, he pitched his third no-hitter, a record at the time, since tied by Feller, broken by Koufax (four) and again by Ryan (seven). Young's second no-hitter (in 1904) was in the middle of an incredible 24 inning hitless stretch covering four games (three starts and a relief effort), still a record.

The Pilgrims of 1908 had returned from mediocrity and were on their way up, but Young was the victim of a youth movement. In early 1909, he was traded to the Cleveland Naps (no relation to the Spiders who expired after their ill-fated 1899 season), a team that would later become the Indians.

Young won 19 games in his first season with Cleveland against 15 losses, completing 30 of 34 starts. The Naps struggled to a sixth place finish. The end of the line was approaching. In 1910, he could start only 20 games and finished 7-10, although his ERA was a respectable 2.53. The Indians released him in August, 1911, and he was picked up by the Boston Braves, returning him to the National League after a 10-year absence. In 11 games with Boston, he managed two shutout victories, and one classic matchup against rookie Grover Cleveland Alexander. Young, with 510 victories behind him, gave up just one run on six hits. However, Alexander, with 350 victories ahead of him, pitched his first career one-hitter, a shutout.

It was to be the final season for Young. The Braves finished last, and the 44-year-old pitcher retired to his native Ohio. He was elected to the Hall of Fame in 1937, the second year of elections, and was in the famous picture taken at the opening of the Hall of Fame building in Cooperstown, 1939, along with nine other Hall of Famers. He died of heart failure in 1955 at the age of 88.

Cy Young's record 511 victories is as safe a record as his 750 complete games and 7,356 innings pitched. Would Young have won 500 games pitching today? Of course not. Over his 19 complete seasons, he averaged 40 starts. Today, he would average maybe 33 games a year, and he would not be allowed to complete anywhere near the 92% of his starts that he did, thus resulting in far fewer decisions. Still, with his ability and, equally important, durability, he surely would be among the winningest pitchers of our time, as he was in his own time.

It is fitting and proper that such an esteemed award is named after this much-esteemed athlete.

Ed Delahanty - 1902

by Tony Blengino

G	AB	R	H	2B	3B	HR	RBI	BB	AVG	OBP	SLG	SB
123	473	103	178	43	14	10	93	62	.376	.454	.590	16

The dead ball era was characterized by rubber-armed pitchers throwing every other day, and singles-hitting spray hitters who played one-base-at-a-time baseball. Ed Delahanty was one of the few players from this era who offered a combination of hitting for average, hitting for power, and speed.

After spending most of his career with the middling Philadelphia Phillies, Delahanty was one of the premier stars to jump to the fledgling American League, joining the Washington Senators in 1902. At age 34, he recorded one of the best individual seasons ever. Less than a year later, he was dead, in some of the most bizarre circumstances ever to befall an active major leaguer.

In 1901, the Western League had expanded eastward, becoming baseball's second major league -- the American. League President Ban Johnson knew that it was imperative to legitimize his league from the outset, and this meant raiding the experienced star talent in the National League. Such studs as Nap Lajoie, John McGraw, Jimmy Collins, Joe McGinnity, Clark Griffith and Cy Young had led a group of about thirty National League regulars over to the new league in 1901. Another key piece of the Ban Johnson Strategy was expansion into the nation's capital. He uprooted the manager and several key players of the Kansas City Western League franchise and moved them to Washington in 1901. A year later, the Senators were bolstered by the arrival of Delahanty, who had been lured away from the National League by a hefty salary increase.

In 1902, the American League batted .275, with a modest .331 on base percentage and .369 slugging percentage. Delahanty in '02 was clearly the league's dominant offensive player, leading the league in on base percentage, slugging percentage, and relative production (with a 186 index; OBP + SLG relative to the league, adjusted for park factor, with league average = 100). Delahanty was second in the league in batting average (two points behind Lajoie at .378). He led the Senators in every major offensive category except steals, pacing them to the third highest run total in the league. Unfortunately, their woeful pitching staff allowed 790 runs, the second worst in the league. Only six pitchers took the mound for the Senators in 1902, and all six had ERA's above the league average of 3.57. The team's overall ERA was 4.36. The end result was a poor 61-75 mark, good for only a sixth-place finish, 22 games behind the champion Philadelphia Athletics.

Delahanty had several great seasons in the 1890's for the National League Phillies. Overall, he led his league five times in slugging percentage (1892, 1893, 1896, 1899, in addition to 1902) and doubles (1895-'96, 1899, 1901 and 1902), four times in relative production (1895-'96, 1899, and 1902), three times in RBI (1893, '96 and '99), twice in homers (1893 and 1896) and on base percentage (1895 and 1902), and once each in hits (1899), triples (1892), batting average (1899) and even steals once (1898 with 58).

Delahanty was a force both in power and speed-related categories. He was as complete a hitter as the dead ball era ever produced. He remains high on the all-time career lists in diverse categories. He finished his career with a .346 average (fourth), 522 doubles (25th), 185 triples (13th), a .412 on base percentage (23rd) and a 153 relative production index (23rd).

Delahanty was considered an above-average defensive player in his younger days, but became more one-dimensional by the turn of the century. For all of his efforts, in the old National League and in the new American, Delahanty had never played on a team that finished higher than third place. As the 1902 season ended, it remained reasonable to hope that Delahanty could someday be part of a championship team; he appeared to have several productive seasons left in his career. Unknown to everyone, his career -- and his life -- were both about to end.

It became apparent early in the 1903 season that the Washington Senators would be an even worse team than the year before. They had done nothing to fortify their weak pitching staff; they would again use only six mediocre pitchers, all with ERA's above the league average. To make matters worse, the Senators offense had become less potent, except for Delahanty, who kept hitting well but began wishing fervently that he could jump back to the National League, and join the contending New York Giants. As it became ever more evident that he was destined to remain a lowly Senator, Delahanty indulged in alcohol. Visibly depressed, on various occasions he talked of taking his own life. Still, his mental state did not affect his play; entering July, he was batting .333 with a .388 on base percentage and .436 slugging.

On July 2, 1903, after a series in Detroit, Delahanty boarded a train to Buffalo, with the stated intention of then catching another train for Washington. The conductor on the train out of Detroit later said that Delahanty already appeared to be tipsy when he got on board, and then went on to consume several shots of whiskey, eventually becoming disorderly and threatening some people with a razor. Instead of being turned over to authorities, Delahanty was simply ejected from the train in Bridgeburg, Ontario, just across the Niagara River from Buffalo. In the pitch dark, he began to walk across the International Bridge, and eventually encountered bridge watchman Sam Kingston. The intoxicated Delahanty confronted Kingston, and a scuffle ensued. Precisely what happened next remains a mystery today. According to various accounts by Kingston, Delahanty either fell, jumped or was pushed into the river. Eight days later, Delahanty's body was found.

Ed Delahanty was the oldest of five brothers who played major league baseball. Frank, Joe and Tom all batted less than .240 in short careers. Jim Delahanty was a good hitter, if a poor field infielder, who lasted 15 major league seasons and compiled a .283 career average. "Big Ed" was different: a genuine superstar. He combined power and speed better than any of his contemporaries. He was a top talent in the National League in the 1890's, and appeared to be on his way to another period of stardom in the American League in the 1900's. Hopes of becoming one of the first great stars to spread his career over the two leagues came to an end, however, in the gloom of that hot July night above the Niagara River.

AMERICAN LEAGUE CHAMPIONS

1905

1906

GEORGE EDWARD WADDELL

ATHLETIC BASE BALL TEAM

Rube Waddell - 1902

by David Gordon

W	L	PCT	G	GS	CG	SV	IP	SO	BB	B/I	ERA
24	7	.774	33	27	26	0	276	210	64	1.04	2.05

In the space of 12 months, Rube Waddell made the decision to pitch in the minor leagues rather than the majors, then won 24 major league games, and finally pitched college ball! Such was the state of baseball at the turn of the century.

Rube Waddell never reached his full potential due to his free-spirited nature and his enthusiastic drinking. He was so easily distracted that it was never known for sure if he would even show up at the ballpark. He was fascinated by fire engines, and reportedly missed games on several occasions because he was following one that went by. He loved fishing as much as baseball, and he often lost track of time on his fishing trips, returning days after a scheduled start. And if those distractions didn't get him, the bottle might.

One manager after another lost patience with Waddell. His major league career had a slow beginning, as he played for three major league clubs and several minor league clubs in his first few seasons. Towards the end of 1901, he found himself suspended for the umpteenth time, this time by the Chicago Cubs. He joined a barnstorming team that was headed to the west coast.

Waddell liked Los Angeles so much that he signed with the Los Angeles Looloos for the 1902 season even though the Cubs wanted him back. However, he was the highest paid player in the league and one of the most popular as well, so he chose to stay, and the Cubs eventually released him. Connie Mack, in the second of his fifty seasons as manager/owner of the Philadelphia A's, needed pitching. It took several

weeks of coaxing, an end run around a watchful Looloos manager, and a substantial offer, but in late June, Rube was in Philadelphia.

The Athletics had already played 50 games of a 140 game schedule (although they ended up playing only 137), yet Rube was about to embark upon an amazing season. He started 27 of Philadelphia's last 87 games, completed 26, relieved in six more, and won a total of 24 victories.

Waddell managed to lead the league in strikeouts and finish second in wins despite his abbreviated time in the league. His earned run average was second only to Ed Siever's 1.91 (the league ERA was 3.57). The only time he was relieved after starting a game was once when he was ahead 9-0 after six innings. Every game he started, he pitched to completion.

That first outing, on June 26th, was a poor showing, a 7-3 loss to Baltimore (soon to move to New York and become first the Highlanders, then the Yankees). However, Waddell won his next 10 appearances (three in relief). Connie Mack somehow managed to get him to the ballpark most days, and he was starting every third game.

From late July until late August, Waddell went through a slump during which his record was 3-4 with one game tied. After that, he began a remarkable stretch where he won 11 and lost only twice. The A's entered September with a half game lead on the St. Louis Browns and a full game lead over the Boston

Pilgrims (soon to be Red Sox). Philadelphia then embarked on a 16-game road trip during which they held onto the league lead despite going 8-8. Rube won all but two of those victories, including two relief wins in one doubleheader.

By this time the Browns had faded, and Boston was the only remaining contender. Waddell's next four games were all against the Pilgrims, and he won three of them while the A's won five of seven games against their rival. This streak all but sewed up the pennant and ended Rube's coming-of-age season. With no World Series (the first ever would be played the next year) there were no worlds left for Rube to conquer.

That winter, Stetson University in Florida brought in some University of Illinois ballplayers exclusively to defeat archrival Rollins College. Rollins countered by bringing Rube Waddell to school and signing him up for business courses! This enrollment was after his brilliant 1902 season, and he was every ounce a professional. Apparently, the 1902 equivalent of the NCAA was not too diligent. Nobody at the school could catch Waddell's fastball and sharply breaking curve, so Rollins then went out and got Rube's batterymate, Ossee Schreckengost (a.k.a. Schreck) and signed him up for some courses, too! It is said that Ossee attended classes far more often then the unpredictable Rube.

When Stetson came to play Rollins, they took one look at Waddell and took the next train back! So much for ringers. However, Waddell did see some action against other schools, and it is rumored that on some occasions, he called in his fielders and proceeded to strike out the side (not unlike a display of skill that Satchel Paige later featured). The A's took their cue from Waddell and Schreck and trained that year in nearby Jacksonville, Florida.

The next six years saw Waddell become one of the premier pitchers in the American League. He led in strikeouts all six of those years, including 302 in 1903, and a record 349 in 1904 (broken by Sandy Koufax in 1965). His ERA was a minuscule 1.62 in 1904 (second to Addie Joss' 1.59) and a league leading 1.48 in 1905. During the years 1902 to 1908, he won 150 games (averaging over 21 per year), struck out 1808 in a contact-hitting era (258 per year), had a remarkable composite ERA of 1.96, and pitched 2155 innings (308 per year).

The A's could capture only one other pennant (in addition to 1902) during that span, in 1905. However, in September of that year, the fun-loving Waddell engaged in horseplay with teammate Andy Coakley and injured his left shoulder, thus ending his season and denying him his only opportunity to pitch in the World Series. Christy Mathewson, of the Giants, dominated that fall classic, hurling three shutouts while leading his team to a 4-1 Series victory. After six years of Waddell's antics, Connie Mack sold his 31-year-old star pitcher to the St. Louis Browns. Still in his prime, Waddell had the last of his seven fine seasons, posting a 19-14 mark with 232 strikeouts and a 1.89 ERA. In 1909, despite a 2.57 ERA, Waddell had a losing season (11-14.) The end of the line came in 1910 as he started only two games, relieved in eight others, and was 3-1 when the Browns ran out of patience. He pitched three more seasons in the minors, but soon contracted tuberculosis and passed away in 1914 at the age of 37. In 1946 he was elected to the Hall of Fame.

Mordecai Brown - 1906

by David Gordon

W	L	PCT	G	GS	CG	SV	IP	SO	BB	B/I	ERA
26	6	.813	36	32	27	3	277	144	61	0.94	1.04

Let's set the record straight about the right hand of Mordecai Peter Centennial Brown. It consisted of a fully intact thumb, a stub where an index finger had been (the finger torn in a corn grinder accident at his uncle's farm at age seven), a slightly mangled middle finger (same accident), a fully intact ring finger, and a slightly mangled pinky (line drive through the box). Hence, he was always known as Three Finger, even though his parents named him after an Old Testament figure (Mordecai), a New Testament figure (Peter), and the year he was born (1876, America's Centennial year).

Brown got into baseball through the recommendation of a brother of an umpire-in-training (scouting was not very comprehensive at the turn of the century) and began his professional career with Terre Haute of the Three-I league in 1901. The next year he spent with Omaha, and in 1903 found himself a rookie with the St. Louis Cardinals at the age of 26. His rookie year was lackluster. Despite a 2.60 ERA, he won only 9 games against 13 defeats with a last place team.

Brown got a boost from being traded to the up-and-coming Chicago Cubs after his rookie season. (These were the Cubbies featuring the "Tinkers to Evers to Chance" infield and several other fine players). In his first year with the Cubs, Brown posted an excellent 1.86 ERA with 15 wins against 10 losses. Brown's strength was in his curveball, which had a unique movement due to both Brown's unusual hand and to his fine control, which he had been improving in each successive year. By 1905, his second year with the Cubs, Brown allowed only 1.59 walks per 9 innings

and saw his record improve to 18-12, even though his ERA rose to 2.17. The Cubs played .600 ball in both 1904 and 1905, but fell significantly short of the Giants both years.

1906 was the breakthrough year for the Cubs, and also for Mordecai Brown. The team won an all-time record 116 games, in a 154-game schedule (of which the Cubs played only 152 games). The 116-win mark looks as unreachable as ever now, 90 years after the fact and three decades after expanding the season to the 162-game schedule [and even amid increasingly clamorous reports that small-market cities are unable to field competitive teams; the small markets must have *really* had a salary squeeze in 1906 - ed.]

The Cubs' .763 winning percentage is a major league high. Far behind, in second place on the all-time list, is the Cleveland Indians' team of 1954 at .721. The 1906 Cubs hitters were not extremely impressive, despite a league-leading team batting average of .262. It was the pitching that made the Cubs. Their team ERA was an amazing 1.76! They were the best-pitching team in the best-pitching era. Only six times since 1900 has a team finished with an ERA under 2.00, and the Cubs did it three times, in 1906, 1907 (with a league record 1.73), and 1909. The top three pitchers in the league in ERA were all Cubs and four of the five leaders in winning percentage were Cubs.

What about the 1906 pennant race? The second place New York Giants finished a distant 20 games behind. The race was more challenging than the end result

indicates. The Cubs did not take over first place for good until May 28th, and led by only 2 1/2 games on July 3rd. A month later, August 4th, the lead was only 4 1/2 games and it was still a race. However, the Cubs then won 37 of their next 39 games to settle the pennant question.

Stated mildly, Brown had a glorious year. His 1.04 ERA is the second best ever; only Dutch Leonard's 1.01 in 1914 was better. Brown completed all but five of his 32 starts, and he led the league with 10 shutouts.

The World Series was disappointing for the Cubs. They faced the crosstown rival White Sox, whose 93 wins would have tied for a distant third in the NL. Brown lost the first game, in snow-flurry weather, despite giving up just two runs on four hits. The next two games were split, and then Brown outdueled Nick Altrock 1-0 with a two-hitter in game four, to even the series. At that point, Cub hurlers had given up a mere six runs on 11 hits in four games. The pitching finally gave way in games five and six as the White Sox scored eight runs in each game to take the series. Brown was the victim in game six, allowing seven runs in 1 2/3 innings. He was working on just one day's rest.

For six seasons Brown was virtually unhittable. From 1906 through 1911, his *average* record was 25-9 and his composite ERA was 1.63 for the six years. During this stretch, the Cubs won pennants in 1906, 1907, 1908, and 1910. They won over 100 games four out of five years from 1906 to 1910, with an all-time best .693 winning percentage over the five year span. The Cubs also set the ten-year record for winning percentage, for the span 1903-1912.

The 1907 and '08 World Series were lopsided contests. The Cubs defeated Cobb's Tigers both times, and the Tigers could muster only one victory in the two years. In 1907, the Cubs gave up only six runs on 36 hits in the five games (a 4-0 sweep with one tie). Brown pitched in only one game that year, the finale, in which he finished his season with a flourish, a seven hit shutout. In 1908, Brown pitched two scoreless innings

in relief in the first game of the series and got credit for the win when the Cubs scored five times in the top of the ninth. He then hurled a shutout in game four to put the Cubs up 3-1. Another shutout the next day by Orval Overall closed out the Tigers. In 1910, the A's needed just two pitchers (Jack Coombs and Chief Bender) to defeat the Cubs, four games to one. Brown was ineffective and lost his two starts, although he did pick up the lone Cub victory with two shutout innings in game four.

In 1912 an injury limited Brown to just 15 appearances. He was never the same again. In 1913, he found himself with the Cincinnati Reds, pitching mostly in relief. Despite a respectable 2.91 ERA, he had a losing record, 11-12. At age 37 and with his best years behind him, Brown was lured by the upstart Federal League in 1914. Pitching first for St. Louis and then for Brooklyn, he had a nondescript year, going 14-11 with a 3.52 ERA. However, in 1915, back in Chicago with the Whales, Brown had one last fling at glory. He posted a 17-8 record for the pennant winners with a 2.09 ERA, a tainted pennant though it was. Here are the strange final standings for the Federal League in 1915:

Chicago	86	66	.566	-
St. Louis	87	67	.565	-
Pittsburgh	86	67	.562	1/2

When the Federal League disbanded, Brown went back to the Cubs for the 1916 season. The only highlight was one more duel with long-time rival Christy Mathewson (they faced each other 25 times over their respective careers, with the Cubs winning 13 and the Giants 12). Both pitchers struggled, and the score ended up 10-8 in favor of the Cubs. Both hurlers retired at the end of the year.

Brown spent his post-baseball years in Terre Haute, Indiana, where he had first played professionally. He operated a garage. Brown died in 1948 at age 71, just one year before he was posthumously inducted into the Hall of Fame.

Christy Mathewson - 1908

by Brian Weaver

W	L	PCT	G	GS	CG	SV	IP	SO	BB	B/I	ERA
37	11	.771	56	44	34	5	390	259	42	0.83	1.43

Christy Mathewson was one of the five players voted into the Hall of Fame in the initial balloting in 1936. The other four have planted mental pictures in the memories of millions of baseball fans: Babe Ruth, Ty Cobb, Walter Johnson, Honus Wagner. For lots of good reasons, Mathewson also was and is a memorable character.

On the field, he won 373 games, tying Pete Alexander for the National League career record. Some contemporaries said Mathewson was too soft for the stereotyped rough life of pro ball right after the turn of the century. He refused to throw at batters, a common practice during that time, because he said he was confident he could get them out without throwing beanballs. The Giants' star righthander's reputation for honesty was so great that umpires sometimes asked his opinion on close plays, while he was playing for one of the teams!

Those qualities carried on beyond the field of play. Mathewson was outspoken about the influence of gamblers on the game during the teens. He was one of the first to suggest that the White Sox might have thrown the 1919 World Series. Even before that, he was among the first to contend that the nefarious Hal Chase should have been thrown out of baseball.

Beyond the gentlemanly personality, he was as recognizable as a player could be in those primitive days before mass media. He had matinee-idol looks. College educated at Bucknell after growing up in a comfortable suburban home in Pennsylvania, he provided a graphic contrast to his long-time manager, the sometimes crude John McGraw. Mathewson was so highly regarded that he was the upstanding model for the "Baseball Joe" novel series. In 1912, a highly regarded instructional volume, "Pitching in a Pinch," was published under his byline.

He and ghostwriter John Wheeler had plenty to write about. Mathewson threw a variety of pitches: a slowball, several different curves, a spitball (legal in those days), a fastball, and his devastating, trademark "fadeaway." That pitch, delivered with a reverse wrist twist so it broke in on righthanded batters and fell away from lefties, is known today as a screwball. Mathewson also had success as a hitter, knocking 362 career hits including seven home runs.

Mathewson became a tragic hero. During the first World War, he inhaled poison gas, which contributed to his death from tuberculosis nine years later at the age of 45. After serving in the war, he didn't pitch again, ending his career at age 36 after 17 seasons. He did manage the Reds for three years (1916-1918, finishing no higher than fourth), and was the Giants' general manager when he died.

Above all, Mathewson was a great pitcher, even among his peers in a pitching-dominated era. The Cy Young Award wasn't initiated until 1956, but the Society for American Baseball Research later conducted retroactive balloting to determine the top pitcher of each year before '56. The results, wrote Lyle Spatz, indicated that Mathewson would have won seven Cy Young Awards, including four in a row from 1907 to 1910.

The first of Mathewson's thirteen 20-win seasons was 1901, his second year in the majors. He won 30 or more games in three consecutive seasons (1903-1905), a feat matched only by Alexander. Mathewson may be most famous for his three shutout wins in a period of six days in the Giants' 1905 World Series triumph over the Athletics. In 27 innings pitched, he allowed just 14 hits and one walk.

There were many great years for Matty, but his best was 1908. It was a year of nail-biting races in both leagues, with three teams all within 1 1/2 games of the lead at season's end. He dominated the National League as never before, leading its pitchers in wins, ERA, innings pitched, games pitched, complete games, strikeouts, shutouts (11) and fewest walks per nine innings (0.97). Statistics determined in later years show that he also had tied for the lead in saves. He also was among the top three in winning percentage, fewest hits per nine innings (6.57) and most strikeouts per nine innings (5.97). His contribution kept the Giants in the race even beyond the final day on the schedule.

Too good to be true? Almost. Mathewson's most marvelous season had an unhappy ending. The single most memorable event of that memorable season came on September 23, when the Cubs, tied with the Giants, visited the Polo Grounds for a critical game. That was the game of the famous "Merkle Boner," when rookie Fred Merkle failed to touch second base after an apparent game-winning hit by Al Bridwell, and Hall-of-Fame second baseman Johnny Evers managed to get both the ball and umpire Hank O'Day's attention to turn the play into a forceout. Amid on-field crowds and confusion, darkness set in, ending the game. A week later, National League president Harry Pulliam ruled that the game was indeed a tie, which would have to be made up if it affected the pennant race.

The tie certainly did affect the race. The regular season ended with the Cubs and Giants tied for first, half a game ahead of the Pirates. But they would have to make up for that tie game. So on October 8th, Mathewson took his 37-10 record to the mound for his 56th appearance.

For once that year, he didn't have it. The Giants went ahead 1-0, but in the third inning, the Cubs reached Mathewson for four runs. Another Hall-of-Famer, Mordecai "Three Finger" Brown, entered the game in relief and stopped New York to give Chicago its third consecutive pennant. For the second year in a row, the Cubs went on to beat the Tigers in the World Series. Those remain the Cubs' only two world titles. Enduring as long as the Cubs' futility are Mathewson's all-time Giants' records: most 20-win seasons; most career wins, shutouts (79), complete games (433), strikeouts (2,499) and innings pitched (4,771 2/3), most strikeouts in a season (267) and game (16). He also is the all-time leader in World Series complete games (10) and shutouts (4).

It's easy to compare Mathewson with the two other most dominant pitchers of his time. Between 1904 and 1912, the Cubs and Giants waged vigorous battles at the top of the league. Each won four pennants in that nine-year period. Mathewson's battles with the Cubs' Brown mirrored that team rivalry. Like the Cubs, who were 26 games better than the Giants during those nine seasons, Brown had a slight advantage over Mathewson in head-to-head matchups, with Chicago winning 13 of the 25 games.

By the end of that period, Alexander too had emerged as an ace. Between 1911 and 1914, Mathewson won 98 games to Alexander's 96, but Old Pete won 31 percent of the Phillies' games. With a better supporting cast, Mathewson's victories represented "only" 25 percent of the Giants' total. Mathewson versus Brown and Mathewson versus Alexander: these were rivalries for the ages.

Honus Wagner - 1908

by Greg Gajus

G	AB	R	H	2B	3B	HR	RBI	BB	AVG	OBP	SLG	SB
151	568	100	201	39	19	10	109	54	.354	.410	.542	53

"He was the best third baseman in the league, the best shortstop, the best outfielder, the best second baseman, and the best first baseman. That was in fielding. Since he led the league in hitting eight times between 1900 and 1911, you knew he was the best hitter, too."

-- Tommy Leach on Honus Wagner

The problem with Honus Wagner's reputation among the general baseball public (besides the fact that he played 90 years ago and not many of his original fans remain in the general baseball public) is the same problem all multi-faceted players have -- that of having no single statistical hook that offers a memory key. In fact, for many casual fans (even in his own time) Wagner's hook was that he was funny looking. Somehow the fact that he could be the greatest player of all time (any time, any position) has been lost.

Who considered Honus Wagner the greatest player ever? Authorities like John McGraw, Branch Rickey, and Ed Barrow (all of whom saw Babe Ruth and Ty Cobb, and Rickey also saw Willie Mays and Hank Aaron) all cited Wagner as the first player they would want. Analyst Craig Wright makes a very interesting case for Wagner as the greatest player of all time in his gem *The Diamond Appraised*. Bill James ranked him second greatest of all time in the *Historical Baseball Abstract* for both peak and career value (behind Ruth) but in the text considered him the first player he would want, although others may have better-looking statistics. Like the other greatest players of all time, picking Wagner's best year is a real challenge (he had

four years of leading the league in batting average, slugging average, and on base percentage).

For true dominance, and for carrying his team, I agree with Craig Wright's assessment that 1908 was Wagner's best year. He led the league in the following categories: hits, doubles (by nine over the next man), triples, total bases (by 40), RBI, batting average (by 20 points), on base percentage, slugging average (by a staggering 100 points), and steals. He was second in runs (by just one) and home runs (by two). Defensively, he was among the best shortstops in the league, although he didn't start playing the position full time until he was 29. The 1908 season featured the famous Giants/Cubs pennant race, but what is forgotten is that Wagner's Pirates were in contention the entire season, and only a last game loss to the Cubs kept them from the pennant (and thus set up the playoff game).

Let's compare the competition in the 1908 race. The Cubs were the dominant team in the league (this was a long time ago), having won the league title in 1906 by 20 games and in 1907 by 17 games. They featured four Hall of Famers and just missed leading the league in runs scored. The Giants featured Christy Mathewson at his peak, and led the league in runs scored. The Pirates didn't have many assets other than a good pitching staff and Wagner. Based on runs scored and allowed, the Pirates had no business being in the race (the Giants should have won), but instead they ended up one game behind the eventual World Champion Cubs (as I said, it was a long time ago).

Wagner had five years nearly comparable to his 1908 season. In 1900 he led the league in average and slugging, and turned in a total of 71 extra base hits, remarkable for the dead ball era. In 1904, 1907, and 1909 he repeated his sweep of the batting, slugging, and on base crowns. In 1909 his team won the World Series over Ty Cobb's Tigers, and in that Series the 35-year-old Wagner clearly outplayed the 23-year-old Cobb. (Wagner: a .333 average with four walks, six stolen bases, six RBI, and four runs; Cobb: a .231 average with two walks, two stolen bases, five RBI, and three runs.)

Why doesn't Wagner have the reputation of a Ruth, or even a Cobb? First of all, he was a modest, quiet player who did not seek media attention, which in his time was still a relatively undeveloped form in American culture. *Total Baseball* suggested that Wagner would have won six MVP awards had such a prize existed in his time.

Wagner did not even play professional baseball until age 21, and he was 26 when he started with the Pirates in 1900. The bulk of his career came after what would now be considered his prime age. Had Wagner come along just a few years later, when baseball was more organized, he probably would have added three or four seasons to his already remarkable career.

The second reason for Wagner's lack of lasting fame is that he played his entire career in the dead ball era. The incredible stats of Wagner's 1908 season were produced in an environment where the league ERA was 2.35. His .354 average in 1908 would be the equivalent of .391 in the National League of 1993. Tony Gwynn with power and speed, leading the league in RBI and playing shortstop like Ozzie Smith in his prime would be a good idea of what Wagner was like as a player.

Third, Wagner is generally lumped into late 20th century thinking with "all those guys who played before Ruth." Wagner was the greatest player whose entire career was inside the dead ball era. Cobb played nearly a third of his career after 1920. Compared to anyone in the live ball era, Wagner's stats don't seem that impressive. But he dominated his time in a manner that was matched only by Ruth and Cobb in their time frames.

Based on the available contemporary evidence, Wagner's contribution to the team off the field was equal to his contribution on the field. In contrast to most players of his time, he was patient and helpful with rookies, and was never a disruptive influence. He stayed in shape and played aggressively at every position he was asked to play (which was every position except pitcher and catcher). He never held out on a contract or had any difficulty with ownership or management.

If I had to choose between Cobb and Wagner, it would be easy to pass up a spectacular hitting but mentally unusual center fielder, who hated his teammates. I would pick the greatest shortstop ever, a man who loved his teammates and was loved by them in return.

Eddie Collins - 1910

By Bill Gray

G	AB	R	H	2B	3B	HR	RBI	BB	SO	AVG	OBP	SLG	SB
153	583	81	188	16	15	3	81	49	NA	.322	.381	.417	81

In any discussion about the greatest second baseman of all time, the name Eddie Collins will inevitably be introduced, usually by someone who appreciates the more cerebral aspects of the game. Collins was a defensive genius and a fine hitter who combined blazing speed with baseball "smarts" to perform at a high level well into his late thirties. Collins' strong suit was his base running. He stole 744 bases in his career, second only to Ty Cobb in the same era, and currently the fourth best record of all time.

Cobb had entered the majors in 1905 at age 18. Collins also arrived at age 18, a year later in 1906 (using an assumed name at first, because he was still enrolled in Columbia University and was violating collegiate sports rules). From that point, the careers of Cobb and Collins while certainly not identical, had a similar pattern. If you look at the two as automobiles, you might conclude that Ty Cobb was the Shelby Cobra of his day, and Collins the Corvette. The Cobra was wildly powerful, mercurial and savagely effective. The Corvette, it's valiant adversary, was innately destined to remain about a level below the Cobra, but impressive in it's own right. Ty Cobra and Eddie Corvette.

Collins honed his skills in his first two years with Connie Mack's Philadelphia A's. By 1908 he emerged as a bonafide star and as a member of Mack's 1909 "$100,000 Infield" (so named because Mack would not accept an offer of $100,000 for Collins, Frank Baker, Jack Barry and Stuffy McInnis). Despite the attachment to his infield, the bigger picture is that

Mack never met a star player he didn't want to sell. Predictably, when Collins was at the peak of his career, Mack sold him to the White Sox before the 1915 season, for $50,000.

In 1910, Collins and the Athletics blossomed together. Philadelphia became one of baseball's all-time great teams. They won 102 games while losing only 48 times. The Athletics stood far atop the American League, winning the pennant by a margin of 14 1/2 games over second place New York.

Collins was a devastating force on both offense and defense. His league-leading total of 81 stolen bases left Cobb third in 1910, with 65. In the World Series, Collins hit .429 and stole four bases as the Athletics pummeled the Chicago Cubs and won in five games. The A's won again in 1911 and 1913, with Collins giving standout performances.

In 1914 the mighty Athletics were stunned by Boston's "Miracle" Braves in a four game sweep. Collins had a fine regular season, hitting .344 with 58 steals, but he batted only .214 in the series. A major distraction for Major League Baseball arrived in 1914, in the form of The Federal League. This new league lasted only two years, but it got off the ground well enough to entice a number of players into jumping, and a number of others considered their options. Mack, fearing he might lose Collins to the Federal League for nothing, decided to sell him to the White Sox for $50,000. Collins reported to Chicago and was instrumental in turning the franchise into a contender.

Charles Comiskey not only shelled out the $50,000 to buy his new star; he also granted Collins a fat new contract to keep him happy and away from the Federal League. In furtherance of the latter purpose, Collins' contract covered a five-year term, an extremely rare condition in those times. Jealousy in the White Sox clubhouse lasted well into the 1919 season, intensified by the players' dissatisfaction with Comiskey's general tightness in financial matters. Collins' precious skills, and the contract reflecting ownership's appreciation of them, were thus ironically linked to the 1919 World Series Black Sox scandal.

The essence of Eddie Collins was consistency: throughout his career he proved himself to be one of the most consistent players ever. That is his greatness. Collins hit under .300 only two times during the years 1909 to 1928 (he became the White Sox manager in 1925). In 1917 Collins hit .289, and in 1918 he dipped to .276, but for anyone preparing to write about the end of his star period, he put a long hold on that story by coming back in 1920 to hit .329 for the Sox. From 1920 through 1927, Collins never batted below .324.

In 1927 Collins' returned to the Athletics. He was nearly 40 years old, but still played in 95 games and hit .336 in 226 at bats. He appeared in pinch hitting situations through the 1930 season. The eyes, hands, and knowledge of pitchers kept him going. Collins other big asset, speed, also stayed with him late into his career. In 1924, Collins at age 37 stole 42 bases.

Yes, Eddie Corvette was still running pretty well in 1927. But he was still no Ty Cobb. In 1927, at the end of their careers, Cobb joined Collins on the Philadelphia roster. Through their careers, anything Eddie could do, Ty could do better.

Eddie Corvette, versus Ty Cobra: the result never changed. But it was a beautiful race.

Ty Cobb - 1911

by Tony Blengino

G	AB	R	H	2B	3B	HR	RBI	BB	AVG	OBP	SLG	SB
146	591	147	248	47	24	8	127	44	.420	.467	.621	83

Today Ty Cobb is perceived as a rough-tempered, base-stealing, singles-hitting dynamo, a Pete Rose type with the aggressive speed of Rickey Henderson. While such characterizations of Cobb's demeanor and foot speed are right on the money, it is an error to describe Cobb as a mere "singles hitter." Cobb was the premier power hitter of the dead ball era, batting cleanup for a strong Tiger club whose lineup included fellow Hall-of-Famer Sam Crawford. Cobb's all-around offensive dominance was never more evident than in 1911, when he posted an array of statistics that will never be matched. First, let's put the 1911 season into proper perspective.

The American League in 1911 batted .273, with a .338 on base percentage and a .358 slugging average. The entire league combined to hit only 198 homers. League-leader Frank 'Home Run' Baker notched only 11 dingers. Within this context, Tyrus Raymond Cobb, then only 24, led the AL in batting average (.420), runs scored (147), hits (248), and stolen bases (83), all categories normally associated with Cobb, and he also led the AL in doubles (47), triples (24), RBI (127), slugging percentage (.621), and relative production (193). He also finished second in homers (8), and on base percentage .467 (just behind Joe Jackson's .468). Though these high rankings in the power categories may surprise some, they were hardly unusual; 1911 was the fifth of six consecutive seasons that Cobb led the AL in slugging percentage. Only a couple of guys, named Babe Ruth and Ted Williams, ever matched that streak. Quite simply, Cobb's 1911 season was just as dominating as say,

Ruth's 1929 season (46 homers) or Williams' 1947 season (32 homers) *relative to the league*. Cobb hit 4% of the league's homers in 1911; to match that feat in a recent year, like 1992 in the AL, one would have had to hit 71 homers. Even after adjusting for the number of teams in the league, Cobb's 1911 home run output equates to a 40+ homer season in 1992 and more in the post-expansion power bonanza.

The 1911 Tigers finished in second place with an 89-65 record, 13 1/2 games behind Connie Mack's Athletics team which featured Hall-of-Famers Eddie Collins, Frank Baker, Eddie Plank and Chief Bender. Besides Cobb, Crawford (.378, 115 RBI, 37 stolen bases) and first baseman Jim Delahanty (.339, 94 RBI), the Tigers could muster precious little offense to support their mediocre pitching staff led by veterans George Mullin (18-10), Ed Willett (13-14), and a fading Wild Bill Donovan (10-9). Tiger fans, however, were far from worried. After all, their franchise player was a mere lad of 24, and had already led his club to three consecutive World Series appearances (all losses) from 1907-09. There certainly would be many more chances.

The 1907 Tigers were embarrassed in four straight games (plus a tie) against the mighty Cubs. Cobb managed only four hits in 20 at bats against the vaunted Chicago staff which held the Tigers to six runs in five games. The two clubs had a rematch in the 1908 World Series, and the Cubs again prevailed decisively, four games to one. Cobb played much better in the 1908 series, batting .368 (7 for 19) with a series-high four RBI. The Cubs were bested by the Pirates, coming off a 110-46 season for NL honors in 1909, and the Bucs continued the NL's World Series dominance over the Tigers, beating them four games to three in a highly competitive series. The pitching of Babe Adams (three complete game victories) proved too much for the Tigers, as Cobb struggled to a .231 average for the series. No one knew it at the time, but at age 22, Cobb had played his last postseason game. There were several more second place finishes to come, but no more championships.

With or without the postseason glory, Cobb's career totals are something to behold. His .366 career batting average and 2,246 runs scored are all-time major league highs. For his line drive hitting and on-base skills, Cobb ranks near the top in hits (4,189, second), doubles (724, fourth), triples (295, second), on base percentage (.433, seventh), and he also stands high in power-reflecting categories like RBI (1,937, fifth), slugging percentage (.512, 34th), and relative production (167, 8th).

Relative production is an excellent measure of batting ability. The only modern players with career marks higher than Cobb were Ruth, Williams, Lou Gehrig, Rogers Hornsby, Mickey Mantle and Joe Jackson. The length of Cobb's career and his extraordinary speed are enough to fill the gap between Cobb and those other players (except for Ruth and Williams) for total career accomplishments. Cobb led the AL ten times in relative production and batting average, eight times in hits and slugging percentage, six times in on base percentage and stolen bases, five times in runs scored, four times in triples and RBI, three times in doubles, and once in homers.

This was no "singles hitter." This was a man whose power was stifled by his home park; he managed only 36 homers at home versus 81 on the road in his career. This was a man who once hit three homers in a game in which he went 6-for-6 with 16 total bases. This was a man who hit a tape measure homer into the streets of Philadelphia in a pivotal game in the 1907 pennant race. When it came time to choose the charter members of the Hall of Fame, Cobb received the most votes, even more than Babe Ruth.

This book concentrates primarily on the on-field exploits of the game's all-time greats, but any essay on Cobb must address some aspects of his much-troubled, paradoxical life away from the field. Cobb was the son of a respected college professor, politician and community leader. Cobb worshiped his father, the only man on earth he feared. His father opposed his involvement in baseball, wishing instead that his precocious son would become a doctor. Tragedy struck in 1905, when in the same week Cobb made the major leagues, his father was shot dead. Apparently, Mrs. Cobb mistook him for a burglar as he climbed a ladder into their bedroom. The feisty Cobb, a rookie who was being hazed and abused by his much older, bigger Tiger teammates at the time, kept the horrible news to himself, and let it swell into a rage that would consume him for the rest of his life. This rage drove him to become the best, but least-liked, player of his day.

The tug of war between the good Cobb and the bad Cobb was fascinating. He was a very early investor in the Coca Cola Bottling Company, which made him a multimillionaire at a relatively young age. He created the Cobb Educational Fund to provide a college education for poor children from his hometown of Royston, Georgia, where he also endowed a hospital. He cared for his crippled sister until she died. He took care of many destitute ex-ballplayers and their families financially for many years.

Cobb also had more than his share of personal problems. He is one of those figures in history who simultaneously evokes conflicting emotions such as awe, compassion, anger and hatred. When it was all said and done, three (count 'em, three) people from his baseball past attended his funeral in 1961.

Joe Jackson - 1911

by Tony Blengino and John Benson

G	AB	R	H	2B	3B	HR	RBI	BB	AVG	OBP	SLG	SB
147	571	126	233	45	19	7	83	56	.408	.468	.590	41

Babe Ruth plainly stated that Joe Jackson was the greatest hitter of his time, and Ruth admitted studying and imitating Jackson's batting stance while developing as a hitter. Ty Cobb, who didn't speak glowingly of many people, allowed that Jackson deserved a place among his personal choices for the all-time greatest outfield.

From a career perspective, Jackson's place in history and any overall assessment of his value must be downgraded for his implication in the 1919 Black Sox scandal. Indeed most biographical writing about Jackson dwells on the question of what might have been, if Shoeless Joe hadn't accepted that money from first baseman Chick Gandil. For this book, however, Jackson in his peak season remains unimpaired, to assess and enjoy for what he was, not what he might have been.

Jackson was just age 21 in 1911, his first full season in the major leagues. He had been obtained by the Indians from the Philadelphia Athletics following the 1909 season. The A's were a tough, no-nonsense team, finishing second to Cobb's three-time champion Tigers in 1909 and then taking the World Series in 1910 and 1911. In such fast company, a raw, illiterate farmboy like Jackson was a natural target for hazing and verbal abuse. The insecurity engendered by such treatment took a toll on Jackson's natural gifts (which were immense in all aspects: hitting, running, fielding, and throwing) and taunting contributed to his flops in two brief trials in 1908 and 1909. A's manager Connie Mack correctly assessed that the big-time high-

pressure situation in Philadelphia (which then had, like New York and Chicago, two major league teams and numerous daily papers competing for penetrating stories) was not the right environment for the talented young Jackson, and shipped him off to Cleveland.

Surrounded by nice-guy teammates and benefiting from the aura of two aging legends, Nap Lajoie and Cy Young, and playing in front of appreciative fans, Jackson blossomed superbly. In a late 1910 callup he hit .387, and then in the following season, delivered his best performance ever.

The dead ball era surrounded the 1911 season. In 1908 to 1910 the American League batted .239, .244, and .243; and in 1913 through 1918 there was no season when the league batted over .260. In 1911 and 1912 there was a minor surge in hitting, as the league reached .273 and .265 respectively, but the composite on base percentage for the league was a soft .338 and .333 in those two years.

Jackson and Cobb were prominent among those who staged the mini-assault on pitchers in 1911. Cobb, the all-time highest average hitter, had his career year, placing a statistical veneer over Jackson's best season. Though basically just a rookie, Jackson finished second to Cobb in hits, doubles, total bases, batting average, slugging percentage, runs scored, and many of the catch-all stats such as total average, relative production, and total player rating. For the first time in history, a player had batted .400 and didn't win the batting title. That has only happened once since then,

in 1922, when Cobb was the victim rather than the victor (George Sisler's .420 bested Cobb's .401 mark). Jackson was slightly better than Cobb in one key category in 1911, producing the league's best on base percentage (and thus taking away something from Cobb's best-ever season).

The 1911 Cleveland Indians soared to the level of respectability in the standings, finishing in third place (after being sixth and then fifth in 1909 and 1910). The Indians batted .282 as a club, but only one regular player other than Jackson hit over .300 (outfielder Joe Birmingham at .304). Lajoie, who played only 90 games including 41 at first base because of a leg injury, hit .365 but didn't qualify for the batting title. Cleveland scored 691 runs, a paltry sum compared to the first place Athletics (861) and second place Tigers (831). Jackson simply didn't have any sluggers among his teammates that year. After Shoeless Joe's .590 slugging, the next highest mark, among the regulars, was second baseman Neal Ball's .396. The Cleveland squad also featured a one-man show in the pitching department; Vean Gregg, who went 23-7 while leading the league in winning percentage (.767) and ERA (1.81). Only one other starter reached double figures in wins (Gene Krapp with 12), and he led the circuit in walks with 136.

After 1911, much was expected from Jackson, who had positioned himself as the league's best player except for Cobb. With a two-and-a-half-year youth advantage, and hardly any major league experience other than the splendid 1911 season, Jackson looked like a great talent ready to climb above Cobb. While Jackson remained second behind Cobb in batting average again in 1912 and 1913, both years he beat Cobb in hits, runs, doubles, triples, and total bases. For claims to being the league's best hitter, Jackson had arrived. He was in a virtual tie with Cobb in the Chalmers MVP award voting in 1912, and finished far ahead of Cobb in 1913, though neither won the Chalmers either year (Cobb had won it in 1911, and the award was eliminated after 1914).

Jackson was in his personal golden era, but soon the money troubles of major league baseball began to work against him. First he was pursued by teams from the new Federal League, but he turned down their generous offers and instead followed the conservative course of loyalty to the Cleveland franchise. That decision backfired. Cleveland ran into financial trouble while the Federal League took away both players and fans, and the wave of higher salaries gave each team the choice of paying players more, or fielding teams without stars. Cleveland chose to be a non-contender. They shipped Lajoie to the Athletics and sent their young superstar Joe Jackson to play for the Chicago White Sox of Charlie Comiskey. For Jackson they got in return some inexpensive players and $31,500 in cash, and finished seventh in 1915.

Jackson was justifiably grieved about being dismissed in this manner, after he had turned down bigger offers and stayed with Cleveland. Hitting .327 when they traded him in mid 1915, Jackson slumped to .272 in his first partial season with the White Sox (finishing the year with a composite .308 average) and then fell to a career-low .301 in 1917. The notoriously tight-fisted Comiskey had little interest in the happiness of Jackson, who stayed away from Chicago in a bitter holdout for most of the 1918 season. He did finally return, both to the team and to the top star level in the American League, in 1919, when he hit .351. By 1920 he was as good as ever, hitting .382 with personal career highs in homers and runs batted in, and coming within one point of that career high .590 slugging percentage that he had reached in 1911.

One benefit of the move to Chicago was that Jackson finally got to play in the World Series. In 1917 he banged out seven hits in a six-game victory over the Giants. He played even better in the 1919 Series, collecting a full dozen hits for a .375 average while leading the White Sox in both runs scored and runs batted in. He did it all.

The problem, of course, was taking that money from Gandil. Before the 1920 season was over, Judge Landis had spoken, and Jackson was out, for good, barely age 31. He finished with a .356 career average, third best of all time, behind only Cobb and Rogers Hornsby. The "what if" analysts may now wonder about Jackson's career, but we know exactly what he did in 1911, and it was marvelous!

Tris Speaker - 1912

by Greg Gajus

G	AB	R	H	2B	3B	HR	RBI	BB	AVG	OBP	SLG	SB
153	580	136	222	53	12	10	90	82	.383	.464	.567	52

''If you can imagine George Brett playing center field like Cesar Geronimo, you'd be pretty close.''

-- Bill James on Tris Speaker

Tris Speaker was one of the biggest stars of pre-1920 baseball, and among many observers of his time he was considered every bit as good a player as Ty Cobb. It's true that Cobb was a better hitter, but Speaker was a much superior fielder, and his teams generally performed better than Cobb's Tigers.

1912 was Speaker's breakout year, after three good years with the Red Sox from 1909-1911. Speaker, then age 24, jumped into the top tier of players with a tremendous performance that typified his career-long, multi-faceted excellence. He was second in the league in runs scored, third in hits, first in doubles, tied for first in home runs, second in total bases, fifth in walks, fourth in steals, third in batting and slugging average and first in on base percentage. He was also the best center fielder in the league, leading the league in assists, double plays, and chances per game in the outfield. Joe Jackson and Ty Cobb had comparable offensive years, but when you include defense Speaker was the best player in the league in 1912.

1912 was the first year of the Boston dynasty that dominated baseball through 1918. The Red Sox won 105 games with only two big stars on the team, Speaker and Smoky Joe Wood (who had one of the greatest years ever for a pitcher). Speaker had a good, but not great, supporting cast with Larry Gardner, Jake Stahl, and Duffy Lewis. Underdogs against the more famous, but aging Giants in the World Series, the Red Sox won one of the best fall classics ever played, lasting eight games (game two was a tie). Speaker hit .300 and drove in the run that tied the final game in the bottom of the 10th inning, off Christy Mathewson. Speaker capped the year by winning the Chalmers award, the equivalent of the MVP in 1912. (In 1910 the Chalmers prize had been decided by the objective measure of batting average, which led to some questionable managerial directions and player performances; in 1911 the decision process was changed to an election with writers voting.)

Following the 1915 season, Speaker was dumped by Boston in a salary-cutting move after the collapse of the Federal League (which had increased salaries across the board in baseball). Traded in 1916 to a poor Cleveland team (57-95 in 1915), Speaker swept the league in batting, slugging, and on base average and also led the league in hits and doubles. Cleveland improved a full 19 games to 77-77, but Boston did just fine without Speaker, winning the World Series for the second straight year behind a pitching staff led by Dutch Leonard, Carl Mays, and a dominant young lefty named Babe Ruth. Speaker's performance faded after 1915, but revived in 1920, with the arrival of the lively ball era and Speaker's renewed attention to his on-field game (he had become a playing manager for in 1919 and initially found the extra duty distracting).

From 1920 to 1923 Speaker hit .388, .362, .378, and .380 with 48 or more doubles in each season and still continued his remarkable center field play. In raw numbers, those years may be as great as his 1912 year, but in the context of the time (the league average was .265 in 1912, compared to .292 in 1921) the 1912 season was clearly his best.

In addition to his great hitting, Speaker's fine defense places him among the immortals. Only Richie Ashburn and Willie Mays can be considered in Speaker's class defensively, and the question of who played the greatest defensive center field of all time is among these three.

As a manager, Speaker was innovative and successful. He was one of the earliest platooners, and he won it all in 1920 in one of the great pennant races of all time. Given the extenuating circumstances, it was one of the most impressive managerial jobs ever. Speaker was in a three-team race the entire season, and had to deal with the midseason death of Ray Chapman. Speaker was able to keep the team focused, overcome his grief (he was close friends with Chapman), and eventually win the race. His managerial career ended in a cloud after 1926, when he and Ty Cobb were accused (but acquitted) of fixing a late-season 1919 game. At age 39 he still was able to hit .327 with 43 doubles for the Senators before a final year with Connie Mack and the Athletics in 1928. He still holds the career record for doubles (792).

Among the position players of his time, I would rank Speaker behind only Wagner, Cobb, and Jackson offensively and behind no one defensively. But like most of the players before Babe Ruth, Tris Speaker is almost forgotten today. He is one of the five greatest center fielders of all time (with Cobb, Mays, Mickey Mantle, and Joe DiMaggio).

Smoky Joe Wood - 1912

by Tony Blengino and Lary Bump

W	L	PCT	G	GS	CG	SV	IP	SO	BB	B/I	ERA
34	5	.872	43	38	35	1	344	258	82	1.04	1.91

Smoky* Joe Wood's story would make an excellent film. Perhaps it already has, in ''The Natural.'' For the story of Wood's career is that of Roy Hobbs, Dizzy Dean and -- for a more recent generation of Red Sox fans -- something like the case of Jim Lonborg: one spectacular year early in a career that later involved an injury and a comeback.

The popular myth, that Red Sox pitcher Joe Wood was a one-year phenom, is essentially incorrect. He had a fine overall career, which included more than the 1912 superlative season. In 1911 Wood won 23 games, had a 2.02 ERA, and would later be cited by *Total Baseball* for having the league's best total pitcher index, and by us, here, for having the best relative control/power. There were also later accomplishments, such as Wood's 15-5 record in 1915, when he had both the league's highest winning percentage at .750 and the lowest ERA at 1.49. His .671 lifetime winning percentage is consistent with the adjective "great."

In a twist of irony, Wood's 1912 performance was so far off the scale of merely "great" as to create an illusion that the remainder of his career was not so great. For our purposes, The Smoky Joe Wood Story is the single most outstanding example of one shining season with fully-realized potential, stretching far above the rest of the career context. Why couldn't Wood go 34-5 every year? Part of the answer is that he fell on wet grass in the spring of 1913 and broke his thumb, but another part of the answer is that nobody could go 34-5 every year. And yet, much analysis has focused on the theoretical question of a Wood career without the thumb injury. Lawrence Ritter and Donald Honig in their classic work, *The 100 Greatest Baseball Players of All Time*, a book that focuses on career total accomplishment as the criterion for evaluating greatness, coined the phrase "Smoky Joe Wood Syndrome" to rationalize including some players whose career stats may not look like one of the best hundred lifetime lines. They ask the reader to make a leap of faith toward what could have happened.

This book, the one that you are now reading, gets to the inclusion of Joe Wood much more directly and easily, just by examining the evidence of what happened during his one greatest year. The only leap of faith required from readers here will be the acceptance of eyewitness accounts from those who saw Wood's velocity in action; the numbers speak for themselves.

There is no videotape to show us just how hard pitchers could throw in 1912. Walter Johnson reputedly had the fastest fastball. But Johnson himself asserted, when asked: ''Can I throw harder than Joe Wood? Listen, my friend, there's no man alive who can throw harder than Smoky Joe Wood.''

Johnson was at the top of his game in 1912. At age 25, he was 33-12 with a 1.39 ERA. He went on a winning streak that reached an American League record 16 games before it ended in late August.

At that time, Wood had a nine-game winning streak of his own that had started on July 8th. By September 6th, Wood's streak had risen to 13 games, and was still alive when Boston had a weekend matchup against Washington, with Johnson scheduled to pitch one of those games. Red Sox manager Jake Stahl moved Wood up a day in the rotation, so Johnson could attempt to preserve his own 16-game record streak by defeating Wood and ending his streak. The confrontation took place in front of a Fenway crowd so large that spectators overflowed from the seats onto the field; before the game, there was almost no room for Wood to make his warmup tosses.

Newspapers had treated the matchup like a prize fight, running "tale of the tape" style segments about the two hurlers. Both pitchers were nearly unhittable that day. The only run scored when Red Sox outfielder Duffy Lewis doubled home Tris Speaker. The 1-0 win kept Wood's streak intact. He finally tied Johnson's 16-game streak later in September, but couldn't pass it.

The Wood-Johnson rivalry was just one of the stories in this a larger-than-life epic. The parallels to Dean, Lonborg, and Hobbs become apparent as the story unfolds. The character of Max Mercy, who was in and out of Hobbs' life in "The Natural," was Rube Marquard in Wood's tale. Marquard, a Hall-of-Fame lefthander, and Wood both arrived in the majors in 1908, after battling each other all season for pitching supremacy in the American Association. By 1911, Marquard was a big 20-game winner in the majors, with a dominant 24-7 record. Wood also cracked the 20-win level that year. In 1912, when Wood and Johnson posted the AL-record 16-game winning streaks that have been matched twice, but never equaled, Marquard established the still-standing major league season record with 19 consecutive victories for the New York Giants.

Wood's greatest season marked the beginning of a dynasty, with four American League pennants and four World Championships in seven years, before the Curse of the Bambino struck the Red Sox. In the 1912 World Series against the Giants, Wood was superb, winning three of his four decisions. In game

one, he went all the way in a 4-3 win, and struck out Art Fletcher and Otis Crandall with the winning run on base in the ninth. In game four, Wood won 3-1 with another complete game. The second game had ended in a tie, so Boston had a 3-2 Series lead going into game seven. Marquard had pitched complete games for both New York victories. Stahl sent his ace to the mound, but this time Wood was bombed for seven runs in one inning plus, and the Sox lost 11-4.

The next day, Wood entered the decisive eighth game with the score tied 1-1 in the eighth inning. The game remained tied until the Giants scratched out a run in the 10th. All appeared lost for the Sox and Wood. But Clyde Engle led off the bottom of the 10th with a routine center field fly, which Fred Snodgrass dropped for his infamous error. The crazy inning then continued with an incredible game-saving catch by Snodgrass. Then on a routine popup by Tris Speaker, pitcher Christy Mathewson, catcher Chief Meyers and first baseman Fred Merkle let the ball fall in fair ground. Speaker then singled in the tying run, and Larry Gardner singled home the winning run.

In 1912 Wood was a mere 22 years old, and appeared to be, like Johnson, headed for one of the greatest all-time pitching careers, maybe even the best ever. Instead, he suffered an injury which, as in the case of Lonborg, transformed him from being a Red Sox World Series hero into a player on the comeback trail. Both Lonborg and Wood did, in fact, stage successful comebacks, but not all the way back.

Wood, returning from the broken thumb incident, attempted to come back too soon. He compensated for pain and weakness in his hand by altering his pitching motion, and hurt his shoulder in the process, much like Dean (one of only seven pitchers since Wood to win 30 games in a season) would later change his arm motion while trying to come back.

The legendary Smoky fastball, possibly harder than Johnson's, just wasn't the same. Wood went to countless physicians, but none had an answer that would work for him. Cortisone wasn't in the dictionary back in 1913. Wood still managed to pitch brilliantly in short spurts during the next three seasons, helping the Red Sox of 1915 win the pennant and go on to a World Championship for the first time in three years. All this time he refused to change his style; despite his pain, Wood still threw mostly heat. The Sox won the World Series in five games over the Phillies, but they did it without Wood, who would never again appear in postseason play.

After the 1915 season, Wood went to a chiropractor, who encouraged Wood to "throw as long and hard as he possibly could." That didn't work, to state the result mildly; he was in such pain that he had to sit out the entire 1916 season.

Roy Hobbs, who threw hard enough as a youth to strike out The Whammer at a railroad siding, finally made it to the majors as an outfielder. In real life, Wood also came back as an outfielder. Like many of the game's top pitchers of that era, he could handle a bat. Another facet of his mythic 1912 season was a .290 batting average, with 13 runs batted in and 15 extra-base hits, including a home run. He went 2-for-7 against the Giants in the 1912 World Series.

That 1912 Series performance at the plate had not been forgotten by Speaker, who went from the Red Sox to Cleveland after the 1915 season. He had been Smoky Joe's only roommate, arriving in Boston from the minors a few weeks after Wood in 1908. Speaker encouraged Wood to make a 1917 trial as an outfielder with Cleveland. He made the team, and played the next six seasons for the Indians. Surprisingly, he once said his greatest thrill was hitting two homers, including the game-winner, in a 19-inning, 3-2 win over the Yankees on May 24th, 1918. Another highlight was his second World Championship, in 1920. Wood scored the first two runs of that year's World Series against the Dodgers after walking and doubling, against Rube Marquard.

Wood pitched only seven times for Cleveland, with minimal effectiveness. He finished with awesome career statistics 116-57 (and the .671 winning percentage) with a 2.03 lifetime ERA. His career relative ERA, adjusted for park factors and compared to league average, was 146, or 46 percent better than the league average, third of all time behind Lefty Grove's 148 and Johnson's 147. At bat, Wood compiled a .283 career average.

Smoky Joe retired in 1923 to become the baseball coach at Yale, and coached the Elis for 20 years, through 1942. In May 1981, when Wood was 91, he met author Roger Angell at a game between Yale and St. John's in an NCAA regional tournament. While talking baseball, they both enjoyed a wonderful game, the now-famous epic struggle between Ron Darling and Frank Viola. Darling pitched 11 no-hit innings for Yale, only to lose 1-0 on a single and steals of second, third and home in the 12th. Wood called it the greatest game he had ever seen at any level. Maybe he wasn't counting one game in which he pitched himself, the legendary pitching duel of September 6, 1912, when he beat Walter Johnson.

Should Smoky Joe Wood be in the Hall of Fame? Yes of course he should. He is *very* famous, and it's a hall of fame, not a hall of milestones.

---

*Footnote for historians: many authoritative sources use the spelling "Smokey" for Joe Wood's nickname. No less an authority that Wood's own son, Bob Wood, assured the editors of this volume that the original spelling, and the only correct spelling, is "definitely without the E." In 1910, Boston *Post* writer Paul Shannon, who had observed that Wood threw real smoke, began using the name Smoky Joe in print. While agreeing that the nickname might be used in media guides and press reports (teammate Cy Young in 1908 had advised Wood that he would go farther in baseball if he had a nickname less common than "Joe") Wood still signed his autograph simply as "Joe Wood" right up until the end of his life, believing that to sign the name "Smoky" would be unnecessarily showy. So if you have any memorabilia items signed with the nickname, you might want to get a second opinion about their provenance (especially if Smoky is spelled with an E).

Walter Johnson - 1913

by Tony Blengino

W	L	PCT	G	GS	CG	SV	IP	SO	BB	B/I	ERA
36	7	.837	48	36	29	2	346	243	38	0.81	1.14

A very strong case can be made that Walter Johnson had the greatest career of any starting pitcher in baseball history. Johnson dominated the American League for two decades, neatly bridging the gap between Cy Young and Lefty Grove, two of his main competitors for the top spot. His career record of 417-299 (.599 winning percentage) highlights his incredible durability, and is particularly amazing because the Senator team averaged just a .501 percentage in the seasons in which he qualified for an ERA title. That .098 gap between Johnson's and his teams' winning percentage is second among retired big leaguers, after Pete Alexander's .107. Johnson led the AL in wins six times, in ERA five times, in strikeouts 12 times, and shutouts seven times. He was the all time strikeout leader (3509) until 1983, and he remains the all time shutout leader (110) by a country mile.

Using the relative control/power factor, a measure which I developed years ago, Johnson's sum of individual season factors is 76.51, by far the highest of all time (see appendix). He led the AL in this category in ten different seasons during the period 1910 to 1925. No one was as dominant for as long as was the Big Train. He reached his apex in 1913.

Despite Johnson's dominance, beginning with his 1907 debut, the Senators were mired near the bottom of the AL. Their climb from mediocrity to contention in 1912 coincided with Johnson's graduation from merely great pitcher to all-time master. Johnson went 32-12 with a league leading 1.39 ERA in 1912,

fashioning a 303/76 strikeout/walk ratio in 368 innings, as the Senators finished second behind the Red Sox who featured Smoky Joe Wood (34-5). What could Johnson do for an encore?

From April 10 through May 13, 1913, over a period of 56 consecutive innings, Johnson did not give up a single run, a record which would stand for 55 years until broken by Don Drysdale. Almost single-handedly, Johnson kept the Senators in contention for the pennant throughout the summer. They again finished second, six and a half games behind the Philadelphia A's, who featured five Hall of Famers: second baseman Eddie Collins, third baseman Home Run Baker, and pitchers Chief Bender, Eddie Plank and Herb Pennock.

The Athletics scored 25% more runs than any other AL club that year, batting .280 as a team in a league that collectively batted only .256. The Senators had, well, they had Walter Johnson. Do the names Ray Morgan, George McBride, Eddie Foster, Danny Moeller, Howard Shanks and John Henry mean anything to you? They were mainstay Senator regulars in 1913. Their other two starting position players, outfielder Clyde Milan and first baseman Chick Gandil, are slightly better known, though Gandil's notoriety came mainly from being one of the Black Sox who fixed the 1919 Series. Pitching-wise, the Senators trotted out 24 different moundsmen in 1913. Johnson and his lieutenant, Joe Boehling (17-7), combined to go 53-14, while the rest of the staff went 37-50. At the tender age of 25, Johnson gave a

performance that was arguably the greatest single season ever by a starting pitcher. In a year when the average ERA in the American League was 2.93, Johnson led the league in wins, ERA, winning percentage, complete games, shutouts, innings, and strikeouts, while walking only 38 batters! He posted his career-best relative control/power factor at 7.11.

Walter Johnson was a farmboy from Kansas who did not play baseball until age 14. At 19 he was pitching in a semipro league in Idaho when his big break came. The Senators' catcher, Cliff Blankenship, one of the worst hitting position players ever (.249 on base percentage with .252 slugging in 218 at bats, with no homers) was injured, so manager Joe Cantillon sent him on a scouting trip. Blankenship proved to be a much better scout than a ballplayer; he signed both Johnson and the aforementioned Clyde Milan (2100 career hits with 495 stolen bases) on the trip.

After signing with the Senators, Johnson was immediately inserted into the rotation. He opened some eyes with his first start on August 2, 1907, despite losing a complete game 3-2 decision to the Tigers on an inside-the-park homer by Sam Crawford. It was then that Ty Cobb uttered his famous comment, ''You can't hit what you can't see,'' regarding Johnson. Johnson's out pitch -- and for most of his career his only pitch -- was his fastball, which was unlike any heater since Rube Waddell. That first season, Johnson was invited to join an honorary "all-star" tour team, despite his 5-9 record for the wretched last-place Senators. After all, he had a 1.88 ERA, and a 71/20 strikeout/walk ratio in 110 innings.

The Senators' second place finishes during Johnson's glory years of 1913 and 1914 proved to be the closest he would come to a World Series until 1924. Johnson was a force on that 1924 team, going 23-7 with a league-leading 2.72 ERA, leading the circuit in wins, winning percentage, strikeouts and shutouts. His presence on the mound, as a reliever, late in game

seven of that exciting series has become legendary. Johnson got the win after escaping a ninth-inning jam, and then benefiting first from Travis Jackson's error and then from Earl McNeely's bad hop hit (bounced off a pebble which belongs in Cooperstown) which went past Freddie Lindstrom in the 12th inning, giving Washington the victory over the Giants.

The next season, Johnson again played a leading role in the pennant and in the Series, winning two games from the Pirates. But this time he failed to deliver in game seven, getting no breaks as he endured a 15-hit barrage in the pouring rain, going all the way in a 9-7 loss to the Pirates.

Walter Johnson was a clean living man who was idolized by many, and respected by all. For writers who wanted a sober, thoughtful and kindly man who performed athletic feats at the highest level, the soft-spoken Johnson was their man. He never had a word of criticism or blame for anyone. He was stately, not shy. To those who were not his friends, he was courteous and open. To those who were his friends, he could display rare acts of kindness, even while a game was in progress. Sam Crawford and others have confessed that Johnson would occasionally tip them off that he was about to throw a hittable pitch just to let someone else look good, but such events occurred only when the Senators had a safe lead, and never against the meanest competitors, like Ty Cobb.

Walter Johnson, though he has strong competition from such luminaries as Lefty Grove, Rube Waddell, and Dazzy Vance for short-term dominance, clearly put together the greatest career of them all. In his early years, the raw Johnson quickly surpassed the aging Cy Young as the best pitcher in baseball, and in his later years, he bravely contended with all-time greats like Grove, and held his own for many years. Johnson's staying power, at a dominant level, has never been equaled, and it is unlikely that baseball fans will ever again see such a player.

Pete Alexander - 1916

by David Gordon

W	L	PCT	G	GS	CG	SV	IP	SO	BB	B/I	ERA
33	12	.733	48	45	38	3	388	167	50	0.99	1.55

Grover Cleveland ("Pete") Alexander was named for a U.S. President, and his character was played in a movie by another President-to-be. His life was hardly presidential, but for several years he did preside over the National League, in a way. Grover Cleveland was the President when Alexander was born (1887), and, of course, it was Ronald Reagan who played Alexander in his life story, *The Winning Team.*

Alexander's career got off to a slow start, but accelerated quickly. His first scheduled major league game, in April, 1911, was delayed by a fire that destroyed a section of the grandstand at the Polo Grounds in New York. It was one of his few setbacks all year. His rookie performance was one of the most impressive of all time, as he led the league in victories, complete games (31), innings pitched, and shutouts (seven). In a symbolic passing of the torch, Alexander hooked up with the legendary Cy Young in what would be the final month of Young's illustrious career. Young, age 44, held the Phillies to one run on six hits, but Alexander pitched his first one-hitter for a 1-0 victory.

For the next two years, Alexander pitched very well (a combined 41-25, 2.80 ERA), but he was not among the league's best hurlers. His control was still improving, and so was his effectiveness. When he finally matured, reaching a long, high peak in the four years 1914 to 1917, he became truly remarkable. Alexander averaged 30 wins per year, leading the league every year. His composite ERA for the four years was 1.74, including a low of 1.22 in 1915. At

the time, many pitchers had low ERA's, but Alexander also dominated the league in strikeouts every year from 1914 to 1917, with a total of 823 -- an average of 206 whiffs per year in the golden age of the contact hitters. Alexander also amassed 42 shutouts, including a record of 16 in 1916. That record still stands.

While much is made of baseball's Triple Crown, there is less discussion of a counterpart for pitchers. If there were, it would be leading the league in wins, ERA, and strikeouts, which has been accomplished this century by 14 pitchers (most recently by Dwight Gooden in 1985). Alexander is the only pitcher to do it four times, 1915, '16, '17 and again in 1920. Sandy Koufax and Walter Johnson are three-time winners.

Alexander was extremely effective in his first World Series, in 1915, against the Red Sox. He won the first game 3-1 against Ernie Shore, and barely lost 2-1 to Dutch Leonard in game three, as the winning run scored with two outs in the ninth. The Red Sox went on to win the next two games and the series, with Alexander watching from the bench.

It is difficult to choose one season from the four-year peak as Alexander's best. In 1915, his minuscule 1.22 ERA and 241 strikeouts were impressive, especially as he led the Phillies to their only pennant to come in the first half of the century. However, it is hard to beat the single season performance of 1916, with those 16 shutouts. Another high-water mark: Alexander's 33 victories that year have not been matched since. Of Alexander's 16 shutouts. His first and last were both against the Boston Braves, on April 18th and October 2nd. Nine of the blanks were at home in the tiny Baker Bowl, with its 40 foot right field fence just 272 feet from the batter. In 11 of the shutouts, Alexander did not walk a single batter, and he walked a total of only nine in all of those 16 games! While throwing the ball over the plate so consistently, at the same time he was a dominant strikeout pitcher, and was also darn tough to hit, allowing an average of just 5.4 hits per game.

Alexander came tantalizingly close to shutouts on several other occasions in 1916. On June 12th, he had two outs and no one on in the ninth when a double and a single (off his shin) scored the lone run. On June 23rd, he allowed just five hits in 11 innings, but one of those was the only homer he allowed over the Baker Bowl "monster" wall all year. On July 11th, the only run against Alexander came on an infield out. On July 26th, the only run got into scoring position on a passed ball. On September 16, a botched double play allowed the lone run to score. And on September 19th, both runs in a 2-0 loss were unearned. While the pitching profession has had 80 years to think about that amazing total of 16 shutouts, the number could easily have been 18, 20 or even 21!

Despite Alexander's heroics, Philadelphia failed to capture the NL flag in 1916. The Giants, who put together winning streaks of 17 games and 26 games, also fell short. The Brooklyn Robins won their first crown that year, finishing two and a half games ahead of the second place Phillies, through no fault of Alexander. From September 16th to October 2nd, he was 5-2, one of those losses the previously described game of September 16th. On September 28th, the Phillies started a three-game series in Brooklyn, trailing by one and one half games. Alexander won the first game, and the team won the second, but Alexander lost the third. The Phillies left trailing by half a game. Two days later they retook the lead on Alexander's final shutout, but then lost it in the nightcap of the doubleheader. Without Alexander, the Phillies lost both games of yet another doubleheader the next day, ending their pennant hopes.

After that all-time great season for the ace of the Phillies staff, Alexander was nearly as effective in 1917, winning 30 games. He also won the untitled pitchers' Triple Crown for the third straight year. Sensing that Alexander might be called for military service, the Phillies sold him to the Cubs in the off-season before 1918. Indeed, he was drafted and pitched only three games in 1918. The war was the turning point of his life. He returned suffering from seizures, and he had a changed personality. The change included an increased use of alcohol.

Alexander still had two good seasons left, going 43-25 in 1919-1920, with a composite 1.84 ERA. He won the ERA title both years and the Triple Crown for the fourth and last time in 1920. Then began the decline. Over the next five years, he won 90 games, nothing like the old days of 30-win seasons. And his ERA now stayed above 3.00. Despite his health problems and overall decline, Alexander's control remained excellent; he averaged just 1.1 walks per nine innings over those five years.

The drinking finally became too much for manager Joe McCarthy, and in June, 1926, Alexander was shipped to the Cards for the waiver price. He was 9-7 for the rest of the season, which saw St. Louis win its first NL pennant. In the World Series, Alexander held the mighty Yankees of Babe Ruth and Lou Gehrig to two runs in the second game again in the sixth game (both of which the Cards won). In game seven, Old Pete came in to relieve with the bases loaded, two outs, and Tony Lazzeri at the plate. With perfectly placed curve balls, he whiffed the budding star. He then closed out the Yankees over the final two innings, with the season's last out coming when Ruth was thrown out stealing. It was the only time a World Series ever ended on a steal attempt. Alexander's strikeout of Lazzeri would become a celebrated tale, often embellished in its retelling.

Alexander never did conquer his epilepsy or drinking. His life after baseball kept sinking lower and lower, from barnstorming with major leaguers down to a side show in a circus. The one high point left in his life was his election to the Hall-of-Fame in 1938 as a member of the third class of inductees. He eventually returned to his native Nebraska and died there in 1950 at the age of 63.

Babe Ruth - 1920

by John Benson

G	AB	R	H	2B	3B	HR	RBI	BB	SO	AVG	OBP	SLG	SB
142	458	158	172	36	9	54	137	148	80	.376	.530	.847	14

Babe Ruth is so far above the rest of the player population, by any objective measure, it can be downright amusing to debate with anyone who believes otherwise. People willing to engage in such a debate must focus on career totals rather than peak seasons, because in peak value Ruth has no peers. A few mortals have approached him on a cumulative basis in some hitting stats, a phenomenon made possible only by the fact that Ruth spent five years as the best lefthanded starting pitcher in the American League. And most of the career debates are confined to fans from Boston, Yankee haters, and modernists trying to dismiss all accomplishments before 1940.

Since the best career is a natural context for the best season, I will briefly address the career question. But rather than fill this whole page with Ruth's career marks, which are the best, I will simply address the question, "Who else?" The alternatives are easily dismissed.

Red Sox fans long ago gravitated toward Ted Williams as the best player ever. When comparing him to Ruth, they need to rationalize the shortfalls in total stats, and they do this by pointing to Williams' military service which robbed him of five seasons and about 165 home runs. "Williams would have had 700 home runs if he hadn't spent five years as a fighter pilot."

Rather than haggle, I concede the Williams 700-homer assertion, but counter with, "Babe Ruth would have had 900 home runs if he hadn't spent five years as a pitcher." And those five years were highly productive on the baseball field, time spent mainly on the pitcher's mound rather than in the batter's box.

Ruth was a great pitcher, not just a good one. In 1916 he won 23 games (including nine shutouts) and led the American League with a 1.75 ERA. For that season he could be in this book as a pitcher. In 1917 Ruth won 24 games with a 2.01 ERA. The facts of this pitching career (94-46 and a 2.28 ERA) tend to end any argument about another player having a better career than Ruth. Supporters of Hank Aaron and Willie Mays, for example, simply have no answer to the challenge: could your man win 90 games in five seasons as a superb starting pitcher, and still have a hitting career like Ruth's? The only answer is "no."

Some critics maintain that "modern" baseball is different from the game Ruth played; they say Babe had it easy. The modern schedule is longer and arguably tougher. Faster travel packs more games closer together (or so it seems; there are fewer days off now, but the disappearance of the double-header from today's schedule has relieved players from one form of playing without rest). Ruth never had to play a night game, and thus he never had to play a day game after a night game. And so on. Such arguments sound appealing, but they are undone by the overriding truth that the pitchers of Ruth's era all enjoyed the same life of leisure, riding on trains, sometimes returning to their families between starts on the road, and living without the media microscope that affects pitchers especially (no hitter has yet been charged with a loss). And the pitchers of Ruth's era all enjoyed pitching off a higher mound and throwing at a much, much larger strike zone. Ruth clobbered the pitchers of his era like no other hitter of his time, and like no hitter has ever dominated in any other era.

While the career marks offer a landscape of Everests, it is the individual season peaks where Ruth stands the highest. It is simply impossible to look at annual totals and come up with any other player. John Thorn and Pete Palmer's *Total Baseball* gives both of the best two seasons ever, and three of the top four since 1900, to Ruth in their overall performance measures of Batting Runs, Adjusted Batting Runs, Adjusted Batting Wins, and Total Average. Ruth gets both of the top two seasons and three of the top four in Runs Created, and all three of best three seasons ever in Total Player Ranking. Larry Thompson in "The Best Year Any Hitter Ever Had" ranks Ruth's 1920, 1921, and 1923 seasons as the top three in both Real Slugging Average (with walks and stolen bases included) and in his Relative Performance measure (Real Slugging Average compared to league average).

The only real question is which of Ruth's great seasons was the greatest? Here we could have a challenging debate. Was the best year 1920, 1921, 1923, or even 1927? I could comfortably argue in favor of any of these years, with ample evidence. Sifting through all the available information, however, I keep coming back to 1920 as the best, and my reasons for this choice will illustrate the types of factors that we considered throughout this book:

1. Babe Ruth in 1920 had the highest slugging percentage in baseball history. Since Ruth himself (in half-a-dozen monster seasons) could never surpass that early record, it must rank among the most unreachable of "records that will never be broken." So there is a prominent high water mark that stands for all time.

2. Ruth in 1920 dominated his league to an extent never approached by any other player (even by himself in later years). Statisticians use the method of standard deviations to measure the degree of excellence in diverse comparisons; while it may be troublesome to compare apples and oranges, it is relatively easy to compare a big apple to a big orange, and say which is really bigger compared to its peers. Ruth's 1920 season beats all others using standard deviations, by any objective measure of total offense. One quick illustration of Ruth's dominance in 1920: he had more home runs than any other TEAM that year. For comparison, Albert Belle would have had to hit 162 home runs to accomplish the same feat in 1994.

3. These feats came in the immediate wake of the 1919 Black Sox scandal. Never was there any time when baseball so needed an innocent, captivating, bigger-than-life hero. As nations and epochs have had their "man of destiny," Babe was that man for baseball. And 1920 marked his emergence, a genuine light in the sky, fulfilling mythic proportion.

4. Ruth's performance transformed the game: what players try to do, what managers want them to do, and what fans come to see. In 1920 "home run" became a synonym for high drama with a successful outcome. And it was The Babe, all by himself, who made it that way. Within two years, three other players had broken the 30-homer mark. Many more soon followed. Major league baseball, at age 50, had suddenly found a whole new kind of hero: the slugger.

5. The Ruthian model of excellence arrived suddenly, like a metaphor for the home run itself. Baseball in 1919 was a different game from what emerged in 1921. Ruth's 1920 season was the watershed.

Compared to 1920, Ruth had more home runs in 1921 and 1927. He had a higher batting average in 1923. He took the Yankees to the World Series seven times, but not in 1920. No matter. With his spectacular play in 1920, Ruth was the main attraction in the first team ever to attract one million fans to watch one season. The show he put on included 54 home runs in just 458 at bats. With the 590 at bats Roger Maris got in 1961, Ruth would have reached 70 -- by far the highest home run percentage by anyone ever.

And the world was never the same.

George Sisler - 1920

by David Gordon

G	AB	R	H	2B	3B	HR	RBI	BB	SO	AVG	OBP	SLG	SB
154	631	137	257	49	18	19	122	46	19	.407	.449	.632	42

In 1915, two pitchers named George arrived in the American League. Ironically, they were both to go on and establish single season batting marks. The record of the "other" George (i.e. George Herman Ruth) of 60 homers in one season has since been surpassed. However, George Sisler's mark of 257 hits in a season still stands. Other comparisons between the two Georges are not as favorable for Sisler. However, Sisler figured in the record of another Yankee icon, for it was Sisler's American League record 41 game hitting streak that Joe DiMaggio passed on the way to his 56 game streak.

Born in 1893 in Manchester, Ohio, Sisler was a creditable pitcher, with experience from high school and the University of Michigan. His career record was 5-6 with a 2.35 ERA. He lost a 1-0 game and two 2-0 games in his career, and even bested Walter Johnson twice by scores of 2-1 and 1-0.

But Sisler's story lies not in his arm but in his bat and his glove. By his second season, he had found a home at first base and was regularly among the league leaders in most fielding categories. At the time, Hal Chase was generally regarded as the best fielding first baseman, and when he retired, that honor was passed on to Sisler.

After batting .305 in 1916, his second season, Sisler then had three excellent years when he hit a composite .349 with a total of 524 hits. Amazingly, he struck out only 56 times in 1,502 at bats in those three years. He was also one the league's best base stealers (a rarity for a first baseman), stealing 110 bases from 1917-1919, including a league leading 45 steals in 1918.

All this was a mere prelude to his biggest year in 1920. He set the all time record with 257 hits that year. The next best is 254 hits, a mark reached by Lefty O'Doul in 1929 and again by Bill Terry in 1930. Sisler's .473 average at home in 1920 is the second best of all time (Joe Jackson hit .483 at home in 1912). 1920 was the only year Sisler's slugging average topped .600 and the first of two years that he hit over .400. Cobb, Hornsby (three times each), Joe Jackson, and Sisler are the only players to hit over .400 in two or more seasons in this century.

Sisler's remarkable season included career highs in RBI, homers, and runs scored. The 42 stolen bases were his third-best season in that category. Despite these numbers, Sisler led the league in only three categories in 1920: hits, total bases, and batting average. He's an obvious contender for the record of finishing second in the most offensive categories (eight, at least). Here's the rundown of categories in which Sisler finished as runner-up in 1920:

Slugging Average	.632	(Ruth, .847)
Home Runs	19	(Ruth, 54)
Runs Batted In	122	(Ruth, 137)
Stolen Bases	42	(Rice, 63)
Home Run Percentage	3.0	(Ruth, 11.8)
Runs Scored	137	(Ruth, 158)
Doubles	49	(Speaker, 50)
Triples	18	(Joe Jackson, 20)

Simply put, Ruth, who also batted .376 and slugged a record .847 in 1920, had the best season by anyone ever. Sisler being dwarfed by Ruth is therefore not remarkable. Sisler finishing ahead of Ruth in any categories was quite a feat.

Sadly, the 1920 St. Louis Browns were only a .500 team, finishing in fourth place, 21 1/2 games behind the Cleveland Indians, despite Sisler's heroics (which inspired the team to bat a league-leading .308) and Urban Shocker's first of four consecutive 20-win seasons. After Shocker and Dixie Davis (18-12), no other Browns pitcher could muster even 10 victories. Meanwhile, the Indians, led by player-manager Tris Speaker, had six regulars batting over .300 and a team average of .303, second only to the Browns. But it was their big three pitchers of Jim Bagby, Stan Coveleski, and Ray Caldwell who combined for 75 wins and led the Indians to the pennant.

As an aside, game five of the 1920 World Series between the Indians and the Dodgers saw the first Series grand slam home run, the first Series homer by a pitcher, and the only Series unassisted triple play. Quite a game. For George Sisler, the year had one more treat. On November 2, 1920, son Dick Sisler, a future major leaguer, was born.

George Sisler went on to bat .371 in 1921 and a near-record .420 in 1922. He amassed an amazing 719 hits in the three years 1920 to 1922, batting a composite .400 (actually .399666). He was 29 years old and already had slugged 1,498 hits. However, an infection of the optic nerve kept him out the 1923 season. When he returned, he was not the same player, as was evident from his hitting and also his fielding. Before

the eye problem he had committed an average of 14 errors per year; afterward he committed an average of 23 misplays, sometimes leading the league in errors.

Still, Sisler was able to put together three more seasons of 200+ hits, and he batted over .300 in six of his final seven seasons (and 13 of 15 years overall). His best season of those last seven was 1925 when he batted .345 with 224 hits, 21 doubles, 15 triples, and 12 home runs. After two more solid seasons, he was sold to Washington, a franchise which turned around and sold him to Boston during the 1928 season. In 1929 he managed 205 hits and 40 doubles with a .326 average for the Red Sox. In his final season of 1930 he still batted .309, playing in 116 games for the Red Sox. He retired at age 37 with 2,812 hits, 375 stolen bases, only 327 strikeouts in 8,267 at bats (1 every 25 at bats), and a .340 lifetime average (14th best ever).

Sisler never played for a pennant winner. The closest he came was 1922 when the Browns finished one game behind the Yanks despite Sisler's .420 average and the Browns leading the league in runs, batting average, slugging average, and ERA. Even teammate Ken Williams' league-leading 39 homers (Ruth had 35 in a suspension-shortened year) was not enough.

Sisler was inducted into the Hall of Fame in 1939, only the fourth year the Hall was accepting inductees. He appeared in the famous Hall of Fame photo at the opening of the building in 1939 along with Honus Wagner, Grover Cleveland Alexander, Tris Speaker, Napoleon Lajoie, Walter Johnson, Eddie Collins, Babe Ruth, Connie Mack, and Cy Young, pretty select company. He died at the age of 80 in Richmond Heights, Missouri.

Harry Heilmann - 1923

by Tony Blengino

G	AB	R	H	2B	3B	HR	RBI	BB	SO	AVG	OBP	SLG	SB
144	524	121	211	44	11	18	115	74	40	.403	.481	.632	8

Anyone reading this book is a serious baseball fan with a bent toward history. So you should be easily able to rattle off the names of the modern era's .400 hitters, right? Let's see, there's Ty Cobb, Ted Williams, George Sisler, Rogers Hornsby, Nap Lajoie, Joe Jackson, Bill Terry and ... Harry Heilmann? Yes. Heilmann is the most-overlooked of the .400 hitters. One would suppose then, he must have been just a pesky but unproductive singles hitter, less worthy of attention than the others. Not so. Heilmann had excellent power. He must have been a one-year wonder then, right? Wrong again. Heilmann batted over .390 four times, a mark matched only by Rogers Hornsby and Ty Cobb, and exceeded by no one!

Heilmann attracted little attention for two main reasons: (1) he played alongside Cobb and was thus totally overshadowed in the early part of his career, and (2) when Heilmann had matured to his peak, that Ruth guy was performing feats that changed the face of baseball; Ruth was capturing the public's attention and adoration. Heilmann's legacy is an excellent career spanning the years from 1914 to 1932, with the quietest lifetime .342 average you will ever see. Like Cobb, Heilmann would never win a World Championship. Unlike Cobb, Heilmann would never even win a pennant. The closest the Tigers would come to a pennant was in 1923, the year that Harry Heilmann overtook Cobb for good as the Tigers' best player.

Heilmann's career had already taken a major step forward in 1921 with the abolition of the spitball. He graduated from very good to excellent that season,

lashing 237 hits and batting .394 with a .444 on base percentage and .606 slugging percentage, becoming the first righty hitter since 1910 to win the American League batting title. This was only an appetizer for what was to follow in 1923. Heilmann batted .403 to lead the AL for the second time, and added 121 runs scored, 211 hits, 44 doubles, 11 triples, 18 homers, 115 RBI, 74 walks, a .481 on base percentage, a .632 slugging percentage, and a 195 relative production index (OBP + SLG relative to the league, adjusted for park factor, with league average = 100). To put Heilmann's relative production of 1923 into context, consider that only 20 players in the current century have ever reached the 195 level. Babe Ruth was routinely at the 220 to 230 level, but 195 was higher than greats like Willie Mays, Hank Aaron, Joe Jackson, and Joe DiMaggio ever got in any season during their careers. Amazingly, in 1923 Heilmann led the American League in only one category, batting average. Ruth's 1923 season (arguably his best, but more likely his third best) with a .393 average, 170 walks, a .545 on base percentage and .764 slugging percentage, and 151 runs scored, to cite a few highlights) totally overshadowed Heilmann. The league as whole that year had an overall .282 batting average, a .351 on base percentage and .388 slugging percentage.

Heilmann's Tigers, now managed by Cobb, finished 83-71, sixteen games behind the mighty Yankees. Heilmann led a strong team offense that batted .300 and finished second in the AL in runs scored with 831 (more than the Yankees). Cobb, at age 36, batted

.344 with 88 RBI, and 21-year-old right fielder Heinie Manush batted .334. The Yanks' offense was still without Gehrig, and not yet at its peak. However, the Yanks had far superior pitching compared to the Tigers. Detroit's 4.09 team ERA was second worst in the league, as the only passable Tigers' starting pitcher was Hooks Dauss, who went 21-13, with 3.62 ERA. Meanwhile, the Yanks had a league-best 3.66 ERA. Four of their five starters had an ERA better that Dauss did, and the fifth pitcher in that rotation was the ace Sad Sam Jones who was 21-8 with a 3.63 ERA, just 0.01 above Dauss. The Tigers did well to finish second.

1923 was the first year of the American League MVP award as we know it. Obviously, Ruth had to be the choice. Heilmann came in third in the voting, behind second baseman Eddie Collins of the seventh place White Sox. Heilmann's next best chance to win an MVP was, ironically, 1927 when Lou Gehrig produced 175 RBI, leaving Heilmann a distant second in the voting. (In those days, you could win only one MVP award, so Ruth, having already won in 1923, was ineligible in 1927.)

The Tigers never made a significant pennant run during Heilmann's productive career, and the Reds were cellar-dwellers with Heilmann in his last two seasons. For his career, Heilmann stands 10th in batting average, 13th in doubles, and 25th all-time for on base percentage. He is 30th all-time for relative production. For the decade of the 1920's, Heilmann averaged an amazing .364. Another potential reason for Heilmann's obscurity was his relative lack of skills outside of the batters' box. Scribe of the times Ken Smith wrote about Heilmann: ''He was not a good

fielder or thrower, and there were several faster players in every game he played. He was a hitter for a pure and simple fact.'' He normally played left field, but also played some in right for the Tigers, and even played center for the woeful Reds at the end of his career.

For a long time, Heilmann was consistently near the top of the league in many statistics, but he was far from consistent when it came to finishing first in any category. He did win four batting titles (1921, 1923, 1925, 1927), and led the league once each in hits (1921) and doubles (1924) and that's it. Virtually every year throughout the 1920's, he finished in the top five in a variety of other measures, only to be upstaged by guys named Ruth, Cobb, Gehrig, etc..

Off the field, Heilmann was one of many stars of his day to dabble in vaudeville. After the end of his playing career, he spent some time as an announcer. Heilmann narrowly missed the requisite number of votes needed to make it into the Hall of Fame in 1951. He died soon after that vote, at age 56, and was inducted posthumously into the Hall in 1952.

Heilmann remains a much-overlooked four-time batting champion, from an era when it took stats like .394, .403, .393, and .398 to win a batting title. He was a forceful line-drive hitter with gap power who soared through the 1920's, but who was lost in the wake of the Babe Ruth Experience. He benefited greatly from the introduction of the lively ball and the banning of the spitball in the early 1920's, but of course, so did Ruth. Harry Heilmann is arguably the most forgotten major league star of the modern era. As a pure hitter, there were few better.

Dazzy Vance - 1924

by Tony Blengino

W	L	PCT	G	GS	CG	SV	IP	SO	BB	B/I	ERA
28	6	.824	35	34	30	0	308	262	77	1.04	2.16

A mere glance at the bottom line of agate type in Clarence Arthur "Dazzy" Vance's entry in *Total Baseball* does not inspire awe. Vance was 197-140 with a 3.24 ERA during his career, which lines up pretty squarely with Catfish Hunter's career numbers (224-166, 3.26). However, that is where the similarity ends. Dazzy Vance was, at his peak, arguably the most dominant pitcher in baseball history. Vance pitched in the foremost offensive era in baseball history when he recorded those numbers: relative to the league, he was phenomenal. He led his league in strikeouts by Ruthian margins. He accomplished all of this despite not winning his first major league game until the age of 31. To put that into perspective, Sandy Koufax had retired at a younger age. Furthermore, Vance pitched for relatively poor teams. During seasons in which he qualified for the ERA title, Vance's teams compiled a cumulative .499 winning percentage.

Vance's signature season took place in 1924, the third of his 11 seasons with the Brooklyn Dodgers. Vance was elected National League MVP that season -- no small feat in a year in which Rogers Hornsby batted a lusty .424. In each of the two previous seasons, the perennial also-ran Dodgers had compiled identical 76-78 marks, placing sixth both seasons. The 1924 edition was a veteran club which was built around the right arms of Vance, then 33, and another future Hall-of-Famer, Burleigh Grimes.

The only two offensive standouts on the Dodgers were future Hall of Fame outfielder Zack Wheat (who hit .375 with 97 RBI at age 38) and first baseman Jack Fournier (who hit .334 with 27 homers and 116 RBI). By contrast, the New York Giants were an offensive juggernaut; they batted .300 as a team. The Giants started five future Hall of Fame position players: first baseman George Kelly, second baseman Frankie Frisch, shortstop Travis Jackson, and outfielders Ross Youngs and Hack Wilson. All five were in full bloom, with ages from 20 to 28.

The tandem of Vance and Grimes were primarily responsible for keeping the 1924 Dodgers in the race all season long. Vance completed 30 of 34 starts in fashioning a 28-6 mark, while Grimes completed 30 of 36 starts in compiling a 22-13 mark. How dominant was Vance? The league batted .283, but only .213 against Vance. Every team in the league gave up more than a hit per inning pitched. Vance gave up 238 hits in 308 innings. The league had an overall 3.87 ERA. Vance's was 2.16.

Vance's career ERA is not truly appreciated until it is placed within the context of the era in which he pitched. *Total Baseball* uses a statistic called Adjusted ERA, which measures a pitcher's ERA compared to the league average (base value of 100) adjusted for park factors. Vance's career Adjusted ERA was 125; Catfish Hunter's was a mediocre 104. Vance's figure lags behind the two best, Lefty Grove (148) and Walter Johnson (147) by a significant margin; but, it is in the same range as greats like Tom Seaver, Eddie Plank and Bob Gibson.

Among Vance's mind-boggling 1924 numbers, the

most impressive is his strikeout total. National League *teams* averaged only 423 strikeouts in 1924. Vance whiffed an amazing 262 (against only 77 walks) all by himself. To put that in perspective, the average NL team whiffed 846 batters in 1994. To exceed that figure by the margin Vance achieved in 1924, a pitcher would have needed 524 strikeouts, in the shortened 1994 season! Grimes, with 135 K's, was the only other hurler to strike out 100. This margin rivals the staggering 54-19 homer advantage Babe Ruth enjoyed over the AL runner-up, George Sisler, in 1920. I have developed and used a statistic, the relative control/power factor (see appendix) Vance led the NL in this statistic for an unmatched nine consecutive years from 1923 to 1931, and his 1924 mark of 9.18 is by far the highest in history. His 1925 factor of 8.49 is the second highest ever, and his 1928 mark of 7.28 is fifth. His career factor (the sum of the individual season factors) of 68.15 is the third highest ever, behind only Walter Johnson (76.51) and Nolan Ryan (69.36).

However, Vance qualified for only 11 ERA titles, while Johnson qualified for 18, and Ryan for 20. What kind of career Vance might have had, if only he had pitched in the majors during his twenties, is a question that inspires awe. We will never know, but we can wonder; he might have been the most dominant pitcher ever. Only three no-hitters were pitched in the offense-laden National League from 1925 to 1937. Vance pitched one of them, and he delivered it in his first start after pitching a one-hitter, in 1925.

So why didn't he pitch in the bigs earlier? Well, Vance was plagued by chronic arm miseries while in the minor leagues. At one point, he pitched five complete games in seven days. Dodger manager Wilbert Robinson saved Vance's career when he took the unusual step of starting Vance every fifth day, instead of every fourth, as was the custom of the time. Vance never started more than 35 games in a season.

As an individual, Dazzy Vance was a piece of work. Characterized by a high leg kick, and an 83 inch reach which featured his trademark tattered sleeve, Vance was both overpowering and deceptive, a killer combination in the pitching profession. He was a notorious partier who took great pride in being the last man back to the hotel the morning after a game. However, he didn't take his craft lightly. Upon learning of his election to the Hall of Fame in 1955, he was overcome with emotion.

Vance is often overlooked in discussions of all-time greats, for a number of reasons: the hitter-dominated era in which he pitched and its effect on his stats, the relative brevity of his career, and the weakness of the teams on which he played. It is clear, however, that Vance was the paramount pitching force of his time. No pitcher will ever again lead the league in strikeouts for seven consecutive seasons, as Vance did from 1922 to 1928. If he was born ten years earlier, or had pitched in the majors by age 22, he would be up there with Grove and Johnson as one of the three best ever. As it is, he is a deserving Hall of Famer, who in his prime was the most dominant pitcher of them all.

Aside from that question of what he might have been, we know with certainty what he was. And in 1924 he was the most accomplished pitcher in the National League, by a very wide margin.

Rogers Hornsby - 1925

by Bill Gilbert

G	AB	R	H	2B	3B	HR	RBI	BB	SO	AVG	OBP	SLG	SB
138	504	133	203	41	10	39	143	83	39	.403	.489	.756	5

Rogers Hornsby's career batting average of .358 is second only to that of Ty Cobb. He led the National League in hitting seven times, in slugging ten times, in home runs twice, in RBI's four times and in runs six times. He twice won the triple crown and was elected to the Hall of Fame in 1942, his first year of eligibility.

With the St. Louis Cardinals, Hornsby had a six-year run from 1920 through 1925 that is unequaled in major league history. In each of those years, he led the National League in batting average, on base average and slugging average. His batting average over the 1921-1925 period was .402. During this period, he also had at least one season when he led the league in runs, hits, doubles, triples, home runs, runs batted in, total bases or bases on balls. After an "off year" in 1926, when he did not lead the league in any category other than expressions of contempt for ownership and front office types (Hornsby had become the Cardinals' player-manager and wanted everyone above him in the organization to stay out of the clubhouse and keep their mouths shut) he was traded to the Giants, and gave New York a .361 average with 125 RBI and again led the league in on base percentage in 1927. He had two more outstanding seasons. With the Boston Braves in 1928 he again led the league in batting average, on base average and slugging, and then with the pennant-winning Chicago Cubs in 1929, he hit .380 with 39 home runs, 149 RBI, and a league-leading .679 slugging average, and again was named the league's MVP.

The task here is to select just one year for Hornsby, the model of consistency. By most of the accepted measures of offensive performance, at least six of Hornsby's seasons rate among the 100 best of all time. The four leading contenders are 1922 when he won the Triple Crown while hitting .401, 1924 when he set a modern major league record with a batting average of .424 and reached his personal peak in relative production (223 based on a league average of 100), 1925 when he again won the Triple Crown and was the league MVP, and 1929 when he won his second MVP award. A good case could be made for each. The envelope please ... The winner is 1925, when Hornsby batted .403 and set the all-time National League record .756 slugging average.

The 1925 season marked a turning point in the long-standing contentiousness between Hornsby and Branch Rickey, who served the Cardinals as both GM and field manager. The differences between these two strong personalities were diverse and complicated, but the public sniping was characterized by Hornsby second-guessing his manager excessively and Rickey expressing concerns about Hornsby's nagging little injuries that often left him unable to play baseball but well enough to enjoy a day at the track. In a critical decision that he would later rethink, St. Louis owner Sam Breadon finally intervened by siding with Hornsby and removing Rickey from the dugout. Hornsby himself was installed as manager. At the time the Cardinals were 13-25 for a pathetic .342 winning percentage. Under Hornsby they played .557 ball for the remainder of the 1925 season and then won a pennant in 1926.

As a player in 1925, Hornsby missed 15 games but still led the league in home runs with a margin of 15 over Gabby Hartnett, and he was first in RBI by 13 over Jack Fournier. He also topped the league in total bases for the sixth time and was second to Kiki Cuyler in runs. Hornsby was second in bases on balls and fourth in both hits and doubles.

Although Hornsby piloted the Cardinals to a long-overdue pennant in 1926, he got on the wrong side of owner Breadon. There were some personality differences (as Hornsby seemed to have with almost everyone above him) but the main issue was money. Hornsby wanted a much higher salary than Breadon felt prepared to offer, and Hornsby wanted a multi-year contract instead the one-year deal that Breadon had put on the table.

In a move that would incur the wrath of St. Louis fans and media, Breadon solved his problem by trading Hornsby to the rival New York Giants, getting back Frankie Frisch and a journeyman pitcher. The public outcry was loud and long, but finally subsided when all could see that Frisch was a pretty good player himself (but that's another story).

Hornsby's Olympian batting feats resulted in only two MVP awards. There were no official awards in the National League until 1924; if there were, Hornsby would have been a logical choice for Most Valuable Player in both 1921 and 1922, when he dominated most of the offensive categories and there was no great standout pitcher in the National League. In 1924, the first year of an official award and the year Hornsby hit .424, he finished second behind Dazzy Vance, who had never before led the league in any category but strikeouts. Vance in 1924 swept the pitchers' Triple Crown of wins, ERA and strikeouts, and also led the league in numerous other categories. Hornsby won the MVP award in 1925, over Cuyler of the pennant-winning Pirates, and again in 1929 over Lefty O'Doul who hit .398. The only other time he came close was in 1927 when he finished third behind Paul Waner and Frisch.

Hornsby set some records that have endured for over 70 years. Of the commonly used measures for offensive performance, many analysts say the most meaningful is slugging average. Hornsby's .756 slugging average in 1925 remains as the National League standard, although it was challenged by Jeff Bagwell's .750 in the shortened, pitching-diluted, juiced-ball season of 1994. Hornsby was the first National League player to record a .700 slugging average in a season, and he was the only one ever to do it more than once (he had slugged .722 back in 1922). The only other National Leaguers to reach .700 in a season were Hack Wilson, Stan Musial and Bagwell. National League sluggers Hank Aaron, Willie Mays, Ernie Banks, Frank Robinson, Willie McCovey, Eddie Mathews, and Mel Ott all hit over 500 home runs but never had a season with a slugging average over .670.

What made Hornsby such a great hitter? In present day sports lexicon, he was focused. He didn't smoke or drink. He disdained movies and avoided reading to preserve his uniquely gifted batting eye. He didn't argue with umpires and was never ejected from a game. He was a perfectionist and expected the same from others, a trait that gave him problems in his generally unsuccessful career as a manager with five different major league teams. He was also contentious, dictatorial and brutally frank. He had a problem dealing with authority and wore out his welcome rather quickly wherever he played or managed.

Despite Hornsby's prodigious batting feats, he is not universally regarded as the top second baseman of all time. Bill James, in his *Historical Abstract*, rates him fourth in career value behind Eddie Collins, Joe Morgan and Nap Lajoie and third in peak value behind Morgan and Jackie Robinson. However, there is no doubt that his 1925 season ranks among the best of all time.

Lou Gehrig - 1927

by John Benson

G	AB	R	H	2B	3B	HR	RBI	BB	SO	AVG	OBP	SLG	SB
155	584	149	218	52	18	47	175	109	84	.373	.474	.765	10

Here's a trivia challenge for grandmasters: How is the following lineup different from the real Murderers Row, which hit a composite .327 while winning 110 games for the Yankees in 1927?

1. Earle Combs CF (.356 average and 137 runs)
2. Mark Koenig SS
3. Babe Ruth RF
4. Bob Meusel LF (former AL home run champ)
5. Lou Gehrig 1B
6. Tony Lazzeri 2B
7. Joe Dugan 3B
8. Pat Collins C

That lineup has all the right names, but it's the 1926 batting order. In 1927 manager Miller Huggins flip-flopped his fourth/fifth hitters, to get his budding star Gehrig the cleanup spot as protection for veteran slugger Ruth, while dropping the 30-year-old Meusel down a notch to fifth. That little shift, combined with the blossoming of youngsters Gehrig, Lazzeri and Koenig, helped the defending champions romp to a 19-game winning margin, an American League record that now looks more unbreakable than ever. Given the same starting eight that took them to the seventh game of the World Series in 1926, the Yankees transformed a very good team into a great team, cited by many as the greatest team of all time.

Gehrig, as the nucleus of that lineup, was the single most critical factor. Ruth's 60 homers were an eye-catcher that attained higher stature as years and decades went by with no one else achieving that level.

Back in 1927, most observers calmly figured that Ruth, the freakish long ball hitter, might well reach 65 or 70 home runs in a year or two. It was Gehrig and his jump from 16 homers to 47 which most impressed the contemporary analysts who marveled at the Yankee hitters' ascendancy to greatness.

Looking back from the 1990's, there is a common perception that, after Ruth smashed 54 home runs in 1920, power hitters began a steady stream of 40+ homer seasons. That picture is essentially inaccurate. George Sisler came in second in the majors with 19 home runs in 1920. Aside from Ruth, the kings of the home run in succeeding seasons were guys like George Kelly of the Giants, who led the National League with 23, his career high, in 1921. Other notables of the early-to-mid 1920's included Ken Williams, who led the AL in 1922, Meusel who won the AL crown with 33 in 1925, and Tilly Walker of the Athletics who had won a dead-ball home run crown before Ruth's emergence and got as high as 23 in 1921 and 37 in 1922 before fading out of sight. Kelly, Williams, Meusel and Walker never reached 40 in any year, and each had just one season over 30. In the National League, Rogers Hornsby broke the 40-homer mark in the National League in 1922 but slipped to 17 in 1923 and averaged only 23 per year from 1923 to 1928. Ruth stood uniquely, even peculiarly, elevated among the rest of the slugger population for most of the decade.

Gehrig was the man who finally joined Babe at the Ruthian level. His presence batting fourth helped

Ruth in the third spot, much as Mickey Mantle would help Roger Maris in 1961. While the concept of lineup protection is exaggerated and over-generalized by many today, there are some remarkable cases from history when the numbers support the theory. In games of 1961 without Mantle batting behind him (in classic Stengelese manner, Maris was dropped to seventh against lefties early in the year, and of course Mantle was out with an injury late in the year) Maris was a .172 hitter who walked with extreme frequency and showed fair power. Ruth in 1926, without Gehrig behind him, was of course more formidable than Maris without Mantle, but it's a fact that from 1926 to 1927, Ruth's walks went down, while his home run and RBI output soared. Give Gehrig a tiny measure of credit for Ruth's 60-homer season.

While Ruth was setting the all-time home run record in 1927, Gehrig was setting the all-time RBI mark, with 175. Ruth's mark eventually fell to Maris. Gehrig's lasted until he broke it himself (184 RBI in 1931) and he is still the American League's all-time best. Hack Wilson got his 190 in the National League in 1930, when a super-juiced ball helped the National League as whole, pitchers included, bat .303.

In addition to the runs batted in, Gehrig in 1927 led the American League in doubles with 52, and in total bases, where he outpaced Ruth 447 to 417 (third best was their teammate, Earl Combs, down at 331). Gehrig was second to Ruth in home runs, and he became only the second player ever (Ruth the first of course) to exceed 42 homers; he was also a close second behind Ruth in slugging percentage in 1927.

The big year culminated perfectly in a big World Series for Gehrig and his New York teammates. The 1927 Yankees were itching for another shot at the world championship. In 1926 they had come down to a one-run deficit with two outs in the ninth inning of game seven; Ruth walked but then got caught stealing when Cardinals catcher Bob O'Farrell made the biggest throw in the history of the catching profession, and Rogers Hornsby made the tag. The next year the Yanks were back, this time facing the Pittsburgh Pirates of Waner brothers, Paul and Lloyd, and Pie

Traynor. The Pirates were a tad short of lefty pitching, however, and the Yankees made short work of them. In the first inning of the first game, Ruth singled and Gehrig tripled to put the Yankees ahead. Pittsburgh went more or less steadily downhill from that point, as New York swept in four games. The greatest team reigned supreme, and Gehrig had arrived.

As a figure in history, Gehrig is known for his consistency and durability, rather than for any high peaks. He scored 100 runs and drove in 100 in every full year in his career, 13 straight seasons. He led the American League in RBI five times and in runs scored four times. He became the first and only hitter ever to exceed 150 RBI seven times. Gehrig's .632 career slugging percentage is the third best in history, 48 points behind Ruth and just two points behind Ted Williams. Gehrig holds the all-time greatest rate of RBI per game with a .920 mark (Ruth had .883 RBI per game).

Gehrig was clearly the greatest first baseman of all time. The alternatives for consideration, led by Jimmie Foxx, offer the same types of credentials in the same measurable categories, and all such candidates fall short of Gehrig. George Sisler, the finest first-sacker of the dead ball era, finished with the same .340 career batting average as Gehrig. Although Sisler hit .400 a couple of times, and Gehrig didn't, the best case for Sisler must be founded on a what-if career projection with upgraded stats for all years following the optic nerve infection that impaired his performance after 1922. Of course Gehrig's case would obviously be strengthened too, with a what-if that excluded diseases. Even in the category of tragic illness, Gehrig beat Sisler.

Was 1927 really Gehrig's best season? He hit more home runs in 1932 and 1934, his batting average was higher in 1928 and 1930, and he had 184 RBI in the Great Pitching Crash of 1931. Numbers-wise, the main feature of 1927 was the .765 slugging percentage; no one but Ruth ever did better, before or after. And 1927 was significant as the year of Gehrig's arrival. He became the Yankees' cleanup hitter (that's what the uniform number four meant) and he became the on-field leader of the greatest team ever.

Mickey Cochrane - 1930

by Fr. Jerome C. Romanowski

G	AB	R	H	2B	3B	HR	RBI	BB	SO	AVG	OBP	SLG	SB
130	487	110	174	42	5	10	85	55	18	.357	.424	.526	5

They called him "Black Mike" because of his coal dark hair and businesslike demeanor on the playing field. He came from Boston University where he starred in football as well as baseball. Connie Mack liked his play so much that he purchased the whole Portland club of the Pacific Coast League just to get Mickey Cochrane. It was a purchase Mack would not regret. For most of his career, which extended from 1925 to 1937, Cochrane dueled with the Yankees' Bill Dickey for "Best Catcher in Baseball" status.

Cochrane excelled offensively and defensively. 1930 was his greatest year and one of the greatest for any catcher ever. In addition to his hitting and catching skills, Cochrane also had to play the role of counselor, to keep pitchers like Lefty Grove, the Athletics' temperamental pitching star, maintaining some kind of poise and concentration. Cochrane was obviously quite successful with the staff ace in 1930. Grove went 28-5, and led the league in ERA. Cochrane's expert handling of pitchers helped prepare him for his later career as player/manager for the Detroit Tigers. Cochrane learned managerial skills not only from Mr. Mack, but also from Ty Cobb, Tris Speaker and Eddie Collins, all of whom were part of Mack's juggernaut of the late twenties and early thirties. Earlier, Cochrane had learned catching from veteran Cy Perkins, who later joined him as a Tigers coach.

Cochrane's .357 batting average in 1930 was the second highest of any catcher playing a full season (over 400 plate appearances). Only Dickey, at .362 in 1936, had a higher mark. Babe Phelps hit .367 in

the same year, but as a part-timer. Cochrane's lifetime average of .320 outranks all catchers in baseball history. The other .300 hitting catchers are: Dickey (.313), Phelps (.310), Bubbles Hargrave (.310), Spud Davis (.308) and Ernie Lombardi (.306).

While producing his career-high batting average in 1930, Cochrane batted third in Connie Mack's set batting order. In addition to being his team's anointed hitting star, Cochrane swept the three primary fielding categories for catchers, leading the AL in fielding percentage (.993), putouts and assists.

Cochrane continued to lead the Athletics in the World Series, hitting homers in each of the first two games (both wins) against the St. Louis Cardinals. Cochrane hit only .222 during the World Series, but he knocked in four runs and caught every inning, with his expert pitcher-handling a key factor, as the Athletics beat the Cardinals in six games.

Cochrane was in his prime, at age 27, during the 1930 season. He had many more outstanding seasons in the major leagues, including his tenure as the Tigers' player/manager, which began in 1934, after Connie Mack broke up his last great team, and sold Cochrane to Detroit.

Cochrane and Dickey, two players who are often compared, were eerily similar. Offensively, Cochrane was slightly more patient (.419 career on base percentage, to Dickey's .382 and 857 walks for Cochrane, versus Dickey's 678), but Dickey had

Gordon (Mickey) Cochrane

slightly better power (.486 slugging percentage, compared to Cochrane's .478 and 202 Dickey home runs to Cochrane's 119). Both players were virtually impossible to strike out. Cochrane whiffed only 217 times in 5469 career at bats, while Dickey struck out only 289 times in 6300 career at bats. Cochrane played a greater percentage of his career in hitters' eras, making their production relative to the league virtually equal.

Cochrane's accomplishments would probably have surpassed Dickey's, if not for a career-shortening beanball in May 1937, which ended Cochrane's career and nearly ended his life. Though Dickey is remembered as one of the catchers with the most postseason experience, Cochrane did well enough for himself; Dickey appeared in eight World Series, and Cochrane in five.

Cochrane was a notorious bench jockey, so notorious that Judge Kenesaw Mountain Landis threatened to suspend him in the 1929 World Series. Cochrane would do whatever it took to win a ball game. And in 1930, he was good enough to help the A's win 106 of them, on their way to their second consecutive world championship. A catcher for all seasons!

Frankie Frisch - 1930

by David W. Alvarez

G	AB	R	H	2B	3B	HR	RBI	BB	SO	AVG	OBP	SLG	SB
133	540	121	187	46	9	10	114	55	16	.346	.407	.520	15

If you want a good trivia question, try this one: what Hall of Famer was traded for Rogers Hornsby? The answer of course was Frankie Frisch. If you want a harder trivia question, try naming the player who was the throw-in with Frisch. That was Jimmy Ring, a journeyman pitcher at the end of his career; Ring went 4-21 with an ERA over six after the trade (at least he had ample opportunity to show off what little talent remained). And then if you want a stumper for a trivia expert who knows names and numbers and not much else, ask him why Jimmy Ring was included in the deal. The answer to that is that Giants manager John McGraw was so angry at his talented second baseman (who had taken a leave of absence without permission in August 1926, following a dispute between the two) that McGraw didn't want to give Frisch the possible pleasure of ever saying he was traded even-up for Hornsby.

Frisch, known as "The Fordham Flash" for his days when he captained three teams at the university, played in the National League from 1919 to 1937 and excelled for the Giants and the Cardinals, appearing in eight World Series.

Frisch was born in 1898 in Queens, New York and did not stray far from home while playing baseball for Fordham, located in the Bronx. It was at Fordham that he first earned his reputation for speedy feet. The speed of Frisch was documented, as speed often is, in the form of an anecdote that became part baseball lore. The Giants were traveling by train, and a man entered the club car to talk to the players. The man said he was a snake expert and added he had with him the fastest snake on the continent. The snake expert said to the players, "None of you could catch this snake." Outfielder Ross Youngs promptly insisted that Frisch could catch any snake. The snake fancier answered Youngs with the statement that he couldn't possibly know what he was talking about, because Youngs had never seen this snake on the loose, to which Youngs immediately replied, "maybe not, but I've seen Frisch."

Frisch's speed was an asset welcomed by the Giants who gave him a full-time job at third base in 1920. McGraw's Giants then proceeded to win four National League flags in a row, from 1921 to 1924. During those four years Frisch never hit less than .327. Frisch excelled in those four World Series also, collecting 37 hits in 102 at bats, for a .363 average.

The Giants eventually fell on hard times. Their pitching weakened in 1925 as the team ERA went from 3.62 to 3.94, although the team hit .283 and led the league in home runs. In 1926 the team dropped to fifth place with a sub-.500 winning percentage. McGraw, upset by his team's play, began publicly criticizing Frisch (who had hit .314 in 1926) among other stars, for their lack of hustle. Frisch had once been McGraw's favorite youngster, but when Frisch missed a defensive signal in St. Louis on August 20, McGraw exploded at him. Frisch took the next train home and the rift between the two became permanent. Frisch returned to the team, paid a $500 fine, but was fully aware and, in essence, glad that his days with the

Giants were numbered. McGraw began shopping Frisch aggressively as soon as the season ended. The Cardinals at the time were offering Rogers Hornsby around, after he had become too assertive in his new role as player-manager, and was making all kinds of financial demands on the club's owners.

The deal was a classic problem-for-problem swap. Hornsby played well enough in 1927 but continued to clash with his superiors, and was traded again, after just one year with the Giants. Frisch, on the other hand, thrived in his new environment. He dedicated his 1927 season as a mission to show up McGraw for trading him, playing with unprecedented passion. Frisch led the Cardinals with a .337 batting average and led the National League with 48 stolen bases. In the field he was a dynamo, making 641 assists (his second best season was 537, and all the others were below 475). Frisch also achieved a career high of 104 double plays in 1927. The Cardinals didn't win the pennant, missing by a game and a half, but they did beat out the Giants for second place. Frisch's acquisition was a successful move. Based on his efforts, the St. Louis papers dropped their harsh criticism of the owner for trading Hornsby. Years later, teammates would call Frisch's 1927 season the finest individual effort they had ever witnessed ... but we found an even better year for Frisch.

As the 1930 season started, the Cardinals, under new manager Gabby Street, were considered serious contenders for the pennant. Sunny Jim Bottomley at first base and Frisch at second base were among the league's top hitters. Chick Hafey and Taylor Douthit were well-known for their outfield speed and strong arms. The pitching was a bit less solid. On the staff that year were Flint Rhem, who would later miss a critical game with the Dodgers because of drinking too much, aging spitballer Burleigh Grimes (a midseason purchase to add strength), Jesse Haines, Bill Hallahan and 13-game winner Sylvester Johnson.

The Redbirds started slowly, dropping 12 of the first 18 games. However they spurted to a 21-13 record by late May, reaching first place. But then came the injuries, including 17 days lost by Frisch in an infield collision. The Cards again fell below .500. As July approached, the defending champion Cubs won 20 of 27 games, taking over first place. Street began imposing fines for lackadaisical play in August, and the team responded. They climbed to second place, 2 1/2 games out, on September 7. The Cardinals came east to play the Giants and Dodgers, and after winning three of four games in the Polo Grounds, they faced the Dodgers, who had just won 11 in a row and jumped to first place. Frisch saved the first game at Ebbets Field, as the middleman in a lightning fast 6-4-3 double play that prevented the tying run from scoring in the bottom of the 10th inning. This double play occurred so fast, wrote a sportswriter of the day, that many fans didn't realize the game was over. The Cards won the second game, although Rhem didn't pitch as scheduled, and blamed his failure on a kidnaping by gangsters who had forced him to imbibe. The next day the first place Redbirds completed their sweep of the demoralized Dodgers, as Frisch tripled to score a run and later scored when Bottomley homered. The Cardinals continued to win regularly and finished first by two games. Frisch, who finished the year at .346, lost the vote for National League MVP by two votes to Hack Wilson, who hit a mere 56 homers with 190 runs batted in to accompany his .356 batting average.

The Cards entered the World Series as underdogs. Babe Ruth was certain that Connie Mack's Athletics would win in four straight. He was almost right. It took six games. Frisch didn't excel offensively in the Series (he batted .208), but still managed to set two World Series records. Despite suffering from lumbago, Frisch managed to play in game one, producing a single and a two-bagger. Frisch got a double in game two, his 43rd hit in World Series play, a new Fall Classic record. In game four Frisch was part of a "sparkling" double play when he barely threw out Jimmie Foxx at first in the third inning. In game five Frisch collected his 34th single in World Series play, also a record at that time. In game six Frisch made a great play on a shot by Mickey Cochrane.

Frisch went on to manage the "Gas House Gang" as a player-manager in 1934, and subsequently he managed the Giants and Cubs. But that 1930 season best displayed the magnitude of his talent and desire.

Hack Wilson - 1930

By Bill Gray

G	AB	R	H	2B	3B	HR	RBI	BB	SO	AVG	OBP	SLG	SB
155	585	146	208	35	6	56	190	105	84	.356	.454	.723	3

It's an accepted fact that the ball was juiced in 1930. But Cubs outfielder Hack Wilson was juiced, too, both in terms of lively distance off the bat, and with the definition implying indulgence in drink. Despite the latter, Wilson holds two seasonal records which have lasted sixty five years: the major league high 190 RBI and the National League high 56 home runs.

Wilson was only 5'6" and weighed over 200 pounds. He was one of the strongest players ever. He got the name Hack for George Hackenschmidt, a wrestler/ strongman of the era, or Hack Miller, another powerful Cubs outfielder, or he was named for a taxicab "hack" in reference to his physique.

Alcohol made his career both funny and tragic. There are many "Hack Wilson stories." He is alleged to have nodded out while standing in right field during a game. His funniest line, oft repeated, came after manager Joe McCarthy tried to illustrate the ravages of alcohol on the human body by dropping a worm into a glass of water. The worm wiggled contentedly in the water. McCarthy commanded Wilson to notice how water does no harm to the worm. "But," intoned McCarthy, "watch what happens when the worm is dropped in a glass off whiskey!" McCarthy plunged the critter into the hooch and it died instantly. "What does that show you?" asked the manager. Wilson replied eagerly: "If you drink whiskey you won't get worms!?"

Because of the 190 RBI mark as a lone peak on the statistical landscape, Wilson's accompanying 56 home runs and .356 batting average are often overlooked. Critics who paint Wilson as a one trick pony like to cite the juiced ball as the reason Wilson made the record books, and when you focus on his nose-dive in 1931 when he hit only .261 with 13 homers and a measly 61 RBI, he may look like a one act play. But Wilson's poor 1931 season interrupted a five year run in which he had reached over 100 runs batted in and over 20 homers every year. Actually he *averaged* 35 homers and 141 RBI per year from 1926 to 1930. He finished with a career batting average of .307.

While his 1930 season is tainted by the rabbit ball, Wilson didn't just suddenly sneak up on baseball. You could almost see it coming in 1929 as he banged out 39 homers and knocked in a hefty 156 runs. His .723 slugging in 1930 is 14th highest all-time.

After the 1931 season, the Cubs traded Wilson to the Cardinals, who then shipped him to Brooklyn before the season began. He had a bit of a rebound in 1932, hitting 23 homers and driving in 123 runs, but by 1933 he was about done. He played in just 67 games for the Dodgers in 1934, and was released. He played another year in the minors before retiring in 1935.

Lewis Robert "Hack" Wilson was one of the great power hitters of the era, and his 65-year-old record of 190 RBI should hold up well, maybe forever. Despite a major league career which lasted only 12 years, Wilson was posthumously elected to the Hall of Fame in 1979, 31 years after his death at the age of 48.

Robert (Lefty) Grove

Lefty Grove - 1931

by Tony Blengino

W	L	PCT	G	GS	CG	SV	IP	SO	BB	B/I	ERA
31	4	.886	41	30	27	5	288	175	62	1.08	2.06

Robert Moses "Lefty" Grove was definitely the premier lefthanded starting pitcher of all time, and it is a close call between Grove and Walter Johnson for best ever. An illustrious minor league tenure, extended by one owner's unwillingness to sell Grove to a major league club, delayed and thus shortened his major league career, preventing any chance for him to become the clear-cut best pitcher of all time.

Grove was among the first "bonus babies." He posted a 109-36 record for the Baltimore Orioles of the International League from 1920-24. Owner Jack Dunn resisted many overtures from big league clubs for Grove's services, and since he was being paid quite well, Grove didn't particularly mind. Dunn finally broke down and sold Grove to the Athletics for $100,600 before the 1925 season. Grove didn't pitch in his first big league game until age 25.

Grove fashioned an imposing 300-141 (.680) lifetime record, easily the highest winning percentage among 300-game winners. He was fortunate in pitching for teams that had a cumulative .589 winning percentage in the years in which he qualified for the ERA title, but the .091 difference between his and his teams' winning percentages ranks behind only Pete Alexander, Walter Johnson and Sandy Koufax among Hall of Fame pitchers. Even more impressive is his career 3.06 ERA, an amazing stat when viewed in the context of his era. With 100 representing the league average, Grove's adjusted ERA index was 148, meaning he was 48% better than the league average, the highest of all time, just nosing out Johnson's 147 index.

Grove neatly bridged the gap between Walter Johnson and Bob Feller, dominating the American League from 1925 to 1939. Grove led the league in wins four times, winning percentage five times, complete games three times, shutouts three times, strikeouts seven consecutive times, ERA nine times (an all time record) and saves once. He led the AL in relative control/power factor seven times.

Grove had a three-year peak from 1929 to 1931, not coincidentally three seasons when the Athletics won the pennant. In that span, Grove went 72-19, for a winning percentage of .791, compared to his teams' .665 mark. Grove's best year of the three was 1931. He led the AL in wins, winning percentage, ERA, complete games, shutouts (4) and strikeouts, winning the MVP award.

Grove had just a little bit of offensive help in 1931. Behind Hall of Famers Jimmie Foxx (30 homers and 120 RBI at age 23), Al Simmons (.390, 22 homers, and 128 RBI) and Mickey Cochrane (.349, 17 homers, and 89 RBI), the Athletics offense was indeed potent, though they scored 209 runs less than the Yankee juggernaut which finished second. Pitching made the difference for Philadelphia.

The Grove-led pitching staff, including 21-game winner George Earnshaw, 20-game winner Rube Walberg and Hall of Famer Waite Hoyt, enabled the A's to finish 13 1/2 games ahead of the Yankee team with Babe Ruth, Lou Gehrig, Tony Lazzeri, Earle Combs, Bill Dickey, Lefty Gomez, Red Ruffing,

Herb Pennock (Hall of Famers all).

Grove had a 16-game winning streak near the season's end, tying the AL record (which still stands). His legendary temper reared its ugly head when his streak ended in a 1-0 loss, as the only run scored on a muffed fly ball by backup outfielder Jim Moore. Moore was playing only because Manager Connie Mack had allowed the regular, Simmons, to take the day off since the pennant had already been clinched. Grove's anger was directed not at Moore, but at Mack and Simmons and, most of all, the unfortunate A's clubhouse, which he remodeled and redecorated quite extensively that day.

Grove's 1931 season was also characterized by Mack's using him as a reliever between starts. Grove made 18 relief appearances in addition to his 32 starts, and went 5-1 with 5 saves working out of the pen. The total of decisions and saves in comparison to the relatively low number of relief appearances (11 of the 18 games) underscores the fact that Grove was used primarily in tight game-on-the-line situations, much like the "closers" of today.

One more amazing aspect of Grove's peak period is his incredible record at Shibe Park. He went 17-1 there in 1931, and 75-11 (.872) there from 1929 through 1933.

Ironically, the Athletics didn't win the World Series in Grove's best-ever season. Going for their third consecutive championship, they fell to the Cardinals. Grove outdueled Paul Derringer 6-2 in game one, battling through a gritty complete game 12-hitter. Burleigh Grimes got the better of Grove with seven no-hit innings in game three, a 5-2 Cardinal triumph. With the A's facing elimination in game six, Grove again beat Derringer, throwing a complete game five-hitter and winning 8-1. Alas, Grimes and Wild Bill Hallahan shut down the Athletics 4-2 in game seven, while Grove sat and watched St. Louis win the title. Grove was 2-1 with a 2.42 ERA for the Series. Though he gave up an unusually high number of hits (28 in 26 innings) he posted an incredible 26/2 strikeout/walk ratio.

For the first phase of his career (through 1933), Grove threw steady heat. There were no hops or dives on his pitches, but it didn't matter. After Connie Mack's legendary clearance sale following the 1933 season, Grove joined the Red Sox, and promptly hurt his arm en route to an 8-8, 6.50 season. Robbed of his legendary fastball, Grove needed to change his style as a pitcher to survive. He became a curveball-throwing finesse/control pitcher in 1935, mixing in just an occasional fastball to keep hitters honest, and did much more than just survive. He remained at the top of his profession, going 85-41 over the next five seasons while pitching for a less-than-spectacular Boston club, and he led the American League in ERA four more times during that span.

Grove won exactly 300 games, and that figure became a magic number of sorts for the first time as he approached it in 1941, his final season. Earlier that year, the media had become absorbed in DiMaggio's 56-game hitting streak, and now thirsted for the next on-field long-term accomplishment that could be a media focal point. Grove's plodding march toward 300 was covered by writers from every major city.

Lefty Grove was a hot-tempered, sensitive man who was completely intolerant of anything he perceived as criticism, no matter how well-intentioned. He often would trek back to his farm in Lonaconing, Maryland, between starts to cool down and re-group. For most of Grove's reign, he had little competition for supremacy among AL hurlers, and his chief rivals came from the two NL franchises in New York City. Dazzy Vance of the Dodgers, and later Carl Hubbell of the Giants, ruled the NL during this period. Vance was possibly a harder thrower, and Hubbell had comparable control, but in virtually every year that Grove and either Vance or Hubbell pitched, Grove came out ahead in the record books.

Grove's place is secure in the pantheon of immortal pitchers. An earlier escape from the minor leagues could have made Grove a clear choice as the greatest pitcher ever. He is, nonetheless, the greatest southpaw ever, and an extremely close second behind Walter Johnson on the all-time list. And in 1931, for sure, he was second to no one.

Al Simmons - 1931

by Fr. Jerome C. Romanowski

G	AB	R	H	2B	3B	HR	RBI	BB	SO	AVG	OBP	SLG	SB
128	513	105	200	37	13	22	128	47	45	.390	.444	.641	3

When Al Simmons joined the Philadelphia Athletics in 1923, practitioners of the art of hitting complained that he hit with his "foot in the bucket." This phrase meant that he slid his front foot away from the plate, thus losing the necessary balance to handle the savage assaults of major league pitchers. When this point was made to Connie Mack, he replied, "I think I will leave Mr. Simmons alone because, so far, I like the results." No one ever changed Simmons' batting approach, and "the results" continued for over 20 years. He finished his career with a .334 average, fifth best among all righthanded hitters since 1901.

Simmons was also regarded as a premier defensive player. Curt Gowdy often compared Carl Yastrzemski to Simmons; both were good enough to play center field at times during their careers, though both were used primarily as left fielders. One of the oldest reporters on the television show "The Sportswriters" said that Simmons was the only outfielder who could routinely throw the ball from the warning track to home plate on the fly.

Al Simmons was a holdout in 1931, and didn't sign his contract until opening day. He signed for $100,000 for three years, one of the highest contracts given in those depression days. In true Roy Hobbs fashion, he won the opener with a tremendous home run onto the roof at Shibe Park. He finished the season by hitting .333 in the World Series, which was won in seven games by the St. Louis Cardinals. Simmons hit two doubles, two homers, and had eight RBI to lead both teams in the Series. For his career, Simmons hit .329 with six home runs and 17 RBI, in World Series competition.

To put Simmons' .390 average in 1931 into proper perspective, consider that only Ted Williams in 1941 and Tony Gwynn in the shortened 1994 season have hit for higher single season averages since. Also, Simmons (who was at the time still only age 29) had already accumulated seasonal averages of .387, .392, .365, .381 and .390. He started 1931 with a career average of .363.

Why then, did Simmons not go on to post career numbers like Ted Williams or Ty Cobb? Simmons freely admitted that his new-found wealth had a negative effect on his development as a player. Simmons stated, "When I finally decided I had it made, I was never again the ballplayer I was when I was hungry." That story has been told by many players, before and after. Simmons' performance tailed off, but he was still a solid major league contributor for many years. Mack disposed of Simmons' expensive contract in 1932 when attendance was declining.

A visitor to Connie Mack's office many years later noticed that the only player's picture in his office was that of Al Simmons. When asked why, Mr. Mack responded, "When the chips were down, Al Simmons was the man I wanted at the plate."

Jimmie Foxx - 1932

by Fr. Jerome C. Romanowski

G	AB	R	H	2B	3B	HR	RBI	BB	SO	AVG	OBP	SLG	SB
154	585	151	213	33	9	58	169	116	96	.364	.469	.749	3

Blame Babe Ruth. Lay the blame at Ruth's feet for being such an enormous presence and exerting such emotional control over baseball fans in the 1920's and 1930's that he would actually cast a shadow big enough to obscure a player with the stature of Jimmie Foxx. Ted Williams once declared that he had never seen anybody who could hit a ball harder than Jimmie Foxx. Such admiring citations from his illustrious peers were common. Lefty Grove once described his astonishment at seeing one of Foxx's howitzer shots, and how after the game he walked all the way up into the upper deck to inspect the damage done where Foxx hit the ball. Grove confirmed with his own eyes what many couldn't believe: the hard wooden seat had been shattered by the impact.

Who would doubt Williams' assessment of a hitter? "Double X" was strong, very strong. Unfortunately, so was his choice of beverage. Drinking accelerated Foxx's decline while he was still in his early thirties. The natural ability that enabled him to enter the major leagues at age 17 was eroded by too many late nights. He was washed up before he reached his mid thirties.

By 1932 Foxx was already known as "the righthanded Babe Ruth." He had led the Athletics to the World Series in 1929, 1930 and 1931, and Foxx hit .344 in those three fall classics, with four home runs and 11 RBI in 64 at bats. But in 1932 the A's vaunted pitching staff started to falter, opening the door for the Yankees to reclaim the pennant and Ruth to play in his final World Series. The Athletics' offense, however, remained awesome. Mickey Cochrane, Al Simmons, Jimmy Dykes, Mule Haas and Eric McNair all had productive years, but 1932 was The Year for James Emory Foxx. In his fourth year as a regular, Foxx reached his peak as a sensational slugger.

After pounding 30 or more home runs in each of the previous three seasons, Foxx challenged the immortal Ruth's single-season home run record. In mid-July, Foxx was 32 games ahead of Ruth's pace. But then a freak household accident intervened. In August Foxx fell from a ladder and sprained his wrist. Though the injury did not force him from the lineup, it visibly affected his power until a resurgence in September.

The "what if" analysts of the time observed that Foxx in 1932 hit eight balls into outfield screens that had been recently erected above the fences in St. Louis and Cleveland -- screens that didn't exist when Ruth collected his 60 home runs in 1927. Could Foxx have hit 66 home runs? Maybe. But that's baseball: things change.

Foxx not only missed the all-time home run record but was also nosed out for the 1932 batting title, and thus the Triple Crown, by Dale Alexander who played less than full-time for the Tigers and Red Sox, hitting .367 overall. Foxx was an obvious choice for the American League's Most Valuable Player in 1932. The Athletics finished in second place, thirteen games behind the Yankees. Connie Mack then dismantled the Athletics at the end of the '32 season by selling Simmons, Haas and Dykes to the White

Sox. Foxx was the last of the 1929-1931 dynasty Hall of Famers to leave the Athletics when he was traded to the suddenly well-financed Red Sox of Tom Yawkey after the 1935 season.

Foxx went on to become a member of the 500 homer club, bashing 534. He hit for a higher lifetime average (.325) than all but two of his fellow club members (Ruth and Williams). Foxx finished with a career .428 on base percentage (eighth all-time) and a .609 slugging average (fourth).

Foxx appeared eminently capable of producing even bigger lifetime numbers, but then came the sudden, dramatic decline in 1942 at the young age of 34. At age 33, Foxx had 519 homers; by comparison Ruth had 470, Willie Mays 445, and Henry Aaron 481. Despite the fact that Foxx won three MVP Awards (1932, 1933, 1938) and finally got his Triple Crown year, in 1933, at no time was he universally regarded as the best player in the game. Early in his career, the nod generally went to Ruth or Lou Gehrig, and near the end, he had to contend with Joe DiMaggio and Ted Williams.

Still, the big 1932 season elevated Foxx to legendary status; he was viewed as a peer of players like Ruth and Ty Cobb, even if classified as a junior partner in the top tier. Foxx was only 24 years old in 1932. His home runs were not only plentiful; they also came with vast dimensions, long and lofty.

Fans of the time often identified Foxx with particularly impressive home runs they had witnessed: the shot over the upper deck at old Comiskey Park, that went beyond 34th Street; the World Series clincher at St. Louis in 1930; the blast clear over the flagpole in Philadelphia; and that immense shot high into the left field upper deck at Yankee Stadium, the one that broke one of the "indestructible" hard wooden seats that were sold as souvenirs when they rebuilt the stadium 40 years later.

Though Foxx had many great years, he never had another like 1932. He reached 50 home runs again in 1938, when he also produced career highs with 175 RBI and 119 walks while winning the batting crown with a .349 average, but 1932 was the best.

Carl Hubbell - 1933

by Marc Bowman

W	L	PCT	G	GS	CG	SV	IP	SO	BB	B/I	ERA
23	12	.657	45	33	22	5	308	156	47	0.99	1.66

The most dominant National League pitcher of the 1930's, Carl Hubbell won 20 games five straight years, leading the league in ERA three times and winning two Most Valuable Player awards. A member of nine All-Star teams, he won 253 games over 16 seasons for the Giants, helping them to three pennants and a World Series championship.

Hubbell had a number of excellent seasons, and choosing the best would be difficult if not for his unusually marvelous 1933 campaign.

In 1933, the New York Giants needed every bit of pitching that Hubbell could give them. Despite featuring a lineup that included future Hall-of-Famers Bill Terry and Mel Ott, the Giants were an average offensive team. Ott had an off year; his 23 homers were the least he would produce in any season of the decade. Meanwhile, the aging Terry hit .322, his worst mark in eight years.

The Giants' fortunes rested on their fine starting rotation that featured Hubbell, Hal Schumacher, Freddie Fitzsimmons and Roy Parmelee. This staff was the best in the National League in virtually every category, including ERA and shutouts. Hubbell was best in the league in most pitching stats and even managed five saves, tied for second best in the NL.

Hubbell was overpowering from start to finish. His strong pitching helped the Giants take hold of the National League lead midway through the season and hold it until the end, finishing the year with a four game bulge over the Pirates. Hubbell fashioned a 46-inning scoreless streak on his way to his league-leading 23 victories.

Among his ten shutouts was an eighteen-inning six-hit whitewashing of the Cardinals; Hubbell struck out 12 and walked none in that game. His eighteen inning stint has been matched just twice since in the majors. Hubbell himself claimed this game to be his finest performance of all, better even than the no-hitter he hurled during his second season in the majors.

The crowning accomplishment for Hubbell came when he led his Giants into the World Series against the favored Washington Senators. Hubbell tossed complete game victories in games one and four, allowing just three unearned runs in twenty innings. The Giants won the Series in five games.

After the season, Hubbell was rewarded with the National League's MVP award. His startling 1.66 ERA is one of the best since the end of the dead ball era. Over the last 75 years, only three National League pitchers have posted better marks. Since 1920, only two National League pitchers have bettered Hubbell's ten shutouts. Hubbell also led the league in innings pitched (308.2) and opponents' on base percentage (.260).

According to the Total Pitcher Index rankings from *Total Baseball* by John Thorn and Pete Palmer, Hubbell's 1933 season ranks ninth best among all pitchers since 1920. In his *Historical Baseball*

Abstract, Bill James ranks Hubbell's peak season as the third best ever by a lefthanded starter.

In the following season Hubbell again led the league in ERA (2.30) and accomplished perhaps his most legendary exploit during that year's All-Star game. He fanned consecutively, over two innings, Babe Ruth, Lou Gehrig, Jimmie Foxx, Al Simmons and Joe Cronin, future Hall-of-Famers all!

Hubbell went on to lead the National League in ERA (2.31) and victories in 1936 when he again won the league's MVP award and carried the Giants to the World Series where they lost to the Yankees in six games. That year Hubbell won his final sixteen games on the way to a 26-6 record. He then won his first eight games in 1937 for a since-unsurpassed 24-game winning streak. Hubbell also led the NL in wins in 1937 (22) and in strikeouts (159).

During the nine year span from 1931 to 1939, Hubbell led National League pitchers with the best opposition on base percentage seven times and posted a lifetime .291 opposition OBP, among the very best of all time. Further testimony to Hubbell's dominance is his 1.79 ERA in World Series play.

Hubbell's .622 career winning percentage ranks eleventh all-time among pitchers with 200 or more victories. He never lost more than 12 games in any season and had just one losing season out of sixteen years in the majors. Hubbell won election to the Hall of Fame in 1947.

Pitching in an era when offense ruled and legendary hitters stalked the ballparks, "King Carl" ruled with an overpowering screwball. While team batting averages soared upwards to .300 (the entire National League hit .303 in 1930), Hubbell thrived and became the most consistent pitcher in the league. His ability to halt the Giants' losing streaks earned Hubbell the sobriquet "the Meal Ticket."

Hubbell's success helped keep the Giants near the top of the National League for more than a decade. During Hubbell's most dominant years, the Giants went 968-711, a .577 winning percentage, and won at least 83 games in all but one of eleven seasons.

Ironically, the "Meal Ticket's" bread-and-butter pitch was one which a former manager forbade Hubbell to throw. Believing that the reverse curveball motion required to throw the pitch would ruin Hubbell's arm, Ty Cobb forced Hubbell to abandon the screwball. It wasn't until a few years later, when he was playing in the Texas League that Hubbell once again began throwing his best pitch.

Once he had mastered his screwball, Hubbell quickly advanced to the majors and thrived under the tutelage of John McGraw. He won 10 games in his rookie campaign and won at least ten games in fifteen consecutive seasons. By the early 1930's, Hubbell had become the league's dominant force on the mound.

He would rule the National League during the next decade before an arm injury turned him into an average pitcher near the end of the 1930's. Among all of Hubbell's fine seasons, 1933 stands out as his best -- and as one of the best of all time.

Chuck Klein - 1933

by Bill Gilbert

G	AB	R	H	2B	3B	HR	RBI	BB	SO	AVG	OBP	SLG	SB
152	606	101	233	44	7	28	120	56	36	.368	.422	.602	15

Most of the players in the Hall of Fame achieved their status through 15 or more years of consistently high performance. Outfielder Chuck Klein followed a somewhat different path into the Hall. Klein is part of a group which includes Hack Wilson, Ralph Kiner, Sandy Koufax and Dizzy Dean: players who made it to the Hall of Fame based on exceptionally high performance over a relatively short period.

While Klein appeared in the majors for 18 consecutive seasons, he established essentially all of his Hall-of-Fame credentials in a five year span early in his career, from 1929 through 1933. He arrived in the majors with the Phillies in 1928 at the age of 23, hitting .360 for a half-season as a replacement for the aging Cy Williams. In the next five years, Klein led the league in homers and total bases four times, runs and slugging average three times, hits and RBI twice and batting average, on base percentage and stolen bases once each. He had over 200 hits each year and set a modern major league record for outfielders with 44 assists in 1930.

These accomplishments were partly attributable to Klein playing in the most generous ballpark for hitters, Baker Bowl with its 280 foot right field fence. Klein's run of success changed abruptly when he was traded to the Chicago Cubs after the 1933 season. From that point on, his performance was affected not so much by the change of stadium (Wrigley Field has always been kind to hitters) as it was diminished by various injuries. Klein continued as a productive hitter for six more years before tailing off; but he never again led the league in any key category as he had done so many times during the years 1929 to 1933.

Selecting Klein's best season is difficult. His best home run year was in 1929 with 43. In 1930 he peaked in runs (158), doubles (59), RBI (170) and batting average (.386). But 1930 was the best year ever for *all* hitters, especially in the National League, and any raw statistics from that season in particular must be regarded with some thought of the context. Klein led the National League in runs, RBI, home runs and slugging average in 1931, and in runs, hits, home runs, slugging average and stolen bases in 1932. Four great years they were, 1929 through 1932, for sure.

In 1933, Klein did not reach a personal high in any category. However, he won the Triple Crown and also led the league in on base percentage, slugging percentage, hits, and doubles. No player has so dominated a league in all seven of these categories since then, and only two did it before Klein: Nap Lajoie in 1901 and Rogers Hornsby in 1922.

Why is Klein's 1933 season (.368-28-120) rated higher than his 1930 season (.386-40-170)? The answer lies in the context. The juiced up ball in 1930 produced a .303 batting average in the National League, a number reduced to .266 by 1933, through further changes in the ball, to make it more suitable for the dimensions of existing ballparks. The 1930 ball was fun for spectators, but it made many of the league's parks appear too small, and it took a serious toll on the pitchers who had to throw many more pitches to get through each game, and face many more batters over the course of a season. It was a bigger workload without any offsetting increase in the number of pitchers on the roster to carry that load, and the game simply got distorted. In 1930, Klein's big numbers were insufficient to dominate the league as he did in 1933. In 1930 he finished third in batting average behind Bill Terry (.401) and Babe Herman (.393) and second behind Hack Wilson in home runs (56) and RBI (190).

1930 was clearly Wilson's year. It was the only year in Klein's five year run when he didn't lead the league in home runs. In 1933, Klein led in all three categories, and his batting average was 102 points above the league average. In the swinging decade of the 1930's, only four other players had a batting average that reached higher than 100 points above the league average: Al Simmons in 1931, Arky Vaughan in 1935, Joe Medwick in 1937, and Joe DiMaggio in 1939.

The Baseball Writers' Association of America established the Most Valuable Player Award for both leagues, as we know that award today, before the 1931 season. Klein finished second behind Frankie Frisch in 1931, won the award in 1932 over Lon Warneke, and finished second behind Carl Hubbell in 1933 when Hubbell recorded his incredible ERA of 1.66 for the pennant winning Giants.

Klein was clearly considered the best offensive player in the league in 1932 and 1933, playing for a team that was not a contender. In Klein's five years of glory, the Phillies never finished higher than fourth. In 1929, the team had four players with over 100 RBI (Klein had 145, Don Hurst 125, Lefty O'Doul 122, and Pinky Whitney 115) and still finished fifth. In 1930, the team had a composite batting average of .315 and finished last, with the pitching staff yielding an all-time high

team ERA of 6.71. The ballpark obviously was a major factor in both hitting and pitching, but the Phillies' pitchers also set a major league record that year for most runs allowed per game on the road. They were clearly just bad pitchers, as a group, but also the aforementioned workload problem, wearing out the pitchers in the toughest circumstances by requiring so many pitches and so many batters faced to get through each game, had a tiring effect that followed the staff even when they went on the road.

By 1933, Philadelphia's other strong offensive players had either faded or departed. The team hit only 60 home runs, with Klein's 28 accounting for almost half of them. While Klein drove in 120 runs, no one else on the team drove in more than 76, for a club that finished seventh, 31 games off the pace. The obvious implication is that Klein had little protection in the lineup, so he could often be pitched around. And the top of the order was also weak at getting on base, meaning a shortage of opportunities for Klein to drive in runs. Klein himself was the only player on the team to score more than 100 runs, leading top-of-the-order man Chick Fullis who scored 91 times and Dick Bartell who scored 78 runs. No one else on the team crossed the plate more than 58 times. The team's scoring dropped from 944 in 1930 to 607 in 1933. For Klein to lead the league in RBI with the framework of this lineup in 1933 was a contextual miracle.

Klein was not elected to the Hall of Fame until 1980, 36 years after he last appeared in the major leagues and 22 years after he died. The rap against Klein was that his numbers were largely a result of the ballpark, and probably no player ever used his home park to greater advantage. However, his accomplishments have too much substance to be ignored. He was a standout hitter in the golden era for hitters. His great '33 season was the icing on the cake, without which, he probably would not have been elected to the Hall.

Dizzy Dean - 1934

by Tony Blengino

W	L	PCT	G	GS	CG	SV	IP	SO	BB	B/I	ERA
30	7	.811	50	33	24	7	311	195	75	1.19	2.66

Dizzy Dean is primarily remembered as a wisecracking country boy who drove his teammates, opponents, and managers crazy with his surprising antics and outrageous commentary. When his playing career ended, he took his show to the airwaves as an announcer, and entertained the next generation of fans as well. His pitching career was simply amazing, especially as it was concentrated in a time span cut short by an injury that is often overlooked in historical retrospectives.

Dean combined phenomenal velocity, movement, *and* fine control, to dominate hitters in an era when batsmen in general were enjoying a heyday. Dean was an easy Hall of Fame selection despite a career so short that he pitched only six seasons with enough innings to qualify for the ERA title, the fewest of any Hall of Fame starting pitcher (Sandy Koufax qualified in eight seasons, for comparison).

A toe injury suffered in the 1937 All Star Game started Dean's downward spiral at age 26. He had already recorded 134 wins, but would get only 16 more in his career. He reached his personal peak in 1934, leading the Gashouse Gang Cardinals (along with his brother Paul) to the World Championship with a succession of late-season heroics. In so doing, he became the last National League pitcher to earn 30 wins in a season.

The St. Louis Cardinals were a solid club in 1934, but appeared to be way overmatched by the mighty New York Giants (featuring Hall of Famers Bill Terry, Mel Ott, Travis Jackson and Carl Hubbell). The Cards were an offensive juggernaut, but their pitching looked suspect. They led the National League in runs, hits, doubles, RBI, steals, average, on base percentage and slugging percentage. First baseman Ripper Collins led the offense with a .333 average, 35 home runs (best in the league), 128 RBI and a .615 slugging percentage. Left fielder Joe Medwick batted .319 with 18 home runs, 106 RBI, 40 doubles and 18 triples. Second baseman Frankie Frisch and third baseman Pepper Martin both batted over .300. Behind the Deans, the Cards pitching staff featured Tex Carleton (who finished the year 16-11), Bill Walker (12-4) and Wild Bill Hallahan (8-12), as well as two Hall of Fame hangers-on, Dazzy Vance (age 43) and Jesse Haines (age 40).

During the first four and a half months of the season, the Cards never led the league, except for one week in early June. St. Louis stayed in the hunt all year, however, and remained clearly within reach of a pennant with two weeks to go. Frisch, the player/manager, decided to roll the dice and send either Dizzy Dean or his brother Paul to the mound in almost every game remaining. This strategy had the Cards sitting just one game behind the Giants entering the season's final weekend.

The schedule favored the Cards, as they were matched up against the last place Reds, while the Giants faced the scrappy Dodgers. In the series' first game, Dizzy Dean shut out the Reds, which pulled the Cards into a tie for first when the Giants lost their game that day.

Now it was Paul Dean's turn to beat the Reds the next day, while Dodgers' ace Van Lingle Mungo beat the Giants, giving the Cards sole possession of first place. Leaving nothing to chance, Frisch sent Dizzy Dean back to the mound on one day's rest to attempt to clinch the NL flag. Dean did not disappoint, again shutting out the Reds, this time by the score of 9-0. It was Dizzy's 30th win.

The Cards completed their amazing surge due mainly to the exploits of the Dean brothers, who won seven games between them in the season's final ten days. For the season, the Deans gave the team 49 victories. Dizzy had deservedly won the MVP Award. What could the Deans do for an encore in the World Series?

There was a two-day break between season's end and the beginning of the World Series, plenty of time for Ole Diz to get rested and ready. The Cards took advantage of five Detroit Tiger errors in game one, and rode Dizzy's complete game effort to an 8-3 win. In game two, for the first time in quite a while, a Dean did not pitch for the Cards. Consistent with the growing tendency to consider Dean starts and victories as one and the same, St. Louis lost game two, 3-2. Then Paul ''Daffy'' Dean got the Cards back on top in game three, with a complete game, 4-1 effort. Neither Dean brother pitched in Game Four, but Dizzy still got himself involved. After entering the game as a pinch-runner, Dizzy promptly broke up a double play -- with his forehead! He was staggered by the relay throw which caught him flush in the head. Legend has it that banner headlines the next day appeared nationwide with the news:

X-RAY OF DEAN'S HEAD
REVEALS NOTHING

The Dean-less Cards lost game four, 10-4. Dizzy recovered in time to pitch the next day, and pitched well, but this time in a losing effort, as Tommy Bridges outdueled him, 3-1. Down three games to two, Frisch knew what he had to do: start Daffy in game six, and Dizzy in game seven. He didn't need a single reliever. Daffy outdueled Schoolboy Rowe, 4-3, and then Dizzy pitched an 11-0 shutout in the Cards' seventh game rout, an event remembered partly for

the spectacle of Tiger fans pelting Cards' left fielder Joe Medwick with food and bottles. The Cards' last seven wins of the season were all credited to the Dean brothers.

Dizzy's 1934 stats were almost as big as the story of his season. He led the league in wins, winning percentage, strikeouts, and shutouts (seven). He finished second in ERA, behind Carl Hubbell's 2.30, and amazingly, second in saves, again behind Hubbell, 7-8. Dean's 312 innings ranked a narrow third (Mungo had 315, and Hubbell 313). Dean ranked second behind brother Paul in relative control/power factor. Dizzy's was 3.39, Paul's 4.01.

On a peak value basis, Bill James ranks Dean as the third best righthanded starter of all time. Any way you slice it, he was one of the game's true greats, despite the shortened career. And he was clearly at his peak in 1934.

The Cards narrowly missed winning pennants in 1935 and 1936, but there appeared to be no need to worry about another title coming down the line, as Dizzy was still only 26 years old. (Daffy had hurt his arm, permanently, during the 1935 season.) Diz was on his way to yet another outstanding season in 1937 when he was struck on the toe by an Earl Averill line drive in the All-Star Game. Dean came back too soon from the broken toe, compensating for the pain by altering his pitching motion. He damaged his arm, and was never again the same. At age 26, Lefty Grove had 26 wins; he went on to win 300. At age 26, Carl Hubbell had 28 wins; he went on to win 253. Dean had 134 wins at age 26, but would win only 16 more.

Dean finished his career with a 150-83 record, a .644 winning percentage, and a 3.02 ERA, all in the midst of a classic hitters' era. Dean's winning percentage was .088 better than his team's, a figure identical to Tom Seaver's career mark, just behind Lefty Grove, and just ahead of Dazzy Vance. Dean's career ERA ended up at an average 30% better than the league average (Lefty Grove was the all time best, at 48% better than the league average).

Dizzy clearly belongs in the all-time top tier of pitchers.

In his short career, he led the league in strikeouts four times (1932 through 1935), led the league in innings three times (1932 and 1935-'36), complete games three times (1933 and 1935-'36), wins twice (1934-1935), shutouts twice (1932 and 1934) and winning percentage (1934) and saves (1936) once. Amazingly, he never led the league in ERA.

Dean's quick humor and down-home manner won over a new generation of fans when he became an announcer following his playing career. His media presence elevated Dean's popularity and added to the lasting impressions that he left behind. The homespun style didn't please everyone, however, and the negative reactions began long before the broadcasting career. Dean's first major league manager, Gabby Street, sent him to the minors in 1931 because he thought Dean didn't take the game seriously enough. Commissioner Kenesaw Mountain Landis, in one of his last official acts before his 1945 death, had Dean removed from the national broadcasting team because he didn't like Dean's mangling of the English language.

Famous Dean quotes included, ''It ain't braggin' if yuh can do it,'' and ''he slud into third.'' Legend has it that, in one day, Dean gave three different reporters three different accounts of his life story, complete with three different birth names, dates and places. He explained that he just wanted to give each reporter an "exclusive."

Dean played dumb, all right, but those close to him maintain that he was far from dumb. Many credit him with exceptional intelligence, and he was obviously sensitive. Dean was simply most at ease when making light of himself. He routinely heaped praise on others, notably his brother Paul, and also on his barnstorming buddy, Satchel Paige, whom Dean called the "best I ever saw."

For all his effervescence off the field, Dean spoke an even more-animated (and more convincing) language with his on-field pitching performances. In 1934 he simply loaded the Cardinals onto his back and carried them all the way to a World Championship. No other pitcher ever lifted a team so successfully, and no pitcher was ever able to squeeze such a great career into just six full seasons, not even Sandy Koufax. Dean was elected to the Hall of Fame in 1953.

Arky Vaughan - 1935

by Marc Bowman

G	AB	R	H	2B	3B	HR	RBI	BB	SO	AVG	OBP	SLG	SB
137	499	108	192	34	10	19	99	97	18	.385	.491	.607	4

Most players reach their peak in their late twenties or early thirties. It usually requires a number of years in the majors to learn all of the nuances of the game and then to combine that knowledge with still-superior physical skills, before the body, the eyes and the reflexes deteriorate. Such was not the case with Arky Vaughan. He reached his peak by turning in the season of a lifetime at the tender age of 23.

When Vaughan joined the Pirates in 1932, his excellent arm and great speed seemed a great fit for the outfield. But the Bucs were overstocked in the outfield with the Waner brothers, Paul (Big Poison) and Lloyd (Little Poison). Vaughan was a lefty hitter, and Pirates brass wanted a righthanded hitter to complement the lefthanded Waners. So the versatile, athletic Vaughan was inserted at shortstop to replace light-hitting Tommy Thevenow.

As a 20-year old rookie in 1932, Vaughan contributed immediately, hitting .318, then emerged as one of the game's best hitters in 1933, placing in the top ten in many offensive categories and leading the National League in triples. In 1934, Vaughan led the league in on base percentage and walks, building up to his fantastic 1935 campaign.

The Pirates relied on good hitting in the early 1930's. The Waner brothers, first baseman Gus Suhr and third baseman Pie Traynor gave Pittsburgh a slashing, high-average offense. From 1932 to 1934, Pittsburgh batters hit .286 and led the league in triples each year. However, they also finished last or next to last each season in home runs, keeping their runs to only slightly above average.

In 1935, the Bucs featured the same kind of offense, but it was much less effective. Traynor had become a full-time manager and part-time player. Suhr's performance had gradually diminished, and the Waner brothers were both having off years. Pittsburgh relied more heavily on a good pitching staff led by Cy Blanton and Bill Swift. But they also relied heavily upon their young star, Vaughan, who led the club in runs, homers and RBI.

That year, Vaughan also managed a trifecta that has been duplicated by only one other National League player in the last sixty years. He led the league in batting average, on base percentage and slugging average. Only Stan Musial (in 1943 and again in 1948) accomplished the same feat after Vaughan.

Vaughan's .385 batting average is the best by a National League shortstop in the 20th century and was the best by any National League hitter since 1935, before Tony Gwynn hit .394 in 1994.

Described by teammate Woody Jensen as ''a natural-born hitter.'' Vaughan had a fluid, easy swing that produced line drives tailor-made for Forbes Field's outfield dimensions. Vaughan was a gap hitter, and Forbes Field was an angular ballpark with a large centerfield. A ball in the gap would often roll far away to the outfield fences, resulting in a disproportionate number of triples in that park. Overall, though,

Forbes Field was not a good hitters' park, while it helped improve Vaughan's triples count, it hurt his home run totals.

Several points need emphasis regarding Vaughan's outstanding play:

1) Strike-zone judgment: In ten years as a regular for the Pirates, he fanned 227 times in 5268 at bats. Meanwhile, he drew 778 walks. In his breakthrough season of 1935 he struck out just 18 times in over 600 plate appearances. Except for the 1934 season when he struck out 38 times (but still led the league with 94 walks and a .431 OBP), Vaughan never struck out more than 26 times in any season. That's one strikeout per week over the course of a career.

Vaughan's batting eye helped him to lead the National League in OBP by 84 points; his .491 mark topped Mel Ott's .407. It is the largest margin of victory in on base percentage in the National League in the 20th century and only one modern day player has ever topped it, the incomparable Ted Williams.

Indeed, one of the minor criticisms that has been leveled at Vaughan by some of his contemporaries was that he wouldn't expand his strike zone with runners on base in order to drive in more runs. The foolishness of this idea is self-evident. While such a tactic might be useful in a few very specific situations, it certainly couldn't be a wise method for regular use. In specific tactical situations, free swinging might add a some RBI to one individual hitter's totals, but would even more certainly reduce his total offensive value in other respects and would ultimately result in his team scoring fewer runs and winning fewer games. For a batter to regularly swing at bad pitches in order to plate more runs, in his one at bat, would necessarily result in fewer run opportunities for later batters should his attempt fail. By drawing walks instead of striking out, Vaughan extended more innings and added more scoring opportunities. For Vaughan in context in 1935, the idea of swinging at bad pitches is even more ludicrous, since he led the league in slugging average. The fact that Vaughan didn't reach the 100 RBI level is more an indictment of the hitters in front him, than of his batting style.

2) Power combined with contact hitting: Few slugging leaders have been able to match Vaughan's low strikeout count. Since the end of the dead ball era, only Stan Musial in 1943 and Tommy Holmes in 1945 have beaten Vaughan's 33.8-to-1 rate of plate appearances to strikeouts while leading the league in slugging average. Vaughan controlled the strike zone like no one else.

3) Power combined with speed: Because of the era in which Vaughan played, his stolen base totals don't look like much. But he had six seasons of double-digit steals at a time when the league leader finished the season with 20 stolen bases, and he led the league in triples three times. The good speed was there.

4) Youth combined with batting eye: It is extremely rare for hitters to lead their league in on base percentage at the age of 23. Vaughan's performance is even more remarkable considering that his .491 on base percentage in 1935 is 24th on the all-time list.

Following his outstanding season in 1935, Vaughan finished third in MVP voting by the Baseball Writers Association of America, but was selected by *The Sporting News* as the National League's MVP and as the outstanding major league shortstop of 1935. Vaughan was elected to the Hall of Fame in 1985.

In his *Historical Baseball Abstract*, Bill James rates Vaughan's peak season as the third best of all time by a shortstop, behind only Honus Wagner and Ernie Banks. He also ranks that season as the 36th best all-time among all players. John Thorn and Pete Palmer, in *Total Baseball*, rank Vaughan 47th all-time among non-pitchers.

Vaughan turned in a very strong season for a young shortstop, one of many in a career in which he batted over .300 for ten straight seasons. Vaughan's career .318 batting average is the second best lifetime mark among shortstops. His relative obscurity among other players rated among the best of all-time is merely a testament to Vaughan's quiet demeanor. He was modest and dignified. What he lacked in brashness and flair off the field, Vaughan more than made up for on the baseball diamond.

Mel Ott - 1936

by Tony Blengino

G	AB	R	H	2B	3B	HR	RBI	BB	SO	AVG	OBP	SLG	SB
150	534	120	175	28	6	33	135	111	41	.328	.448	.588	6

If you were to gather all of baseball's 500-home run hitters in a room, the others would probably look in awe at Mel Ott. Standing five feet, nine inches tall and weighing just 170 pounds, he didn't look the part of a prolific slugger. Ott combined a textbook left-handed swing with an unorthodox batting style (featuring a high front leg kick) and a refusal to swing at bad pitches. He also played in a home park highly conducive to home runs. This combination resulted in 511 home runs over a career which spanned 22 seasons, all with the New York Giants.

Though he is rarely mentioned in discussions of the all-time great hitters, Ott matches up quite evenly on a per-at-bat basis with players like Hank Aaron and Willie Mays, who had even longer careers than Ott and amassed higher raw power totals. Ott's career was virtually the same length as Frank Robinson's, and their numbers are so similar, it's eerie. Ott was extremely consistent, and had about ten seasons which could be considered his best. However, his value as a player was never greater than in 1936, when he carried an aging offensive nucleus to the National League pennant and a World Series with the mighty New York Yankees.

Ott was still relatively young, at age 27, in 1936. Yet he was already in his ninth season as the Giants' regular right fielder, and had accumulated 242 career home runs. The Giants had kept most of their team nucleus intact since 1928, when they finished second in Ott's rookie season, and though they had been perennial contenders, they had won only one pennant and one World Championship, in 1933 (along with three second-place and three third-place finishes).

The 1936 Giants featured Ott, 37-year-old Bill Terry who managed the team and played first base, shortstop Travis Jackson at age 32, and pitchers Carl Hubbell then 33, and Freddie Fitzsimmons at age 34, all still around from the 1928 club. All but Fitzsimmons would eventually be enshrined in the Hall of Fame. In 1936 the Giants' pitching was far and away the best in the National League; the staff's 3.46 ERA led the league. Hubbell was its unquestioned leader, going 26-6, with a 2.31 ERA, leading the league in wins and ERA in one of his best-ever seasons.

As Hubbell led the pitchers, Ott led the hitters. The offense ranked only fourth in the league in runs scored, but they would have ranked much lower without Ott. The entire team hit 97 homers, and Ott produced more than a third of them. No one else had as many as ten. The somewhat forgettable tandem of outfielder Hank Leiber and catcher Gus Mancuso tied for second on the squad with nine each. Ott's 135 RBI were more than twice as many as the second most productive Giants hitter (Leiber had 67). Ott's 111 walks were nearly three times as many as the next best Giant in the bases-on-balls category (shortstop Dick Bartell had 40). Terry missed almost half of the season with a knee injury, and Jackson, now at third base, was experiencing a severe downturn in his abilities, struggling through a .230 season. So the Giants really depended on Ott.

Ott's home run total led the league. He ranked second in RBI, and third in runs (only two behind the leader, the Pirates' Arky Vaughan). The 111 walks ranked third, also behind Vaughan.

Unlike most power hitters, Ott was tough to strike out. He did so only 41 times in 1936. He ranked second in on base percentage, again right behind Vaughan (.453), and Ott led the league in slugging percentage and relative production (179). There have been very few cases of a pennant-winning ballclub being so dependent on one player for offense, to the extent the Giants depended on Ott in 1936. However, Ott received only a sixth place finish in the MVP voting, which was won by teammate Hubbell. The Giants rode Ott and Hubbell to a 92-62 record, good enough for a five-game advantage over the second-place Cubs and a berth opposite the Yanks in the World Series.

The 1936 Yankees had gone an eternity (or so it seemed for them) without winning a championship, three seasons. They had yet to win a pennant without Babe Ruth. The 1936 season was the start of a new era of Yankee dominance. Lou Gehrig, Tony Lazzeri, Bill Dickey, and Red Ruffing and other luminaries were still around from the 1932 team that had swept the World Series in four games but hadn't been back since. But 1936 was also the first year in the career of Joe DiMaggio, then a 21-year-old graduate of the Pacific Coast League. The Yankees rolled to a 102-51 record, winning the pennant with a 19 1/2 game bulge. They simply had too much for the Giants in the World Series, winning in six games. Gehrig was the heart of a murderous offensive lineup, while Ott stood comparatively alone in his batting order. In the Series Ott batted .304, and he homered in the final game, a 13-5 Giants' loss. This was the first of four consecutive Yankee World Championships, and the first two of that streak were won against the Giants.

After another World Series loss to the Yankees in 1937, Ott's post-season career was over, but his playing career lasted through 1947, and he was the Giants' player-manager from 1942-48. He amassed a set of career statistics impossible to ignore. He posted a .304 career average, with 511 homers (14th all-time), with 1860 RBI (ninth), 1859 runs (also ninth), and 1708 walks (sixth) with only 896 lifetime whiffs. Ott had a .414 career on base percentage (21st on the all-time list) and a .533 slugging percentage (23rd), and his career relative production figure of 155 ties him for 20th. Somehow, despite these numbers, his name is often overlooked when all-time great outfielders are discussed. Hank Aaron and Willie Mays rank first and third on the all-time home run list, and they clearly had better careers than Ott. Playing longer, Aaron had 12,364 at bats; Mays had 10,881; Ott had only 9456.

The two key components of offensive performance are getting to first base (measured by on base percentage) and advancing past first base and around to home (measured by slugging percentage). Ott was superior to Mays and Aaron in the former skill. Despite the significant shortfall in at bats, he still walked more than Aaron or Mays. Ott had 100 or more walks ten times, while Mays reached that level only once, and Aaron never did. Ott also made contact much more frequently. Aaron and Mays were clearly better power hitters than Ott, but Ott, quite interestingly, came within 43 RBI of Mays' lifetime total, despite having many fewer career at bats.

Frank Robinson is Ott's right-handed hitting twin, statistically, though not an identical twin. Ott had just a slightly better eye, made slightly better contact, and hit for a slightly better average, while Robinson had slightly better power. The bottom line is that Ott is an all-time great. Bill James ranked Ott the 24th best player for career value and 28th best for peak value, in the James *Historical Baseball Abstract*.

Ott led the National League in homers six times (1932, 1934, 1936-38, 1942), relative production six times (1931-32, 1934, 1936, 1938, 1942), walks six times (1929 at age 20, 1931-33, 1937, 1942), on base percentage four times (1930, 1932, 1938-39), runs twice (1938, 1942), RBI once (1934) and slugging percentage once (1936). He hit over .300 ten times, but never won a batting title. With Hubbell, Ott led the Giants to the World Championship in 1933, batting .389 with two homers in the five-game demolition of the Senators. His two-run homer in the first inning of game one set the tone, and his series-winning homer in the tenth inning of game five put it away.

Ott was a great defensive outfielder who mastered the art of playing the ball off the short right field fence at the Polo Grounds. He routinely put up high assist totals, defying the conventional wisdom that, once you have thrown out enough baserunners, the opposition will stop testing your arm. Ott amassed 256 assists in his career, and exceeded 20 in four different seasons.

Offensively, of course, he also benefited extensively from the short porch at the Polo Grounds. Of his 511 career home runs, 323 were hit in New York, the highest home-park percentage by far among the 500-homer club. This imbalance became most extreme late in Ott's career when his skills began to erode. In his career year of 1936, he hit 18 home runs at home and 15 on the road. However, from 1940 on, he hit an amazing 111 of his final 144 homers at home. In 1943, all 18 of his homers were hit at the Polo Grounds. Obviously, his power numbers were helped by his home park, but Ott was much more than a power hitter. In an average offensive environment, he would never have been a 500-homer man, but he could have reached 400 with almost any other home park. And Ott consistently hit for a high batting average, and consistently had a high on base percentage. Throw in the good defense with a strong throwing arm, and you've still got a Hall of Famer.

Ott's first manager, the legendary John McGraw, kept Ott in the majors at age 17 in 1926 because he didn't want any minor league managers messing with his quirky leg kick which preceded his swing. A wise decision it was, too. The little lefty remained the all-time National League home run leader until Willie Mays finally passed him in 1967. Along with Eddie Mathews, Ott was one of the few major leaguers to establish himself as a star while still a teenager.

Mel Ott's life ended prematurely in 1958, at age 49, in an auto accident. He left behind an all-around legacy that, unfortunately, has been downgraded by some baseball historians and largely ignored by others. Ott could, however, hit for average, hit for power, work the count, draw a walk, and cut down many a surprised baserunner who shouldn't have been surprised. In 1936, he and Carl Hubbell loaded the Giants on their backs and carried them to a National League pennant. It was the foremost season of Ott's long and wonderful career.

Vernon Gomez

Lefty Gomez - 1937

by John Benson

W	L	PCT	G	GS	CG	SV	IP	SO	BB	B/I	ERA
21	11	.656	34	34	25	0	278	194	93	1.17	2.33

The Yankee dynasty of the 1920's took a three-year leave from 1929 to 1931, while the Philadelphia Athletics of Jimmie Foxx, Al Simmons, Mickey Cochrane and Lefty Grove dominated the American League. When the Yankees finally got back on top with the beginning of another dynasty for the 1930's, they had their own "Lefty" in Vernon Louis Gomez, to anchor a revitalized pitching staff. Gomez and righty Red Ruffing were the biggest winners for a team that took pennants in 1932, 1934, 1936, 1937, 1938 and 1939. Gomez was at his best in 1937 when New York won their second of four consecutive world championships.

Gomez emerged as a rookie sensation in 1931, blowing away the game's top hitters with his quick fastball, and capturing the hearts of New York's fans and media with his quick wit. He was a slender figure with surprising velocity, utilizing a high kick and a whip of an arm. He won 21 games in 1931, including three against the fearsome Philadelphia team. The Yankees would not be looking up at the Athletics again until 1966.

In 1932 Gomez made sure of New York's revival by personally beating the Athletics seven times. With that feat he solidified his reputation as a big-game pitcher and added to the growing mystique of Yankee supremacy. Reaching full blossom in 1934, Gomez led the American League in complete games, shutouts, innings, strikeouts, lowest opponents' batting average and lowest ratio of baserunners per inning. His 2.33 ERA was also a league best, while his 26-5 record gave him the most wins and the best percentage.

Some would say 1934 was Gomez's best year, but he had another 2.33 ERA in 1937, when the league's hitters were better in just about every category, including 17% more home runs than they had in 1934. Gomez in 1937 again won the pitchers' Triple Crown, leading the league in wins and strikeouts (with a career high) in addition to the glittering ERA. And again he led the league in shutouts and lowest opponents batting average.

In the 1937 World Series, Gomez pitched a complete game, one-run gem to beat Carl Hubbell in the series opener at Yankee Stadium. Gomez was on the mound again for the fifth and final game at the Polo Grounds, matched against Cliff Melton as the Giants had spent Hubbell in game four to avoid a sweep. Gomez held the Giants to just two runs in another complete game, as the Yankees took the series.

In a career marred and shortened by arm trouble, Gomez was nonetheless 6-0 in World Series competition, and likewise dominated All-Star games, of which he won three. He survived with guile and a big, slow curve, long after his fastball left him. "I'm throwing as hard as ever; the ball just isn't getting there as fast," explained Gomez. His career looked finished in 1940, but Gomez came back for one more great season in 1941, going 15-5 to lead the league in winning percentage and lead the Yankees to another championship. Gomez was a winner, plain and simple.

Joe DiMaggio - 1939
by Tony Blengino

G	AB	R	H	2B	3B	HR	RBI	BB	SO	AVG	OBP	SLG	SB
120	462	108	176	32	6	30	126	52	20	.381	.448	.671	3

As the best player on a team that won ten world championships in his thirteen seasons, Joe DiMaggio's place among baseball immortals has long been secure. DiMaggio was a superb all-around player who combined hitting for average with hitting for power, was "the best base runner I ever saw" in the eyes of Joe McCarthy, and was one of the greatest defensive center fielders of all time. In 1939, he was simply the best player on the best team ever.

Ironically, the Yankees reached the apex of their dominance in 1939, the year in which they lost their Iron Horse, Lou Gehrig. All the Yankees did that season was post a 106-45 record, good enough to win the American League pennant by a comfortable 17-game cushion. More impressively, the Yankees outscored their opponents by a mind-boggling 411 runs (967-556), by far the largest margin in baseball history. By Yankee standards, the talent on this club wasn't all that remarkable; after all, there were only four Hall of Famers on this team. DiMaggio, at 24, was the only one then under age 30. Catcher Bill Dickey, 32, and pitchers Red Ruffing, 35, and Lefty Gomez, 30, were all key contributors to the club, but all were on the downside of their careers. How dominant were the 1939 Yankees? Well, they batted .287 as a team, with a .374 on base percentage and a .451 slugging percentage, easily the league's best offensive team. They also led the league in runs scored, homers, and walks.

Such domination in the offensive categories might suggest a hitters' home park, but we all know that old Yankee Stadium was very much a friend of the pitchers. The Yankee mound staff topped the league in complete games, shutouts, saves, and fewest runs allowed. Most telling among the pitcher stats -- and validating the offensive accomplishments of the hitters with a big exclamation mark -- is the Yankees' team ERA of 3.31, so much better than the second-best 4.08 team ERA in the league as to suggest that the pitchers enjoyed not just a different kind of ballpark, but also pitched in a different kind of league. In a way, the Yankee pitchers of 1939 were indeed in their own unique league; they did not have to pitch against the Yankee hitters like all their peers did.

In today's age of parity and player turnover, it is difficult for many fans to grasp the possibility of one team having the league's best hitter at every position. The 1939 Yankees didn't have Ted Williams in left field, but they still came remarkably close to having an all-star lineup. In 1939 only 31 players in the American League hit 10 or more home runs, and eight of them were the Yankee regulars. Five of the eight Yankee regulars hit .300 or better: DiMaggio, outfielders Charlie Keller (.334) and George Selkirk (.329), third baseman Red Rolfe (.329), and catcher Dickey (.302). The second baseman, Joe Gordon, hit .284 with 28 home runs and 111 RBI, not exactly a weak link in the batting order.

DiMaggio had his best season in 1939, delivering his career high .381 average. In addition to his league-leading average, DiMaggio also led the league in relative production, at 185. DiMaggio finished near the top in several categories. He racked up his massive totals despite missing 34 games with torn leg muscles. And with the big home run and RBI totals and the lofty slugging percentage, DiMaggio rarely struck out, whiffing just 20 times in 514 plate appearances.

DiMaggio's leg injury occurred on April 29th. He was off to a flying start, batting .435 with a seven-game hitting streak. He didn't get back into centerfield until June 7th but produced well as a pinch hitter. By June 9th, the Yankees had opened a nine-game lead. DiMaggio led the way with a .464 average. The Yanks were so completely dominating, six of them started for the American League All-Star team: DiMaggio, Rolfe, Dickey, Selkirk, Gordon and Gomez. By August 30th, New York's record stood at 87-35, and DiMaggio's batting average stood at .408. But then DiMaggio slumped the final two weeks of the season, with his average dropping another 27 points. Still there was little if any disappointment in New York. DiMaggio and the rest of the team were already focused on the coming World Series.

The Yankees totally dominated the Cincinnati Reds in the Series, sweeping them in four games and outscoring them by a 20-8 margin. The Yankees' fourth consecutive World Championship came, not coincidentally, in DiMaggio's fourth major league season. DiMaggio acquitted himself well in the series, going 5-for-16 (.313) with a homer and three RBI, generating more favorable writing in the New York papers than did Charlie Keller's performance which included bigger numbers.

DiMaggio's career totals were diminished by the loss of three seasons (1943-45) to military service. Nevertheless, he's in the record books with the sixth highest career slugging percentage of all time, a .579 mark, higher than Willie Mays, Hank Aaron, and Mickey Mantle. Only Babe Ruth, Williams, Gehrig, Foxx and Hank Greenberg had higher slugging averages.

Just how powerful was DiMaggio? If the sixth highest

career slugging percentage doesn't conjure up any distinct image, try thinking about the fact that DiMaggio in 1948 (playing most of the year with a sore heel) out-homered the entire Senators team, by a margin of eight. As a righthanded slugger in Yankee Stadium (think how many of the great Yankee sluggers batted from the right side; it's quite a short list) DiMaggio's power was much diminished by the vast expanses in "Death Valley" as righty hitters of the era had nicknamed the left-centerfield pasture extending to the 457-foot mark. Clearly this was a park designed to help lefty pull hitters, and to break the hearts of righty sluggers. DiMaggio had too much heart and too much power to be broken by anything as mundane as the distance of fences, but it's a fact he got 213 of his career homers on the road, and only 148 at home. Writers have noted various reasons why DiMaggio got "only" 361 career home runs, namely the time missed for World War II service and his retirement when the Yankees still wanted him to play. But when it comes to power output, forget about the ifs and buts; Joe DiMaggio doesn't need them.

The oversized outfield in New York may have cut into DiMaggio's home run output, but it also offered a perfect stage for his defense. To say that the big field allowed him to showcase his talents would be missing an important subtlety, however: DiMaggio made it all look easy. Many fans never appreciated the perfect positioning and intense study that gave him such great range (better than Willie Mays, for example, 2.71 to 2.56). The Yankee Clipper was never a flashy or showy fielder. Fans who saw DiMaggio remember him for being a smoothly gliding, omnipresent defensive angel, even more than for being a murderous power hitter, which he surely was.

DiMaggio was always an extremely private person. He never would have liked today's intense media scrutiny of athletes. He was not an easy interview, but the local media simply idolized him. He remains a symbol of the game's golden era, leader of its most important team, in the biggest city. There will never be another like him. He was at his best for a long time, but especially in 1939.

Hank Greenberg - 1940

By Bill Gray

G	AB	R	H	2B	3B	HR	RBI	BB	SO	AVG	OBP	SLG	SB
148	573	129	195	50	8	41	150	93	75	.340	.433	.670	6

Only two players have ever reached the 60-homer mark, hardly enough to be called a "club" or to invite comparisons. There are, however, 11 sluggers who have reached 50 or more in a season, and 10 more who came tantalizingly close, getting 48 or 49 in their peak year. All-time home run champion Hank Aaron is not among these 21 great power hitters, although he did once get 47 homers in a season.

Just for fun, I decided to compare Hank Greenberg with Aaron and Ruth, the two players who stand first and second on the career homer list, and who also stand like bookends for the single-season leaders, with 20 great sluggers sandwiched between them. Since this book is all about peaks, and because Greenberg's career was shorter than Ruth's and Aaron's, I decided to create a mythical peak season for each of the three sluggers, using his actual peak one-year performance in batting average, slugging, hits, doubles, triples, runs batted in, runs scored and of course, homers, to create a single "season" line. This is more an exercise in fun, then sabermetric science, though the method might offer a new way of looking at players, possibly for a SABR research presentation. We could call this index the *Harry Caray, MCI "Might Be, Could Be"* method.

Before getting to the Greenberg-Aaron-Ruth comparison, here for the record are the 21 names above Aaron's 47 homer mark: Roger Maris, Babe Ruth, Jimmie Foxx, Greenberg, Hack Wilson, Ralph Kiner, Mickey Mantle, Willie Mays, George Foster, Johnny Mize, Cecil Fielder, Lou Gehrig, Ted

Kluszewski, Harmon Killebrew, Frank Robinson, Andre Dawson, Mark McGwire, Frank Howard, Willie Stargell, Dave Kingman, and Mike Schmidt. If your favorite player isn't in this group, take consolation in the well-established truth that pitchers tend to work around hitters who have already passed the 40-homer level any given year. The tight pack that got stuck at 48 or 49 (every name from Gehrig through Schmidt on that list) indicates the extent to which pitchers will tighten up their offerings when any hitter gets near 50. Without further ado, those three composite seasons:

BEST CAREER PERFORMANCE

Ruth:

SLG.	H	2B	3B	HR	RBI	RUNS	AVG
.847	205	45	16	60	171	177	.393

Greenberg:

SLG.	H	2B	3B	HR	RBI	RUNS	AVG
.683	203	63	16	58	183	144	.348

Aaron:

SLG.	H	2B	3B	HR	RBI	RUNS	AVG
.669	223	46	14	47	132	127	.355

Greenberg comes out pretty well, and that's really no surprise. The doubles might be a surprise to some who think of Greenberg only in terms of his 58 homer season in 1938. Greenberg's 63 doubles in 1934 are the fourth highest total of all time, and that includes the handlebar mustache, dead ball crowd. You might score an easy trivia point if you ask "Who is the all-time Detroit Tigers leader in doubles for one season?" The right answer is *not* Ty Cobb!

Truly, Greenberg was one of the most complete hitters ever. It is difficult to choose his best season, and almost too tempting to go straight to the 58-homer season without stopping to look at the others. All of them were good, and four were awesome. He became a regular for the Tigers in 1933, and from then until WW II interrupted things, he hit over .300 every year. He smacked 247 of his 331 career homers from 1931 to 1940. What was his greatest season? Let's take the four great ones. In 1935, Greenberg was 24 years old. He batted .328, with 46 doubles, 16 triples and 36 home runs. All this firepower drove in 170 runners. The Tigers won the Pennant and the World Series.

Greenberg missed almost all of 1936 with a broken wrist. His return in 1937 didn't help the Tigers win a pennant, but he dispelled a rumor that his wrist injury was career threatening. In 1937, Greenberg batted .337 with 49 doubles, 14 triples and 40 homers. He drove in an astonishing 183 runs, just one short of Lou Gehrig's all-time AL record of 184. Greenberg later said as far as individual records were concerned, he was more disappointed in failing to tie Gehrig than in not hitting 60 homers.

"I ran out of gas." That is how Greenberg described his shortfall in the home run race of 1938. His 58 homers that year are still the record (tied with Jimmie Foxx) for a righthanded hitter. Many will point to 1938 as being Greenberg's best season, given his assault on the Babe's record. But Greenberg was off in some other categories. He hit "only" .315 (right around his career average, thus not at all prominent within the career context) with 23 doubles and four triples. He drove in 146 runs, which sounds fantastic until you realize it was about 40 less than he had the year before. On the plus side, Greenberg in 1938 had his career high slugging percentage, 13 points higher than he had in 1940; but in '38 he didn't lead the league in slugging (the top spot went to Foxx with a .704 slugging percentage) while in 1940 Greenberg was very clearly atop the American League, beating runner-up teammate Rudy York by 41 points and dwarfing the efforts of Ted Williams and Joe DiMaggio who finished third and fourth, respectively. Greenberg's on base percentage in 1938 was five points higher than in 1940, but it wasn't a career high.

1940 gets our nod as Greenberg's best campaign. The Tigers won the pennant and nearly won the World Series. Critical to the Tigers' success was Greenberg's willingness to vacate first base, making room for the bat of the 26-year-old York, who simply wasn't developing as a major league catcher. York had been limited to 329 at bats in 1939, and had never gotten over 470, much to the chagrin of Detroit management who had seen York's potential when he hit 18 home runs in August, 1937, the biggest monthly output of any player ever. In 1940 York got 588 at bats and drove in 134 runs, solidifying the heart of the order. Meanwhile Greenberg proved that he was both willing, and able, to learn the skills of a left fielder, actually doing an above-average job compared to his peers.

In the 1940 World Series, the Reds won in seven games, despite being outscored overall 28-22. Greenberg led the Tigers with 10 hits and had a .357 average.

Greenberg joined the Army early in 1941. He returned to the Tigers in 1945. At age 34 he was still a fine hitter, but a level below what he was before the war. Joining the Tigers in July, Greenberg helped keep the team in the race. He hit a grand slam on the final day to clinch the pennant for the Tigers, then had a fine World Series as Detroit defeated the Cubs. 1946 was Greenberg's final year in Detroit. The Tigers decided Greenberg's salary demands were too high, and he was waived after the 1946 season. The only team willing to pay for Greenberg's services was the Pittsburgh Pirates, who made Greenberg the National League's first $100,000 player. The Pirates shortened the distance to the left field wall by erecting a cyclone fence in front of the Forbes Field scoreboard. They called it Greenberg's Garden. Hank hit only .249 for the Bucs, but he managed 25 homers and led the league in walks. He announced his retirement following the season, but he had an enormous positive impact on the development of Ralph Kiner, who would go on to join Greenberg as a member of that distinguished 50-homer club.

Bob Feller - 1940

by Fred Matos

W	L	PCT	G	GS	CG	SV	IP	SO	BB	B/I	ERA
27	11	.711	43	37	31	4	320	261	118	1.14	2.61

The Bob Feller story -- a teenage farm boy with a blazing fastball reaching the major leagues while still in high school -- reads like a fiction from one of those children's adventure books of long ago. Even in that context, the story is hard to believe. Indeed, Feller was a true product of the healthy life of an Iowa farm where he honed his pitching skills on a real "field of dreams" built by his father.

Feller's best pitch was his amazing fastball, usually thrown from a windup with a very high leg kick, frequently including a windmill motion. He learned how to throw a curve at age eight, and by age 16, it was a very sharp, near major-league quality curveball. His exaggerated pitching mechanics made him occasionally wild, but the unpredictable quality served the very useful purpose of keeping the hitters just a little fearful, preventing them from digging in on him.

Feller got his first exposure to the major leagues in an exhibition game in the summer of 1936 when he was a 17-year-old high school student between his junior and senior years. He pitched three innings against the famed St. Louis Cardinals "Gas House Gang" that included Leo Durocher, Johnny Mize and Pepper Martin. The teenage fireballer shocked everyone present, as he struck out eight batters. Late in the year, getting a callup to the majors, he whiffed 15 in his first major league start, and before his brief 1936 stint ended, he had set a new American League record by striking out 17 Philadelphia Athletics in one game. Only a year later in 1937, at age 18, Feller struck out 18 Tigers in a game, setting a new major

league record that stood until the free swinging era of the 1960's.

Feller had many outstanding seasons and set numerous records that stood for decades. In choosing a best year, one must consider 1946, when Feller struck out 348 while posting a 26-15 record and a sharp 2.18 ERA in 377 innings. The 348 strikeouts broke Rube Waddell's 1904 record of 343, although Waddell's total was later adjusted upwards to 349 following an official recount. Feller's 26 wins in 1946 tied for the league lead, and he also led the league in shutouts, innings pitched, games started, games pitched, and complete games. He pitched a no-hitter against the tough Yankees on April 30th.

The case for 1946 as Feller's best year includes several contextual facts: he won those 26 games while pitching for a poor, sixth-place team, unlike the 1940 Indians who finished second, one game out. The 1946 Indians were a weak-hitting bunch, with a league-low .245 batting average, and they ranked next-to-last in runs scored. Feller's 2.18 ERA in 1946 ranked third in the league. The overall league ERA was a relatively low 3.50. One more argument against Feller's 1946 season as his best-ever is that he lagged behind Hal Newhouser (26-9 with a 1.94 ERA) in several key measures.

So we go back to 1940. Feller had his career high in wins and held the opposition to a measly .285 on base percentage, also a career best for Feller. The 2.61 ERA in 1940 looks even better when compared to the league average of 4.38. He led the league in wins, ERA, strikeouts, complete games, games pitched, innings, most strikeouts per nine innings, lowest opponents' batting average (.210) and lowest on base percentage, and he also tied for the lead in shutouts.

Feller's 1940 ERA title was not bestowed immediately; at the time it took only 45 innings to qualify, and the Yankees had a rookie forkballer named Ernie Bonham, who crafted a 1.91 ERA while making 12 starts totalling 99 innings. At first Bonham was credited with the league's best ERA of 1940, but the qualifying rule was changed in 1951, requiring one inning pitched for each scheduled game, e.g. 154 innings for a 154 game season. So Feller got his crown, just a little late.

The widespread use of computers today has led to the development of a number of new statistics measuring pitcher performances. The "total pitcher index" is one such newly-developed measure, based on innings pitched, the league ERA, and the pitcher's ERA. For comparative purposes, Feller had a total pitcher index of 6.1 in 1940, the best in the league, far ahead of the second place Bobo Newsom with 4.6. In 1946, Feller's index was 4.9, third in the league, behind Newhouser's league-leading 7.1.

Despite missing all of 1942, 1943, and 1944, and almost all of 1945, serving his country gallantly, Feller led the league in wins six times and strikeouts seven times. He was number one in wins and strikeouts all three of the years before his military service and both of his first two after returning. Feller's *average* season from this five-year period was 24 wins and 262 strikeouts per year. In essays telling the effect of war-year absences in baseball careers, Feller is a major topic. The before-and-after performances suggest he missed about a hundred wins and 1300 strikeouts.

In the 1940 era, it was unthinkable to baby a young pitcher, bringing him along slowly and carefully as is the normal practice today. It was a "sink-or-swim" approach in Feller's day. He proved very early that he could swim with best of them. At ages 18 and 19 he looked like a seasoned veteran, maybe just a little on

the wild side of the pitching profession:

Year	Age	Record	Innings	K's	BB	ERA
1936	17	5-3	62	76	47	3.34
1937	18	9-7	148 2/3	150	106	3.39
1938	19	17-11	277 2/3	240*	208*	4.08
1939	20	24*-9	296 2/3*	246*	142*	2.85
1940	21	27*-11	320 1/3*	260*	118	2.61

* League leader.

The substantial decline in walks in 1939 indicates that Feller was developing into more of a pitcher than just a super-hard thrower overpowering the hitters. His fastball enabled him to be a winning pitcher while still learning and perfecting his craft. Along the way he set several records for youthful pitchers that stood untouchable until the Mets' Dwight Gooden came along in 1984 and 1985. For example:

Record for youngest pitcher to lead his league in strikeouts

1938 - 240 - Bob Feller - age 19 and 11 months
1984 - 276 - Dwight Gooden - age 19 and 10 months

Record for youngest pitcher to win 20 games or more

1939 - 24 - Bob Feller - age 20 and 10 months
1985 - 24 - Dwight Gooden - age 20 and 9 months

Feller and Gooden were both born in November, but the differences result from the 13 days between their birthdays and the different dates during the seasons when the records were set.

Gooden didn't have to face the likes of Joe DiMaggio, Ted Williams, Hank Greenberg, Jimmie Foxx, Rudy York, Charlie Gehringer, Bill Dickey, and Luke Appling. Hitters in Feller's era struck out much less frequently than they do today. The old style was different, and the expectations were different. It was simply unacceptable for any hitter to strike out a hundred times in a season; such a performance would mean a quick return to the minors for any young slugger. Mickey Mantle in 1951 went back down largely because he was on a pace toward 100 whiffs. There were a few rare exceptions. Hank Greenberg, two years after leading the league with 170 RBI in 1935, was allowed to stay in the majors while striking out 101 times in 1937, but he never got to 100 again, not even in 1938 when he hit 58 home runs. Coaching and player development favored slap hitters during the 1940's. It took a long time to change. Mantle during his career passed 120 strikeouts in a season four times; once he went over 130. But *nobody* broke the 150 whiff barrier until 1963, and of the 66 individual cases of 150+ strikeout seasons going into 1995, only eight occurred before 1970, fifteen during the 1970's, and 43 in the period 1980 to 1994.

Bob Feller pitched in a different world. No pitcher now can ever go back to that world, so no pitcher will ever be able to match Feller's strikeout dominance.

Feller began the 1940 season with a bang, pitching a no-hitter on Opening Day, April 16th, against the White Sox. The masterpiece was even more rewarding for Feller as his parents and sister were in attendance. ''I didn't feel as if I had as much stuff as I've had before. Couldn't grip my curve just right and that wind bothered me a little,'' said Feller.

Feller continued his sharp pitching through the season, becoming the first in the majors to reach the 10 win mark as he four-hit the Senators on June 20th. He hurled a second masterpiece on July 12, giving up only a scratch eighth-inning single to the Philadelphia Athletics; he struck out 13 that day, winning 1-0. He developed a blister on his finger before the eighth inning, so he threw nothing but fastballs in the last two innings. Dick Siebert, who hit the single, was a well known fastball hitter, and would normally have seen a lot of Feller's curve, which was untouchable earlier in the game.

Feller had a notable personal achievement on July 26th when he pitched his career-first complete game without issuing a base-on-balls. He won his 20th

game on August 12th, becoming the first major league pitcher to reach the 20-victory mark that year. He won his 23rd on August 30th in the stretch drive as the Tribe was leading the league, with the Tigers, Yankees, and White Sox in a cat-and-dog fight for the pennant.

Feller was 23-7 on August 30th, and starting every fourth day. He had seven more starts in the season, and an outside chance to win 30, one of his personal goals. Since the Indians were in a pennant race, Manager Oscar Vitt announced that Feller would spend every other day in the bullpen, just in case he was needed to finish up a close game and preserve a victory. It was thought possible that he might pick up a win or two in relief.

The Indians were in first place following the Labor Day weekend, but went into a tailspin thereafter, dropping seven out of eight, including three critical games to the surging Tigers that turned the race around. Unfortunately, Feller couldn't pitch every day. He won in relief on September 8th, and started against the Yankees on the 11th, losing 3-1. Feller gave up only five hits, but the Yankees bunched them together to score their runs. Only one game now separated the Indians, Tigers and Yankees.

Feller won his 25th by shutting out the Philadelphia A's 5-0 with a two-hitter on September 15th, narrowly missing a no-hitter. He retired the first 22 batters, tired in the 8th and yielded a scratch single and then a line drive that the centerfielder just missed catching. Pitching with only two days rest, Feller came right back to pitch a beautiful complete game against the Washington Senators on September 18th. He scattered five hits while winning the game 2-1. His record was now 26-9, and he had pitched 302 innings.

On September 20th, the Indians and Tigers were tied for first place, and began a crucial three-game series in Detroit. The Indians had eight games remaining, and six were against the Tigers. With the Indians leading the first game 4-1, Feller relieved in the 8th inning. Pitching only two days after a complete game, he gave up singles to Hank Greenberg, Rudy York, and Pinky Higgins, and with an outfielder's error mixed in, he blew the lead. But he came back only two days later on the 22nd, pitching a 10-5 complete game victory over the Tigers, giving up eight hits and helping his own cause with a home run.

The pennant race would be settled in the final three-game series between the Tigers and Indians beginning September 27th, with the Tigers needing only one victory to clinch the pennant. Feller started for the Indians, and the Tigers' strategy was to hold out Schoolboy Rowe, their pitching ace, for a game against somebody other than Feller, to give Rowe a better chance of winning. The Tigers gambled by starting Floyd Giebell, a rookie just called up. The gamble worked, as Giebell surprised everyone, out-pitching Feller and winning 2-0. Feller pitched a beautiful game giving up only three hits, but one was a two-run homer by Rudy York.

Undoubtedly tired, but still pitching very well until the very last, Feller didn't finish his 1940 season quite as gloriously as he began. An appropriate ending to the year would have been a pennant-clincher and two or three victories in the World Series. The Indians were a scrappy bunch, but overall, not nearly as talented as the Yankees or Tigers, especially in power hitting. One footnote to the season was the midsummer near-mutiny of a group of Indians players who went to the owner, calling for the firing of Manager Vitt, but that's another story. Suffice it to say that whatever distraction resulted, it didn't help Feller or the team. After the season, Feller experienced one final shortfall in 1940, finishing second to Greenberg in the MVP voting, 292 to 222.

Because of the time lost to war years, and considering the change in hitting style that occurred later in the 20th century, it is safe to say that we will never know just how great Bob Feller might have been. And no one can look at his strikeout feats in today's context and fully appreciate the extent of his domination. We do know, however, that he was one of the all-time greats for more than a decade, and he was at his peak in 1940.

Ted Williams - 1941

by Lary Bump

G	AB	R	H	2B	3B	HR	RBI	BB	SO	AVG	OBP	SLG	SB
143	456	135	185	33	3	37	120	145	27	.406	.551	.735	2

My generation has seen most of baseball's sacred numbers fade into obscurity and be cast aside like old newspapers. Babe Ruth's 60 home runs in a season and 714 in a career no longer remain as standards. Ty Cobb's 20th century record of 96 stolen bases in a season has been passed by four players who moved the mark upward. Cobb's career stolen base mark of 892 was exceeded by Lou Brock, who in turn was passed (somewhat disrespectfully) by Rickey Henderson. It took 34 years, but the seemingly unattainable goal (for modern-day baseball) of 30 victories in a season also was reached, in 1968. Even that most sacrosanct of numbers, the mark that everyone (except Bill James) said was eternally unreachable, Lou Gehrig's 2,130 games, turned out to be just another number for future generations to file with all those others that aren't current any more.

However, two numbers that do remain after more than half a century seem as far away as ever: 56 and .406. Both were achieved in 1941, when Joe DiMaggio's crafted his 56-game hitting streak and Ted Williams' produced his .406 batting average.

Which was, and is, the more impressive feat?

After the season, DiMaggio was voted the American League Most Valuable Player, with 291 points in the balloting to 254 for runner-up Williams. But that award was derived largely from the success of DiMaggio's team (the Yankees clinched the pennant September 4, and finished 17 games ahead of Williams' second-place Red Sox). Rationally, the voters for MVP could suppose that DiMaggio was the best and most indispensable player on a wonderful, winning team, while Williams' presence didn't do the Red Sox a whole lot of good, other than helping ticket sales. But what about pure individual achievement?

Williams' 1941 on base percentage is the highest in major league history. His slugging percentage ranks 11th on the all-time list, and was the highest of his career. His batting average was only 18th all-time, but eighth in the 20th century and the highest since Rogers Hornsby hit .424 in 1924. Williams' 1.286 total average (on base percentage plus slugging percentage) has been exceeded only three times -- by Ruth in 1920, '21 and '23.

Clearly, Williams had the better individual season in 1941 (career being a different question) and that's why he, not MVP DiMaggio, ranks second only to The Babe in our listing of the best seasons ever.

In the 54 years since Williams and DiMaggio accomplished their dual feats, no one has come very close to matching either. Pete Rose created a stir with his 44-game hitting streak, but that still was 12 games and about 21 per cent short of DiMaggio's all-time mark. For the next 35 years after 1941, only one batter came closer than 24 points to .400 -- and that was a 39-year-old Ted Williams at .388 in 1957! Then Rod Carew also batted .388 in 1977 and George Brett hit .390 while playing in just 117 games in 1980. Tony Gwynn reached .394 in 1994, but that also was in only three-fourths of a season, and his

slow start in 1995 showed the difficulty of maintaining a .400 pace for even 154 games, let alone 162.

Before the 1941 season, what was the perceived likelihood of Williams batting .400? It wasn't considered as remote a possibility as today that *somebody* would reach that level. The most recent .400 season had been just 11 years earlier, and players had exceeded .380 four times (including DiMaggio's .381 in 1939) during the intervening years. However, there was no compelling reason to think that Williams would be the one to attain that lofty level. He had come into the league with a bang, with a major league leading 145 RBI as a rookie in 1939, and a major league high 134 runs scored the next season. But he had batted just .327 and .344. And he would be playing almost all of the 1941 season before his 23rd birthday on August 30.

Compare that to the phenoms of the 1990's. At a age 22, Frank Thomas batted .318 with 32 homers, 109 RBI, 104 runs, 138 walks and 112 strikeouts. Ken Griffey Jr. was at .308-27-103, with just 83 runs and 44 walks. Manny Ramirez played the 1995 season about three months older than Williams was in '41. Chipper Jones had eight major league at bats when he reached age 23. All of these players are noted for youth.

Before Ted, in the history of baseball, the only player younger than 24 who ever had batted .400 was Joe Jackson, who turned 22 on July 16, 1911. (Oh, yes, there was Ross Barnes' 1872 and 1873 seasons in the National Association, when he had just 240 and 338 at bats, respectively.) Of the 18 players besides Williams who have compiled .400 seasons, their average age was 27 years, 0 months at the start of their first year reaching that .400 level.

There are three reasons why Williams never again batted .400:

1) *No one* has ever done it, in 54 years;

2) His singlemindedness about baseball is missing from later generations of players. He wasn't seeking endorsements or taping advertisements on his days off, though he did find time to catch a 374-pound tuna during the 1941 season.

3) Most important, during his prime years, Williams was flying combat missions, not hitting baseballs. During that prime age of 26 to 27, when so many of the other greats reached their peak, Williams was finishing his military career in 1945.

Williams followed his 1941 batting championship with a more modest .356 mark in 1942, throwing in a Triple Crown despite a major league high 145 walks. After three years away from the game, he had an adjustment period in '46, falling all the way to .342, second in the league to Mickey Vernon. Williams was back in Triple Crown form in 1947. By that time, he was well on his way to his goal of being "the greatest hitter who ever lived." Bernard Malamud mirrored Williams' mythic character for *The Natural*, Roy Hobbs, who wanted to be "the best there ever was in the game."

No matter how much better his career numbers might have been had he played in the majors during World War II and the Korean War (absences from the game only slightly shorter than Hobbs had), Williams still might not have matched the individual excellence of his 1941 season. After all, only the Mighty Ruth ever had a better one.

There was little to foreshadow anything remotely like what would happen when Williams started the 1941 season. He had come to the majors as a gangly (6'-3", 178 pounds) 20-year-old, soon nicknamed "The Kid" by Red Sox equipment manager Johnny Orlando. It didn't take long for Williams' innocence to be shattered, or to begin his career-long sparring with the Boston media (it was such that at one time his nickname of "The Splendid Splinter" was corrupted to "The Splendid Spitter" in reference to his allegedly expectorating in the direction of some fans).

Ted's home life growing up in San Diego wasn't very easy, and his parents finally separated during his rookie year. To stay away from that unpleasant situation, Williams didn't go home during the winter of 1939-40. In *My Turn at Bat*, which is equal parts autobiography and treatise on hitting, he and John

Underwood recalled:

And do you know what (Boston writer) Harold Kaese wrote the first time I did something to displease him? "Well, what do you expect from a guy who won't even go see his mother in the off season?"

That bitterness was on hold during most of 1941, a year which Williams wrote was "fun again." His season was slow in unfolding. He chipped a bone in his ankle sliding into second base during a March 19 exhibition game, so he started just one game during the first two weeks.

On opening day, Williams pinch-hit for pitcher Earl Johnson and contributed a run-scoring single to a three-run ninth-inning rally that gave Boston a 7-6 win over the Senators. Pete Fox, who shared time with Stan Spence while Ted was out, started that game in left field.

During that time, Williams wasn't idle, but was laying the groundwork for his big year. Every day, he'd take batting practice with righthander Joe Dobson, who also wasn't playing much. Williams wrote that his long BP sessions developed the calluses on his hands that he liked in those pre-batting-glove days. "When I finally got back into the lineup, the weather had turned warm, and I mean I got off to a flying start."

He was right at .400 (4-for-10) when he returned to the starting lineup in Detroit April 29. He went 2-for-3 with a double and a home run in a 5-3 loss. Three days later, going 0-for-3 in a 7-3 loss at Cleveland dropped him to a season-low .308. A modest six-game hitting streak preceded an 0-for-5 game against the White Sox May 14. That left him at .339. When DiMaggio started his streak the next day, Williams was beginning his own 23-game streak. He re-crossed the .400 level with a 4-for-5 game at Yankee Stadium May 25, peaked at .436 and was at .431 before the streak ended in an 0-for-5 doubleheader June 8 in Chicago.

Williams then hit in another seven straight games before Detroit's Schoolboy Rowe threw an 0-for-3 collar around him June 18. Ted also had mini-streaks

of five and seven games, during DiMaggio's streak of 56 straight. When the DiMaggio streak ended July 17, Williams was having his longest dry spell of the year, going 0-for-7 during five games, four of them as a pinch hitter, and one in which he drew a walk.

During DiMaggio's streak, Williams actually outhit The Yankee Clipper, .412-.408. Williams hit safely in 45 of 55 games, and went 77-for-187.

As it became clear that he was a serious contender to bat .400, Williams felt only minimal pressure from the media. Showing the generally casual attitude toward the .400 mark itself, radio talk show host Harry Von Zell asked Ted if he could exceed Hugh Duffy's all-time record of .440 compiled in 1894, when a walk literally was as good as a hit. Williams replied that he hoped not, because he liked Duffy, a Red Sox coach when The Kid first came up. He related that Duffy told him, "Son, you've got form and power. But the form is the most important. With it you get the power. Don't monkey with your form." Anyone who ever saw Williams bat knows he heeded those words.

Williams also had some advice from Harry Heilmann, the last American Leaguer before Williams to bat .400 (.403 in 1923). In 1941 Heilmann was a Tigers broadcaster, and he'd caution the lefthanded-hitting Williams against swinging for the right field fence in Detroit: "Now, forget about that short fence, just hit the ball where you want it, hit your pitch, get those base hits. You can hit .400."

Surprisingly, Williams also credited Boston's Fenway Park, with its short left field distance that favored righthanded batters and tortured lefthanded pitchers, with making it easier for him to scale the .400 plateau that has become a mountain. He reasoned that because he could swing late and still hit a ball off or over Fenway's Green Monster, he could wait longer on pitches, and couldn't be fooled, because his bat was so quick. To him, that was a bigger factor than his vaunted eyesight. When he went for his Navy physical in 1942, doctors determined that he had 20-10 vision. That meant that from 20 feet away, he could see an object -- a baseball, let's say -- the way a person with normally healthy eyes could see it at 10 feet. Combined with his classic form, his bat speed and his ability to wait on pitches, his eyesight would indeed seem to be a tremendous asset. Yet Williams wrote, ''Writers always gave my eyes more credit than they deserved for the hitting I did.''

And did he ever hit in 1941! His average, .405 at the All-Star break, fell to .393 on July 19. It would never be that low again. He was up to .400 after a 2-for-3 performance, including his 19th home run, on July 25. How's this for consistency? From that point on, more than two months, Williams' average was never higher than .414 nor lower than .400.

But what about that final day of the season, you ask. Wasn't he below .400 then? It's a matter of baseball folklore, true in this case, that a 9-for-34 skid left him technically below .400 on the evening of September 27. But his average of .3995535 would have been rounded off to .400, and Red Sox player-manager Joe Cronin offered Williams the choice to sit out the next day's season-ending doubleheader against Connie Mack's Philadelphia Athletics to preserve a .400 average. Williams declined the offer, and worked off his nervous energy by walking what he said must have been 10 miles through the streets of Philadelphia with equipment manager Orlando. He no doubt was thinking that he was going against the A's, who had not treated his .400 bid kindly. On August 31, after his 31st home run had beaten Philadelphia in the first game of a doubleheader, manager Connie Mack had ordered Williams walked intentionally three times in the nightcap. And A's coach Al Simmons, whose own .400 bids had fallen 19 and 10 points short in 1930 and '31, was the one person who openly expressed to Williams that he hoped The Kid also would fail to finish at .400.

Sure enough, when he came to bat for the first time, Williams wrote, Athletics catcher Frankie Hayes said, ''Ted, Mr. Mack told us if we let up on you he'll run us out of baseball. I wish you all the luck in the world, but we're not giving you a damn thing.''

Nonetheless, Philadelphia pitchers didn't intentionally walk Williams this time. In his first at bat, he singled

against Dick Fowler. He could have left the game then, with his average securely above .400 at .4008908. Instead he stayed in to hit a home run against Fowler and two more singles against lefthander Porter Vaughn in the first game. There was no sitting out the second game, either, and Williams added a double and a single to complete a 6-for-8 day and finish the year at .406.

That October, DiMaggio had another World Series, almost an annual event during his time with the Yankees (10 in 13 seasons). In 19 years, Williams would play in only one frustrating Series, in 1946. But in '41 he had the spotlight in the other interleague showcase, the All-Star game, which was much more hotly contested in days of yore than today. At the All-Star break, DiMaggio already had his record streak -- at 48 games, four better than Willie Keeler's mark. Batting .405, Williams was barely halfway home.

In the All-Star game Williams had a run-scoring double and a walk early in the game. In the eighth he had to face Claude Passeau, whom he had never seen. Williams maintained that the pitchers who gave him the most trouble were those who weren't familiar to him. Passeau also was one of the first to throw a slider, the pitch that has helped to keep batters under .400 ever since. And on a low slider, plate umpire Babe Pinelli called Williams out. He had a chance for revenge in the bottom of the ninth. Even though manager Bill McKechnie had available lefthander Carl Hubbell, whom Williams hadn't faced, Passeau stayed in the game with two out, runners at first and third and the NL clinging to a 5-4 lead. With a 2-1 count, Passeau threw a slider on the inside half of the plate. (Williams said belt-high, Passeau letter-high). Williams drove the ball off the edge of Briggs Stadium's right field roof, 118 feet above the field, for a three-run homer.

The American League had a dramatic 7-5 victory. Williams bounced around the bases, windmilling his arms in joy. He was so excited after the game that he couldn't stop talking to the press. That day, for perhaps the last time ever in his career, he was still The Kid, after all.

Hal Newhouser - 1945

by Bill Gilbert

W	L	PCT	G	GS	CG	SV	IP	SO	BB	B/I	ERA
25	9	.735	40	36	29	2	313	212	110	1.12	1.81

Hal Newhouser started playing for his hometown Detroit Tigers right out of high school. He was rushed to the majors in his first season, making his debut in 1939 at the age of 18, and he never returned to the minor leagues. He struggled with his control in his early years, leading the league in bases on balls in 1943. At the end of the 1943 season, he had a record of 34-52.

Newhouser had a congenital heart ailment which exempted him from military service. For many years, his achievements were devalued because two of his best years came during the war years when the major leagues had a large contingent of what we now call ''replacement players.'' However, over half of his 207 major league wins came after the war was over. He had a blazing fastball and an outstanding overhand curve, a pitch that prompted Ted Williams to call him one of the three best pitchers he ever faced. Newhouser's accomplishments were finally rewarded with his election to the Hall of Fame in 1992, 31 years after he first became eligible.

Beginning in 1944, Newhouser had a three year run that ranks as one of the greatest ever, in any player population. He compiled records of 29-9, 25-9 and 26-9 with ERA's of 2.22, 1.81 and 1.94. His 80 wins over those three seasons have not been matched in any three-year period since then. Newhouser was voted the Most Valuable Player in the American League in both 1944 and 1945, the only pitcher ever to win the award in successive seasons, and he finished second to Williams in 1946. Thus, he was clearly recognized as the best pitcher in his league for three successive years, a feat matched in this century only by Cy Young, Christy Mathewson, Walter Johnson, Pete Alexander, Lefty Grove, Newhouser and Greg Maddux. Newhouser had another 20-win season in 1948 with a 21-12 record.

Each of the seasons in Newhouser's three year run had distinguishing features. The 29 wins and MVP award in 1944 stand out. However, teammate Dizzy Trout had 27 wins with a lower ERA and more shutouts and complete games than Newhouser. The 1946 season, when Newhouser led the league in ERA and tied for the lead in wins, after the return of players like Williams, Joe DiMaggio and Bob Feller, validated Newhouser's status as more than just a standout wartime pitcher.

However, the 1945 season was clearly the gem in Newhouser's career, even though he had more wins in both 1944 and 1946. Newhouser was just totally dominant in 1945, leading the league in virtually every category, in most cases by a wide margin over his nearest competitor. He led the league in wins, winning percentage, ERA, strikeouts, innings pitched, complete games, shutouts (8) and opponents' batting average (.211).

The icing on the cake was an American League pennant and World Series win over the Chicago Cubs. The pennant was captured after four days of rain in St. Louis, when Newhouser came on in relief to post his 25th win, the game in which Hank

Greenberg hit the winning home run in the ninth inning. In the World Series, Newhouser started the first game but got hammered, yielding seven runs in less than three innings in a 9-0 loss to Cub ace Hank Borowy. Newhouser took the mound again in the pivotal fifth game with the series tied at two games apiece. This time, in Chicago, he prevailed over Borowy, 8-4 with nine strikeouts in a complete game win. In game six, the Cubs tied the series at three wins apiece, with an 8-7 victory in 12 innings as Borowy came out of the bullpen to take the win over Trout with four scoreless innings of relief.

After a day of rest, the Series came down to game seven at Wrigley Field. Newhouser was on the mound for Detroit, against the weary Borowy. The first three Tiger batters singled. Chicago manager Charlie Grimm saw the error of starting Borowy, and relieved him with Paul Derringer, but Detroit went on to score five runs in the first inning. Newhouser cruised all the way with a ten-strikeout performance in a 9-3 win, putting a perfect cap on his brilliant season. Newhouser made one more World Series appearance in his career, nine years later.

After arm problems resulted in his release from the Tigers in mid-season in 1953, he signed with Cleveland for the 1954 season and became a part of one of the best pitching staffs of all time, when the Indians won an American League record 111 games. Newhouser was one of four future Hall of Fame pitchers on the Indian staff with Feller, Bob Lemon and Early Wynn, and Newhouser was a valuable contributor with seven wins, seven saves and an ERA of 2.51. He made one relief appearance in the 1954 series and pitched in two games in 1955 before ending his playing career at the age of 33. He later worked as a scout for several major league teams, and then had a 20-year career in banking.

Various measures have been devised to evaluate overall pitching performance. One is the Total Pitcher Index (TPI) used in *Total Baseball*. Newhouser had a TPI of 7.8 in 1945, which ranks 21st on the all-time best season list, and has not been topped since (not even by Greg Maddux in 1994). The only others with a TPI over 7.0 since 1945 were Dwight Gooden with 7.3 in 1985 and Bob Gibson with 7.5 in 1968 (Maddux in '94 got a 7.1). In his book *Baseball's Best Pitchers*, Ralph Horton ranks Newhouser's 1945 season in a tie for 22nd place on the all-time list. Clearly, Newhouser's 1945 season ranks among the best ever, particularly when considered in light of his team's success.

Jackie Robinson - 1947

by John Benson

G	AB	R	H	2B	3B	HR	RBI	BB	SO	AVG	OBP	SLG	SB
151	590	125	175	31	5	12	48	74	36	.297	.383	.427	29

Jackie Robinson's 1947 season is baseball's most powerful reminder that numbers never tell the whole story. Robinson's statistics were merely good, yet his performance holds a place of greatness -- not just in baseball, but in the course of human events. A thousand years from now, even if baseball has gone the way of chariot racing and jousting, people will remember Jackie Robinson.

The essence of this book is context. The lesson of these hundred stories is that circumstances define greatness. To understand Jackie Robinson's circumstances, we must go back to 1886, when Cap Anson refused to play in a game with a black man on the field. From that moment until April 15, 1947, there were no blacks in major league baseball.

The longer a line stands without being crossed, the more pressure is put on anyone who comes close to crossing it. We have marveled at how Roger Maris, a nervous wreck with his hair falling out, finally overcame the shadow of Babe Ruth and crossed the line of 60 home runs, after so many great hitters had approached that line and faltered. How much more significant was Robinson's crossing the color line, a barrier reinforced by time, underlined by the major leagues' commissioner-endorsed ''gentlemen's agreement,'' and further emphasized by the whole tradition of the Negro Leagues? As an experienced evaluator of player performance under diverse circumstances, I can only describe the pressure on Robinson as unimaginable. Only one person could ever comment on the situation with any actual knowledge, and that was Robinson himself.

Consider the unique pressures brought to bear on no other player in history:

- Dodger president Branch Rickey made Robinson's whole presence conditional on a promise to take abuse, insults and even threats without retaliating, for one full year. The promise was: there would be no ''incidents,'' meaning that any participation in the verbal and physical give-and-take, which are fundamental in every ballgame, would be totally forbidden for Robinson during his rookie season.

- Fans and opponents poured their racial venom profusely onto rookie Robinson at every opportunity. Most disturbing were the many anonymous threats of violence and death against Jackie, his wife, and his son. Never a joking matter, threats of racial violence in the world of 1947 had to be regarded as seriously close to the actual commitment of the threatened deeds.

- Even Robinson's teammates, initially, joined in opposition to his presence on the field. The infamous petition drawn up by Dixie Walker, Bobby Bragan, and Eddie Stanky was among the first of many barriers he had to overcome (which he did, successfully).

- Robinson was barred from using the same basic facilities as his teammates for meals and housing.

The list goes on and on, and the point is overwhelming:

Jackie Robinson played under the most extremely negative conditions ever experienced by any athlete, before or since. For perspective, I reflect on the marvelous accomplishments of superstars like Barry Bonds and Ken Griffey Jr., in today's world, and wonder how much of their success depended on supportive environments beginning with father figures offering major league star role models. I can't help wondering how Bonds and Griffey could have performed, if isolated and threatened, in 1947, and I conclude that no one will ever know, or can even imagine.

While Robinson's statistics from 1947 do not tell the story of his season, they were quite good, nonetheless. He led the league in stolen bases. He amassed 42 bunt singles. He won the first-ever Rookie-of-the-Year award. He helped the Dodgers win the pennant. His exciting play increased attendance dramatically. Records were set, not just in Brooklyn but in cities throughout the National League. Baseball became more popular, nationwide.

Later in his career, Robinson excelled statistically. In 1949 he hit .342, winning the National League batting title, the MVP award, and leading the Dodgers to the World Series. He also led the league in stolen bases again that year. For six years, beginning in '49, he averaged .327 at the plate and finished with a career mark of .311. Four years in a row Robinson finished first, second, third and fourth in the NL batting race, and for five consecutive years he was among the top three in on base percentage. He led the league in OBP in 1952. Robinson got the highest Thorn-Palmer *Total Baseball* player rating in the National League in 1950 and 1952; in 1951 he finished second to Stan Musial. The reason that we pick 1947 as his most impressive season is the same reason the we have him in this book: the circumstances were uniquely challenging and simply beyond comparison to any other player at any other time.

Robinson's greatest strengths in 1947, and throughout his career, were in aspects of the game that had been long neglected: working the count to draw a walk; dropping a bunt or slapping a single; taking a hit-by-pitch for the team ... anything to get on base; and then using that presence on the bases to create runs in any way possible. Robinson was incessantly probing for any exploitable weakness in the opponents' pitching or defense. He would use the fake steal to get fielders out of position, take huge leads to distract pitchers, and pick the cleverest, most unnerving times to be off and running. Robinson stole home 19 times in his career. Taking two bases on a sacrifice bunt was another of his common but thrilling exploits.

The emergence of Jackie Robinson changed the style of play in the majors. Since Babe Ruth and his home runs had introduced a new way of winning, baseball had become a game of long, quiet periods broken by occasional explosive longballs. Players on the field and fans in the seats had fallen into various forms of waiting, then suddenly watching, then waiting again. Robinson made it impossible to be a good player or an astute fan without paying attention all the time, hanging on every pitch.

Robinson's integration of the game encompassed more than just crossing the color line. He brought with him the style of play from the Negro leagues, a style that had vanished from the majors after the retirement of Ty Cobb. The blacks, who became the standard-bearers for the scratch-one-run style that emphasized pitching, speed, defense, timely hitting, and sensational baserunning -- and who emphasized a deep understanding of the fact that professional baseball is, ultimately, a form of show business -- brought these same qualities back to the major leagues after a long absence. Fans appreciated.

The Negro leaguers called the Robinson style of play "tricky" baseball. Today, scouts use words like aggressive and heads-up, or simply "smart" baseball. Whatever you call it, Robinson was the master who brought it back for enjoyment in the second half of the 20th century.

And, a thousand years from now, he will be remembered.

Lou Boudreau - 1948

by Fred Matos

G	AB	R	H	2B	3B	HR	RBI	BB	SO	AVG	OBP	SLG	SB
152	560	116	199	34	6	18	106	98	9	.355	.453	.534	3

The many diverse personas and talents of the 1948 Cleveland Indians made up a very exciting team with a near-mystical magnetism that captivated Ohio, much of middle America and even parts of Canada. The owner was Bill Veeck, a flamboyant, iconoclastic, 34-year-old promoter and former Marine with a wooden leg replacing the one he lost fighting World War II in the Pacific. Gene Bearden, a 28-year-old rookie and Purple Heart war veteran who emerged as the star pitcher, four years previously was floating aimlessly in a life raft in the Pacific following the sinking of his Navy ship. Ace righthander Bob Lemon was a mediocre outfielder only two years before. Usually dependable Bob "Rapid Robert" Feller was having a mysterious up-and-down year. The team's center fielder was hard-hitting Larry Doby, the first black to play in the American League. And in mid-year, the Indians signed a tall gangly righthanded veteran of a jillion pitches in the Negro Leagues and barnstorming tours: Satchel Paige.

But the heart and soul of this great team was the shortstop, a charismatic fellow named Lou Boudreau. He was more than just the shortstop -- he was the leading hitter, batting third. He was also the manager, and already in his seventh year of managing at the relatively tender age of 31, then and still holding the record as the youngest manager at age 25 when appointed in 1942.

Boudreau's '48 offensive stats were outstanding, but not the best in the American League. Joe DiMaggio and Ted Williams were having good years, leading the league in numerous categories with Boudreau finishing second or third in many of them. But Boudreau had an outstanding year in the field, and with his strong leadership and clutch hitting, led the Indians to a world championship. Taking everything into consideration, Boudreau's 1948 season easily ranks as one the top 100 greatest years.

Boudreau describes himself as a hitter who always tried to make contact, but he is not using the latest definition of contact hitter, meaning a slap-and-spray type singles hitter. Boudreau had good power in the gaps and down the lines. He led the league in doubles three times from 1941 to 1947. Boudreau is proud that he rarely struck out. For example, in 1948, he struck out only nine times in 560 at bats.

Boudreau began the year with a bang, having a big day on April 26 against the White Sox, going five for six with two doubles, two triples and a single, good for four RBI. Three days later he got four hits and slammed a prodigious homer to the top of the pavilion against the St. Louis Browns in old Sportsman's Park. He was hitting .440 a month into the season, with Williams second at .397. The Indians and Philadelphia A's were tied for the league lead. Mid-June saw the Tribe in first with some pennant optimism, three games ahead of the A's, with Williams at .394 and Boudreau at .374. Cleveland fans were now excited and setting attendance records to see the charismatic Boudreau and the exciting Tribe.

Boudreau was elected to the All-Star team, and went

0-for-2 with an RBI in the midsummer classic. The Tribe now had a half-game lead over the A's, and Boudreau was hitting .359, second to Williams at .388. The pennant race got hotter with the weather, and at July's end, Boston, New York, the A's and Indians were all fighting for the lead. On August 4th, all four were tied for the lead!

On August 5th, Boudreau suffered leg and shoulder bruises in a collision with the Senators' Gil Coan. A key series with the Yankees followed, and Boudreau sat out the series -- with the exception of one pinch hit appearance. In the seventh inning of the first game of a doubleheader on August 8th, still hurting, he inserted himself as a pinch hitter with two men on and two outs. He delivered a clean single to center driving in two runs, and the Indians went on to win 8-6. When I asked Boudreau about his fondest memories of the season, this key pinch hit was one of the games that came to mind immediately.

In mid-August, Boudreau went 7-for-9 with two triples in a doubleheader win over the White Sox, as Cleveland had a lead of 1/2 game over the A's and was 2 1/2 games ahead of the Red Sox. Boudreau was hitting .363 and Williams .377. At the end of August, Boudreau was up to .371, edging Williams at .370. In early September, Boudreau was hitting .366, tied with Williams. But that's as close Boudreau came to the batting title as Williams kept up his pace finishing at .369 to win it. Boudreau went into a mild slump in the pennant race, but came on strong at the end to finish at .355, leading the Indians to the pennant and an eventual World Series victory.

As the manager, Boudreau the hitter had to be the ultimate team player. The Indians top hitter, he batted third, but he was not averse to calling on himself for a sacrifice bunt when the situation required it.

Boudreau was known for his great clutch hitting, and the best example of Boudreau's ability to come through in the clutch came in the playoff game for the pennant. He went 4-for-4, with two homers, two singles, two RBI, and three runs scored as the Indians trounced the Red Sox 8-3. Years later, Red Sox fans blame the ''curse of the Bambino'' for Manager Joe McCarthy's selection of journeyman pitcher Denny Galehouse to start the important game.

Boudreau's defensive skills were recognized very early in his career. In spring training in 1939, Indians Manager Oscar Vitt described the new rookie by observing ''that kid has the greatest pair of hands I've ever seen.''

Boudreau was not very fast, so he had to use his brainpower to stretch his physical limitations. For example he used superior defensive positioning, based on a careful study of all the league's hitters and all of his team's pitchers, to squeeze out more range from his fielding. On the bases he could do better than just "not hurt the team, by remaining alert" as so many not-so-fast runners have been described; Boudreau could actually win a game with a surprising jump or a tricky slide, even with his lack of raw speed.

Boudreau was a basketball and baseball star at the University of Illinois, and he brought his athleticism to the baseball field. Before the days of the 11:00 o'clock news highlight video clips, fans relied largely on in-person observations by others, especially from radio broadcasts and the vivid descriptions in print media, to learn about details like a fielder's skill. Two short but highly illustrative pieces from the 1948 New York *Times* offer excellent examples of Boudreau's first-rate fielding skills.

During a spring training game against the New York Giants on April 7, 1948, James Dawson, the *Times* writer, provided this highlight clip:

The tying run was at the plate when Manager Lou Boudreau made one of those plays on which he seems to have a monopoly -- a daring grab of Conway's rap to his right, a toss over his shoulder in midair before he went somersaulting near the foul line, as his peg forced Hartung to end the game.

-- New York *Times*, April 8, 1948

Following a World Series game when Boudreau had a bad day, the respected *Times* sports columnist Arthur Daley observed:

Boudreau had such an off day that he slapped into a double-play in the first inning and then saw his incredible powers of anticipation desert him in the second when he failed to get his usual jump on Frank McCormick's simple single to the left of second, the kind he ordinarily gobbles up in one gulp.

In an interview for this essay, Boudreau told me that his great anticipation skill came from years of experience. From the catcher's signal for a particular pitch, the pitch count, and his knowledge of the hitters and his pitcher, he could anticipate where the ball was going to be hit, moving with the pitch. He had a prescient sense of where the ball was going, thus making many otherwise difficult plays look easy as he was in the right place at the right time. The anticipation skills were developed out of necessity to make up for his slowness, although he had first and second step quickness.

Boudreau elaborated on his anticipation skills, recalling that he made adjustments according to different counts on the hitter. With two strikes on a righthanded batter, he would look for a defensive contact swing aimed up the middle, and he therefore protected the middle of the diamond. With the pitcher behind in the count, say three-and-one, he protected the hole as the hitter could be expected to pull the ball. Of course, not all hitters were pulling, and the catcher may be calling for a pitch on the outside corner to a righthand batter, so Boudreau's dynamic anticipation adjustments depended on many factors.

Boudreau developed a great pick-off play with his righthanded pitchers, and it frequently worked to perfection, picking off unsuspecting runners at second base. The play was very simple but required perfect timing. Following a signal, on a certain count the pitcher quickly wheeled and threw to the bag with Boudreau already moving behind the runner and arriving at the bag at the same time as the ball. It was critical that the umpires be prepared for the play, so Boudreau gave the secret signal to American League umpires so they would be ready. But the most famous example of the play was in the first game of the 1948 World Series, with Bob Feller pitching. That case resulted in a safe call by a National League umpire who was not previously alerted to the play. Movies later clearly showed Boston Braves runner Phil Masi to be out, and many years later, following the death of umpire Bill Stewart, Masi admitted that he was out.

As a manager, Boudreau was sometimes forced into lineup juggling. On one occasion on May 30, he lifted catcher Jim Hegan for a pinch hitter, and Joe Tipton, the backup catcher, who was then hit on the wrist and had to leave the game. Since the Indians carried only two catchers, Boudreau caught for the last two innings. The strategy paid off anyway, as the Tribe scored nine runs in the eighth inning to defeat the White Sox 13-8. Boudreau had no problems catching, as he had begun as a catcher on the Chicago sandlots many years before.

Boudreau's leadership skills were developed in high school when he was the captain of the basketball team in his junior and senior years. As a college junior, he was captain of the basketball team at the University of Illinois, a position normally given to a senior. Thus, the strong character and leadership skills were already developed, and were readily recognized when he was a baseball rookie in 1939. Very early in his baseball career, Boudreau was described as a "fiery Frenchman" with an extraordinary personality that made him the vital catalyst, the much-needed sparkplug of the team.

In 1942, Boudreau applied for the Indians manager's job in a very convincing letter to owner Alva Bradley. Bradley agreed, and appointed Boudreau as the manager prior to the 1942 season, making him at age 25, the youngest manager ever, a record that he still holds today. There have been other player-managers, but they have been old veterans nearing the end of their playing careers who obtained managerial jobs. Boudreau was truly unique.

Boudreau was an imaginative manager, exemplified by his invention of the radical Williams shift in the second game of a doubleheader in Boston in August 1946, after Williams had torn the Indians apart in the first game. The shift moved all infielders to the right side of second base with the second baseman moving to short right field, and all the outfielders were moved to the right of center. The radical shift dared the pull-hitting Williams to alter his batting style and hit to left field. Williams refused to alter his batting style, and admitted that the shift affected his hitting.

Boudreau was also known for taking risks on rookies, and they frequently worked out. In 1948, Gene Bearden was an unknown lefthanded knuckleballer who had been released by the Yankees. Boudreau gave him a chance, and he came through with a 20-win season.

During the 1948 season, Boudreau demonstrated his extraordinary patience with the struggling Bob Feller who had a 9-11 record at one point, with a seven-game losing streak. Boudreau stuck with Feller, and his confidence was rewarded as Feller responded by winning seven in a row during the stretch run.

Boudreau's gutsiest managerial decision came in the playoff game for the pennant as he selected as the Indians' starter, the rookie Gene Bearden, with one day rest, over more seasoned and well rested veterans Lemon and Feller. Furthermore, Bearden was a lefthander and the game was in Fenway Park, long noted as a place where southpaws often faced disaster. The selection defied all odds and percentages, but the smooth lefty scattered five hits and went all the way for the victory, making Boudreau look like a genius.

For his great season, Boudreau was voted the Most Valuable Player (MVP) in the American League over Williams, obtaining 324 points out of a possible 366.

Boudreau's 1948 season was indeed an extraordinary one combining his hitting, defense, and management talents, a year unique in baseball history.

Harry Brecheen - 1948

by Fred Matos

W	L	PCT	G	GS	CG	SV	IP	SO	BB	B/I	ERA
20	7	.741	33	30	21	1	233	149	193	1.04	2.24

Harry ("The Cat") Brecheen is most remembered as the winner of three World Series games against the Boston Red Sox in 1946, but the smooth southpaw had a more extraordinary year in 1948 while leading the St. Louis Cardinals to a second place finish. His 2.24 ERA was the best in the major leagues, and he ranked first in the National League in strikeouts, shutouts (seven) and winning percentage. His 20 wins and 21 complete games both ranked second in the National League. Looking further, we can see that Brecheen ranked high in the National League in several other of the key statistical categories:
- fewest hits per nine innings, 7.44, ranking third;
- fewest walks per nine innings, 1.89, ranking fourth;
- most strikeouts per nine innings: 5.75, ranking first.

As the facts illustrate, Brecheen had excellent control and was always around the plate, but it was still difficult to get a hit off him, let alone a base on balls. The numbers match the pitcher; Brecheen was fast but not overpowering, and he had a great deal of movement on his pitches. Brecheen was a lefthander who stood at 5'10" and weighed 160 pounds. He gave definition to the phrase "crafty lefty" with his fine control and ability to change speeds while hitting spots precisely. Brecheen was also a master at working on the individual weaknesses of each hitter.

Brecheen bested some outstanding colleagues among National League pitchers in 1948. Among the top hurlers were future Hall-of-Famer Warren Spahn, Johnny Sain, Preacher Roe, Johnny Vander Meer, Ralph Branca, and Rex Barney.

In 1948 strikeouts were not as common as they are today. In 1948, 11.2 percent of all at bats resulted in strikeouts, whereas in 1993, the rate was 17.2 percent. An increase of such magnitude indicates that there are many more free swingers nowadays, and far fewer contact hitters who can punch the ball and use all fields.

Comparing the top home run hitters and their strikeout percentages:

1948 Hitter	HR	AB	K - Percentage	
Ralph Kiner	40	555	61	11.0%
Johnny Mize	40	560	37	6.6%

1993 Hitter	HR	AB	K - Percentage	
Barry Bonds	46	539	79	14.6%
David Justice	40	585	90	15.4%

Modern day sluggers are typically more free swinging than their 1948 counterparts, especially after they have two strikes. The one exception from the top sluggers of 1948 who would fit nicely into the 1993 model was Hank Sauer, who struck out 16 percent of the time. One reason for the difference is that today's hitters use light, thin-handled bats for greater bat speed and power, whereas in 1948 there were more contact hitters, even some using the extra-heavy ''bottle-handled'' bats.

The point of this contrast in hitting styles: appreciate what Brecheen's skills would equate to, against today's hitters. With the same pitching repertoire, he would be a big winner on any team, and would have many more strikeouts if the team used a four-man rotation.

Brecheen had many excellent games in 1948, including his seven shutouts. One very sharp 3-0 game against the New York Giants on August 3rd at the Polo Grounds stands out. The hard-hitting Giants were led by Johnny Mize, Sid Gordon and Whitey Lockman. Brecheen was unhittable through four perfect innings before Mize opened the fifth with a scratch single. There was one walk in the sixth, and the only other Giant to reach base was Walker Cooper, who lined a clean single to left-center in the ninth. The pinch-runner was quickly erased in a double play, so Brecheen faced only 29 men in this masterful outing.

Another memorable performance was a 4-0 shutout on September 9th against the tough Cubs led by Andy Pafko, Phil Cavaretta, and Peanuts Lowery. Brecheen scattered six hits and whiffed 10 Cubs. No runner reached second until the ninth.

Now at home in Ada, Oklahoma, Harry Brecheen shared some of his memories of this outstanding season. Brecheen said he featured a fastball, curve and screwball. He varied his delivery, frequently coming over the top with his curve, but three-quarters was his natural delivery. His threw a four-seam fastball that moved upward and tailed away from right handed hitters. He had two distinct speeds on his screwball, using it as changeup to keep the toughest hitters off balance. He found that throwing the screwball slower gave it a much bigger break than the faster version. The screwball was frequently his out pitch against righty batters, and he could throw it for a strike at almost any time.

Brecheen recalled that even in this great season there were many days when not all of his pitches were working. He would then use whatever was working best. He said that there are certain key points in a game when a pitcher must make good pitches to win the game, and winners make those key pitches.

Brecheen said his pitching style was to mix up his pitches and move the ball around. He worked the inside corner extensively, and if hitters were crowding the plate he pushed them back, but he said that he never tried to hit anybody intentionally. He liked to move the ball in and out, hitting his chosen spots, especially against the good, smart hitters. Brecheen revealed that the pesky hitters (he called them "choke-up" hitters) gave him the most difficulty. The choke-up hitter who gave Brecheen the most difficulty was Richie Ashburn, the Hall-of-Fame Phillie outfielder and lefthanded hitter who sprayed the ball all over the place. Brecheen recalled that Pee Wee Reese and Alvin Dark were also difficult spray hitters.

Brecheen was clever enough to fool most of the big power swingers, but Bob Elliott, Boston Braves third baseman, and Sid Gordon, New York Giants third baseman/outfielder, came to mind as exceptions. Both Elliott and Gordon were right-handed power hitters, and Brecheen called them "overpowering." He remembered slugger Ralph Kiner hitting long fly balls that carried like fungoes with a back spin, so he kept the ball low on Kiner to keep it in the park. He said Jackie Robinson was a great hitter, hitting many line drives over the infielders' gloves. Brecheen said that Robinson was "a real headache" on the bases, and that he had to keep him close to the bag with repeated pickoff throws. Johnny Mize was another great hitter, and Brecheen recalled that "Big Jawn" couldn't get out of the way of inside pitches. He said that he accidently hit Mize in the head with a pitch as Mize just stood there like a statue. He recalled other particularly tough hitters such as Hank Sauer, Del Ennis, and Gil Hodges.

Brecheen had the good fortune to be backed up by an excellent Cardinal defense, especially in the middle infield with Marty (Slats, The Octopus) Marion at shortstop and Red Schoendienst at second base. The outfield was anchored by Enos Slaughter and Stan Musial. The Cardinals had a strong offensive team led by Musial, Schoendienst and Slaughter, all of whom are now in the Hall of Fame. Despite the hitting strength and Brecheen's pitching, the Cards finished a distant second, 6 1/2 games behind the pennant-winning Boston Braves with the "Spahn-and-Sain-and-pray-for-rain" pitching rotation. Other than Brecheen, the Cardinals were thin in starting pitching with Howie Pollet, Murray Dickson, Jim Hearn, and Al Brazle the other main starters.

As was the practice in the 1940's and early '50's, even the top starters were occasionally called on to relieve between starts. Brecheen got such a call and came through as a reliever in the last week of the season when the Cards were fighting for second place. Second place money mattered in those days, so the games meant something even though the Cards were hopelessly out of the pennant race.

Brecheen has a place in history as a classic "smart" pitcher who carefully studied hitters and pitchers. He later used his extensive knowledge to become a successful pitching coach for 14 years, beginning with the St. Louis Browns where he was both a pitcher and a coach for several years, and remained with the team when they moved to Baltimore. He coached the Oriole pitchers under Paul Richards, Billy Hitchcock, Jimmy Dykes and Hank Bauer. Any pitching coach capable of holding his job through such a succession of different managers with diverse styles must be an obvious asset.

As a coach, Brecheen was responsible for the early development of numerous pitchers, most notably Bob Turley, Don Larsen, Jim Palmer, Dave McNally, Jack Fisher, Milt Pappas, Chuck Estrada, and Wally Bunker, all of whom had some good years, and one (Palmer), who was later enshrined in the Hall of Fame. But Brecheen didn't teach any of them the screwball, believing that the strain on the elbow would eventually hurt them.

Asked if any pitcher of recent vintage reminded him of his pitching style, Brecheen came up with only one name: Fernando Valenzuela, the only recent major league starter with a screwball featured in his repertoire.

Brecheen recalled picking up his nickname, ''The Cat,'' during spring training early in his career. The pitchers were practicing fielding bunts, and Brecheen was so good at pouncing on the ball that the other players began referring to him as ''The Cat.'' A St. Louis sports writer picked it up and the rest is history.

Stan Musial - 1948

by John Benson

G	AB	R	H	2B	3B	HR	RBI	BB	SO	AVG	OBP	SLG	SB
155	611	135	230	46	18	39	131	79	34	.376	.450	.702	7

Stan Musial had the best career of any player ever, based on MVP voting. He won the award outright in 1943, 1946 and 1948, came in second in the voting four times, and six times he finished third to ninth. That's seven years standing as the top one or two players in his league, and 13 years among the top nine. No one else attracted so many high value assessments from baseball writers nationwide, not Mickey Mantle or Yogi Berra, or Roy Campanella or Joe DiMaggio, each whom won three MVP awards. Ted Williams, who won two MVP awards and had a number of close calls, ranks second to Musial in overall voting consideration.

Much of this book is given to explaining how statistics may differ from true player performance and value. The MVP award offers a window to the world of subjective wisdom, a quantitative catch-all for the elusive facts that may not appear in box scores, as Bill James has most fully explicated. Musial was the exact opposite of today's flashy, self-absorbed stars. He was friendly, quiet without being aloof, and totally unassuming.

In the case of Musial, we can offer some new objective evidence here in these pages, with some of the latest findings from those baseball archaeologists, Retrosheet. Stan The Man might have earned a more lasting place in media memory if he had spent his career in New York or Los Angeles, instead of 22 years in St. Louis. But he made a lasting impression on New York writers with unique excellence in beating the Brooklyn Dodgers, especially in 1948.

The Cardinals came in second to the Boston Braves that year, but the defending champion Dodgers slipped to third. Not coincidentally, Musial hit .522 at Ebbets field in 1948, with a .560 on base percentage and 1.022 slugging -- these stats unearthed by Retrosheet (see page 317). No statistical fluke, Musial in 1949 again enjoyed visiting Brooklyn, producing a .523 batting average, a .632 on base percentage, and 1.114 slugging.

According to researchers at the *Total Baseball* office, Musial got his nickname ''The Man'' on May 20, 1948, when he got four hits in a 13-4 trouncing of the Dodgers at Ebbets Field. Whether or not fans heard voices coming from the Brooklyn dugout, ''That man, [expletive] that man,'' it is a recorded fact that the crowd began a collective murmur of, "That man, that man," when Musial came to bat.

The Dodgers' starting pitcher Preacher Roe, also emerging as a star in 1948, suggested, half seriously, that the smartest way to pitch Musial was to walk him intentionally and then try to pick him off first base. Considering what he did in Brooklyn, that method would simply have traded a few walks for some doubles, triples, homers, and runs batted in. And, there would still be the remote hope of that pick-off, so the trade-off isn't all that laughable within the context of Ebbets Field.

Musial, in 1948, led the National League in runs, hits, doubles, triples, total bases, batting average, on base percentage, slugging percentage -- you get the idea,

just about every offensive stat there is (he was just one home run behind Ralph Kiner and Johnny Mize). It was a classic breakout year from a maturing hitter; Musial was age 26 that summer, turning 27 in September. He had won two batting titles before 1948, but never had hit more than 19 homers.

Musial explained his hitting prowess with the simple explanation that he could see the ball well, picking up the rotation on every pitch. His batting stance clearly featured an outstretched head with alert, peering eyes, prompting one pitcher to say he looked like ''a kid peeking around the corner to see if the cops are coming.''

The stance was often a topic of debate and ironic humor. One future Hall-of-Fame pitcher stood at the batting cage one day, watching Musial take his cuts. ''Kid,'' he said, ''you will never become a good hitter with that funny-looking stance.'' The pitcher was Warren Spahn, and the year was 1961. ''Too late for me, pal,'' was Musial's good-natured retort. Stanley Frank Musial had his own idea, one that speaks volumes to current players and coaches: ''If a batter hits well with a particular stance, think twice before changing it.''

Musial's 1948 season is prominent both within the context of his career and in comparison to other NL hitters of 1948. The peak within career context is the strongest framing of this great one-year performance, because Musial was so noted for all-around consistency throughout his 22 years in the big leagues. He hit .330 at the age of 41, for example, just before calling it quits the next year. When he retired, his 3,630 hits were the National League record, and he had split them precisely, 1,815 at home and 1,815 on the road, while collecting his seven batting titles and .331 career average.

The .376 mark was the career peak, as were the 39 home runs, and the .450 on base percentage, and the .702 slugging percentage among other numbers. Musial's 1948 season was a classic blossoming of pure and innocent talent, a line drive hitter whose accomplishments included accidentally knocking the ball over the fence 39 times. Musial said he never once tried to hit a home run before 1949. ''After the 1948 season, I got to thinking about the 39 home runs,'' said Musial, ''and asked myself, if I hit 39 without trying, how many could I hit with an earnest effort?'' He found out in 1949, by trying. Half way through the season, he had only a dozen homers and was hitting barely .300. That was the end of his swinging for the fences. Nonetheless, he proceeded to average 31 round-trippers a year for seven years, and amassed 475 in his career.

There was one more occasion, however, when Musial was suspected of trying to hit a home run. It was in an All-Star game, and thus forgivable. He came to the plate in the 12th inning of a marathon tie game, and (he loved to chatter with catchers) commiserated with Yogi Berra on the subject of aching feet. ''Relax, and I'll get you out of here in a hurry,'' said The Man, and he promptly deposited the next pitch in the seats for a game-ender.

It was the prolific output of line drive doubles and triples, not the home runs, for which Musial is most remembered. Joe Garagiola described the Musial Method this way: ''Stan comes sauntering up to the plate and asks me how my family's making out. Before I can answer him, he's on third base.'' Soft-spoken, modest, and undramatic especially when compared to many lesser heroes, Musial's on-field conduct set the tone for the quiet, great place he has taken in baseball history. Today, it seems as if his 22 years passed through the National League with that same elusive quality that kept landing him on third base.

Ralph Kiner - 1949

by Lary Bump

G	AB	R	H	2B	3B	HR	RBI	BB	SO	AVG	OBP	SLG	SB
152	549	116	170	19	5	54	127	117	61	.310	.432	.658	6

Resting under glass, inside a library on the University of Pittsburgh campus, is home plate from Forbes Field, the Pirates' home from 1909 to 1970. From there, you can walk down a corridor, through two sets of doors, down the steps and most of the way to the street before you come to several rows of bricks embedded in the sidewalk. Those bricks are all that remain of Forbes Field's wall down the left field line. They seem to be a long way from home plate, and they are -- 365 feet away.

The 365-foot left field line was just part of the problem for batters at Forbes Field. The original park had a 376-foot right field line and a distance of 442 feet to center field. The deepest part of the ballpark, to the left of center, was 462 feet from home plate. With its deep gaps, Forbes Field was a haven for triples, as Owen Wilson found out in 1912, when he established the major league record of 36. But it was death to home run hitters. No Pirate hit as many as 20 home runs in a season until Johnny Rizzo banged 23 in 1938. And in the Forbes Field years, no Bucco led the National League until rookie Ralph Kiner cranked 23 in 1946, when the entire team totaled 60. He won the homer crown by one over Johnny Mize, whose career would parallel Kiner's over the next several years.

Kiner's rise up the minor league ladder was interrupted by World War II when he enlisted in the Navy. Returning to civilian life in 1946, he was expected to start the season in the Pacific Coast League with the Hollywood Stars, but after he cranked 13 homers and batted over .400 in spring training, the Pirates took Kiner north with them.

Before the 1947 season, the Pirates had obtained Hall of Fame slugger Hank Greenberg. They decided fans might like to see more homers, so they moved a bullpen from foul territory down the left field line to fair ground in the left field corner. The fence in front of the new bullpen was 335 feet from home plate down the line. The new home run target area was initially known as Greenberg Gardens, but its greatest beneficiary would be Kiner. 1947 was Greenberg's final season, when he produced 25 homers. But he made a far more important and lasting contribution to Pittsburgh baseball. He asked to room with Kiner, and talked hitting with him. Greenberg told the young slugger the value of proper sleep, and suggested that he spread his feet, stand closer to the plate, and above all, relax.

Said Kiner: "In 1946, I was afraid that when the pitcher got two strikes on me, the next pitch would come at me. I'd bite and strike out. With Hank's coaching, I learned to swing only when the ball was over the plate." Kiner learned the lessons well. That very season, 1947, he smashed Pittsburgh's season record with 51 home runs. For the first time since Hack Wilson set the National League record with 56 in 1930, the NL had an individual 50-homer season. Two, in fact, for Kiner and Mize tied for the league lead with 51 each.

Kiner and Mize led the league again in 1948 with 40

home runs apiece, but Kiner broke loose and won the home run crown alone in each of the next three seasons, and tied 1952 MVP Hank Sauer, with 37 homers. That made seven consecutive seasons leading the league. No one, not even Babe Ruth, ever matched Kiner's long run of domination. None of the NL's sluggers matched Kiner's total of seven home run titles until Mike Schmidt took his seventh in 1984, and his eighth in '86.

In the March 1961 issue of *Sport* magazine, Warren Spahn rated Kiner the fourth-toughest batter he faced, behind Stan Musial, Willie Mays and Ernie Banks. Said Spahn, "Every time Ralph came up he endangered any lead that you had." Bill James rates Kiner as the second-greatest home run hitter of all time -- and he does have the second-highest ratio of homers to at bats, behind only Babe Ruth.

The zenith of Kiner's dominating period was 1949, when he powered 54 home runs, 18 more than runner-up Musial. Kiner had produced a big September in 1947, including eight home runs in four games September 10-12. But that was nothing compared to what he did in the final month of the '49 season.

He entered September with 38 home runs, which would have given him the home run title even if he didn't play another game. Then on September 1, he hammered a grand slam against Hank Behrman in a 9-5 loss at the Polo Grounds. In the Pirates' next game, Kiner powered number 40, then hit two more the next day. On September 11, Kiner helped the Bucs stop a slide of 13 losses in 14 games by bashing two two-run homers in a 7-3 win over the Cubs. In Pittsburgh's next game, he smashed a grand slam and a solo home run against the Phillies' Hank Borowy and Curt Simmons, respectively, giving Kiner 48 homers for the season and, for the third time in his career, four in four consecutive at bats. The grand slam was his fourth of the season, tying a major league record then held by six others including Ruth and Lou Gehrig. Kiner hit his 49th homer against Robin Roberts off the football clock above the scoreboard September 14. Five days later, Kiner became the first National Leaguer with two 50-home run seasons when he blasted a Kirby Higbe offering

out of Forbes Field. The Pirates season record fell on September 21, when Kiner hit two more homers. In the first game of a doubleheader September 25 in Cincinnati, home run number 53 tied Cy Williams' NL record of 15 homers in one month. That record fell September 30, when Kiner belted a Herm Wehmeier pitch for a solo home run, his 54th (and 47th against a righthanded pitcher).

Two games, an October 2 doubleheader against Cincinnati, remained for Kiner to take aim at Wilson's league record of 56. But starters Howie Fox and Ken Raffensberger held the Pirates slugger to three singles in eight at bats. That 1949 performance completed a stretch when Kiner smashed a record 168 home runs in his first four seasons. He would hit 47 the next year, for a two-year NL mark of 101. He and Willie Mays are the only National Leaguers with two seasons of 50 or more homers, and Kiner and Duke Snider are the only players in league history with five consecutive seasons of 40 or more. In 1949, Kiner also edged MVP Jackie Robinson for the RBI title, 127-124, and Pee Wee Reese for the league lead in walks, 117-116. And the Pittsburgh outfielder had 12 assists.

But it was home runs that attracted fans. In 1947, Kiner and Greenberg helped bring a Pittsburgh record 1,283,531 fans into Forbes Field. With Kiner alone as the drawing card the next season, the Pirates drew 1,517,021 at home. Many of them would stay until what they figured was Kiner's last at bat, then leave in droves. Said general manager Roy Hamey, "He's the franchise."

Kiner has been quoted as saying, "Home run hitters drive Cadillacs, and singles hitters drive Fords," but he credited pitcher Fritz Ostermueller with coining the expression. Kiner could drive just about any car he wanted. His early-'50s salaries have been reported as high as $100,000. During his playing days, he was somewhat of a man about town, and in towns bigger than Pittsburgh. In California, where he made his off-season home, he was linked romantically with actresses, including Elizabeth Taylor.

One thing he couldn't do was lift his team into a pennant race. The last wartime edition of the Pirates finished fourth in the NL. Pittsburgh would get that high in the standings only once during Kiner's years there. From 1946 to '53, the Bucs were seventh, seventh, fourth, sixth, eighth, seventh and eighth, with a franchise-low 42-112 record in 1952. The team's lack of success led to one of the best-known contract negotiation stories in sports history, right there with Vince Lombardi's trading Jim Ringo when he showed up with an agent.

Kiner asked for a raise, but Branch Rickey replied: "I know you hit all those homers, but remember, we could have finished last without you." The Pirates did finish last in 1953 without Kiner, after they traded him and three other players to the Cubs for six players and a much-needed $100,000.

After that 1953 season, both Kiner and Kiner's Corner were gone. With no bullpen in fair ground, the distance down the left field line again was 365 feet. No Pirate remotely approached 50 homers until the team moved to Three Rivers Stadium.

In '53, Chicago placed seventh, ahead of only the Pirates. Kiner totaled 35 homers and finished fifth in a league led by Eddie Mathews' 47. The Cubs were seventh again in 1954.

Kiner faded further after he was traded to Cleveland. He played 113 games in '55, batting .243-18-54, but the Indians started their long downward spiral by finishing second by three games to the Yankees. That was the last season for Kiner. Battling back problems, he retired, still short of his 33rd birthday.

As brief as Kiner's playing career was, he has proven to be a durable part of the baseball scene since then. He was the general manager of the Pacific Coast League's San Diego Padres from 1956 to 1960. After

that he joined Bob Elson in the Chicago White Sox broadcast booth for one year.

When the New York Mets entered the National League in 1962, Kiner became part of their broadcast team. He outlasted career professional announcer Lindsay Nelson. Another pro, third man on the broadcast team Bob Murphy, remained a Mets announcer into the 1990's, but on radio only. It was Kiner -- the malapropist and mispronouncer -- who remained on the Mets TV team. Through the 1994 season, he also had a postgame show -- Kiner's Korner.

It's tempting (and in some quarters, popular) to discount Kiner's 1975 election to the Hall of Fame as the result of his post-playing-career television exposure in the world's greatest media center.

He was perceived as a poor fielder. Enos Slaughter said he could score on a fly ball to Kiner 30 feet past third base. Indeed, Kiner had a less-than-terrific throwing arm. But he was not a lumbering outfielder in the Harmon Killebrew mode. Kiner led NL outfielders with 390 putouts in 1947.

Another perception was that he hit cheap home runs onto a Charles O. Finley Pennant Porch. But in 1949 Kiner set a National League record with 25 road home runs (exceeded by George Foster's 31 in 1977). And even with Kiner's Corner in place, Forbes Field's 335-foot left field line still was slightly longer than the current average distance in the National League.

In the history of the big-park league, Hack Wilson still is the only batter to exceed Kiner's 54 home runs in 1949. And no park in the league is as big as old Forbes Field -- with or without Kiner's Corner.

Roy Campanella - 1953

by Bill Gray

G	AB	R	H	2B	3B	HR	RBI	BB	SO	AVG	OBP	SLG	SB
144	519	103	162	26	3	41	142	67	58	.312	.395	.611	4

Major League Baseball entered the summer of 1994 with the promise of thrilling pennant races, record setting paces for home runs, and a serious run at .400 by Tony Gwynn. It ended with a strike in August, and without a World Series in October. In March 1995 spring training games were played by replacement players. The real players were still hunkered down, in month eight of their strike. While the news was filled with lengthy daily ranting from owners and players alike, one item appearing on the news wire lent some much-needed dignity to the tattered sport. A boy named Aaron Desmond had sent 10 letters to some baseball greats, past and present. To each, young Desmond had made a polite and simple request for an autograph. He received only one reply. It came from a woman named Roxie, the widow of Roy Campanella. She sent an autographed picture of the great Brooklyn Dodger catcher and wrote Aaron a note which read:

"I'm very unhappy to inform you that Roy has passed away and is no longer with us. I miss him so very much. I'll send you what I have - a photo. The signature on the card is the way he wrote before he left us."

Aaron Desmond still has Campanella's autograph, as do thousands of fans whom Campy touched during his life. While the players and owners continued the agonizing dismemberment of the National Pastime, Roy Campanella made another little boy happy, the way baseball players used to.

Campanella, the second black man to play in the majors, played for Brooklyn from 1948 until 1957 when an automobile accident left him paralyzed. Campanella would never wear a Los Angeles Dodger uniform as a player. This man was a *Brooklyn* Dodger. It was in Brooklyn where he crouched behind the plate in Ebbets Field, catching Newk, "Oisk," Preacher, Labine and two youngsters named Drysdale and Koufax. The Boys of Summer chased the hated Yankees every year of Roy's career, only winning the World Series in 1955, the same year Campanella won his third MVP.

Campanella, despite a friendly, easygoing manner, did not suffer fools lightly. But at the same time he knew he had to keep his cool in response to the barrage of insults and taunts from white players. In the minors at Nashua, New Hampshire, Campanella was behind the plate as a player named Sal Yvars stepped up to hit. Yvars had a well deserved reputation as a crude, bad-tempered player. He had previously been responsible for ending the playing career of future Dodger manager Walter Alston by veering far off course and crashing full speed into Alston as he tried to catch Yvars' foul pop near first base. The impact broke a bone in Alston's back.

In Nashua, Campanella crouched and waited for Yvars to complete his preparations before flashing the sign to his pitcher. Yvars bent down and picked up a handful of dirt, but instead of performing the normal ritual of rubbing the dirt into his palms, he turned toward Campanella and disdainfully flung the dirt into Campanella's face. Campy tensed, ready to

ROY CAMPANELLA

vent his rage on the smirking Yvars. He collected himself and remembered Branch Rickey's admonishment to avoid taking the bait. The smirk quickly disappeared from Yvars' face when Campanella snarled; ''If you ever do that again, I'm going to beat the living blood out of you.'' Yvars usually responded to such a challenge, but in this case knew he had gone too far, and that the powerful Campanella was ready and able to hammer him. Yvars turned away without a word.

Campanella reached the majors in 1948. Then 26, he was a rookie only by definition. He played with the skill of a veteran, having served since 1941 as a catcher and four time All Star in the Negro Leagues. Campanella was not the premier catcher in the Negro Leagues. That title belonged to Josh Gibson, the ''Black Babe Ruth.'' Based on talent, it had been assumed that Gibson would be the first black player to break the color line and enter major league baseball. But in 1946 Gibson suffered a massive stroke and died at 35. Some say his death was connected to the bitter disappointment he felt upon learning that Robinson would be the first black man to play major league ball in the modern era. Gibson's skill was not in question, but his age was against him. Robinson joined the Dodgers in 1947, and a year later Campanella joined him.

Both Robinson and Campanella were pioneers, and while Robinson was to bear the burden of breaking the color line, all black players entering the major leagues in that era were subject to bad treatment and often had to turn the other cheek. They also had to play at a high level to substantiate the ''worthiness'' of the black man to play major league ball.

Campanella played in 83 games for the 1948 Dodgers and stroked nine home runs in 279 at bats. His average was .258. The following year Campanella began to assert himself more, collecting 22 home runs and 82 RBI. His average shot up to .287 and his slugging percentage was .498. He reached 31 homers with another batting average in the .280's and another RBI mark in the 80's in 1950, and then burst to a higher level in 1951 when he and the Dodgers began to run away with the NL race ... until the Giants made

up a 13-game deficit and won the pennant against the Dodgers on Bobby Thomson's shot heard around the world (hit when Campanella was not catching, because of a bad leg). Campanella hit 33 home runs, batted .325 and drove in 108 runs while slugging .590. He was named the National League's Most Valuable Player.

A pattern emerged for Campanella after capturing the MVP award. He followed each MVP season with a significant decline, then followed the off year with another MVP season. In 1952 he fell to 22 homers, and his batting average dipped to .269, down 56 points. He continued steady in the RBI department with 97, although his slugging fell from .590 to .453.

In 1953, at age 31, Campanella produced his career season. His 144 games played and 519 at bats were both career highs -- and an incredible workload for an over-30-year-old catcher. The Dodgers won 105 games and lost only 49 in winning the pennant by 13 games. They scored 955 runs. The next highest run total belonged to the Cardinals and the Giants tied at 768. Brooklyn fielded an awesome combination of power and speed. The Dodgers produced 205 homers and stole 90 bases, both far above the league average.

In the '53 World Series, Campanella played all six games at catcher for Brooklyn, collecting six hits including a home run that gave the Dodgers a 3-2 win in game three.

Campanella undeniably was overworked in 1953. In 1954 he and the Dodgers paid the price. He played only 111 games and his batting average dropped 105 points to .207. The Dodgers fell to second place, five games behind the Giants. Campanella, always a free swinger, still managed 19 home runs, but knocked in only 51, a shocking decline of 91 RBI. His on base percentage plummeted to .286, dipping 26 points below his 1953 *batting* average, and 109 points below his OBP the previous year. His slugging plunged from .611 to .401. At 33, the two-time MVP was thought to be at the end of the road. It seemed as if the entire Dodger team was fading and had yielded their seat on the New York Sock Exchange to the World Champion Giants.

But coming into 1955, the Dodgers had learned something. Give Campy a day off every now and then, and he can still hit pretty well. You'd be hard pressed to find a catcher not plagued by injuries at different times during a season. Campanella's age compounded the aches. But instead of playing with pain as he had for his entire career, he accepted the rest. He played in only 123 games in 1955, but showed he had plenty of pop left in the bat. His average shot back up to .318, the second highest of his career. He drove in 107 runs, hit 32 home runs (in 446 at bats), boosted his on base percentage to .402, slugged .583, and won his third MVP award.

To find the last time when a Brooklyn team had won baseball's championship, one had to go back to 1900. The team wasn't then called the Dodgers; they were the Superbas. Since that 1900 championship the Brooklyn franchise appeared in, and lost, the World Series' of 1916, 1920 and 1941. The entrance of Jackie Robinson in 1947 and Campanella in 1948 propelled Brooklyn to six more World Series appearances over the next ten seasons.

The 1955 World Series began like another chapter in the same old story. The Yankees won the first two games at Yankee Stadium, and it looked bad for the Dodgers. But Campanella began the turnaround at Ebbets with a first inning homer against "Bullet Bob" Turley. Johnny Podres went the distance, scattering seven hits and three runs as the Dodgers won 8-3. Duke Snider, Gil Hodges and Campanella each homered in Game Four as the Dodgers evened the series at two apiece. Snider whacked two more homers as Brooklyn won Game Five. The Yanks returned home and won Game Six, and it was back to Ebbets for the final game. The hero was again Johnny Podres, who pitched a dramatic eight-hit shutout as the Dodgers took their first championship in 55 years.

In 1955, the World Series began on September 28. For seven consecutive days there was a game played every day. It would be the last time a World Series was played without a day off, there being no need for a travel day between Ebbets Field and Yankee Stadium. Campanella played all seven games, leading the Dodgers in at bats, and Brooklyn won. The catcher who had played his best season when he got very little rest, came through again while carrying an extra workload -- just like he had in 1953.

Eddie Mathews - 1953

by Tony Blengino

G	AB	R	H	2B	3B	HR	RBI	BB	SO	AVG	OBP	SLG	SB
157	579	110	175	31	8	47	135	99	83	.302	.406	.627	1

Whenever a discussion regarding all-time great third basemen gets underway, the names of Mike Schmidt and Brooks Robinson immediately surface. For some reason, the name of Eddie Mathews is less frequently mentioned. It should be impossible for anyone with 512 career homers to be underrated -- but that description fits Mathews perfectly. Mathews was an almost identical player to Schmidt offensively, and he swung a vastly more potent bat than Robinson. Though Mathews was not up to their level defensively, he worked very hard to make himself into an above average defensive third baseman.

There were various reasons for the lack of attention given Mathews. One big reason: for most of his career he toiled in the shadow of his teammate, all-time home run leader Hank Aaron. Secondly, the fact that Mathews' career started with such big production so early, made his career home run total almost disappointing to those who had first evaluated him.

Eddie Mathews had his best season in 1953, as a mere lad of 21, in his second year in the big leagues. After 1952, the Boston Braves packed up and moved to Milwaukee. It was a clean break with the mediocrity that the Braves had comfortably settled into in the few years preceding the move. The 1953 team featured an array of young talent that would form the nucleus of a new team that would post winning records in every one of their 13 seasons in Milwaukee, as well as their first season in Atlanta. First baseman Joe Adcock, 25, (.285, 18 homers, 80 RBI), center fielder Bill Bruton, 27, (league-leading 26 steals),

and catcher Del Crandall, 23, (.272, 15 HR, 51 RBI), were all in their first full season as Braves' regulars. In addition to old standby Warren Spahn, 32, (23-7, league-leading 2.10 ERA), the pitching staff featured Lew Burdette, 26, (15-5, 3.24), Bob Buhl, 24, (13-8, 2.97), and Johnny Antonelli, 23, (12-12, 3.18). The pitching staff led the NL in ERA at 3.30, but the offense finished in the middle of the pack in runs scored. They might have finished dead last if not for the massive campaign posted by their sophomore third sacker, the 21-year-old Mathews.

Mathews led the league in homers, while his 135 RBI ranked second to Roy Campanella (142), and his .302 average gave Mathews one of his three seasons above the .300 mark. His .406 on base percentage was fourth in the NL (Musial led at .437), the .627 slugging percentage was just .001 behind league leader Duke Snider. Mathews drew 99 walks (fourth best to Musial's 105), and scored 110 runs. His relative production of 175 led the National League. Musial and Snider, of course, didn't play third base.

Mathews did not benefit from playing in a hitters' park. In 1953, he hit 30 of his 47 homers on the road, and lifetime 275 of his 512 blasts, giving him the highest road percentage of any 500-homer man.

Due in large part to Mathews' contributions, the Braves jumped from next-to-last in 1952 to second place in 1953. The Braves would win at least 85 games and finish third or better every year until 1961. At the end of the season, Campanella was named the

National League MVP, with Mathews finishing second. Mathews would also finish second in 1959, and never won an MVP award. If Mathews had posted similar numbers in 1957 or 1958, when the Braves won two NL pennants, he would likely have won the award. Instead, the missing accolade is just one more reason why Mathews is underrated.

Mathews was quickly heralded as the next challenger to Babe Ruth's career home run record. No such attention was paid to Ruth's actual successor, Hank Aaron, who joined the Braves in 1954. Mathews continued on his power rampage for several years, amassing a whopping 370 homers before he turned 30! By comparison, Aaron had 342 at the same age, Mays 279, Ruth 284, and Schmidt 235. Mathews hit more than 30 homers in nine consecutive seasons (1953-61), an all-time NL record. In 1962, he fell just short of that mark, with 29 homers.

In 1963, Mathews began a gradual decline in power, as he hit only 23 homers, and posted a slugging percentage of only .453, his lowest mark since his rookie year. He was only 31, an age at which most members of the 500 Homer Club were still highly productive. Aaron, three years younger than Mathews, began to pick up the home run pace at about the same time Mathews began to decline. After age 30, Mathews never hit higher than .265 and eventually dragged his career average down to .271. Aaron, in contrast, hit over .300 six times after age 30. After age 31, Mathews managed only 90 homers. Aaron hit an amazing 389 home runs after the age of 31.

Despite the early career downturn, Mathews had big lifetime totals, especially for a third baseman. His career lines are eerily similar to Mike Schmidt's. And although his defense wasn't the best of all time, for overall value Mathews can be rated the second best third-sacker ever, behind Schmidt and ahead of George Brett and Brooks Robinson. In his *Historical Baseball Abstract*, Bill James also ranks Schmidt and Mathews first and second for both peak and career value.

Mathews led the league in homers twice (1953 and 1959), walks four times (1955, 1961-63), OBP once (1963), and relative production three times (1953-54 and 1960). Players who consistently finish in the top five in various offensive categories, but don't win league crowns, tend to get overlooked. And Mathews drew attention to himself only once in the postseason. Though he hit only .227 in the 1957 World Series, he won game four with a 10th inning homer, and in game seven he doubled in the first two runs and made a diving stab of a Bill Skowron grounder, with the bases loaded, for the last out of the Series. In the 1958 Series, he hit a meager .160.

In answer to a now-popular trivia question, Mathews went on to become the only player ever to take the field for the Boston, Milwaukee and Atlanta Braves. He finished his career as a reserve with the 1968 Tigers, and fittingly ended his career as a World Champion.

From the very beginning, Mathews was touted as a potential king of the home run. After being chased by nine teams, he signed his first pro contract with the Boston Braves at 12:01 AM on the morning after his high school graduation. At 17, he hit a lusty .363 as a minor leaguer. No less an authority than Ty Cobb declared that Mathews had a ''perfect'' swing. Somehow, with all these expectations, which were only heightened by his career's incredible beginning, Mathews was actually considered to be a disappointment by many. Though the presence of Hank Aaron eventually relegated him to supporting player status, with similarities to the career of Lou Gehrig, Mathews was a true all-time great.

By a razor-thin margin, Mike Schmidt probably squeaks through as the best third baseman ever, but in no way can Eddie Mathews be asked to take a back seat to any other third sacker, and in 1953 he was far and away the best anyone had ever seen.

Al Rosen - 1953

by Fred Matos

G	AB	R	H	2B	3B	HR	RBI	BB	SO	AVG	OBP	SLG	SB
155	599	115	201	27	5	43	145	85	48	.336	.422	.613	8

"I've been studying the figures. This fellow Rosen leads the Indians in just about everything. It's a shame, not for us but for Cleveland, that the other fellows haven't helped him.

"If you think those pitchers aren't working hard on Rosen, you're wrong. But think if the club had a few others who were willing, how much easier it would be for Rosen. If he had some help they wouldn't bear down so hard on him.

"What I like about the fellow is that he has taught himself to hit to all fields. He can shoot 'em from one foul line to another. Makes it tough to put your men in the right place for him. He doesn't play too bad in the field either.

"Another thing I noticed. I saw him put on his uniform at the All-Star Game in Cincinnati a couple weeks ago. Why, that boy is all black and blue. Yet he never misses a game. Must be made of the stuff that was in those old Orioles.

"That fellow hasn't been given enough credit."
-- Casey Stengel, Yankee manager, August 1953

There have been only 13 triple-crown winners since the turn of the century, and being so rare, they usually deserve special recognition. Unfortunately, for want of one more base hit, Cleveland Indian third baseman Al Rosen is not part of the elite group. He fell short of the 1953 triple crown by a whisker, narrowly missing the batting title when he hit .336, second only to Mickey Vernon's .337. But the near-triple-crown, the records he set, and his strong statistics make Rosen's 1953 season stand out as one of the 100 greatest years in baseball.

Prior to 1953, Rosen had won a home run title and an RBI title, but they were in different years, and he hit .302 only the year before. But in 1953, everything came together. He hit .336-43-145, leading the league in homers and RBI, and finished second in batting average, and all this despite formidable competition from the likes of Mickey Mantle, Yogi Berra, Minnie Minoso, George Kell, Ray Boone, and even teammate Larry Doby. In case you're wondering, Ted Williams spent most of the year in Korea as a Marine Corps pilot, returning to baseball late in the season, in time to get 91 at-bats.

Rosen had an explosive bat, as shown by the four grand slams in 1951 and his many great games in the past, but his 1953 year was a model of consistency. There were no real outstanding games of two or three home runs and seven or eight RBI. He went 2-for-4 here and 3-for-5 there, with many clutch doubles and homers, and frequently two, three, or four RBI. His home runs were spread out, and nothing came in bunches. As Indian outfielder Bob Kennedy observed, "when you needed a single, he hit a single, when you needed a double he hit a double, and when you needed a home run, he hit a home run."

Rosen kept the Indians in pennant contention almost singlehandedly, carrying them to a second place finish. The Indians had been contenders for some time, and as such, were much more likely to see the opponent's ace pitchers in a series than would, for example, the lowly St. Louis Browns. Thus Rosen faced many top pitchers often over the course of the season, making his season even more remarkable.

Rosen was the Indians' clean-up hitter, but he wasn't given much protection from the fifth spot in the batting order, usually occupied by the likes of Harry Simpson, Wally Westlake and Bob Kennedy, weak to mediocre hitters at best. Power hitter Larry Doby sometimes batted fifth, but he was usually in the third slot. As Casey Stengel correctly observed, the pitchers could bear down on Rosen. There were many times when the pitchers worked around Rosen, not giving him any good pitches to hit, a big handicap that he had to overcome.

Rosen's 43 home runs remains the record for American League third basemen. Harmon Killebrew hit 49 homers in 1969, but he played 105 games at third base and 80 at first base (some at both) and the homers were divided. The Phillies' Mike Schmidt hit 48 in 1980, setting the major league record. Matt Williams was well on his way towards breaking Schmidt's record with his great 1994 season when he had 43 homers, but the strike cut the season short.

The 145 RBI is another very strong statistic, high enough for Rosen to set a major league record for RBI by a third baseman, that still stands. The 145 RBI level was rather common in the American League back in the 1930's and 1940's with the likes of Lou Gehrig, Hank Greenberg, Ted Williams, Jimmy Foxx and Vern Stephens exceeding it almost routinely. But 145 RBI has been achieved in the AL only one other time since Rosen did it in 1953: Don Mattingly had 145 RBI in 1985. In the National League, the 145 level has been surpassed only three times since 1953, by Johnny Bench, George Foster and Tommy Davis.

Hall of Fame hitters Mickey Mantle, Roger Maris, Harmon Killebrew, Frank Robinson, Ernie Banks, Hank Aaron, and Mike Schmidt never reached 145 RBI. Some of the great hitters who never reached 145 RBI played on rather poor teams and can be excused because the lead-off and other top spots in the batting order may have been weak, so the RBI opportunities were not as frequent as on the teams with strong table setters. But that reasoning cannot be used for Mantle, Maris, Robinson and the others who played on strong pennant-winning teams.

The 1953 home run and batting titles came down to dramatic endings in the last three games of the season, games that were otherwise meaningless. Following the Indians clinching of second place, important then because second-place money was relatively significant, Rosen asked Manager Al Lopez to bat him in the lead-off slot to get more at-bats. The lead-off strategy paid off immediately as Rosen went 4-for-6 on Friday, September 25th, against the Tigers, slamming two home runs and passing the A's Gus Zernial 43 to 42, and moving up to .332, within one point of Vernon at .333 following his 0-for-4 day.

On Saturday, September 26th, in the next-to-last game of the year, Rosen went 2-for-4 against the Tigers, and was now hitting .333 with 198 hits in 594 at-bats. Vernon went 3-for-4 against the A's, raising his average to .336 with 203 hits in 604 at-bats.

That the batting title would be settled in the last game with a Triple Crown on the line created a tense atmosphere not unlike that of a 7th game of a World Series. On Sunday, September 27th, Vernon's last game was completed before the Indians game, and the results were telegraphed to Cleveland Stadium where they were announced to the crowd, further intensifying their excitement, as the crowd sensed that they could be witnessing something of real magnitude that could go down as one of the great moments in baseball history.

Vernon went 2-for-4 against the A's raising his average to .337, actually .33717 resulting from 205 hits in 608 at-bats. So Rosen and the crowd now knew exactly what he had to do to win the crown. Earlier in the game, Rosen beat out an infield hit, hit a ground-rule double, and laid down a perfect bunt single against the overshifted Tigers infield. On Rosen's final at-bat, in the 9th inning, everyone knew that a hit was needed as he was now at .336, needing a base hit to win the title (by reaching .33723 from 202 hits in 599 at-bats). Indians' coach Tony Cuccinello noticed the Tigers infield again overshifted and playing deep, and suggested another bunt. But Rosen said, "I can't, Tony. I don't want to win this thing with a bunt. I'd like to win it with a solid hit -- a homer, if possible."

Tigers' pitcher Al Aber became nervous and threw a number of bad pitches, and Rosen would have walked under normal circumstances. But, needing a hit, he refused to walk and fouled off the pitches. He hit the next pitch, also a bad one, on the ground to Gerry Priddy playing a deep third base, and raced to first base. He would have been safe, but he stepped over the bag, and umpire Hank Soar called him out, upsetting the fans who believed he was safe. "Don't blame him," Rosen said later, "Soar knew I was out. I knew I was out. I wouldn't want to win the title from Mickey on that play. I would know in my heart always that I didn't really make it."

It's not surprising that Rosen would have refused to win the Triple Crown with a bunt single, as it would have been totally out of character for him. His strong character is rooted in a deep athletic background that includes football and amateur boxing, sports requiring a great deal of mental and physical toughness. His football skills were good enough for him to play end for the Miami Hurricanes for a year. He was an amateur boxer in prep school and college, and he had his nose broken seven times. He brought his toughness to the baseball diamond, always playing hard and frequently playing hurt. Indeed, his statistics in some years suffered because he played with injuries that would have landed most other players on the disabled list.

The toughness and strong work ethic were reflected in his defense. Although Rosen worked very hard to improve his fielding, he still wasn't very graceful. But the hard work paid off as he was the 1953 league leader in assists and double plays by a third baseman.

"I wasn't exactly a Brooks Robinson with the glove, so I stopped many balls with my chest," remembered Rosen. That explains the bruised body that Casey Stengel observed at the All-Star game.

Rosen choked up on the bat, rare but not unheard of for a power hitter. New York Giant slugger Mel Ott was a choke hitter, as was Rocky Colavito in the late 1950's and '60's, and more recently, Barry Bonds. Rosen said that he began the season using a 35 ounce, 35 inch bat, changing to a lighter 33 ounce bat in hot weather. He choked up about an inch, and even more with two strikes, depending on the pitcher. He also moved around in the batter's box depending on the pitcher and the count. He was a "smart" hitter, always studying and thinking about pitchers. Rosen believed strikeouts were a waste. "Striking out is like taking a shower with your raincoat on," he said.

Questioned about difficult pitchers, Rosen said that, when he was going good as in 1953, he could hit anybody. And in 1953, this included Eddie Lopat, Vic Raschi, Mel Parnell, Bob Porterfield, Virgil Trucks and Whitey Ford. But Rosen admitted that hard throwing Yankee Allie Reynolds and smooth Tiger Ned Garver were a little harder to hit than the others.

As a baseball executive in recent years, Rosen has been close to the game and has seen and evaluated many players. I asked Rosen if any recent player reminded him of himself of years ago. He thought for a while and finally said that Giants' third baseman Matt Williams is about the closest. Rosen said that he likes Williams' toughness, and his approach to, and love of the game.

Rosen was unanimously selected as the league Most Valuable Player (MVP) in 1953, receiving all of the 336 available votes. In the history of baseball, only 14 players have had such outstanding years, so far exceeding the others that they received all of the first-place votes.

"Rosen was a great ball player who always gave 110 percent," recalled Al Lopez, the 1953 Indians manager, and the only manager to beat Casey Stengel out of a pennant any year from 1949 through 1960.

WILLIE MAYS
outfield NEW YORK GIANTS

Courtesy - The Topps Company, Inc.

Willie Mays - 1954

by Alan Boodman

G	AB	R	H	2B	3B	HR	RBI	BB	SO	AVG	OBP	SLG	SB
151	565	119	195	33	13	41	110	66	57	.345	.415	.667	8

"If somebody hit .450, stole a hundred bases, and performed a miracle in the field every day, I would still look you in the eye and say Willie was better." Leo Durocher's point was that traditional objective measures simply failed to capture the combination of skills that made Willie Mays arguably the best all-around player in history.

Mays really could do it all -- hit for average, hit for power, run, field, and throw -- and he did it all for 23 years. And he had fun doing it!

The apex of this magnificent career came early. Mays was just age 22 on Opening Day 1954 (he turned 23 on May 6th). After barely establishing himself as a rookie in 1951, he played only 34 games in 1952 and none in 1953 due to military service. His major league career totals before 1954, in about one full season's worth of playing time, were 24 homers, 91 RBI and a .266 average. His defensive prowess, however, was clearly proven. Mays covered as much outfield territory as anyone in the league; only Richie Ashburn was comparable.

The debate about who was the best player in New York bounced between Mickey Mantle and Duke Snider before 1954; but, the focus of that debate was soon to be altered. Despite the fact that Mays had faced no major league pitching since May of 1952, Giants' manager Leo Durocher predicted in the spring of '54 that Willie would bat over .300 and deliver 30 homers that season. That prediction would prove accurate, and not just in 1954; Mays would

meet those twin standards in seven of the next ten seasons as well.

The '54 Giants won 97 games and the pennant in a year that started with the Brooklyn Dodgers heavily favored to repeat their 1953 dominance. The Mays-less Giants had placed a distant fifth in 1953. The '54 New York team got off to a slow start, playing below .500 through May. They were fortunate that no other club could jump out to a big lead.

Although Mays had homered against Brooklyn on Opening Day, he was not at his best during the first few weeks of the season. He emerged as a truly terrorizing hitter after Durocher convinced the youngster to use the whole ballpark to hit line drives. And, enough of them flew over the fences anyway, especially at the Polo Grounds.

The Giants soared in June, going 24-4, coinciding with a torrid streak by Mays. By June 30 all other contenders, save Brooklyn, had fallen some distance off the pace, and Mays had already reached the Durocher-predicted level of 30 home runs. Willie was suddenly ahead of the record homer pace set by you-know-who. The resulting media onslaught upon a young man not accustomed to star treatment, and the lack of privacy that comes with it, along with the mid-season death of his very close "Aunt" Sarah, wore Mays down mentally and physically as the season progressed.

Durocher kept urging Mays to go for base hits rather

than long balls, and Willie obliged, hitting .379 over his final 55 games, continuing to spray extra-base hits to all corners of the field. He hit six round-trippers in July, and only five more over the remainder of the season. Mays went three-for-four on the season's final day to narrowly win the batting title, ahead of teammate Don Mueller and the Bums' Duke Snider.

The Giants survived late charges from Brooklyn and Milwaukee. The Braves bowed out in early September when their second-best run producer, Joe Adcock (who had often been a target for Dodger pitchers) was nailed by Don Newcombe, ending Adcock's season. Brooklyn stayed close, but the wheels finally came off around the 140-game mark, and Giants had an easy last couple of weeks.

In the World Series, Mays' performance was strong but unspectacular except for "The Catch" and some other defensive gems. In the four-game sweep, Mays got four hits, drew four walks, scored four runs, and got the only stolen base in the Series. Giants' pitching and defense, and Dusty Rhodes' hitting spoiled the final days of the '54 Cleveland Indians, who had amassed an amazing 111 regular season victories while dethroning the five-time World Champion Yankees.

Mays was elected the 1954 National League MVP with 283 of a possible 336 points, beating Ted Kluszewski with 217. The Dodgers' Snider had slightly better offensive stats than Mays in runs, hits, doubles, total bases, and on base percentage, but Snider finished fourth in MVP voting with 135 points. The biggest factor separating Mays from Snider was defense: 448 putouts, 13 assists, and 9 double plays for Mays, versus 360 putouts, 8 assists, and just one double play for Snider.

At the tender age of 23, Mays had reached his career high in slugging percentage and produced what would be his second highest batting average, just two points off his career high of .347 in 1958. The peak continued at about the same level into 1955, when he hit 51 home runs and again led the league in slugging.

A major distinguishing characteristic of Mays' career is that his peak lasted so long. Arguably, the 12 years from 1954 through 1965 (both MVP seasons) could be the longest hot streak in history. In 11 of those 12 years Mays was among the top half dozen MVP vote-getters in the National League. Pete Palmer's Total Player Ranking classifies Mays as being the best player (pitcher or hitter) in either league in 1954, and again in 1955, 1958, 1960 and 1964. Nine times he was the highest-rated position player in the National League. But 1954 was the best year of all.

Duke Snider - 1955

by Richard Burnham

G	AB	R	H	2B	3B	HR	RBI	BB	SO	AVG	OBP	SLG	SB
148	538	126	166	34	6	42	136	104	87	.309	.421	.628	9

In the early summer of 1955, my father took me to see the Brooklyn Dodgers play the Cincinnati Reds. Ebbets Field was then the most exciting a place any eleven year old was allowed to experience. The Reds jumped out to a lead, but the Dodgers chipped away through the middle innings. By the eighth the Bums had tied the game, only to have the Reds regain the lead in the top of the ninth. Dad, who had to make the long drive back to Connecticut, announced that we would have to be leaving at the end of the 10th.

The Dodgers tied the game in the ninth, but were unable to win it by the tenth, and so we left Ebbets Field. On the radio on the ride home, Vin Scully kept us informed. Somewhere in Greenwich, on the Merritt Parkway, came his call: ''And here is the pitch to the Duke. Look out Bedford Avenue, you have company! And the Dodgers win in fourteen innings on a Snider home run!''

Yes, 1955 was Next Year for us long-suffering Dodger fans, and 1955 was Duke Snider's peak year in his Hall of Fame career. Before looking more closely at Snider's 1955 season, recall New York in the 1950's, the only city ever to have three major league teams. And all three teams had great players, but center field was *the* glamour position -- Willie, Mickey and the Duke. The arguments raged as to who was the best.

In hindsight based on career accomplishments, it is clear that the ranking *was* indeed Willie, then Mickey then The Duke. And in 1955 when Mantle reached his brief but magnificent plateau, it may have been Mickey, Willie, and then the Duke, but, to a man, they were all Hall of Fame. Clearly their prowess has made it extremely difficult for a great player like Richie Ashburn to make the Hall, though recently at last, he too made it.

Given the sad fact of life that a Giant and a Yankee were judged better than the Brooklyn center fielder, let us nonetheless enjoy reviewing Duke's wonderful 1955 season.

Carefully looking at his stats, a case can be made for any of three years, 1953, 1954 or 1955 as Snider's best. In 1954 he had his best statistical year, but the Dodgers finished five games behind Mays and the Giants. In both '53 and '55 the Bums won the National League flag, finishing ahead of the Braves by 13 and 13.5 games respectively.

But in 1955 with the Duke batting third, the Dodgers led from wire to wire, and capped the season with their World Series victory. Obviously, even more important than winning the NL Pennant was winning Brooklyn's first and only Series. Duke's contributions to both of those successes were considerable.

In 1955, Snider led the league in runs and RBI. He was second in on base percentage and slugging, and also second in the more comprehensive measures of total production and runs created. He was third in doubles; fourth in home runs and fifth in total bases. Snider had similar ranking's in '53, '54 and '56.

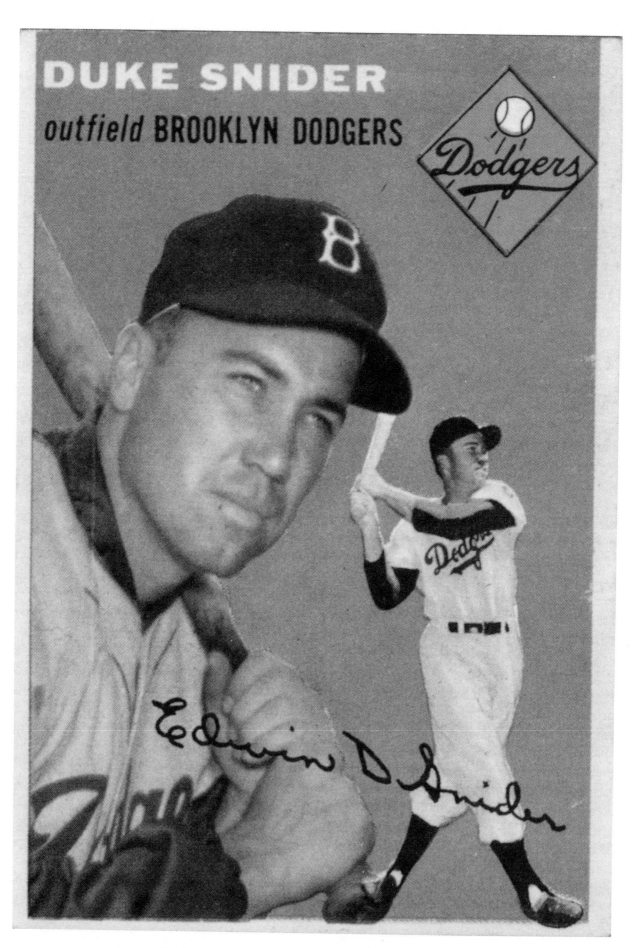

In 1954, for example - which was one of his best years, he was first in the league in total bases; tied for first in runs; second in hits, slugging, and RBI, third in doubles, triples, and batting average; and fifth in home runs. In 1956, by contrast, Snider ranked in the top five in six categories: home runs; slugging; runs, total bases; doubles and RBI.

A key reason that 1955 is Duke's great year is his performance in the World Series against the dreaded Yankees. In the 1955 series, Duke was as consistent as he had been during the regular season. He hit .320, the highest of any Dodger starter. For the second time in a World Series he hit four home runs, becoming the only man in history to accomplish that feat (he had already done it in the '52 series.) Two of those blasts came in game five, in the third and fifth innings, to put the Bums in the lead to stay. And Snider's seven RBI were tops for any player in the Series.

After the series, Duke was named Player of the Year by the *Sporting News*, the only major post-season award he was ever to win. He was surrounded by great company both on the Dodger team and in the National League as a whole.

In 1955 Snider came in second in the MVP voting, just behind teammate Roy Campanella, 226 to 221. A newly-emerging superstar shortstop with the Cubs, Ernie Banks, came in third.

Snider was a glamorous player in a unique time and place. He was conscious of his physical appearance, enjoying both genuine physical conditioning and the aura that comes with a good sun tan, and he much appreciated the adulation of the fans. He showed an understanding of baseball as show business, years before other players grasped the concept, and Snider enjoyed his role of star player on a popular team. With the media he was less popular than he was with the fans, mainly because he spoke his mind freely -- another trait making him ahead of his time in baseball.

Fans remember Edwin Duke Snider mainly for his consistent power hitting. With the game on the line and the team needing a home run, having Snider at the plate was what every Dodger fan would wish for. During his 18 years in the big leagues, he had his ups and downs and was in the shadow of Mays and Mantle more often than not. But in 1955, it was The Duke who was in the limelight, and for that one year, at least, he really was Royalty.

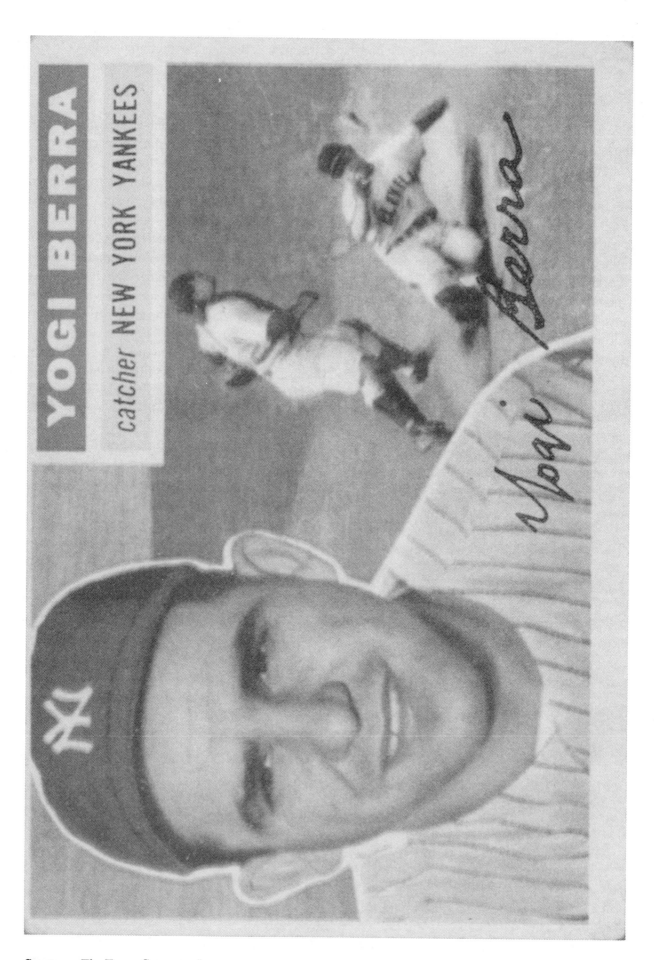

YOGI BERRA

catcher NEW YORK YANKEES

Yogi Berra - 1956

by Bill Gray

G	AB	R	H	2B	3B	HR	RBI	BB	SO	AVG	OBP	SLG	SB
140	521	93	155	29	2	30	105	65	29	.298	.381	.534	3

When Ty Cobb retired, who replaced him? When Babe Ruth was let go by the Yankees, who replaced him? How about Willie Mays? Henry Aaron? Brooks Robinson? Imagine the pressure felt by the unlucky individual who had to take a position that had last been occupied by a living legend. When a brilliant career ends, it usually takes a while until a successor is accepted by the fans. Fan acceptance is crucial; some good players have been literally run out of town just because they aren't as good as their predecessors.

Exception noted in the case of Bill Dickey, who is ranked by many as the greatest catcher in history. The guy who replaced him turned out to be even better. But Yogi Berra, despite being in the Hall of Fame, and playing on 10 World Championship teams, is widely underappreciated.

I'm not going to make the case for Berra over Dickey. Bill James did that several years ago, and brilliantly. His essay on Berra/Dickey, in *The Historical Baseball Abstract*, is a gem. Dickey was not just one of the Bronx Bombers of the 1930's and 1940's, though. He was also one of the Ruthian Yankees, by far the most magical and venerated team in the history of sport. Dickey played with Ruth, Gehrig and DiMaggio. Later Dickey became Berra's tutor. And Yogi needed the help. While Dickey was smooth and certain in his movements, Berra was, in his early days, awkward and uneasy. While Dickey was a legend, Berra was, for his first three years in the majors, just a platoon catcher and backup left fielder.

Berra was never regarded with the same awe and reverence as Dickey was, but Yogi was a player Casey Stengel coveted so much, he said he wouldn't trade him for anybody, not even Ted Williams. Casey tended to blow smoke at times, but he was being sincere about Berra's value. Aside from the obvious fact that Berra could play left field as well as Williams, what would the Yankees have gained with Williams that they didn't have with Berra? A pennant? Nope. Yogi played on 14 pennant winners. A World Series? Again, no. Berra has a World Series victory ring for every finger and thumb.

But among the Yankees, Berra was never the main attraction. He won three MVP's, but first he played on *DiMaggio's* Yankees, and then he played on *Mantle's* Yankees. Berra never *owned* the team, with evidence in possessive phrases like Ruth's Yankees, Mays' Giants, and Clemente's Pirates. Considering Berra's three MVP seasons and on-field leadership, he remains in the shadow of Mantle and Whitey Ford. Berra deserves recognition similar to Jimmie Foxx, DiMaggio, Stan Musial, Mantle, Mike Schmidt and Barry Bonds. All have won the MVP award three times. All except Berra and Schmidt were outfielders.

1951 in the Bronx was a cataclysmic time. It was New York after all, and it was Joe DiMaggio who was stepping down. Regular ballplayers quit or retire. Yankee gods, corporate chairmen and kings ''step down." So Berra's first MVP award, while nice, was minor news compared to bidding DiMaggio goodbye. Berra's next MVP citation in 1954 also became a bit diluted because the Indians won the AL pennant, and the Giants took the series and the championship of New York City. Berra's MVP season in 1955 also lacked the quality of an historic exclamation mark, because the Dodgers finally broke through and beat them, in a great seven-game World Series.

It's the 1956 season that gets the nod in this book, even though it wasn't one of Berra's MVP years. The Yankees won it all of course, with Berra at the top of his game. One of the most memorable pictures in baseball history is Yogi hugging Don Larsen after the perfect game in the '56 series. The number 8 on Berra's back is prominent in all photos of this event, just as Berra himself had been prominent throughout the season and in the series. (For the record, he hit .360 in that series, with three home runs and 10 RBI, clearly the Yankees' offensive workhorse.)

Berra was in full bloom in 1956. His early awkwardness around home plate had been quickly overcome and replaced by cat-like agility. By 1956 he was a grandmaster at covering his position and, on a separate but even more important level, he had become a grandmaster at pitcher-handling. Yogi was a genius for knowing the right style for each pitcher; he left some alone to do their work with minimal intervention, while others received frequent and pointed words of motivation. And of course, Berra knew all the hitters in the league and how to pitch to them.

The defensive mastery showed up quantitatively in Berra's assists and fielding percentages, categories in which he often led American League catchers. The pitcher-handling is more elusive to quantify. The only numbers where the skills bear fruit are in the pitchers' stats. Berra deserves much of the credit for getting an 18-9 season out of Johnny Kucks in 1956; Kucks would never again win more than eight games in a season. Larsen also reached his career high in wins and had his best season in '56. In other years, Berra and Stengel crafted big winning pitching staffs with the likes of Bob Grim, Tom Sturdivant, Tommy Byrne, Bob Turley, and Tom Morgan. There is a good reason why Yankee pitchers of this era did not

get Hall of Fame consideration, while Berra was a shoo-in. Ford, Mantle, and Berra were the only big stars on the winning roster of 1956 and many other years when the Yankees won it all. Credit Berra for much of the pitching magic.

Yet it was Mantle, not Berra, who took ownership of the Yankees with his Triple Crown performance in 1956. Mantle's huge season had been long awaited, and even though Berra had the best year of his career, Mantle easily won the AL MVP with 336 votes to 186 for Berra. Was Mickey a better player (not just a better hitter) than Berra? It's a tough question, the more you think about it, but the perception then and now is that it's an easy question: Mantle was better. End of argument? I wonder.

From 1950 to 1956 Berra was the Yankees' best player, as the MVP's show. But the Yankee Throne was in storage, and Berra, no matter how many MVP's he collected, never ascended to it. When Mantle unleashed his talents in 1956, it was "Long Live The King!" Berra was again a supporting player. From 1951 to 1955 Berra hit 133 home runs to 121 for Mantle, and Yogi had more RBI (527 to 445). Berra had a reputation as a bad ball hitter who would swing at anything. The rep was nonsense. His judgment of the strike zone was superb. In fact throughout his entire career, Berra always walked more than he struck out, even at the end. He walked 704 times in his career while striking out only 404 times, an average of just 21 strikeouts per season. Mantle averaged 134 strikeouts per year over his career. Berra got his bad ball reputation because he didn't walk much either, averaging only 37 free passes a year, and he was happy to drive a pitch he liked when the game situation called for it. The fact is that he put the ball in play and made things happen.

It is said of many players who toiled in smaller markets; "If he had played in Yankee Stadium, he'd be the next Babe Ruth." Maybe if Yogi had *not* played in Yankee Stadium, in their golden era with Mantle, Ford and other stars, then he would have been given his due as the best catcher of all time.

Mickey Mantle - 1956

by Tony Blengino

G	AB	R	H	2B	3B	HR	RBI	BB	SO	AVG	OBP	SLG	SB
150	533	132	188	22	5	52	130	112	99	.353	.467	.705	10

When he reached the majors in 1951, teenager Mickey Mantle was greeted with high expectations. Since Babe Ruth arrived in 1920, New York had been led by a parade of all-time greats: #3 Ruth; #4 Lou Gehrig; #5 Joe DiMaggio; and then #6 (later #7) Mickey Mantle. Mantle possessed awesome power from both sides of the plate, plus blazing raw speed and baserunning ability. In the field he had outstanding range and a great arm -- two big assets in Yankee Stadium's deep expanses.

It took a while for Mantle to mature, but by 1955 he had blossomed, and the three years 1955 through 1957 were his personal golden era. In the middle year of this long peak, 1956, he won the Triple Crown while leading the Yanks to yet another World Championship.

Mantle was still just age 24 when the 1956 season opened. The Yanks were in a championship drought; they hadn't won a World Series in either of the two previous seasons, after winning five straight from 1949 to 1953. For this storied franchise, the ''losing streak" going into 1956 was a genuine concern.

Fans were gratified soon enough. Mantle exploded from the chute, blasting 16 homers in May and nailing number 20 on May 30th. That homer was widely described as the hardest-hit in Yankee Stadium history. It would have gone about 600 feet if the roof had been just 18 inches lower; the ball was still rising when it struck the facade. Classic Ruth-style home runs had been high and majestic, going, going, then gone, while fans watched with big eyes and open-mouthed admiration of the never-ending rainbows. Mantle blasts, by contrast, were quick and shot-like. If you blinked you might miss one. There was a crack and a blur. Fan reaction was often just a gasping, "Did you see that?"

Through the summer of '56, Mantle was on a pace with Ruth's single-season 60-homer record. Mickey maintained a pace of two homers per week, and he clinched the pennant with his 50th homer, a 500 foot shot in Comiskey Park, giving the Yanks a 3-2 victory over Billy Pierce. The league home run title had long been clinched, but Mantle was locked in tight contests with Ted Williams for the batting crown and Al Kaline for the RBI title. On September 12, Mantle was batting .352 to Williams' .349, and had 118 RBI to Kaline's 116. Mantle then slumped briefly, and Williams surged ahead in the batting race, as the two prepared for a head-to-head showdown in the season's final week. The Yanks' pitchers held Williams in check while Mantle ravaged the Red Sox staff in the three-game series. With a six point lead in average, Mantle then strained a hamstring and played sparingly for the remainder of the regular season. Williams settled back to .345 and lost that race by eight points.

In the end Mantle's 130 RBI nosed out Kaline by two, and his 52 homers dwarfed Vic Wertz by 20. Mantle had become the only player in history to win the Triple Crown and hit 50 homers in the same season. His 52 homers are still the most ever hit by a batting

champion. Besides leading in the Triple Crown categories, Mantle also paced the league in runs scored, slugging percentage, and in relative production with 213. No player since Ted Williams in 1957 has posted a higher relative production figure. Williams finished a distant second in 1956, down at 164.

The Yanks would not be denied in the 1956 World Series, winning in seven games over the defending champion Brooklyn Dodgers. Mantle contributed three home runs, including one in Game 5 to win Don Larsen's perfect game 2-0. In addition to the homer, Mantle preserved the perfecto with a dazzling running catch on a drive to left center by Gil Hodges.

At his tender age, Mantle in 1956 was already playing his fifth World Series. He went on to play in a total of 12, of which the Yankees won seven. Mantle remains the all time World Series leader in homers, walks, runs and RBI. He stands second to Yogi Berra in World Series hits and at bats.

Mantle ranks eighth in career home runs with 536. His career relative production of 173 is fifth best in history, behind only Ruth, Williams, Lou Gehrig, and Rogers Hornsby. Even with his high totals in many career categories, Mantle is more noted for his early ascendancy and lofty peaks than for consistency and longevity, especially when compared to all-time greats like Willie Mays and Hank Aaron. At age 29, Mantle had 374 homers, while Aaron had 342 and Mays 279. Aaron never walked 100 times, while Mays did so only once; Mantle did it ten times. Mays' highest relative production was 184 in 1965, and Aaron's highest was 190 in 1971, compared to Mantle's 223 in 1957 and 213 in 1956. Mays' career relative production was 157, Aaron's was 156, both well behind Mantle's 173.

Mantle seemed destined for stardom from birth. Named after Mickey Cochrane, he learned to switch-hit at age five, and was a minor league superstar at age 18. As a rookie in 1951 he played right field alongside DiMaggio, who was in his final year. Despite a return to the minors for a confidence boost in '51, Mantle was expected to pick up the torch of greatness immediately in 1952. He didn't disappoint. In addition

to the power and ability to hit for average, there was blazing speed which produced many a drag-bunt single. Mantle was widely regarded as the fastest runner in the American League, but Casey Stengel and his successors had such awesome lineups that attempting a steal was a rare event reserved for late-inning one-run situations. Waiting for a home run was usually the correct managerial strategy. Being on base so often with his fine speed, Mantle could have amassed many stolen bases with ease (he had a career success rate over 80%). Long after retiring, when the media were buzzing about the amazing notion of a "40/40 man," Mickey stated matter-of-factly (and with a transparent modesty rarely found in today's players) that he could have been a 50/50 man, if he ever thought anyone would be excited about it. Another asset often overlooked is Mantle's prodigious ability to draw walks. He had good strike zone judgment and, again because of his terrific speed and the strength of the batting orders around him, Mantle was much encouraged to take a free pass. Though he was known for his whiffs, Mantle actually walked more than he struck out in his career (1733 to 1710).

Mantle was not always the Big Apple's hometown hero; he was sometimes handled roughly by the media and often booed by the fans. He wasn't widely adored until the scribes and fans began to compare him to Roger Maris in 1961.

With a fear of dying young (a somewhat rational fear considering the short life spans in his family) Mantle embraced a present-oriented life-style. He enjoyed partying with his buddies, especially Whitey Ford and Billy Martin. "If I knew I was going to live so long, I would have taken better care of myself," Mantle said later in life. Indeed, his legacy includes an immortal testimony for youths to follow. But in 1956, young and in his prime, Mantle treated America to one of the most awesome single-season individual performances in baseball history. He reached his peak when New York was the capital of the baseball world, home to three great teams. It was the era of Willie, Mickey and the Duke. There has never been another city or another era like it, and there has never been another player like Mickey Mantle -- and there never will be.

Herb Score - 1956

by John Benson

W	L	PCT	G	GS	CG	SV	IP	SO	BB	B/I	ERA
20	9	.690	35	33	16	0	249	263	129	1.17	2.53

Herb Score burst upon the baseball scene with the same speed that his fastball exploded into the strike zone. His arrival in 1955 was especially exciting because the Indians of 1954 were already awesome, having set an American League record with 111 victories while terminating the Yankees' five-year reign at the top of the baseball world. If beating the Yankees had seemed near impossible, improving on the team that beat them was beyond comprehension. Score nonetheless offered a clear hope that the 1954 team might actually be improved.

Fate intervened, however. The 1955 Cleveland franchise suffered more than its fair share of slumps and injuries, so that even with the best rookie in the league, they could manage only a second place finish behind Casey Stengel's resilient Bronx team. In a managerial rivalry that had Stengel and the Indians' Al Lopez juggling rosters and searching for replacement parts all summer, Yankee depth proved the deciding factor.

While the Indians slipped to second, finishing three games back, Herb Score in 1955 was nonetheless astonishing. He led the league in strikeouts, setting an all-time rookie strikeout record of 245 that would stand for 30 years. Rookie of the Year honors became an easy choice; if there had been an AL Rookie of the Decade for the 1950's, Score was it.

Anyone looking for a sophomore slump from Score in 1956 was on the wrong track. The fireballing lefty, who had joined Whitey Ford and Billy Pierce as the most-feared southpaws in the league, simply got better in his second year -- much better. Despite missing more than a week with a stomach ailment that put him in the hospital, Score won 20 games and led the league with five shutouts. The opposition hit only .186 against him. And there were all those strikeouts: 263 of them, combined with a notable reduction in walks.

Score's 1956 season has aged nicely. The growing mystique has bothered some sabermetric observers, because the numbers (other than the strikeouts) appear less impressive when stacked up in direct comparison against other pitchers who haven't achieved the same stature that Score has. Furthermore, writers at the time commonly rated Score below Ford and Pierce for 1956 performance. If he wasn't clearly dominant in 1956, how could he be clearly dominant now?

I can suggest one plausible explanation for the apparently retroactive elevation of Score's 1956 performance. In 1956 Score was getting amazing results while he was still an unrefined talent. To the eyes of the most astute observers in 1956, there was marvelous potential -- and a visible probability that it would be attained. Score's control of his blazing fastball was improving; yet he was still a long way from obtaining all the benefits that come from pitching to spots, working the count, and studying opposition hitters.

"I never really knew where the ball was going,"

Score said in an interview for this essay, "so we wouldn't do much in trying to prepare for games or work hitters." Score nonetheless credits catcher Jim Hegan for calling a good target, and knowing when to mix in a breaking ball. Later in his career, Score would spend more time studying hitters and working on the finer points of pitching, but after the long layoff following his batted ball injury in early 1957, he was never the same.

The greatness of Score's 1956 season lies partly in the context of a career that never developed. While it may sound funny to mix potential and performance for evaluative purposes, contemporary statements of potential are certainly part of the context within which performance occurs. In the case of Pete Reiser in 1941, for example, we have not only a 22-year-old batting champion, who today's sabermetricians would generally agree was on an upward career path; we also have the written and spoken raves of those who saw Reiser in 1941.

In the case of Herb Score, we have some highly significant statements offering evidence that his achievements in 1956 were founded on still-developing skills, pointing toward peaks that were likely to follow. One such statement came on March 19, 1957, in the form of an offer from the Red Sox to buy Herb Score for $1 million, at a time when the entire Cleveland franchise was valued at only $3 million. Nothing like that happened in the case of Reiser. Another such statement came from veteran pitcher Hal Newhouser, at the end of his career and Score's teammate briefly in 1955. Newhouser, who led his league in wins four times, ERA twice (1.94 and 1.81) and who averaged 22 wins a year for six years in his prime, said he would gladly trade his entire past for Herb Score's future. Again, Reiser didn't attract that kind of testimonial.

Cleveland manager Lopez (the only skipper to interrupt Casey Stengel's dominant grip on the American League pennant from 1949 through 1960, a unique 12-year run broken only by Lopez's 1954 Indians and 1959 White Sox) gave a testimonial to Score's long-term future in the way he handled his young star pitcher. Lopez was obviously looking into the long-term future, working on subtle aspects that would later make his talented lefty even better.

One incident, which shows the classic Lopez attention to detail and building for the future, made quite an impression on Score. "I had just pitched a complete game shutout," recalled Score, "and was leaving the field, when Lopez stopped me and said, 'Stay right here.' He said I didn't bunt well enough and needed to practice. So we stayed, and I practiced my bunting. And after that, he said, in the next game that I pitched, he wanted me to bunt every time I was up, to get some more practice. As luck would have it, in the next game we jumped out to a lead of like 19 to nothing against the Red Sox, before I came to bat for the first time. The third baseman was way back there. I had to do what the manager told me, of course, but I didn't want anyone to misunderstand ... so I told the catcher, there's going to be a bunt, so get ready to throw me out, and everyone will be happy." That incident is just one reflection of the many ways in which Al Lopez was preparing Herb Score for a long and productive career.

So we can say that Score's 1956 season was not only excellent, but also promising. His performance conjured up images of unlimited possibilities, and thinking about those possibilities was part of what made it so much fun to watch him.

Rocky Colavito - 1958

by Fred Matos

G	AB	R	H	2B	3B	HR	RBI	BB	SO	AVG	OBP	SLG	SB
143	489	80	148	26	3	41	113	84	89	.303	.407	.620	0

Cleveland fans enjoying their 1995 powerhouse recalled all too well that the Indians hadn't won a pennant since 1954, and before 1994 they hadn't fielded a prime slugger since the days of Rocky Colavito. The 1954 Indians won the pennant with the likes of Al Rosen, Early Wynn, Bob Lemon, Mike Garcia, Larry Doby and Bobby Avila leading the way. That generation of Indians peaked in 1954. Within three years, many of the veterans were finishing their careers or were retired or traded, being replaced with a new generation. Hopes for the future were initially pinned on talented southpaw Herb Score and the young slugger Colavito, but Score suffered a tragic injury getting hit by a batted ball and was never the same again. That left the legacy on Colavito's shoulders.

Colavito had a good year as a rookie in 1956 and again in 1957, but he established himself as a legitimate slugging star with an outstanding break-out year in 1958 at age 25, emerging as the type of charismatic young star who can capture the imagination of a whole city and even a nation. The 1958 season began oddly for the Indians, as new manager Bobby Bragan was unfamiliar with his Indians and the American League as a whole. Colavito began the season in the Indians doghouse and was nearly traded by GM "Trader" Frank Lane. Lane was very close to trading both Roger Maris and Colavito to the Senators, a trade that could have changed baseball history. Bragan didn't recognize Colavito's skills for the first few months, and had him platooning, riding the bench, pinch hitting, and even playing some first base, an unusual slot for such a good defensive outfielder with a rifle arm.

Frustrated, the bold Colavito told Bragan "If I play regularly, I'll hit 35 homers and knock in 100 runs." It was already six weeks into the season at the time, and he had only two homers. Bragan finally realized what an extraordinary talent Colavito was, and made him the starting right fielder, usually batting fifth or cleanup. At mid-year, Colavito's statistics were:

G	AB	H	HR	RBI	AVG
69	237	72	14	48	.304

Since Colavito hit 41 home runs for the season, he obviously had a superb second half with 27 homers.

The out-of-place Bragan was fired at the All-Star break, and was replaced by Joe Gordon, himself a former Indians slugger. Gordon recognized Colavito's talents. He cut down on Colavito's swing, and then the homers started coming in bunches. Gordon sometimes batted him clean-up, but he hit sixth or seventh much of the time. Since the tail-end of the batting order had poor hitters, he was unprotected and many pitchers walked him or pitched around him, not giving him anything good to hit. Also, the hitters ahead of Colavito were not the league's best for getting on base; The Rock frequently hit with the bases empty, wasting his terrific slugging ability. Although Colavito's first half was good, he didn't make the All-Star team. Perennial All-Star manager Casey Stengel selected others as his reserves, although

Colavito compared favorably with some of those chosen, such as Harvey Kuenn, Elston Howard, and Ted Williams. (The All-Star starters were selected by a joint poll of players, managers and coaches.)

Colavito had numerous great games in the second half of 1958, including a two-homer and four-RBI game on July 17th; two homers, including a grand slam, and five RBI in a July 27th doubleheader as the Indians swept the Yankees; two homers versus Detroit on August 14th, and a home run and five RBI against the Senators on August 25th.

Colavito finished the year very strongly, and his 41 homers were second only to Mickey Mantle's 42, and his 113 RBI were second to Jackie Jensen's 122. Colavito's .620 slugging average was the best in the league. He led the Tribe to a surprising fourth place finish, and he more than made up for the All-Star slight as he finished third in the MVP balloting behind Jensen and Yankee pitcher Bob Turley.

In right field Colavito was known for his rifle arm, with many expert observers saying it was the best in baseball. He liked to show off his flat trajectory throws from deep right field to home plate, a feat usually drawing ''ooh's'' from the crowd. Colavito got his share of assists, but his arm was so strong that runners rarely ran on him. He did lead the league in outfield double plays, indicating that he could easily cut down on a runner attempting to score from third following his catch of a flyball.

Colavito's arm was so strong and he had such good aim that the Indians considered using him as a relief pitcher. He first pitched in an August exhibition game against Cincinnati when he went two innings, giving up only two hits and striking out five. He even showed a curve ball. A sportscaster wanted to set up an electronic system to measure the speed of his fastball, but the idea was nixed by the Indians management. Colavito pitched only once in a 1958 regular season game, going three innings without surrendering a hit. It was a close 3-1 game, indicating that the Indians had confidence in his pitching. Ten years later with the Yankees, he would relieve again for one inning and came away as the winning pitcher

as the Yankees rallied to win the game helped by Colavito's key home run. It marked the last time a position player pitching won a game.

Colavito went through numerous stretching exercises at every time at bat. He would hold the bat at the ends with each hand and stretch it behind his back. After a number of practice swings, he would ominously point the bat at the pitcher. For better bat control, he choked up on the bat an inch or so, reminiscent of former Indians slugger Al Rosen.

Colavito established himself as a star in 1958, and he was soon a fan favorite. He was from the Bronx, the home of the hated Yankees, making him even more attractive. It helped that he was boyishly handsome, swarthy and muscular, very appealing to the Cleveland fans, desperate for a star attraction. This persona is similar to the attraction of Jose Canseco in the late 1980's.

Colavito followed 1958 with another fine season in 1959, leading the league in home runs and helping Cleveland to a second place finish. The highlight of 1959 came on June 10 when he hit four consecutive home runs in a game. The feat was even more remarkable as it came in Baltimore's Memorial Stadium, then a stadium not friendly to power hitters.

The slugger with sex appeal made the cover of *Time* magazine on August 24, 1959. *Time* recognized him as perhaps the most attractive of a group of emerging new baseball stars such as Frank Robinson, Harmon Killebrew, and Don Drysdale.

Indians' management was not uniformly happy with Colavito's hitting. GM Lane claimed that Colavito was always swinging for the fences, and he gave Colavito a 1959 contract that provided a bonus if he hit LESS than 40 home runs. It was one of the strangest clauses ever in a baseball contract. So strong were Lane's feelings, that in 1960 he traded Colavito to Detroit for singles hitter Harvey Kuenn.

After Colavito's departure, fans missed him. There wasn't another slugger of his class in Cleveland again until Albert Belle emerged in 1994.

Ernie Banks - 1958

by Peter Golenbock

G	AB	R	H	2B	3B	HR	RBI	BB	SO	AVG	OBP	SLG	SB
154	617	119	193	23	11	47	129	52	87	.313	.370	.614	4

Born on January 31, 1931, Ernie Banks was the second of twelve children. His father, Eddie, had been a semi-pro ball player around Dallas. As a child, Ernie worked with his father in the fields picking cotton, doing backbreaking work from six in the morning till sundown for a couple of dollars a day.

When he was high school age Banks starred as a softball player, barnstorming with an all-black team called the Amarillo Colts. At age 19, he played with the Kansas City Monarchs of the Negro leagues for $300 a month, which at the time seemed to his family like a fortune. Among his teammates were black stars Satchell Paige, Josh Gibson, and Elston Howard. After the season he barnstormed with the Jackie Robinson All Stars, a collection of black greats, as he at short and Robinson at second formed an exciting double play combination.

Banks spent two years in the U.S. army with a black unit. After basic training he was asked by Abe Saperstein, the owner of the Harlem Globetrotters, to play in a Globetrotter basketball game. According to Banks, at the meeting Saperstein, who was white, asked to sit down next to him.

Said Banks, "I'd never sat down next to a white man, and I wasn't sure what to do."

Banks was shipped to Germany, where he was assigned the job of playing baseball. Bill Veeck was the first major league owner to approach Banks. He wrote him a letter telling him to try out with the Indians when he returned from overseas. The Brooklyn Dodgers also contacted him.

But when Banks returned home to Dallas in March of 1953, he ignored the invitations and made a beeline to his old team, the Kansas City Monarchs, where he hit .386 and hit 20 home runs.

On September 7, 1953, the Cubs Wid Matthews met with Monarch owner Tom Baird, manager Buck O'Neill, and Banks. Banks was offered a major league contract to play for the Cubs for $800 a month. The Cubs paid the Monarch's $20,000 for the rights to sign Banks and a young pitcher, Bill Dickey, who never made it.

When the 22-year-old Banks first reported to the Cubs, he didn't have a glove of his own. Eddie Miksis, an infielder, lent him one. Ray Blades, a Cub coach, offered his help by giving him a book called *How to Play Baseball*. That was how deeply racism was ingrained into the soul of America.

Ernie Banks didn't need an instructional manual, of course. All he needed was an opportunity and an equal chance. Banks played for the Cubs from 1953 through 1971, nineteen years (and twelve different managers) during which he played in 2,528 games, breaking Cap Anson's long standing record (an irony considering that it had been Anson who had set the policy of keeping blacks out of baseball in the 1880's); smote 512 home runs, including twelve grand slams, drove in 1,636 runs, was named Most Valuable

Player in the National League in 1958 and 1959, and in 1977 was elected into the Hall of Fame.

Ernie Banks shone like a beacon during so many years of Cub ineptitude that White Sox manager Jimmy Dykes once was prompted to say "Without Ernie Banks, the Cubs would finish in Albuquerque."

With a glove Banks was decent, but what the fans came out to see was Ernie Banks swinging the bat. In his hands, it was a powerful weapon. He snapped the bat at the ball, like cracking a whip. The ball would leap off the bat and be propelled as if shot into the left field bleachers. About his wrists and forearms, Cub manager Bob Scheffing once said, "You grip them and they feel like steel."

In his time Ernie Banks had not merely played the game of baseball -- he had revolutionized it. He was the first great slugger in the "Era of the Lively Bat," which he had introduced by going to a lighter, snappier bat.

As a result, he became the hardest hitting shortstop in the history of the major leagues. Consider the history of the game. What other shortstops could hit like Banks? There was Honus Wagner, who hit .327 lifetime, but Honus only hit 101 homers. Cal Ripken has been a great hitter, but Ripken won't hit 500 homers. There isn't another shortstop anywhere near Banks.

Noted for consistency and longevity, Banks nonetheless had a definite peak in his career. The only problem for this book is that his peak lasted three full years: 1957 to 1959. In 1958, conveniently in the center of his three-year surge, Banks reached his career highs in at bats, runs, hits, triples, home runs, total bases, batting average and slugging percentage. Naturally Banks won the MVP award in 1958. His 47 homers and 129 RBI dwarfed the runner-up in both categories, Frank Thomas of Pittsburgh who had 35 and 109. The other statistical standouts in the National League in 1958 included Milwaukee pitchers Warren Spahn and Lew Burdette who led the Braves to their second consecutive pennant, and Richie Ashburn who won the batting crown (.350) while the Phillies finished last. Willie Mays had a great year, as usual,

in 1958, but was a step below Banks in almost every measurable category. Banks' 1959 MVP reflected appreciation for his improving defense (dramatically reduced errors with a simultaneous increase in range) and was a special tribute because he beat out the now fully-blossomed superstar Hank Aaron.

The fans, unlike any skeptical teammates, loved Banks for always having had a kind word for the inept Cub organization and a corny phrase or slogan for the media and fans. "Let's play two," became his watchword. Even if his teammates could never figure out whether Ernie was sincere or not, the fans didn't care. He liked to repeat, "In the bee-yoo-ti-ful confines of Wrigley Field." The fans loved it. Every spring Banks predicted the Cubs would win the pennant. One year his slogan was, "The Cubs will come alive in sixty-five." (They finished eighth.) Then it was, "The Cubs will be heavenly in sixty-seven-ly." (That year, they only finished fourteen games out.) Every year the fans believed him.

The other aspect that the fans loved about Ernie Banks was that though he may have played in more losing games than any other player in the history of the game, he seemed unaffected by the losses and at the same time appeared utterly convinced that tomorrow the team would win.

By the time Ernie Banks took the field as a regular in 1954 the fans had come to recognize that losing was something that seemed to come with being a Cub. But with Ernie Banks out on the field playing for them, there was ALWAYS hope for the future. And it is Ernie Bank's hope that has come to symbolize the Chicago Cubs.

Like Banks, Cub fans don't get angry. Banks seemed almost sweet. Cub fans take the same approach toward their team. Banks never complained. Cub fans never complain.

Ernie Banks was a regular guy who went along in the face of adversity, just like the fans. He became their Moses, leading them to the Promised Land, and like Moses, never quite got there. But like Moses, Ernie was the moral and spiritual leader of his people. He always did and said the right thing. During games Ernie Banks even chewed Wrigley spearmint gum.

Oh, how the fans loved him.

Jim Shapiro: "When Ernie Banks joined the Cubs, I never gave it much thought that he was black. The Cubs were one of the last teams to get black ballplayers so by the time you had black ballplayers joining the Cubs, it was so standard in major league baseball that it wasn't any big thing to even talk about.

"The thing Cub fans still remember about Banks was the fact that there were many, many years when there wasn't a lot for Cub fans to talk about. You talked about the vines, the tradition, the die-hard fans, and that was about it. They had a long drought of losing seasons, with an appropriate level of negativism and handwringing both in the newspapers and from the fans. But Ernie Banks brought an unquenchable spirit to the team and to the fans. His famous, "Let's play two" was another way of saying, "Hey, there is more to this than winning." Banks was giving us a reason to go on, saying, "What's important is being out there, having fun, enjoying what you're doing. It's not getting yourself down cause you didn't win." And of course, the longer that went on, and the fact that his spirit never seemed to flag at all, he became an even greater phenomenon.

"What I remember most about Ernie was that he smiled a lot. He was a happy-faced kind of guy, when there were a lot of Cub players and Cub fans and Cub managers and Cub reporters and Cub commentators with long faces. He was hustling when not everyone was hustling. He wasn't given a nickname like Charlie Hustle like they did for Mr. Cincinnati (Pete Rose), but anyone going to the park could see he was running out every grounder, hustling on every play. You had a much better appreciation for it when you were at the park, not watching it on television.

"Since the Cubs had so many lean years, you had a special appreciation for ANYONE who gave you not just hope, but a little spirit and a little joy, when at times no joy was there.

"There are a lot of people who have a special reverence for Ernie Banks and his spirit and his optimism who have no idea what his batting averages were, or how well he played, or exactly when he played or even what position he played. They just remember, "Ernie Banks was the guy who kept the team together."

"And there's a lot to be said for that."

This essay includes excerpts from Peter Golenbock's new book, WRIGLEYVILLE, coming from St. Martins Press in 1996, appearing here with the kind permission of the author.

Warren Spahn - 1958

by Bill Gray

W	L	PCT	G	GS	CG	SV	IP	SO	BB	B/I	ERA
21	11	.667	38	36	23	0	290	150	76	1.20	3.07

His name appears on page 279 in an essay about baseball players and World War II. Next, he appears on page 334 in an essay about Willie Mays, and only because he gave up Willie's first home run. He is last mentioned on page 358, his name woven into a list about the best players of the 1950's. The book is called *Baseball, An Illustrated History*. It runs about 450 pages. It's a companion to the 18-hour *Baseball - A Film by Ken Burns*. In the same book, Sandy Koufax and Don Drysdale are mentioned five times as often as Spahn. Lou Gehrig, The Babe, Cy, Big Train and Grover Cleveland Alexander are all covered lavishly, but no such coverage is given to Warren Edward Spahn.

We are not talking about a player who made a small mark on the game. We are talking about Warren Spahn, possibly the game's greatest pitcher. As Bill James put it in his *Historical Baseball Abstract*, Spahn's career record is "about the same as Don Drysdale's and Sandy Koufax's added together." Still, citing ERA as "the one best indicator of a pitcher's ability," James likes Lefty Grove as "the greatest pitcher of all time, period." He mentions Koufax as being the most comparable recent pitcher to Grove. Without doubt, Koufax and Grove were brilliant. Heck, together they won 20 games 11 times, almost as good as Spahn's 13 seasons with 20 wins.

To pick the best year from Spahn's long career, I gave some thought to hanging his career record on the wall and throwing a dart at it. Chances are wherever the dart landed, one could make the case for a great year.

The 1958 season was special. But I also like 1953 when Spahn was 23-7 at the age of 32. And I like 1963 when he was 23-7 at the age of 42.

Spahn's career dovetails neatly with baseball's so-called postwar era (1946-1961). Most baseball fans can rattle off the names of the great pitchers from that era: Bob Feller, Bob Lemon, Robin Roberts, Whitey Ford, Early Wynn, and Don Newcombe. Yet, Spahn was so much more consistent over the entire postwar period and beyond, it's startling. His first great season was 1947 when he went 21-10 for the Boston Braves. Over the next 16 seasons, Warren Spahn failed to win 20 games only four times! He still posted 64 wins in those four "off" years.

Spahn's 363 career victories rank fifth on the list of all time behind Cy Young, Walter Johnson, Grover Alexander, and Christy Mathewson. Spahn owns the record for wins by a lefthanded pitcher. In the modern, lively ball era, nobody, righty or lefty, is anywhere even close.

In 1957 Spahn was 21-11 with a 2.69 ERA. He won the Cy Young award, and Milwaukee defeated the Yankees in a great seven-game series. Spahn was clearly the best pitcher in the game, but, in the 1957 World Series, Spahn was just 1-1. He was scheduled to start the seventh game, but came down with the flu. Instead, Lew Burdette, pitching on two days rest, started and won game seven, for his third Series win. Burdette had 2 shutouts in the series, a 0.67 ERA and won the Series MVP award.

Burdette went on to win 20 games in 1958, but Spahn proved he was a long way from being the number two starter on any team, by winning 22 games. His workload was incredible as he pitched a major league leading 290 innings, the fifth highest total of his career. He started 36 games and completed 21 with two shutouts. He held batters to a combined .237 average. Despite all the work, he was brilliant in the '58 World Series. In the opener, he went 10 innings to beat Whitey Ford 4-3.

Spahn was better in game four, again beating Ford, with a two hit, 3-0 shutout. The Braves needed one more win to repeat as champions, and Spahn took the mound in the sixth game. Again, he was superb, holding a 2-1 lead into the sixth inning, but an error by Bill Bruton allowed Mickey Mantle to reach third, and Yogi Berra's sacrifice fly tied it at two. Spahn continued to shut down the Yankees into the 10th, but the Yankees finally got to him for a couple of runs and won the game. They won the seventh game and the series the next day.

After 290 regular season innings, Spahn responded with another 28.2 in the World Series. He allowed only 19 hits and 8 walks. During that year, Spahn worked 318.2 innings and won 24 games.

For the 37 year old Spahn, it could have been a fitting way to end his career. But, Warren Spahn wasn't quite ready for the rocking chair. Down the road were four more 20 win seasons, and along with his 300th win, he threw two no-hitters, one at age 39 and another at age 40.

Of the 20 pitchers in history with 300 or more wins, 11 of them pitched all or part of their career in the dead ball era. Another six 300 game winners, Tom Seaver, Gaylord Perry, Nolan Ryan, Phil Niekro, Steve Carlton and Don Sutton, began their careers after the 1961-62 expansion and were reaching their prime as baseball added more expansion teams in 1968. Only Lefty Grove (300), and Spahn (363) won 300 after the dead ball era and before expansion.

Usually pitchers with a shot at 300 wins are running on fumes. Note that after notching his final 20-win season, it took Grove seven more seasons to win his 300th, and then he promptly quit, as did Wynn, who also struggled for four years to get his 300th. Carlton pitched another five seasons after his 300th win, winning only 29 more games. But Spahn approached his 300th win at the top of his game, cruising past 300 at age 40. It was his twelfth 20-win season, and sixth in a row. He won 18 in 1962, and 23 more in 1963.

Unquestionably, of all pitchers who have reached 300 wins, Spahn continued to pitch effectively much longer than any pitcher in modern times. He remains the only modern day pitcher to have a 20 win season after achieving 300 wins.

Now, where did I put that dart?

Hank Aaron - 1959

by David Luciani

G	AB	R	H	2B	3B	HR	RBI	BB	SO	AVG	OBP	SLG	SB
154	629	116	223	46	7	39	123	51	54	.355	.406	.636	8

When Hank Aaron's name is mentioned, people usually think home runs. It's inevitable. Aaron, in case you forgot, is the man who broke Babe Ruth's mark for home runs in a career. For a guy who led his league in home runs four times, RBI's four times and runs scored three times, it's ironic that his best year was one in which he didn't lead the league in any of those categories. The year was 1959 and Hank Aaron compiled the best average of his career to win his second batting title.

1959 was his best year for several reasons. He hit fifty points higher than his final career average of .305. His slugging percentage, while he didn't lead the league in home runs, was still the best in the league. He won his second of three straight Gold Gloves. He led the league in hits (a career high) and his closest competitor that year was Cincinnati's Vada Pinson, who trailed by 18 hits. 1959 was also the only year in which Aaron ever hit three home runs in a game. Aaron posted an early-season twenty-two game hit streak and was hitting over .500 into May. Even the first of the two All-Star games (there were two each year from 1959-1962) turned out to be a highlight. Aaron knocked in the tying run in the first midsummer classic and scored what would prove to be the deciding run on a Willie Mays triple. That year, Aaron became the first player ever elected to the All-Star team unanimously, in those days by a vote of the players.

Perhaps the best authority on that season is Aaron himself. "Ernie [Banks] had to have a great year to beat me out for the MVP award in 1959," Aaron writes in his autobiography *I Had A Hammer* "because I was never a better hitter."

Aaron was part of a very strong Milwaukee Braves team that included home-run leader Eddie Mathews and two 21-game winners, Warren Spahn (the tenth time he had won twenty or more) and Lew Burdette. 1959 was also the year of Harvey Haddix's near-perfect game (Aaron was walked intentionally, just after the perfect game was lost on an error).

1959 was the year of Ernie Banks' second-straight MVP award, and it was the year of the Dodgers, just their second season in LA. The Braves battled with the Dodgers and Giants all summer. The Giants, led by Mays, Orlando Cepeda and Willie Kirkland, were strengthened by a 21-year-old named Willie McCovey, called up late in the season. The Dodgers, who had finished seventh a year before, were a well-balanced team that enjoyed the presence of Don Drysdale, Sandy Koufax, Roger Craig, Gil Hodges and Duke Snider. Hank Aaron's Braves were after their third straight pennant, but it wasn't to be.

At the start of the final weekend of the season, the Dodgers had a one game lead. By Saturday night, the Braves and Dodgers were tied and both teams, forced to the limit, won their games on Sunday. Tied with 86-68 records, a best-of-three playoff series was set up with the Braves heavily favored to take the pennant. But the Braves were upset by the Dodgers in the first two games 3-2 and 6-5 (in 12 innings). The Braves of 1959 were so much taken for granted as a great team that only 19,000 people showed up at County Stadium to see the first game of the Braves-Dodgers series, even with tie-breaking playoffs a rarity.

Aaron's season looked different to fans of his era than it does to modern historians. We have the benefit of knowing what his career would become. Going into 1959, Aaron had won as many batting titles as he had home run crowns (one each) and he was generally viewed as a consistent batting title contender who might add a good number of home runs. Aaron wasn't known for tremendous power, but more for consistency in contact that could get the ball out of the park or get a clutch single. Later, he would also become more of a runner, accomplishing the ''30-30'' mark in 1963. Hindsight lets us look back and determine that among the many great years Aaron was to have, 1959 would stand out as the offensive season you'd most want to have in your lineup and the one that he himself recognized as his best year.

Ironically, the fact that Aaron went on to become the all-time home run champ diminishes the appreciation of many baseball fans for the '59 season. What Aaron has become known for is the long ball, so fans look more at his four home run championships, naturally assuming that his best season must have been a year featuring home runs. In comparison to other players, there are only a few players with similar seasons. Obviously, Ernie Banks, who won the MVP over Aaron, had a better year because he put up tremendous offensive numbers as a shortstop. 1959 was simply the greatest year in one of the greatest careers ever.

Roy Face - 1959

by Bill Gray

W	L	PCT	G	GS	CG	SV	IP	SO	BB	B/I	ERA
18	1	.947	57	0	0	10	93	69	25	1.25	2.70

If you were a relief pitcher, and in one amazing year you won 17 games in a row, you'd call it your greatest season, right? Even if you weren't a relief pitcher, you'd say 17 in a row must make a career best. Well, not if your name is Roy Face. Face did win 17 in a row in 1959, yet he called the 1962 season, when he led the majors with 28 saves for the Pirates and had a brilliant 1.88 ERA, his best. Nevertheless, to win 17 in a row, especially in relief, is one of the single greatest accomplishments in major league history.

Face was among the most effective relief pitchers ever. He and contemporaries Lindy McDaniel and Hoyt Wilhelm were the dominant relievers of the late 1950's, and all pitched well into the late '60's. Their careers spanned the era when the role of the reliever was more clearly defined and took on added importance. The game finisher became a star on many teams, and words like "closer" and "ace reliever" became widely used. Before that, the word "fireman" was used, with the implication that such pitchers wouldn't get into a game unless the starter was getting bombed.

In the 1950's save totals were modest. Fifteen saves led the majors as recently as 1959, as opposed to the 35 to 40 or even 50 saves now required to lead a league. In the 1960's a good reliever was a guy who could warm up in a hurry and pitch a few effective innings, often working several days in a row. Nobody did that job better than Roy Face.

The new emphasis on big save statistics is only relevant when discussing relievers of the current era.

During that time when the job was different, the greatest single season for a relief pitcher was surely 1959, when Roy Face won 17 straight games before he lost one. He had "only" 10 saves, five short of the major league leader. Face received 67 votes for the MVP that year, but a starter; Sam Jones of the Giants, received more. Jones' record was 21-15. He started 35 games and relieved in 15 games adding 4 saves coupled with a 2.83 ERA. Face, at 18-1 had 10 saves with a 2.71 ERA. Unlike today, the Cy Young award went to the best pitcher in the majors, not in each league. Early Wynn won the Cy that year, and Jones received 2 votes. Bob Shaw of the Braves got one vote. Shaw, like Face, recorded 18 wins, but had 6 losses. He started 26 games and also relieved in 21, getting 3 saves, and a 2.63 ERA.

Maybe if Face had started a few games he might have been recognized, but relievers then were the Rodney Dangerfields of baseball. From a historical perspective, Face's incredible win total in 1959 undoubtedly drew attention to the relief corps. The following year, the Cardinals' McDaniel became the first reliever to receive a vote in the Cy Young balloting.

But it wasn't until 1974 when a reliever, Mike Marshall of the Dodgers, won a Cy Young award. Marshall had 21 saves and a 15-12 record. His award can be attributed less to his record than to his workload, an incredible 208.3 innings pitched over 106 relief appearances. There was so much hype regarding Marshall's ''bionic'' arm, that his effort became more important than his results, as far as the

Cy Young Award voters were concerned. Strangely, that was just the opposite reaction to Face's amazing 18-1 record of 1959. His result was considered to be too good, and the effort too little!

Face's money pitch was a forkball. While Face did not invent the forkball, he certainly perfected it. After Dick Groat was traded to St. Louis, he made this observation about Face's forkball: "Coming at you, it looked exactly like a fastball. And then, when it got to the plate, it absolutely died. No way you could hit it." Today pitchers throw a variety of split-finger pitches with different grips and varying velocities, but none of the newer versions is any better than Face's.

In 1958, Face ended the season with a five game winning streak, and the Pirates finished second. The Pirates teams of the 1940's and 1950's were among the most inept in history, so second place was more than a moral victory, it signaled the solidification of a young, talented team. Roberto Clemente, Bill Virdon, Bill Mazeroski, Frank Thomas and Dick Groat led the Pirates offense, and Face came out of the bullpen in relief of solid starters Vern Law, Bob Friend, and Ron Kline. Like all relievers, Face made the starters better by allowing the manager to make a change before disaster had struck. The Pirates were finally contenders, and would win the World Series just two years later.

Although they were a team with rising talent, the Pirates in 1959 were disappointing. The team fell back, to fourth place. It was a season in which the Pirates often would blow leads and then with Face on the mound, come back to win. His winning streak began on April 22. The Pirates, down 7-0 to Cincinnati, came back to tie the game in the seventh. Face came on in the eighth. He allowed the Reds to go ahead 8-7 on a home run by Gus Bell, but then, in the bottom of the ninth, the Bucs scored twice to win and Face was 1-0. There would be other games where Face would see a lead evaporate, only to have the Pirates roar back to win. As a result, many descriptions of the streak characterize Face as the undeserving beneficiary of rare good fortune, creating the impression that he blew lead after lead only to have the Pirates come back in the ninth to win it for him. Certainly there were some games like June 11th when he gave up a 3 run homer to a pinch hitter named Willie Mays, which put the Pirates behind 7-5. But they came back to score five in the 8th and win it for Face 12-9. Pirate broadcaster Bob Prince began to stamp such a win as "The Luck of Elroy!" Other media picked up on the luck theme and featured it extensively. Yet, after that June 11th game, Face got into a groove and didn't allow another run until mid July. Lucky? A look at his 2.70 ERA in 1959 suggests otherwise.

A longer winning streak actually began on May 30, 1958, and ended on September 11th 1959 with a 4-3 loss to the Dodgers. In that span Face made 98 appearances in relief and won 22 straight games.

Vernon Law said of Face, "As far as I'm concerned, there hasn't been anybody that has been as effective as Roy in a relief role. Bases loaded, nobody out, more than once the bases were still loaded and three outs."

Face continued to pitch effectively through 1963. In 1964 and 1965 he appeared to be at the end of the road, yielding his stopper role on the Pirates to Al McBean. But in 1966, at age 38, he returned to form and continued to pitch well until he was 40. In 1968 he made his 802nd and final appearance for the Pirates, tying him with Walter Johnson for the most games pitched for one team. Before he could break the record, the Pirates sent him to the Detroit Tigers for their pennant run. Montreal picked him up in 1969 and he recorded his final five saves, then retired. Over his career, he saved 193 games and won 104, 96 in relief.

Roy Face's career record stands up very well, and bears out his value to the Pirates. Face elevated the position of relief pitcher, and he merits enshrinement in the Hall of Fame. Yet, at this point, the relief pitcher is just beginning to be regarded as worthy of induction. While Face's save totals don't equal those of Lee Smith, Dennis Eckersley, Jeff Reardon et al, his longevity and career effectiveness certainly do. Whether you call him a "fireman," or a "closer," the Pirates' "Baron of the Bullpen" had a solid career, and a truly magnificent 1959 season.

Norm Cash - 1961

by John Benson

G	AB	R	H	2B	3B	HR	RBI	BB	SO	AVG	OBP	SLG	SB
159	535	119	193	22	8	41	132	124	85	.361	.488	.662	11

Lost in the home run binge of 1961, and overshadowed in particular by Roger Maris' 61-homer season, Norm Cash's accomplishments from that same summer were not fully appreciated when they occurred and have not aged well, either, partly because Cash's career didn't age well. He became less of a superstar as his long and productive career unfolded. With a little scrutiny and open-minded appreciation, however, the Cash of 1961 looks better. It possesses that special characteristic, more than many others in this book: the more you look at it, the better it looks.

There is a general perception that "everybody hit well" in the American League in 1961, but in fact the league batting average clicked upward only one point, rising from .255 to .256 in 1960 to 1961, and the league's on base percentage remained steady through those two years at .331. Batting average and OBP were the categories that Cash dominated, so any tendency to discount his marks on account of a contextual surge simply isn't appropriate. The Tigers as a team hit .266 to lead the league in 1961, modest compared to what you see in newspapers today. There simply was no general inflation of batting and on base averages in 1961.

Cash ran away with the AL batting crown, finishing 37 points ahead of teammate Al Kaline's .324, and he similarly dwarfed his nearest competitor in on base percentage, Mickey Mantle, by 36 points, finishing .488 to .452. The .488 mark stood as the highest in the majors for 33 years, until Frank Thomas weighed in with a .494 in the shortened season of 1994.

If Cash had been a high-average, singles-type hitter in the mold of Rod Carew, then there might be another reason to downplay his batting average and OBP, but Cash was obviously a great slugger in 1961. He finished a close second to Maris in total bases, came in fourth in RBI, just ten behind Maris, and finished ahead of Maris, second only to Mickey Mantle, in slugging percentage. Using some of the more comprehensive measures such as Pete Palmer's batter runs, adjusted batter runs and total player rating, and Bill James' runs created, Cash was the best hitter in the American League in 1961. Partly because such measures were not available to journalists in 1961 (and probably would have been dismissed, even if they were available) Cash finished fourth in MVP voting, behind Maris, Mantle, and Jim Gentile.

The 1961 Everests of Cash's career gained stature with the passing of time in one important context: the remainder of Cash's own career. His average dropped 118 points, from .361 to .243 in 1962, a record fall among batting champs. Cash remained a good but not great player for a career that spanned 17 major league seasons. He never went on the disabled list, hit over 30 home runs five times and exceeded 20 homers 11 times, including nine consecutive years starting in '61. He led the league in home run percentage in 1965 and 1971, coincidentally winning the Comeback Player of the Year award in both of those seasons. Cash lasted long enough to prove that his 1961 accomplishments were not pure flukes, although they were indeed very special.

WHITEY FORD
Pitcher

New York
Yankees

Courtesy - The Topps Company, Inc.

Whitey Ford - 1961

By Joey Kusnick

W	L	PCT	G	GS	CG	SV	IP	SO	BB	B/I	ERA
25	4	.862	39	39	11	0	283	209	92	1.18	3.21

In a sport littered with broken dreams, Edward Charles "Whitey" Ford enjoyed more than his share of success.

Ford anchored Yankee pitching staffs that won eleven pennants in his sixteen-year career, notching a 236-106 lifetime record to go with a 2.75 ERA. However, it cannot be said that Whitey's good fortune came from the teams he played for. If anything, the Yankee teams he pitched for were big winners, because they had Whitey Ford.

Blessed with great control of his pitches and an even greater composure on the mound, Ford was a master at getting batters out, one batter at a time, one pitch at a time. Ford was the prototypical Thinking Pitcher. He also possessed an uncanny ability to position his fielders, earning him the nickname "The Chairman of the Board." And when he needed a good pitch, Whitey wasn't above cutting a ball or throwing a spitter. He simply did what he needed to win.

And though much was made of the drinking careers of Ford and teammate Mickey Mantle, Whitey did not let the night life interfere with his pitching. He made an effort to stay in on the two nights before his starts, and often convinced Mantle to do so as well.

Whitey joined the Yankees in 1950, coming up from their farm club in Binghamton, New York. He enjoyed a fine rookie season, posting nine wins, including two shutouts, against only one loss. Ford capped off the year by winning the final game of the World Series

against the Phillies, completing the Yankee sweep. Following the season, however, Ford's career had to be put on hold. The young left-hander was drafted, and spent the next two years doing military service.

Back with the Bombers in 1953, Ford quickly emerged as the Yankees' ace. He went 18-6 for the season as the Yankees captured another World Series title. His 3.00 ERA was fourth-best in the league, and his .750 winning percentage was second only to teammate Eddie Lopat.

The following year, the Yanks won an impressive 103 games, but came in second behind the powerful 1954 Cleveland Indians club. Ford bolstered the Yankee staff that year, turning in a 16-8 record to go with a 2.82 ERA.

By 1955, Whitey had become one of the American League's premier hurlers, leading the junior circuit that year with 18 victories (against 7 losses) and 18 complete games. He finished second in the majors in ERA (2.63), third in winning percentage (.720) and finished fourth in the American League in strikeouts (137). Ford also posted two wins against the Dodgers in a rare Series defeat for the Yanks.

The next season saw the Yankees win another pennant, taking the flag by eight games over the second-place Indians. Ford paced the staff with 19 wins to go with his six losses, and registered the lowest ERA in the majors at 2.47. He was also fourth in the AL in complete games with 18. In the World Series, New

York dropped the first two games to the Dodgers. Ford took the mound in game three at Yankee Stadium and turned in a complete-game win, paving the way for a seven-game Bomber victory.

Despite Whitey's masterful pitching, a 20-win season continued to elude him. Manager Casey Stengel refused to pitch Ford on only three days' rest, believing the pitcher to be too small for the task (with his height of 5' 10" and weight of 175). The result for Ford was fewer starts and, subsequently, fewer opportunities for victories.

Another reason for the limited use involved Ford's opposition. Stengel chose to rest Whitey against weaker teams from time to time, opting instead to save him for action versus first-division clubs. Nonetheless, Ford continued to ring up victories.

Ford posted a 41-22 record over the next three years, despite seeing limited action in the 1957 campaign. He averaged a 2.52 ERA during the span, and led the majors with a 2.01 mark in 1958.

Whitey struggled a little in the 1960 season, notching only a 12-9 record. Though he led the AL in shutouts and his 3.08 ERA was the league's fifth-best, rumors abounded that Ford's career was winding down. Ford's best days, it was widely believed, were behind him. The experts with this opinion were all proved wrong.

Ford's 1960 World Series performance against the Pirates began to dispel the notion that Ford was fading. He pitched superbly in game three, registering a complete-game shutout and scattering only four hits as the Yankees won, 10-0. Ford duplicated the feat four days later, going the full nine innings to notch a 12-0 win in game six. Sadly, Ford's shutouts were all-but forgotten when Bill Mazeroski's dramatic ninth-inning, game seven home run wrested the Series from the Yanks.

Shortly after the heartbreaking Series loss, Stengel was dismissed as Yankee skipper. Replacing Stengel as the Yanks' new field boss was Ralph Houk, who was intent on using Ford more often in 1961.

The Yankees tallied 109 wins in 1961, taking the American League by nine games over second-place Detroit. And for the first time in his career, Whitey worked regularly on three days' rest. The result was Whitey's most productive season, if not his finest.

With all attention that year focused on Yankee teammates Mickey Mantle and Roger Maris and their mounting home run totals, Ford quietly captured the Cy Young Award. He led the majors with 25 wins (against only four losses) and in winning percentage at .862, while posting a 3.21 ERA. He was also third in the majors with 209 strikeouts.

Game one of the World Series saw Ford turn in a brilliant 2-0 complete-game shutout, outdueling the Reds' Jim O'Toole and allowing only two hits. Ford returned in game four to pitch five more shutout innings and pick up his second win. In doing so, Ford set a World Series record of 32 consecutive scoreless innings, eclipsing Babe Ruth's record of 29 2/3.

Ford continued his success for three more seasons, compiling a 58-21 record while the Yankees won three more pennants. During the span, Ford tallied a 2.60 ERA and 521 strikeouts. He also notched his second 20-win season in 1963, leading the AL with 24 victories and a .774 winning percentage.

With the arrival of the 1965 season came the crumbling of the Yankee dynasty. Gone were many of the stars who had helped New York to so many pennants. Those that remained were nearing the end of their careers. Ford was no exception. Whitey managed one last full season in 1965, going 16-13 while tallying a career-high 3.24 ERA.

During his final two seasons, Ford was bothered by shoulder problems, and pitched infrequently. He was only able to muster a 4-9 record in that time, despite a 2.16 ERA. After appearing in only seven games during the 1967 campaign, Ford decided that it was time to retire.

Ford, along with his friend and teammate Mantle, was elected to the Hall of Fame in 1974.

Roger Maris - 1961

by David Wetter

G	AB	R	H	2B	3B	HR	RBI	BB	SO	AVG	OBP	SLG	SB
161	590	132	159	16	4	61	142	94	67	.269	376	.620	0

In 1961, President Kennedy and Premier Kruschev rattled their sabers over Castro and Cuba, Yuri Gagarin was the first man to circle the earth, Adolf Eichmann finally went on trial for his war crimes, and Roger Maris hit 61 home runs.

I bought my Topps Roger Maris baseball card at Tompkins grocery store in the Bronx that spring. This was before children purchased the entire sealed box of cards and tossed it up on the closet shelf as an investment. My friends and I waited outside Tompkins' for the Topps driver to deliver the new shipment. I bought five packs, a 25 cents outlay. Roger was in the very first one. He wasn't Mickey Mantle-- in my mind, he was the ''other'' Yankee outfielder, even though he had won the 1960 American League MVP.

I was eight years old that spring and summer, my second year of collecting cards, my third as a Yankee fan. My father took me to my first game in 1959, and from then on, we attended one each year, and listened to or watched countless others.

Maris started slowly in '61. Then he found a Paul Foytack fastball up in the strike zone and hit his first home run April 27, the same day that Mantle was connecting for numbers 6 and 7. After the first 27 games of the season, Maris collected only three home runs. The expansion of the American League from eight teams to 10, with some 20 new pitchers on rosters, spread the mound talent a bit thin, but the dilution had not benefited Maris in the early going. He

was batting .208 on May 16. The news of the spring thus far had been 40-year-old Warren Spahn pitching a no-hitter for his 290th lifetime victory, and in the Bay Area, the ''Say-Hey'' Kid, Willie Mays, exploding on May 1 for four home runs in one game. Roger's outfield companion Mickey Mantle was making the most of the watered-down rotations and had already collected his ninth round-tripper of the young season.

But then it started. In the next 12 games, the Rajah rapped out nine home runs, Mantle had seven. And on May 31, Roger stood at 12, Mickey at 14. It was way too early for the newspapers to bite. Then, in early June, while the team itself was breaking an American League record, hitting 28 home runs in 14 games, Maris passed Mantle for the first time. On Sunday, June 11, Maris hit his 19th and 20th of the season. He also leaped over the short right-field fence and into the stands to take away a sure home run from Ken Hunt of the expansion Los Angeles Angels. The *New York Daily News* had a series of pictures of the catch the next day on the back page, and I cut it out and tacked it onto my bulletin board between my poster of the flags of the world and a photo clipped from a magazine of ex-Mouseketeer Cheryl posing in a white two-piece.

That month, it seemed that every Yankee box score had either an entry for ''HR-Maris'' or ''HR-Mantle.'' Or just as often, ''HR-Mantle, Maris.'' In late June, when Roger was threatening to slug 30 home runs by the end of the month--Babe Ruth had done it twice-- the newspapers began to take notice. An assault on

Ruth's almighty mark of 60 home runs was once again being mounted, this time by two ballplayers at once. Reporters began to chart Maris' and Mantle's pace. No sooner did the stories begin on the dual challenge than Commissioner Ford Frick announced that in light of the expanded 162 game schedule, the record would have to be broken in 154 games to surpass the previous mark. Otherwise, there would be two entries for most home runs in a season: Ruth's record, and the expanded season record.

In July, the home run race continued, Mantle and Maris answering each other's blasts--two club-wielding ballplayers locked in mortal (albeit friendly) combat. Maris had his finest day of the season on July 25th, hitting four home runs, to reach 40, the last coming off the aptly named ''Happy'' Hacker. Mantle responded a few days later, with three in a twin-bill on August 7th.

On the morning of August 11, Roger Maris had 42 on his side of the ledger; Mickey Mantle had 44. Most writers were picking Mantle to be the one to break the Bambino's mark. That week Maris hit seven home runs in six games, and when the smoke cleared, he had 48 on August 17th. Mantle was hanging tough at 45. Ford Frick's 154-game deadline continued to be an issue as defenders of Babe Ruth decried the expanded schedule and suspected a livelier bat and ball as the culprits causing the home run explosion.

They even blamed poorer pitching that season, choosing to ignore the fact that in 1927 the Boston Red Sox (51 wins and 103 losses) and the St. Louis Browns (59-94) fed up more than their share of gopher balls to the Bambino. Hank Greenberg, who had hit 58 back in 1938, had his say: ''No matter who throws the ball, the hitter must be able to put it out of the park....''

On August 22, Roger hit his 50th off the Angels' Ken McBride, the same day his second son, Randy, was born. The pressure was beginning to build. With a slew of rainouts earlier in the season and an added eight games, the Yankees were playing an exhausting number of double-headers (unfathomable by today's standard). As a result of the stress, Maris's hair began to fall out in clumps.

The pack of sportswriters following the ''M&M boys'' grew exponentially. The same questions were asked over and over again. Maris, a quiet man born in North Dakota, was wholly unaccustomed to the attention. (In fact, in early September, *Daily News* sportswriter Dick Young, under the headline ''Maris's 55th Leaves Scribes Agape,'' wrote that reporters simply watched as Maris sipped a cold beer, unable to think of anything new to ask.

On September 20, in the 154th game of the season, Maris hit his 59th home run. Mantle, plagued by injuries, was stopped at 54. With three more at bats in the game, the Rajah failed to connect, enabling Ford Frick to preserve a portion of the Babe's home run record. Six days later, Roger tied Ruth at 60. And on October 1, 1961, in the third inning of a scoreless game at Yankee stadium, before a crowd of only 23,154 fans, Roger Maris swung at the third offering from Red Sox pitcher Tracy Stallard and drove the ball into the right-field seats, into the waiting arms of thrilled truck driver Sal Durante.

I was in school that day, so I didn't hear the news until I got home that afternoon. My father, who worked the early shift at the Murray Hill Post Office, greeted me at the door and smiled: ''He did it.''

After the first 27 games of the season, when he had managed only three home runs, Maris went on to hit 58 more over the course of the next 135 games. Astounding. It is 1995, 34 years since Roger Maris hit 61 home runs, the same number of years between his record and Ruth's. In that time, George Foster and Willie Mays each hit 52 in a season. No one else has come close.

Maury Wills - 1962

by David Smith

G	AB	R	H	2B	3B	HR	RBI	BB	SO	AVG	OBP	SLG	SB
165	695	130	208	13	10	6	48	51	57	.299	.349	.373	104

It's one thing to put up big numbers and win awards for having a fine season. It's quite another to do things so special that you receive credit for changing the way the game is played. Maury Wills turned in that kind of transforming performance in 1962.

Even though Luis Aparicio had stolen a lot of bases for the White Sox in the previous six seasons, the stolen base was still a seldom-used tactic, quite unlike the 1980's and 1990's when many players steal 50 bases in a season. Maury Wills' baserunning was a major weapon in the arsenal of the 1962 Dodgers, and others learned from his example that greater daring on the basepaths could pay off.

The raw numbers on Maury Wills in 1962 are extraordinary. He stole 104 bases, but was caught only 13 times and picked off 3 times, which is a success rate of 86.7%, well above the league norm (62% in 1961 and 65% in 1962). To see how often Wills used the steal attempt, examine how often he tried to run as a function of the number of chances he had. For this purpose we can say that a runner has a stolen base opportunity whenever he is on base with no one on the base immediately in front of him. For current players the overall average is a stolen base attempt in about 10% of the opportunities, with the league leaders running about 25% of the time. In 1962 Maury Wills attempted to steal in 49% of the situations when he had an open base in front of him. Furthermore, his exceptionally high attempt rate increased near the end of the season as he neared Ty Cobb's 1915 total of 96, the previous record. In

August he ran 57% of the time, and in September-October he attempted to steal an incredible 73% of the time.

It would be a mistake, however, to conclude that Wills' running was selfish and not beneficial to the team. Situational analysis of his 244 chances to run shows that 58% of his steal attempts came when the score was tied or the Dodgers were ahead by one run, that is, when the extra base was most needed. In addition, the opposition was obviously affected by his presence. Opposing teams committed four balks, eight wild pitches, one passed ball, seven errors on pickoff attempts, and six errors while he was actually stealing. These 26 additional advances accounted for 25% of all such mistakes made by Dodger opponents in 1962, even though the number of times Maury was on base was only about 12% of the team total.

Wills was the Dodgers' leadoff man, and it is fair to ask if his propensity for running had an effect on the men batting behind him. The most frequent number two batter for the Dodgers in 1962 was Jim Gilliam, a man with a reputation for a careful batting eye, who struck out rarely. These are ideal characteristics to have in the batter behind a prolific base stealer, because he won't be afraid to take the extra pitch or two that may be necessary for Wills to steal. When the number two Dodger batter appeared with the bases empty, he batted .267. When Wills was on first, but did not steal, he batted .322. When Wills stole second, the batting average was .189, but the on base average was increased as many more walks were received. How are these numbers to be interpreted? It appears that the presence of Wills on first made it easier to get a hit, theoretically because the opposing pitcher would throw more fastballs. The lower batting average after a successful steal might seem negative, but the greater number of walks reflects the larger number of pitches taken while waiting for Wills to steal (3.4 pitches per appearance as opposed to 2.0). Also, with first base open, and Maury Wills in scoring position, and Gilliam at the plate, not many pitchers would be inclined to throw many hittable pitches. Gilliam drew 93 walks in 1962, second in the National League after Eddie Mathews with 101.

Of course, we must also remember that Wills was an effective offensive force with his bat, too. His 208 hits (179 of them singles) were the most in the National League, except for teammate Tommy Davis. His 130 runs tied for second in that category with Willie Mays while Frank Robinson led the league with 134. Although the Dodgers of 1965 and 1966 depended very heavily on excellent pitching for their success, the 1962 team was a much greater offensive force than they are usually given credit for being. For example, their 842 runs (5.1 per game) were second only to the Giants' 878. For comparison, the 1961 Yankees, known for their fearsome power, scored only 827 runs. All those singles, walks, and stolen bases added up to a large offensive output. What matters more than anything else is whether or not Maury's running was of noticeable benefit to the success of the team. When Wills played but did not attempt a steal, the Dodgers had a winning percentage of .554. When he did make an attempt, even if he was thrown out, their winning percentage was over .700. Of course, to have an attempt to steal, one must first be on base, so these percentages reflect his general offensive contribution as well as his running ability.

Many baseball analyses have been done, such as those by John Thorn and Pete Palmer in *The Hidden Game of Baseball*, which show that stolen bases don't add a lot to a team's season wins. However, the 1962 performance by Maury Wills appears to be the exception to this general pattern. In 1979 Leonard Koppett wrote in *The Sporting News* that Wills had changed the game simply because he was the first in modern times to be allowed to run at will. The consequences of this running were not only the often-cited intangibles of upsetting the opponents, but also the clearly measurable improvements in the scoring of runs and winning of games.

Note: Some of the data cited here were published in an article written by David Smith for the 1980 Baseball Research Journal, a publication of the Society for American Baseball Research. Other information came from the files of Retrosheet.

Sandy Koufax - 1965

by David Smith

W	L	PCT	G	GS	CG	SV	IP	SO	BB	B/I	ERA
26	8	.765	43	41	27	2	335	382	71	0.87	2.04

It is difficult to choose a single best year for Sandy Koufax, because each of his last five was excellent. For example he led the National League in ERA all five of those seasons. 1965 is usually cited as his best season, even though it was the only year of his final four in which his ERA rose above 2.00 (all the way up to 2.04).

The number most often noted from Sandy's 1965 performance is the 382 strikeouts, setting the major league record which was surpassed by Nolan Ryan's 383 for the Angels in 1973. Of course, Koufax also pitched his fourth no-hitter in as many years in 1965, this one a perfect game against the Cubs on September 9th, when he struck out 14. Koufax piled up some other outstanding numbers in 1965. He had a win-loss record of 26-8 with 27 complete games in 41 starts (Juan Marichal completed 24 for the Giants, Bob Gibson of the Cardinals had 20, as did Sandy's teammate, Don Drysdale). Koufax averaged over 8.0 innings pitched in his starts and his eight shutouts were second only to Marichal's 10.

Early in his career Koufax was extremely wild. Through the 1960 season he allowed 405 walks in 692 innings, an average of 5.3 per nine innings. That problem was gone by 1965, when he allowed only 1.9 walks per nine innings and in 14 of his 27 complete games he walked no more than one batter.

On the award front, Sandy received the second of his three Cy Young awards in 1965, and it must be remembered that before 1967 there was only one Cy Young given each season, not one in each league as has been the case since. He also pitched one inning in that year's All-Star game and received credit for the win when the NL rallied in the seventh inning.

Big strikeout performances are always attention-getters, but Sandy's real domination is seen in the paltry number of opposition batters that he permitted to reach base. In 335 2/3 innings he allowed 216 hits, 71 bases on balls and hit five batters for an average of 5.8 hits and 7.8 runners per nine innings. To put that performance into perspective, note that the rest of the National League pitchers allowed 8.5 hits and 11.7 runners per nine innings in 1965 and in 1994 the two leagues combined for values of 9.1 hits and 12.8 runners per nine innings.

The National League had a collective .179 batting average against Koufax in 1965, an on base average of .227 and a slugging average of .279. Sandy was consistent throughout the year (his worst monthly ERA was 2.55 in August). In September and October, with the Dodgers fighting off the Giants on their way to an ultimate two-game margin at the end of the season, he appeared in 10 games, compiling a record of 5-2 (plus a save!) and an ERA of 1.51. He was especially dominant at Dodger Stadium, where he had an ERA of 1.38 in 20 starts and held the opposition to a batting average of .152 and an on base average of .196. If ever any pitcher generated ticket sales with an implicit guarantee of fans getting their money's worth, that pitcher was Koufax in 1965.

Courtesy - The Topps Company, Inc.

The 1965 season and the winter that followed were memorable for Sandy, the Dodgers, and all of baseball for two events that don't show up in the statistics. The first of these was the attack by Juan Marichal on John Roseboro and the other is the joint holdout by Koufax and Drysdale before the 1966 season.

On August 22 the Dodgers were in Candlestick for the finale of a four game showdown between the two league leaders. The pitching matchup was a publicist's dream and a fan's delight: Koufax versus Marichal on a sunny Sunday afternoon in a close pennant race.

Unfortunately that game will forever be remembered as the one in which Marichal hit Roseboro on the head with his bat in the third inning. Koufax came down from the mound to intercede and protect his catcher. *The Sporting News 1966 Baseball Guide* has a picture of the incident on page 19, showing Koufax holding up his bare hand to deflect the bats of Marichal and Tito Fuentes, although the latter did not land any blows. When the game resumed, with Roseboro and Marichal both replaced, Koufax had Roseboro's blood covering his pitching hand. He issued two walks and a home run to Willie Mays, effectively settling the issue. Although fights on the field are inevitable, this event thankfully remains the only occurrence of assault with a bat.

The development of the Players Association into a union and the use of agents to negotiate contracts are complicated issues today, and were strange ideas when Koufax and Drysdale, who had both pitched over 300 innings and between them accounted for 49 of the Dodgers' 97 wins, took the extraordinary step of entering into salary negotiations as a tandem. Furthermore, they informed the Dodgers that they would be represented by an agent. As surprising as it may seem today, the use of an agent to conduct salary negotiations was nearly unheard of at that time. In the end they signed separate contracts for substantial raises, each earning in the neighborhood of $125,000 for 1966. As Koufax points out in the book he wrote with Ed Linn in 1966, the most significant part of the whole process was that the Dodgers agreed to bargain with an agent for the first time in their history. It was also the first time the Dodgers had ever paid anyone a salary above the $100,000 barrier.

The 1965 season was certainly an eventful one for Sandy Koufax, both on the field and off. The Dodgers won three pennants in the four seasons from 1963-1966, and it is usually noted that superior pitching played a disproportionately important role. Unlike most world championship teams which pull together the right mix of pitching and hitting, the 1965 Dodgers were unquestionably weak on offense.

The 1965 team was seventh in batting average in the 10 team league. They were eighth in runs scored, surpassing only the Mets and the Astros. The team co-leaders in home runs had 12 each: rookie Jim Lefebvre and the much-traveled Lou Johnson, who joined the Dodgers for a Cinderella-like comeback season after Tommy Davis' terrible ankle break on May 1. Los Angeles was, however, the runaway leader in team ERA with a 2.81 mark and in fewest runs allowed, yielding 59 fewer than their nearest competitors, the Pirates, for a season average of 3.2 runs per game. There were other talented pitchers on the team, of course, notably Drysdale and Ron Perranoski, but Koufax was the ace of the staff in every sense. The esteem in which he was held may be seen in the last game of that year, the seventh game of the World Series against the Twins. Pitching on only two days rest, Sandy took Drysdale's spot in the rotation and pitched a three-hitter, striking out 10, for his second shutout in three days. His biggest season ended with a sharp exclamation point.

Note: Most of the information presented here comes from the files of Retrosheet (see appendix).

Juan Marichal - 1966

by Tony Blengino

W	L	PCT	G	GS	CG	SV	IP	SO	BB	B/I	ERA
25	6	.806	37	36	25	0	307	222	36	0.88	2.23

The word "bridesmaid" applied to both the San Francisco Giants and Juan Marichal, their star hurler, throughout the mid-to-late 1960's. No matter how well the Giants played or Marichal pitched, the Los Angeles Dodgers or St. Louis Cardinals and their star pitchers, Sandy Koufax and Bob Gibson, generally managed to stay a step ahead. Between 1963 and 1969, Marichal combined durability and impeccable control to accumulate an amazing 154-65 record, winning 20 games in six of those seven seasons. During that period, he somehow managed to avoid winning any MVP or Cy Young Awards, and the Giants finished in second place five times, third place once, and fourth place once, never bringing home any award hardware. Marichal's peak dominance coincided with the foremost pitcher-dominated era in the last half-century, so some of his statistics must be taken with a grain of salt. However, there was no arguing his brilliance in the aforementioned seven-year span, most especially in 1966, when he anchored the Giants' staff through a season-long three-way pennant race with the Dodgers and Pirates which would not be decided until the season's last day.

Juan Marichal came of age in the sweet summer of 1962, when the Giants outdueled the arch-rival Dodgers in a three-game playoff for the National League pennant, only to lose the World Series in seven games to the mighty Yankees. Marichal was only 24 that year, and won 18 games. In 1963, Marichal took another step up the ladder, closer to the Koufax level, as he went 25-8, with a 2.41 ERA. Koufax was even better, at 25-5, 1.88, as the Dodgers

won the World Series and the Giants finished third. In 1964, Marichal went 21-8, 2.48. However, the Giants could only manage to finish fourth, three games behind Bob Gibson and the Cards, who went on to win the World Series. Marichal was spectacular again in 1965, going 22-13, 2.13. Of course, Koufax and the Dodgers outdid them again, Koufax posting a 26-8, 2.04, record as the Dodgers nosed out the Giants by two games, and again went on to win the World Series. The 1965 pennant race was embellished by an incident which would dog Marichal throughout the remainder of his career. During a key late season game with the Dodgers, Marichal clubbed Dodgers' catcher Johnny Roseboro over the head with a bat after Roseboro buzzed his return throw to the pitcher a little too close to Marichal's head. The ensuing nine-day suspension (and unprecedented $1,750 fine) in the heat of the pennant race helped cook the Giants. The two strong, veteran teams were primed for another battle to the death in 1966.

In addition to the strong tradition of the rivalry between the Dodgers and Giants which extended back to their New York City days, the stark distinction between the styles in which these two teams played the game made the battles even more fascinating. The Dodgers were a run-and-gun, speed, pitching and defense kind of team. They finished next to last in the NL in homers in 1966 with 108. Their leading home run hitter was a middle infielder, Jim Lefebvre, with 24. In fact, all but two NL teams scored more runs than the Dodgers. They scraped for runs with the aid of an aggressive running game, unusual for the

1960's. Maury Wills stole 38 bases, and Willie Davis added another 21 as the Dodgers were second in the National League in steals. The Dodgers, however, were far above average defensively, and possessed an awesome pitching staff. Their team ERA of 2.62 was a run better than the league average of 3.61. Of course, they were anchored by Koufax, who had his one of his very best years, at 27-9, 1.73. Claude Osteen chipped in with a 17-14, 2.85 mark, covering up a disappointing 13-16 campaign for Don Drysdale. Phil "The Vulture" Regan, later the Baltimore Orioles' manager, was the bullpen ace, going 14-1, 1.62, with 21 saves in 117 relief innings.

The Giants, on the other hand, relied on the longball. Their one-two punch was delivered in the form of Willie Mays and Willie McCovey. McCovey finally had first base to himself thanks to the early season trade of Orlando Cepeda to the Cards, and he stepped up with a 36 homer, 96 RBI season. Mays contributed 37 home runs, 103 RBI, and a pair of more unlikely sources, third baseman Jim Ray Hart and catcher Tom Haller, chipped in with 33 and 27 homers, respectively. However, the Giants were seriously lacking team speed. Shortstop Tito Fuentes led the team with six steals, and as a group, the Giants stole only 29. The Giants also were weak defensively; their 168 errors trailed only the lowly Houston Astros. Their pitching staff was solid, but not at the Dodgers' level. Marichal posted a 25-6, 2.23, mark, and was joined by Gaylord Perry (21-8, 2.99) in the 20-win club. However, the acquisition of Ray Sadecki in the Cepeda trade, which was expected to vault the Giants into the Dodgers' class with regard to pitching, was a failure. Sadecki was 3-7, 5.40 as a Giant, allowing 164 baserunners in 105 innings.

The Giants and Dodgers were joined by the Pirates in a season-long thriller of a pennant race. As late as August 23, the Dodgers were mired in third place, three games behind both the Pirates and Giants. From that point forward, though, the Dodgers were virtually unbeatable. They racked up a seven game, and later a six game winning streak in September to assume control. They couldn't finish it off until the last day of the season, when guess who -- Koufax -- pitched the Dodgers to the pennant-clinching victory. No one

knew it at the time, but this was the last time the Giants and the rest of the National League would need to contend with Koufax, who announced his retirement after pitching the Dodgers to another World Series.

Unlike the previous season, no one in 1966 could point to Juan Marichal as the reason for the Giants' annual pennant race shortcomings. Marichal's .806 winning percentage (25-6) paced the league, and his figure of 7.9 baserunners allowed per nine innings to this day remains the best mark posted since 1915. He finished second in wins (Koufax led with 27), and complete games (25, to Koufax' 27), third in ERA (2.23; Koufax led at 1.73), and innings pitched (307; Koufax led with 323), fifth in strikeouts (222; Koufax led with 317). His strikeout/walk ratio was 222/36, enabling him to lead the National League in relative control/power factor (see appendix) with a 3.49 mark. Marichal allowed only 1.05 walks per nine innings, which remains the sixth-best figure posted since 1961.

For his career, Marichal posted a 243-142 (.631) mark. His winning percentage exceeded his teams' winning percentages by an impressive margin of .095. He posted a career ERA of 2.89 in a pitching-dominated era. His control was legendary. He posted a career 2303/709 strikeout/walk ratio in 3507 innings. He allowed only 1.82 walks per nine innings in his career, third best since 1961, behind Bret Saberhagen (1.68) and control artist Fritz Peterson (1.73). Marichal also managed to complete an amazing total of 244 of his 457 starts.

As with many young finesse pitchers, Marichal experienced a swift, painless decline phase when his marginal power broke down in his early 30's. In 1970, he struck out only 123 in 248 innings. Within two years, it was batting-practice time, as he went 6-16, with only 72 whiffs in 146 innings in 1972. At age 34, Marichal was about finished. Conversely, teammate Gaylord Perry, a power pitcher in his younger days, was able to successfully convert to a finesse pitcher (with the help of various abrasives and lubricants) and pitch well into his forties.

Though he was always in Koufax' or Gibson's shadow, Marichal did manage to lead the National League in various categories over his career. He led the NL twice in wins (1963, 1968), complete games (1964, 1968), shutouts (1965, 1969), innings (1963, 1968), and relative control/power factor (1966, 1967) and once in winning percentage (1966) and ERA (1969), but he never led in strikeouts. He was also somewhat obscured by his limited postseason experience. He had only one World Series outing, in 1962, following the dramatic playoff win over the Dodgers. He pitched four shutout innings in game four, then injured his finger trying to bunt, forcing him to leave the game. He returned to the playoffs in 1971, and pitched wonderfully in game three against the Pirates, only to lose 2-1 on solo homers by Bob Robertson and Richie Hebner. In both series, the Giants fell short.

Juan Marichal burst onto the baseball scene in 1960, pitching a one-hitter against the Phillies in his first major league start. He was famous for his high leg kick (which he abandoned for one start in 1963, resulting in a no-hitter against Houston), and was normally a fun-loving, friendly guy both on and off the field, though this is rarely remembered in the aftermath of the Roseboro incident. It appears to be his destiny to be known as the second or third-best pitcher in the National League during the '60's, despite the fact that he posted a 37-18 career mark against the hated Dodgers, 17-5 during Koufax' glory years of 1962 through 1966. Marichal was one of the most durable and precise pitchers of all time. It's no disgrace to be obscured by Sandy Koufax, in whose all-too-familiar shadow Marichal spent his signature 1966 season.

ORIOLES

FRANK ROBINSON outfield

Courtesy - The Topps Company, Inc.

Frank Robinson - 1966

by Bill Gilbert

G	AB	R	H	2B	3B	HR	RBI	BB	SO	AVG	OBP	SLG	SB
155	576	122	182	34	2	49	122	87	90	.316	.415	.637	8

Frank Robinson first emerged on the major league scene in 1956 as a 20-year-old Rookie-of-the-Year with the Cincinnati Reds. That year he tied Wally Berger's major league record for rookies with 38 home runs.

Robinson was one of an exceptional group of four Hall of Fame outfielders who arrived in the National League between 1951 to 1956. Willie Mays appeared first in 1951, followed by Hank Aaron in 1954, Roberto Clemente in 1955, and Robinson in 1956. Aaron, Mays and Robinson occupy the first, third and fourth spots on the all time home run list. Aaron is the leader of this group in home runs, runs batted in and runs. Clemente had the highest batting average, Mays had the highest slugging average and Robinson, the only one with a career batting average under .300, had the highest on base percentage, too.

Robinson played ten years in Cincinnati before being traded to Baltimore. During this period, he twice led the National League in runs scored and led the league once each in doubles and on base percentage. He led the league in slugging average for three straight years (1960, '61 and '62), but never led the league in any of the Triple Crown categories. Robinson was overshadowed by Aaron and Mays and, to some extent, Clemente. He did win the National League MVP award in 1961, leading the Reds to their first pennant in 21 years.

The trade of Robinson to the Orioles in December 1965 for pitchers Milt Pappas and Jack Baldschun

and outfielder Dick Simpson was viewed unfavorably in Cincinnati at the time. It turned out even worse than most expected for the Reds, as they tumbled from a respectable fourth place finish in 1965 to seventh in 1966.

Robinson's impact in Baltimore was immediate. The Orioles had been contenders for several years when Robinson arrived in 1966, but they had not yet reached the top. In 1965, they finished third, eight games behind Minnesota. In 1966, they were ahead by 13 games at the end of July and coasted to their first AL pennant, finishing nine games ahead of the Twins. Frank Robinson, Boog Powell and Brooks Robinson all reached the 100 RBI milestone. The Orioles crowned the season by upsetting the Los Angeles Dodgers in a four game sweep in the World Series, and Frank Robinson capped his dream season by being named the series MVP. Robinson became the first and only player to win the award in both leagues.

While the story of Baltimore's World Series win was pitching, Robinson provided some timely offense. He set the tone with a two-run homer off fellow Hall-of-Famer Don Drysdale in the top of the first inning of game one, and after that, the Orioles never trailed in a game throughout the series. In game four, Robinson hit another homer off Drysdale which was all the Orioles needed for a 1-0 series clinching victory.

Robinson's big season in 1966, after arriving in

Baltimore, ushered in a new era in the American League. The long-dominant Yankees had begun their descent, falling from first in 1964 to sixth in 1965, and landing with a thud in the cellar in 1966. The Orioles became the league's dominant team, winning the AL pennant four times in Robinson's six years with the club.

In the long history of baseball, only eight players have won the Triple Crown and also led their league in on base percentage and slugging average. Robinson in 1966 was one of them along with Nap Lajoie (1901), Ty Cobb (1909), Rogers Hornsby (1922 and 1925), Chuck Klein (1933), Lou Gehrig (1934), Ted Williams (1942 and 1947) and Carl Yastrzemski (1967). The only three players ahead of Robinson on the all-time home run list, Aaron, Babe Ruth and Mays, are noticeably absent.

In Robinson's case, there is no doubt about which was his greatest season. As the obvious best year in the career of one of the game's best players, it clearly ranks as one of the top seasons of all time. In addition to the individual accomplishments, Robinson's 1966 performance had as great an impact on his team and league as any season in recent memory.

After leaving Baltimore, Robinson played with the Dodgers, Angels and Indians before becoming a playing manager at Cleveland in 1975. The leadership he demonstrated when he came to Baltimore in 1966 was undoubtedly a factor in getting the managerial opportunity. He was the first black manager in the majors and later also managed the San Francisco Giants and the Orioles, before moving up to the O's front office.

Roberto Clemente - 1966

by Bill Gray

G	AB	R	H	2B	3B	HR	RBI	BB	SO	AVG	OBP	SLG	SB
154	638	105	202	31	11	29	119	46	109	.317	.363	.536	7

How do you measure this? Situation: Astros versus Pirates, 1964, Houston runners on first and second. The hitter blunders a bunt attempt, looping a pop-up toward second. But there's nobody near the ball! The second baseman is over by first, and the first baseman has charged in. The runner on second, Walter Bonds, breaks for third, looks back instinctively, and is shocked to see rightfielder Roberto Clemente behind second base, diving to get the ball. The runner accelerates, but Clemente scoops the ball and fires accurately to third. The runner is out. How do we measure that play? Just another assist? When Clemente was on the field, every play was "clutch" and no game was ever meaningless.

Clemente was nicknamed ''The Great One'' by Pirates broadcaster Bob Prince. Was it hype? Sure. Was Prince wrong? No. Was Clemente a great hitter? Yes. Did he hit a lot of home runs? No. Did he have power? Yes. Did he steal a lot of bases? No. Was he fast? Yes. Did he ever win a Gold Glove Award? Yes, thirteen in a row. Clemente was superb at everything. But how do we describe his throwing ability? Saying "superb" is faint praise. If any runner was foolish enough to test that arm, the throw by Clemente became a poison dart. Zip. Smack. Dead.

Joining the Pirates in 1955, the 20-year-old Clemente sized up Forbes Field, and decided it would be unwise to swing for home runs. Forbes' spacious outfield was made for line drives to right field and right center. That's just what Clemente did. Thorn and Palmer's *Total Baseball* defines Home Run Factor; a park HRF of 100 being the average park. The lower the HRF, the more difficult it is to hit home runs there. Forbes Field was a 69, near the all-time low. Willie Mays' Polo Grounds got a 170 rating. Hank Aaron played first in Milwaukee County Stadium, an 82, and then later in Atlanta's Fulton County Stadium, a very friendly 143.

As a contemporary of Mays, Aaron, and Mickey Mantle, Clemente's ''lack of power'' was always mentioned by his detractors. As he reached stardom in the early 1960's, writers often opined that Clemente wasn't quite in the same league as Willie, Hank, and Mickey. Clemente, his pride wounded by such writing, once exclaimed: ''The fans have seen me play ... they know the truth! If I listen to the writers, no matter what I do ... I must be the worst ballplayer ever!''

Clemente's presence in Pittsburgh revitalized a pathetic franchise. By 1958, the Pirates were a contender. In 1960 Pittsburgh won the World Series. Clemente hit .314 with 16 homers and 94 RBI during the regular season, and .310 in the World Series. Clemente won batting titles in 1961, 1964 and 1965, and became the team leader. A new manager, Harry Walker, arrived in 1965 and immediately treated Clemente like the star he was, something former manager Danny Murtaugh wouldn't do. The four-time batting champion had his finest seasons under Walker, who later reflected on those two and a half years, ''People always talked about the things he couldn't do, but he played for me.'' That's what he did: he *played*.

In 1966 Clemente led the Bucs through one of the most exhausting and exciting three-team pennant races in history. Pittsburgh acquired center fielder Matty Alou from the Giants. While Alou had once been productive for the Giants, he'd hit only .231 in 1965. Clemente and Walker, a batting champ himself, rebuilt Alou as a hitter. Walker told Alou, a lefty hitter, to stop pulling to right, use a heavier bat, and slap the ball to the opposite field. But Clemente went beyond advice. With Alou at the plate, Clemente spent hours in left field shagging balls for him, yelling "hit it at me!" It worked. Alou won the batting title with a .342 average, and was frequently on base for Clemente, Willie Stargell or Donn Clendenon.

Walker wanted Clemente to hit for more power, and took action when Clemente complained about the soft and sandy ground around the batter's box at Forbes Field. Walker ordered the sand replaced with good, hard clay. With solid footing, Clemente exploded. In Phil Musick's excellent, unvarnished biography of Clemente, *Who Was Roberto?* he noted after the batter's box was changed, Clemente "went on an immediate tear, hitting at a .414 clip and hammering six home runs during an eleven game homestand in June. Two of the home runs disappeared over the huge, iron exit gate in right-center field, 436 feet from home plate. No veteran observer could recall anyone hitting two home runs in that location."

The Pirates reached the 1966 All-Star break just a game out of first with a 52-33 record. The Dodgers, Pirates and Giants, led by Sandy Koufax, Clemente and Mays, respectively, battled into the season's final weekend. Koufax won his 27th game that week, and notched his third season with 300 strikeouts, a record. He also felt something pop in his shoulder. Mays, the 1965 MVP, hit his 37th homer, and Clemente hit numbers 28 and 29.

A rainout at Forbes Field on October 1st forced a Pirates-Giants Saturday doubleheader. In the crucial first game, Clemente accounted for all four Pirate runs, going 3-for-3 with a double, and a home run off 25-game winner Juan Marichal. But the Pirates lost in the 10th, 5-4. A one-hitter by Bob Bolin in the second game finally eliminated the Pirates

Unlike 1960 there was no lack of appreciation for Clemente. He'd carried his team almost to the top. He'd hit the home runs Walker wanted. And he did all the things only Clemente could do. On November 16th, Clemente received 218 MVP votes to 208 for Koufax. Mays was third with 111. That year marked the passing of an era. Koufax was forced to retire at 31. And Mays, at 35, had displayed all his magnificent skills for the last time; he began a long decline in 1967. Clemente meanwhile was gaining recognition as the best player in the game. He solidified his reputation in 1967 by winning his fourth batting title.

Injuries slowed Clemente in 1968, and he hit just .291. Retirement seemed a possibility to be faced soon, but he came back strong, hitting .345 and just missing his fifth batting title. In 1970 the 36-year-old Clemente hit .352. Still writers dogged the "old man" about retirement. "Let's see," said Clemente. "I hit .345 last year, and .350 this year. No, I don't think I want to quit now."

Pittsburgh faced Baltimore in the 1971 World Series, and Clemente took the spotlight. The world finally saw what we in Pittsburgh had been seeing since 1955, what Puerto Rico had seen even longer: a unique brilliance on the field, one man shaping a baseball game around his own unrelenting efforts and unmatched ability. At 37, he had lost nothing. Finally the world saw Clemente's game, and appreciated.

Rusty Staub: "He makes it all look so easy. He's great at everything. He just beats you and beats you at everything you can do in baseball. There is no player comparable to him."

Brooks Robinson said; "I thought he was great, but now that I've seen him more than I ever had, he's greater than I thought."

Don Buford: "When a guy gets older, you usually see him slow up, but not Clemente."

Dick Williams: "Clemente was the greatest player I have ever watched."

Measure that.

Orlando Cepeda - 1967

by Steven Rubio

G	AB	R	H	2B	3B	HR	RBI	BB	SO	AVG	OBP	SLG	SB
151	563	91	183	37	0	25	111	62	75	.325	.403	.524	11

Much has been written about Orlando Cepeda's popularity with young Giants fans when the team arrived in San Francisco in 1958. Willie Mays belonged to New York, a new local hero was required, and Cepeda delivered. Young (he was 20 years old when he hit the big leagues), good-looking and talented, the Baby Bull hit a massive home run on Opening Day (the first major-league game played on the West Coast) and never looked back. For the season, Cepeda hit .312 with 25 homers and 96 RBI, led the league in doubles, and was the unanimous choice for National League Rookie of the Year.

The 1959 season started just as auspiciously. In June he became the first player to blast a home run over the left field bleachers at Milwaukee's County Stadium, and in early July he played in his first All-Star game. But the Giants had a big talent at Triple A, future Hall-of-Famer Willie McCovey, and McCovey played first base. Mac was called up on July 30, and had one of the most celebrated debuts in Giants' history, going 4-for-4 and starting on the road to his own Rookie of the Year award.

The Giants spent the next five-and-a-half seasons trying to figure out how to get both young sluggers' bats in the lineup at the same time. Cepeda meanwhile had some great years. In 1961 he led the National League in home runs and RBI; in 1962 he helped the Giants to the World Series; he hit 30 or more homers four straight seasons (Bill James notes in his *Historical Abstract* that Cepeda was "the last man to be significantly ahead of [Hank] Aaron's home run pace

at any age"); and he was an All-Star every season from 1959 through 1964. In 1965 the McCovey-Cepeda shuffling became a non-issue when Cepeda suffered a serious knee injury, and missed most of the season.

In 1966, amid management grumbling that perhaps Cepeda wasn't trying hard enough to come back from that injury, he was traded to the Cardinals. Cepeda got hotter after going to St. Louis. In his first season there, he finished with a .301 average, played 142 games, and won the Comeback Player of the Year award. The stage was set for the greatest season of Cepeda's career, 1967.

Modern statistical analysis offers much of value to the intelligent baseball fan. In particular, the importance of getting on base (and the significance of on base percentage as an evaluative tool, as opposed to the older, more conventional measure of batting average). Also, the need to view RBI totals within the context of a team's entire offense has led many analysts to question the real value of offensive contributions from low-OBP, high-RBI sluggers like Joe Carter, for example.

Cepeda's career ended just before the widespread appreciation of "new" stats, and so during his career he was not subjected to the kind of statistical scrutiny and value assessments a player like Carter receives. Cepeda was a much better hitter than Carter, of course; while he didn't walk much, Cepeda's career OBP of .353 is very respectable, and his .499 lifetime

Courtesy - The Topps Company, Inc.

slugging percentage is more than respectable. Nevertheless, over time I have come to view my favorite player's career achievements as offering a good illustration of the fine line which separates the Hall of Famers from those who fall just short. I don't believe the Hall of Fame would be cheapened by Cepeda's presence, but it would be a shame if the only reason Orlando fell a few votes short was because of his post-career drug bust, unrelated to his on-field performance. I have never been able to state with assurance that I would vote for Cepeda for the Hall if given the vote, but that 1967 season surely belongs in a one-year hall of fame.

The 1967 Cardinals were one of the finest teams in baseball history. The pitching staff included future Hall-of-Famers Bob Gibson and Steve Carlton. Another future Hall of Famer, Lou Brock (like Cepeda, acquired through a lopsided trade) led the league with 52 steals and 113 runs scored while knocking 206 hits, including 12 triples and 21 home runs. Center fielder Curt Flood hit .335 while winning his fifth of seven straight Gold Gloves. A 29 year old rookie named Dick Hughes came out of nowhere to post a 16-6 record, leading the league in W-L Percentage. Even the fading star in right field made his share of important contributions; his name was Roger Maris.

Evidence of the team's greatness: at least three Hall of Famers and a noteworthy supporting cast on a team which won 101 games while running off with the NL pennant by 10 1/2 games; a team which went on to win the World Series that year from Boston, and would come within three innings of the seventh game of winning the Series again the following year. They were a great team. The leader of that team was Orlando Cepeda.

In 1967, Cepeda posted the highest on base percentage of his career. He led the National League in RBI, was second in the league in doubles, and was among the leaders in slugging and runs created. And Cepeda was best at things the MVP voters notice most: in addition to the RBI title, he was the clubhouse leader on a pennant-winning team.

What happened in the 1967 MVP vote was remarkable, and speaks volumes about why Cepeda might be considered Hall-of-Fame material. Just look at the competition: Roberto Clemente, the 1966 MVP, hit .357 to lead the league. He also led the league in hits with 209, was an All-Star for the eighth straight season, and won his seventh consecutive Gold Glove (leading the league's outfielders in assists). His slugging percentage was 30 points higher than Cepeda's.

Dick Allen led the league in on base percentage and was second in slugging, beating Orlando in both categories. He hit .307 and stole 20 bases in 25 attempts. Hank Aaron led the league in home runs, runs scored, and slugging. He was an All-Star for the 13th straight season, hitting .307 and knocking in 109 runs. Ron Santo, the "*Total Baseball* MVP" based on overall ranking, would have been the darling of the stat-heads, if we'd known who we were in the late-sixties. The Gold Glove winner set a record for assists by a third baseman (since broken) with 393, led the league in bases on balls while compiling a .401 on-base percentage, was among the league leaders in home runs and total bases, and hit .300.

Given the above information, when the ballots for league MVP were counted, it turned out that every voter had placed the same name at the top: Orlando Cepeda. As Bill James put it, "You've got to respect that."

Cepeda's numbers weren't as good as some in that summer of 1967, though they were plenty good. Similarly, his career numbers aren't as good as some, though they too are plenty good. If I had to choose one piece of non-statistical information to finalize my evaluation of the career of Orlando Cepeda, I think that 1967 MVP vote should carry more weight than the substance law problem, for which he long ago paid the price.

For one year, with no doubt whatsoever, Orlando Cepeda was the best player in the National League.

Carl Yastrzemski - 1967

by John Benson

G	AB	R	H	2B	3B	HR	RBI	BB	SO	AVG	OBP	SLG	SB
161	579	112	189	31	4	44	121	91	69	.326	.421	.622	10

No scriptwriter could pen a better story: a four-way pennant race, down to the wire (in days when a pennant race meant something, and "clinching a playoff berth" was a phrase decades away from the game of baseball). America watched, and large numbers nationwide embraced the underdog Boston team, ninth-place finishers in 1966. Fans everywhere called it The Great Race; in Boston they called it The Impossible Dream.

The force that transformed 21 years of painful reality into one summer of magical fantasy was the 27-year-old left fielder who had stepped into the void left by Ted Williams in 1961. Carl Yastrzemski was signed as a shortstop out of Notre Dame. He reached the majors quickly, but in his first six big league seasons never passed 20 home runs or reached 100 runs scored or driven-in. Then suddenly in 1967 it all came together for him. Yaz had spent the winter lifting weights, and when the season opened, his line drives were clearly going farther faster, and many of his long flies were landing on the far side of American League fences.

The arrival of Yastrzemski lifted his teammates, too. Pitcher Jim Lonborg, who had never won more than ten games in a season (and would never win more than ten again for the Red Sox before leaving after 1971) surged to 22 victories and led the league in strikeouts in 1967. George Scott, age 23, and Rico Petrocelli, 24, solidified a young infield that also included rookie Mike Andrews at second base and 24-year-old Joe Foy at third.

In addition to Yastrzemski, the outfield featured a pair of 22-year-olds in Reggie Smith and Tony Conigliaro, the latter playing in only 95 games before a Jack Hamilton fastball ended his season. But there were positives to offset such losses. Elston Howard came over from the Yankees and solidified the catching. Jerry Adair, acquired from Chicago in June, provided depth at the infield skill positions, and hit .291 for Boston after batting just .204 for the White Sox early in the year. Gary Bell, a 30-year-old starter, left a 1-5 record behind him in Cleveland and went 12-8 for Boston while chipping in three saves in five relief appearances. Veteran John Wyatt anchored the pen with 20 saves. Simply stated, everything clicked for a team that had no business contending with the much-favored Tigers of Norm Cash, Al Kaline, Denny McLain, Mickey Lolich, and company (but their year was yet to come).

The real story was Yaz himself, however. Especially late in the season, through that marvelous four-way stretch run, Yastrzemski surpassed himself. In the final dozen games he hit .523, and he gave definition to the phrase "timely hitting." He scored 14 times and drove in 16 runners in those last 12 games.

After Chicago dropped both ends of a doubleheader on September 27, three teams remained. The Twins were one game ahead going into the incredible final weekend. On Saturday the Tigers split a doubleheader with California, falling a half game off the pace, while Boston overcame an injury-shortened start by Jim Kaat and got to the Twins relief corps for a 6-4 victory and a tie for first. On Sunday the Red Sox won again, behind Lonborg, eliminating Minnesota. But the Tigers had yet another doubleheader with the Angels on that final day; Detroit won their first game, and one more Tiger win would end the season with Boston and Detroit locked in an even 92-70 tie for the year. But the Angels finally pulled one out and helped Boston to their first pennant since 1946. The Impossible Dream had come true.

Where was Yastrzemski during this final drama? In those last two games versus the Twins, he merely went seven for eight, with five runs batted in. His three-run homer in the Saturday game capped the Boston victory, and a shockingly strong throw, cutting down Bob Allison at second base, punctuated the Twins' undoing in 1967.

In the World Series against the Cardinals of Bob Gibson, Lou Brock, Curt Flood, and Orlando Cepeda, the Red Sox were again cast in the role of underdogs, but again Yastrzemski elevated his team to incredible heights. He hit .400, led both teams with three home runs and an .840 slugging percentage, and collected two assists in the field (the Cardinals outfielders as a group had none). All that work was enough to maintain a 3-3 tie after six games, but an overworked Lonborg simply couldn't do the job in game seven, losing to a better-rested Gibson.

When the dust settled after a season that was arguably the most exciting and most-followed of all time, Yastrzemski had won a Triple Crown while also leading his league in hits, runs, total bases, and slugging. He fell one vote short of unanimous election as Most Valuable Player (The versatility of the Twins' Cesar Tovar, who hit .267 with six homers, had apparently impressed one writer quite immensely) but there was no dissent whatsoever in public opinion. There was no argument about who was MVP in 1967. It was Yaz.

Captain Carl won three batting titles, including his .301 mark in 1968 (the lowest average ever to lead a league) that remains as ''proof'' that the pitcher's mound had to be lowered. He starred in the 1975 LCS and World Series, went four-for-four with two walks in the 1970 All-Star game, and amassed records making him easily worthy of his own media guide. Overall it was durability and consistency that made him special, not flashy achievements. Although his career lasted 23 years and crossed many milestones, there was never again anything like his 1967 season. He made a hundred-to-one shot come true, as you would expect to happen about once in every century.

Bob Gibson - 1968

by Marc Bowman

W	L	PCT	G	GS	CG	SV	IP	SO	BB	B/I	ERA
22	9	.710	34	34	28	0	304	268	62	0.88	1.12

Ask a baseball fan to name the best single season pitching performance of all time and the answer will almost always be "Bob Gibson, 1968," and many will top it off with "1.12." Gibson's 1.12 ERA was one of the very best in baseball history and stands out as an example of his mastery that year. But, it is hardly the only thing that makes his 1968 performance memorable.

The 1968 St. Louis Cardinals were defending a World Series championship, which was largely due to three complete game victories by Gibson over the Boston Red Sox in the 1967 series. Nevertheless, the Cards were anything but a dominant team in 1968.

The St. Louis offense was led by Lou Brock, the league's stolen base champion, and Curt Flood, one of only five National League hitters to reach the .300 mark in batting average. It was an offense fueled by speed; while the Cardinals' 73 homers were eighth best in the ten team National League, they stole 110 bases in 1968, second only to Pittsburgh's 130.

In their championship year of 1967, the Cardinals scored 695 runs, placing slightly behind the league-leading offense of the Cubs who tallied 702 runs. A year later St. Louis managed just 583 runs, tied with the Pirates for fourth, far behind the Reds' pace of 690 runs scored. The Cards great speed improved an otherwise mediocre offense, but more than anything else they relied on strong pitching to repeat as Senior Circuit champions in 1968.

In addition to Gibson, the Cardinals rotation sported 19-game winner Nelson Briles, Ray Washburn and a young lefty on his way to the Hall-of-Fame, Steve Carlton. The Cardinals' team ERA of 2.49 was the best by any National League team since 1919. But it was Gibson's performance that shines above all.

Gibson was known as a fireballer who was unafraid to pitch inside. His overpowering fastball was intimidating, but he also displayed uncanny control for such a hard thrower. Gibson walked just 62 in his 305 innings, less than two per game. Only Juan Marichal posted a better strikeout/walk ratio than Gibson's 4.3-to-1. Gibson led the league in many pitching categories, including strikeouts, ERA, shutouts, opponent batting average (.184) and opponent on base percentage (.233). Only the Cardinals' sometimes-sputtering offense prevented him from matching Marichal for the league lead in victories; Gibson got less than three runs support per game in 1968.

Once he got rolling, Gibson was unstoppable. At one point he strung together fifteen straight wins including a streak of ten games during which he allowed just two earned runs. With a small bit of luck it could have been zero earned runs in ten games.

After hurling five straight shutouts, Gibson allowed a run on a wild pitch. Then, following another whitewashing, he allowed one more run on a slicing double that landed just fair down the left field line. Gibson finished the string with two more shutouts,

compiling a total of 95 innings during which he allowed just two earned runs.

Gibson completed 28 of his 34 starts while posting that 1.12 ERA, the best mark since 1914 when the Red Sox' Dutch Leonard led the American League with a 0.96 ERA. Thirteen times Gibson shut out his opponents; only one pitcher in this century managed more shutouts in a season: Pete Alexander in 1916 posted sixteen whitewashings in 45 starts.

With a flair for the dramatic, Gibson saved his best for last. Coasting to a nine game bulge over Marichal's Giants for the National League crown, Gibson's Cardinals entered the World Series against the Detroit Tigers who were led by the cocky Denny McLain and a very potent offense. Baseball fans greatly anticipated pitching duels between Gibson and 31-game winner McLain.

Gibson helped the Cardinals take a three-games-to-one lead by beating McLain 4-0 and 10-1 with a pair of five-hitters; Gibson himself homered in the game four rout. Mickey Lolich kept the Tigers in the series by hurling complete game victories in games two and five, setting up a series finale between Gibson and himself. They matched goose-eggs into the seventh inning when a misplayed Jim Northrup triple highlighted a three-run seventh inning and led the Tigers to a 4-1 victory and the 1968 championship. Both Lolich and Gibson went the distance and both finished the series with 1.67 ERA's. Gibson fanned 35 Tigers in the series including 17 in the opening game shutout, breaking two World Series records.

It would be Gibson's last World Series showing and capped a post-season record of 7-2 with a 1.89 ERA. He allowed just 55 hits while striking out 92 in nine World Series appearances, all complete games.

More than just a great pitcher, Gibson was a complete player; he was a fine fielder who also handled the bat well. Over his 17-year career he batted .206 with 24 homers and earned nine straight Gold Gloves from 1965 to 1973. Gibson won election to the Hall of Fame in 1981, six years after his 1975 retirement.

In 1968 post-season balloting, Gibson was unanimously selected for the Cy Young award, then won the MVP over NL batting champion Pete Rose and home run champ Willie McCovey. (Gibson would win the Cy Young award again in 1970.)

However, the most significant event to result from this phenomenal year of pitching in 1968 occurred well after postseason honors had been awarded. Runs, batting averages and earned run averages had been steadily decreasing over the previous decade, culminating in the most frugal offensive year since the end of the dead ball era. Indicative of this trend were the 339 shutouts in 1968. Mid-September saw back-to-back no-hitters in games between the Cardinals and Giants. Don Drysdale set a consecutive shutout innings streak with 58 and two-thirds scoreless frames. Gibson had combined with Marichal, McLain, Lolich, and Drysdale to help create the "Year of the Pitcher".

Pitchers appeared to have the upper hand, and the rules committee hoped to reverse the anemic hitting trend. Two rules were amended: the height of the pitching rubber was reduced from fifteen inches to just ten inches, while the strike zone was reduced from the top of the batter's shoulders to the armpits. The effect was profound if not immediate; two years later offense had increased by more than a run per game.

In the Year of the Pitcher, Gibson was the pitcher of the year. Only Dwight Gooden in 1985 and Greg Maddux in 1994 have approached Gibson's 1.12 ERA. Using Pete Palmer's Total Pitcher Index ranking, Gibson's '68 season was the ninth best since the end of the dead ball era, tied with Gooden's '85 campaign and just marginally ahead of Maddux' 1994 season. Yet, to many baseball fans, Bob Gibson's performance in 1968 was simply the best ever.

DENNY
McLAIN

PITCHER
TIGERS

Courtesy - The Topps Company, Inc.

Denny McLain - 1968

by Tony Blengino

W	L	PCT	G	GS	CG	SV	IP	SO	BB	B/I	ERA
31	6	.838	41	41	28	0	336	280	63	0.92	1.96

Following the 1969 season, Denny McLain seemingly had the baseball world by the tail. Only 25 years old, he already had a 30-win season under his belt, and had accumulated a 114-57 career won-lost record. At the same age, Cy Young was 72-41, Lefty Grove was 10-12, and Warren Spahn was 8-5.

McLain was a durable four-pitch hurler who appeared to be built for the long haul. He was a controversial loose cannon off the field, but the general consensus was that he was a harmless playboy who would stay on the right side of the fine line between the good life and the dark side. The unseen reality, however, was that McLain had been developing bad habits and keeping bad company.

Though some of the seeds of his eventual decay had already been planted before the 1968 season, they were far removed from that magical season when he led the Tigers on a delightful ride to a World Championship, and ensured himself of baseball immortality by becoming the first pitcher since 1934 to win 30 games.

The 1967 season had ended on a sour note for the Tigers, as they were nosed out for the AL pennant on the last day of the season by the Red Sox. It was a particularly bitter end for McLain, who lost 8-5 to the Angels in that final, critical game. McLain's 17-16 campaign in 1967 was disappointing in comparison to his 16-6 rookie year in 1965 and a 20-win season in 1966. A trend toward pitcher dominance had been developing in both leagues during the mid-to-late sixties, and this trend accelerated dramatically in 1968. Partly due to the general surge in pitching prowess, the 1968 Tigers became the only offensive league-leading team ever to bat as low as .235. They also lacked speed, stealing only 26 bases all year. But this team had power. They scored 671 runs, a full 57 runs better than any other team, and they smashed 185 homers, 52 more than the next best team. Left fielder Willie Horton led the way, batting .285 with 36 home runs, and 85 RBI, and he was supported by catcher Bill Freehan (.263, 25 homers, 84 RBI), right fielder Jim Northrup (.264, 21 home runs, 90 RBI), first baseman Norm Cash (.263, 25 homers, 63 RBI) and second baseman Dick McAuliffe (.249, 16 home runs, 56 RBI, and a league-leading 95 runs scored).

The Tigers were well positioned in the pitching department, with a durable four-man rotation of McLain, Mickey Lolich, Earl Wilson and Joe Sparma. The hefty lefty Lolich was a solid number two starter, going 17-9 with a 3.19 ERA, but the story during the regular season was McLain. The Tigers and McLain led the American League from the beginning in 1968. McLain possessed an above average fastball, curve, changeup and slider, and he threw each from three different release points. He won his 20th game before the end of July.

With the Tigers leading the AL by a wide margin, talk quickly turned to the far-fetched notion that this guy McLain might actually win 30 games, something that hadn't been accomplished in the majors since Dizzy Dean did it in 1934, winning 30 precisely.

The Tigers clinched the AL pennant with over two weeks left to play, and McLain had by now accumulated 28 wins, with four starts remaining. Like clockwork, McLain cashed in win number 29, against only five losses, setting him up for his first crack at win number 30, a nationally televised Saturday afternoon home game against the Oakland A's. The A's were by far the youngest team in the AL, and were just starting to form the nucleus of their early-1970's dynasty, with Reggie Jackson, Bert Campaneris, Sal Bando, and Catfish Hunter, all aged 26 or younger. McLain didn't have his best stuff against the A's. He fell behind 2-0 in the fourth on a two-run homer by the 22-year-old Jackson. In the bottom half of the inning, Norm Cash struck back, nailing a three-run homer, chasing A's starter Chuck Dobson, to give the Tigers a 3-2 lead. The lead was short-lived, as Campaneris' RBI single tied the score at three in the fifth. McLain then settled down, and he and A's reliever Diego Segui traded zeroes until the ninth. Jackson put the A's back in front in the top of the ninth with a solo homer, meaning that a dramatic ninth inning comeback would be the only way for McLain to prevail on the national TV stage. Veteran Al Kaline, pinch-hitting for McLain, led off the ninth with a walk. After McAuliffe fouled out, center fielder Mickey Stanley stroked a single, moving Kaline around to third. A's Manager Bob Kennedy elected to stay with Segui, figuring that the sinkerballer was their best bet to induce a game-ending double play ball. Northrup did hit the ball on the ground, but it was a slow dribbler to third baseman Danny Cater, who threw the ball away in his haste to cut down the tying run at the plate. Kaline scored, and Stanley made it all the way to third with some aggressive baserunning. Kennedy let Segui continue, and let him pitch to Willie Horton rather than allow an intentional walk to set up a potential double play. Horton drilled a line shot over the pulled-in outfield to plate the winning run and make McLain a baseball immortal. He had given up four runs on this day, but had allowed only six hits, walked only one, and had ten well-placed strikeouts.

In his last two starts, McLain won one and lost one, and wound up with a 31-6 record (leading the AL in wins and in winning percentage). His 1.96 ERA was fourth best, behind Luis Tiant's 1.60. McLain also led the AL in starts, complete games (28), and innings, and finished second to Sam McDowell in strikeouts, just three short of the league lead. For his efforts, McLain swept both the AL Cy Young and MVP awards in unanimous votes. The 103-59 Tigers coasted to the pennant, beating out the emerging Orioles by twelve games. Next came the Cardinals in the World Series.

McLain got the nod in Series game one in St. Louis, and was the victim of a dominant performance by Cards' starter Bob Gibson, who tossed a five-hitter and notched 17 strikeouts in pacing the Cards to a 4-0 win. Lolich got the Tigers even in game two, hitting a homer and pitching a complete-game, 8-1 win. After the Cards jumped back ahead with a 7-3 win, the Tigers again called on McLain in game four, and he didn't last three innings. Gibson whiffed ten, hit a homer of his own, and led the Cards to a 10-1 win, giving St. Louis a commanding 3-1 series lead. Savior Lolich bought the Tigers and McLain another day with a 5-3 complete-game win in game five.

The Cards elected to save Gibson for a potential seventh game, instead using Ray Washburn in game six against McLain. Big mistake. By the third inning, it was 12-0 Tigers. McLain cruised to a 13-1, complete-game victory. It was now Lolich versus Gibson for all the marbles, and Lolich prevailed, earning his third Series victory by a 4-1 score.

McLain was excellent again in 1969, posting a 24-9 mark and sharing the Cy Young Award with the Orioles' Mike Cuellar, as the Tigers finished a distant second to the O's in the AL East in the first year of divisional play. McLain had now led the AL in wins and innings pitched for two consecutive seasons, and added the 1969 AL shutouts lead to his growing list of accomplishments. McLain had also continued his outrageous commentary, which seemingly spared no one. He called himself "the greatest pitcher in the world," his teammates "a country-club team," and the Tiger fans "the worst in the world" (though he later recanted that statement). However, the offseason brought some developments which would no longer allow baseball to smile at McLain's antics and look the other way.

New Commissioner Bowie Kuhn launched an investigation into McLain's involvement in a bookmaking operation at a bar in Flint, Michigan. McLain admitted investing $5,700 in the operation, and was suspended by Kuhn for the first half of the 1970 season. But there was more. A *Sports Illustrated* article alleged that McLain had failed to pay out $46,600 on a winning bet late in the 1967 season, and had his toes broken by a mob henchman as punishment. The injury kept him out of at least two starts late in the 1967 pennant race. The toe-breaking mobster's brother allegedly then placed huge bets on the Red Sox to win the pennant - and against the Tigers in the season's last game, which was started by McLain. He was never accused of betting on baseball, or of conspiring to fix games, but he was too close to the center of this storm.

As a pitcher, he was never the same. McLain returned in the second half of 1970 woefully overweight and about a yard short on his fastball. His off-the-field conduct remained a problem, and he was suspended twice more. The Tigers gave up on him, trading him to the Senators before the 1971 season. He went 10-22 in 1971, and then bounced through Oakland and Atlanta in 1972, posting ERA's over 6.00 in both locales. That was it. He was done as a player at age 28. After the suspension, his total won/lost mark was a dismal 17-34.

McLain's troubles, however, were far from over. In 1985, he was found guilty of various racketeering and drug offenses, and spent some time in prison. McLain's legal problems gave baseball history an unfortunate bridging of the gap between the old-time ballplayers' occasional problems associating with gamblers, and the modern ballplayers' ongoing difficulties involving drugs.

The Denny McLain story is a sobering reminder that sports journalists are prone to use words like "superhuman" and "immortal" too freely. The performance and statistics of young Denny McLain in 1968 were indeed monumental. Maybe they will last forever, within the context of sports performance. But the person behind the numbers was very human indeed, and very mortal, a lesson for today's best athletes to learn from.

Harmon Killebrew - 1969

by Tony Blengino

G	AB	R	H	2B	3B	HR	RBI	BB	SO	AVG	OBP	SLG	SB
162	555	106	153	20	2	49	140	145	84	.276	.430	.584	8

Idaho Senator Herman Welker once tipped off the Washington Senators owner, Clark Griffith, about a young pitching prospect named Vernon Law, and Griffith didn't listen. When Welker again touched base with Griffith and told him of a young Idaho-born slugger named Killebrew, Griffith bit. After four years of shuttling between the minors and the nation's capital, Killebrew arrived on the American League scene with a flourish, tying Rocky Colavito for the league home run lead in his first full season in 1959. For the next dozen years, Killebrew enjoyed a legendary power rampage.

Despite the fact that Harmon Killebrew ranks fifth on the all-time home run list (with 573), some baseball historians have a hard time ranking him among baseball's all-time greats. "Just a power hitter ... too one-dimensional," they say.

Killebrew was indeed one-dimensional, but power is a fairly important dimension, to understate the case. Killebrew was a bit below average defensively at first base, third base, and in the outfield, and he lacked speed. However, he managed to hit over 40 homers eight times in a 13-year span, drive in 100 or more runs nine times, and draw huge numbers of walks out of sheer respect (i.e. fear) from pitchers. The foremost of his many great seasons was 1969, when ''Killer'' led the Minnesota Twins to the AL West title in the first year of divisional play.

The 1969 Twins were an extremely well-rounded ballclub. Their pitching staff was solid, taking a back seat only to the mighty Orioles in the AL. Minnesota had two 20-game winners, Jim Perry (20-6, 2.82) and Dave Boswell (20-12, 3.23), as well as the reliable Jim Kaat (14-13, 3.50). Their bullpen was anchored by Ron Perranoski, who led the AL with 31 saves while fashioning an impressive 2.10 ERA. The Twins' offense scored 790 runs to lead the American League. They also paced the circuit in hits, batting average, on base percentage and doubles, and possessed good power and speed. Tony Oliva batted .309, led the league in hits (197), and nailed 24 homers with 101 RBI. The multipositional Cesar Tovar batted .288 and finished third in the league with 45 steals, and young second baseman Rod Carew won his first of many batting titles with a .332 mark. It was the mighty Killebrew, though, who was the unquestioned centerpiece of this offensive juggernaut.

After his injury-plagued 1968 season, it was feared that the 33-year-old Killebrew was in decline. No questions remained after 1969, however. Killebrew played 162 games and led the AL in homers, RBI, on base percentage and walks. He finished third in slugging percentage, fourth in runs scored, and third in relative production; in these last three categories he trailed a blossoming 23-year-old slugger named Reggie Jackson.

For their fine season, the 1969 Twins won the privilege of meeting Baltimore in the first-ever ALCS. The Orioles were emerging as a dynasty. Earl Weaver was in his first full season as their manager. The O's pitching staff was beginning a five-year reign with the league's best ERA, and in 1969 they were almost a full run below the league average. With hitting that included Boog Powell and Frank Robinson, defense featuring Brooks Robinson, and pitching that featured Jim Palmer, Mike Cuellar, and Dave McNally, they swept their division by 19 games, tallied 109 victories, and despite losing the World Series in a letdown reminiscent of the 1954 Indians, earned a place among the greatest teams of all time.

The Twins nonetheless led 3-2 entering the bottom of the 9th of Game 1, and brought in closer Perranoski to nail it down for Perry. Boog Powell spoiled the party, tying the game with a homer, sending it into extra innings. The Twins' own up-and-coming manager, Billy Martin, rode Perranoski all the way into the 12th, when he was beaten by Paul Blair's two-out squeeze bunt. In Game 2, Boswell and McNally engaged in a spectacular pitching duel, tossing blanks at each other through ten innings. McNally kept his shutout intact through the 11th, but Boswell gave way to a tired Perranoski with two outs and the winning run on second in the 11th. Pinch hitter Curt Motton earned a day of fame with the game-winning single that scored Boog Powell. The two gut-wrenching losses were too much for the Twins. They had nothing left for Game 3 back in Minnesota, and were annihilated 11-2 in the clincher.

Notice the absence of the name ''Killebrew'' in the story of the first ALCS. The Killer managed only a double in eight RBI-less at bats, though he walked six times. The O's had elected to let someone other than Killebrew beat them, and no one else could.

The disappointing postseason of 1969 couldn't prevent Killebrew from earning his only MVP award for his regular season exploits. Killebrew's only other postseason performances, in 1965 and 1970, were better than his 1969 disappointment. In 1965, he hit .286 with a homer, two RBI, and six walks. In the 1970 rematch against the Orioles (Baltimore won with total scoring of 27-10) Killebrew was a lone bright spot, launching two homers.

For his career, Killebrew had more home runs per at bat than anyone except Babe Ruth and Ralph Kiner. Hank Aaron and Willie Mays accumulated larger career totals than Killebrew because they remained extremely productive until age 39, while Killebrew tailed off dramatically after age 36. For a dozen seasons, though, the Killer enjoyed a power roll matched only by the Babe himself. Killebrew hit 45 or more homers in four consecutive seasons (1961-64) and five times overall (including 1969). Both feats were bettered only by Ruth. Building on power and walks, Killebrew was productive enough to be ranked as the 37th best player ever, both for his career and for peak value, in Bill James' *Historical Abstract.*

Killebrew's .256 career batting average is the lowest in the 500-homer club, and he is one of only three players in history (along with Darrell Evans and Gorman Thomas) ever to hit 40 homers in a season and bat below .250. However, Killebrew's ability to draw a walk made him an above-average on base performer. His .379 career OBP was better than Hank Aaron's .377 mark, and Aaron had a .305 career batting average.

Killebrew hit homers, and he drew walks. Basically, he created runs, which is what the game is all about. Few did it better. In 1969, he led one of modern baseball's most well-rounded offenses into the postseason in the first year of divisional play.

Willie McCovey - 1969

by Tony Blengino

G	AB	R	H	2B	3B	HR	RBI	BB	SO	AVG	OBP	SLG	SB
149	491	101	157	26	2	45	126	121	66	.320	.458	.656	0

Willie McCovey was one of baseball's preeminent sluggers in one of the most pitcher-dominated eras of all time. He reached his zenith in 1969, at age 31. McCovey was young enough to expect that he would enjoy several more highly productive years, but as events unfolded he would have only two more full and healthy seasons.

1969 was the first year of divisional play, and featured the inaugural seasons of the Montreal Expos, San Diego Padres, Kansas City Royals and Seattle Pilots. Along with the rule change lowering the height of the pitcher's mound that same season, expansion diluted major league pitching. Nevertheless, it was still an era of pitcher dominance. In 1968, the National League batted .243, with a .302 on-base percentage and .341 slugging percentage. The 1969 offensive "explosion" lifted the league batting average up to .250, the on base percentage to .321, and the slugging percentage to .369. In the midst of this unfriendly environment, Willie McCovey had his career year.

McCovey was never known as a high average hitter. In 1969, he posted the only .300+ season of his career. His .320 average was good for fifth in the National League (Pete Rose led at .348). McCovey led the National League in homers and RBI, while achieving his personal career highs in both categories. He had a large enough number of walks to lead the league in both on base percentage and slugging. His relative production was a massive 212, which still ranks as the highest single season mark since 1957. At the end of the year, he was named the National

League MVP for the only time in his career.

Despite McCovey's tour de force, the Giants possessed only an average offense in 1969, ranking fourth in runs (713), and tied for seventh in average (.242). They were carried by McCovey and center fielder Bobby Bonds, then in his first full season. Bonds complemented McCovey with 32 homers, 90 RBI, 45 steals, a league-leading 120 runs, and a National League-high 187 strikeouts. The other regulars were much less potent, including 38-year old Willie Mays, who batted .283 with only 13 homers and 58 RBI. Starting pitchers Juan Marichal and Gaylord Perry were absolutely wonderful, combining for a 40-25 record and 2.31 ERA -- in an amazing 625 innings. However, much like the 1994 Giants of Barry Bonds, Matt Williams, John Burkett and Bill Swift, the Giants' roster was very strong at the top, and weak in the middle and bottom. The end result was a 90-72 record and a second place finish, three games behind the Atlanta Braves.

For his career, McCovey hit 521 homers, good enough to tie for 10th on the all-time list. He finished with 1,555 RBI (28th), a .270 career average, .377 on base percentage, .515 slugging percentage (32nd), and career relative production of 148 (four-way tie for 29th with Harry Heilmann, Ralph Kiner and Sam Thompson).

Compared to players with similar career numbers, McCovey led the league in specific offensive categories relatively infrequently. He led the National

League three times in homers (1963, '68, '69), slugging percentage (1968, '69, '70) and relative production (1968, '69, '70), and once in walks (1970) and on base percentage (1969). McCovey was extremely patient at the plate, and was actually quite difficult to strike out for a player with such power, as evidenced by his 1555/1345 strikeout/walk ratio. However, for a player with such lofty lifetime totals, McCovey had a material impact on relatively few seasons. He had enough at bats to qualify for the batting title only eight times, due to platooning early, and injuries late in his career. It is a wonderful puzzle to consider the numbers he could have amassed if he had assumed the Giants' first base job full-time upon his promotion to the majors in 1959, and held onto it, remaining healthy through his last productive season in 1979.

It was midway through the 1959 season when the Giants recalled the 21-year-old McCovey from Phoenix of the Pacific Coast League, where he had been tutored by Ted Williams. McCovey was an instant sensation, winning the Rookie of the Year Award despite appearing in only 52 games, in which he hit .354 with 13 home runs, 38 RBI, a .431 on base percentage and .656 slugging percentage. To make room for McCovey in the lineup, the Giants moved fellow 21-year-old rookie first baseman Orlando Cepeda to left field. However, McCovey played himself out of the position in 1960, winding up back in the minor leagues. In 1961 and 1962, the lefthanded McCovey and righthanded Cepeda platooned at first, with Cepeda moving to left field when McCovey entered the lineup. McCovey made the last out of Game 7 of the 1962 World Series, on a screaming liner to Yanks' second baseman Bobby Richardson.

The man they called "Stretch" had his coming-out party in 1963, when he smashed 44 homers (38 of them against righties) as a left fielder to lead the National League in his first season as a full-timer. McCovey was plagued by an assortment of injuries in 1964, and then got his big break for playing time when his good friend Cepeda suffered a serious knee injury in 1965. Early in the 1966 season, the Giants finally addressed the issue of the duplication of skills possessed by Cepeda and McCovey by dealing the

Baby Bull Cepeda to St. Louis, for the meager return of Ray Sadecki. Between 1965 and 1970, McCovey nailed 187 homers, and was basically injury-free. A bad knee injury in 1971 sent him on a downward spiral. Between 1971 and 1976, he never had enough at bats to qualify for the batting title, and recorded unhelpful batting averages as low as .204 (in 1976) and .213 (in 1972).

McCovey had one more highlight left in his long career. Realizing little or no success after leaving the Giants prior to the 1973 season, McCovey came home to wind down his career in 1977. Much to the surprise of the Giants, this sentimental journey became a very productive one, too. He stayed healthy all year, and won the Comeback Player of the Year Award, batting .280 with 28 home runs, 86 RBI, a .369 on base percentage and .500 slugging percentage. The quiet, seldom-quotable McCovey showed his tender side when he wept openly upon his return to his beloved San Francisco. Always overshadowed by Mays in his previous tour with the Giants, McCovey finally had the stage to himself at age 39, and he did not disappoint.

You will find the name of Willie McCovey near names like Ted Williams, Mike Schmidt and Lou Gehrig on lists of the most prolific power hitters of all time. However, while these players generally remained healthy and consistent over a long period of time, McCovey's production came in spurts as he first struggled to gain a full-time job, and later struggled with injuries. Of his 521 career home runs, 223 of them came in seasons in which McCovey was at the plate less than 450 times. In contrast, only 37 of Mike Schmidt's -- and only ONE of Gehrig's -- homers came in such truncated seasons.

Despite the limits on his playing time, Willie McCovey has a place in history as one of the most feared sluggers in an era most often remembered for its dominant pitching. Though muted by platooning, injuries and a relative lack of postseason experience, McCovey's slugging legacy is secure. And he was clearly at his peak in 1969.

Tom Seaver - 1969

by Joe Nunziata III

W	L	PCT	G	GS	CG	SV	IP	SO	BB	B/I	ERA
25	7	.781	36	35	18	0	273	208	82	1.07	2.21

There can be no arguments about whether Tom Seaver should be included in this book. Any book that lists baseball's greatest this or that, or biggest impacts or whatever, must include Tom Seaver. And, if it includes Tom Seaver, it necessarily includes some mention (probably lots of mention) of 1969. Tom Terrific. The Franchise. The Miracle Mets, etc. etc.

No one is going to argue against 1969 being Seaver's greatest season. Of course there are probably some esoteric mathematical ways of showing that his wonderful 1981 strike-shortened campaign was his best, and seasons like 1971 and 1973 have lots of bold faced statistics in my copy of *Total Baseball*. But the argument is silly. Of course 1969 was his best year.

So what's the point? Why take up the space to flesh out details of the obvious choices, when we could just list the easiest choices and then have some entertaining arguments about which marginal seasons should be included? Wouldn't it be more fun to worry over the relative merits of Jim Konstanty in 1950 versus Tug McGraw in 1973, for example?

Or we could take the sabermetric high road and compare Seaver's 1969 season to Walter Johnson's best, or that of Lefty Grove or Koufax or Gibson or Marichal or Clemens or any number of other greats. I'm guessing I wouldn't be the first to compare Seaver to his contemporaries and be sure to adjust for ball park effect. Or, we could engage in a very serious discussion of the lowering of the mound after 1968, and the effects of expansion on 1969's statistics.

How about a thorough discussion of Tom Seaver and the '69 Mets' impact on New York City during one of the most turbulent times in social history? Evolution, revolution, Woodstock, moonwalks, Vietnam and lots of other important things were going on in 1969. Why were the Mets so important to the national psyche? Who knows, but they were. And 1969 was Seaver's year.

The Cy Young Award was nearly unanimous, 23 out of 24 votes going to Seaver. Who voted for Phil Niekro, anyway? Seaver's year included five shutouts, the glittering 2.21 ERA, and the *Sports Illustrated* Sportsman of the Year award, the first of nine 200 strikeout seasons, and a dirty knee on almost every pitch.

The perfect game of July 9, 1969, broken up when Jimmy Qualls collected one of his 31 career hits, is worthy of several paragraphs. (Maybe a Jimmy Qualls ''Where is he now?'' section belongs in this book's appendices.) Anyway, I have personally interviewed at least 60,000 of the 55,800 in attendance that night.

Elaboration on some of the interesting occurrences in the 1969 Mets season would frame the Seaver story nicely: Jerry Koosman and Don Cardwell's twin doubleheader 1-0 shutouts where they both knocked in the run was weird to say the least, Hodges' walk out to left field to yank Cleon Jones out of a game for not hustling, the black cat walks in front of the Cubs' dugout. Two days after the near-perfect game Leo Durocher was asked if ''those were the real Cubs'' and he replied "No, but those were the real Mets." Joe Torre, future Met manager, grounded into the division clinching double play. Davey Johnson, future Met manager, flied out to Jones to end the World Series. And the answer to that popular trivia question is: Tom Seaver was the only Mets pitcher to be charged with a loss in the 1969 World Series, adds a little irony to the end of the story.

So is there really need for me to reiterate lots of Seaver's stats, or to try to justify his inclusion in this book in a historical way? Does Tom Seaver need me to state his case? When Bill James ranks you third in career value for right handed pitchers (behind The Big Train and the guy they named the Cy Young award after) well, who am I to argue?

To a Mets fan then an elementary student at "Our Lady of the Snows," Tom Seaver's 1969 season was the coolest event of my short life. I was allowed to stay up past the appointed bedtime to watch his starts. I knew something was special about the guy who was old enough to be a baseball player, but young enough for me to think I could be his friend. I didn't understand how he could ever lose a game, and when he won, I bragged to my buddies as if he was my big brother. My dad would schedule our trips to Shea with a keen eye on Hodges' pitching rotation weeks in advance. Every year we made a point to be at the "200th strikeout" game. I couldn't fathom why he was traded in '77, and I felt like a child again when he won on Opening Day in '83. I was proud when he won number 300 on Phil Rizzuto Day in the home of the team I hated with a religious zeal. I understood when, on the day they retired his number, he felt the only way he could thank the fans was bowing to us from the mound. And the day they put the only Met in Cooperstown is right up there on the "Important Days of My Life" list along with turning eighteen, buying my first new car and meeting my future wife. Tom Seaver was the reason I became a baseball fan.

Reggie Jackson - 1969

by Tony Blengino

G	AB	R	H	2B	3B	HR	RBI	BB	SO	AVG	OBP	SLG	SB
152	549	123	151	36	3	47	118	114	142	.275	.410	.608	13

Reggie Jackson was a walking exclamation point of a ballplayer. The amazing frequency, distance and timeliness of his homers earned him the moniker "Mr. October." He amused with his braggadocio and pointed wit. He elicited every emotion except indifference from baseball fans, who either loved him or hated him.

Reginald Martinez Jackson was the second overall pick in the 1966 draft, chosen by the then Kansas City A's. In 1967, his first full pro season, he played for one of the most talented minor league clubs ever, featuring many of the players who became the nucleus of the A's World Championship clubs of the early 1970's. Jackson struggled mightily in a late 1967 callup to the big club, striking out 46 times in 118 at bats, while batting only .178 with one homer.

The 1967 A's finished 10th and last in the AL, and decided to begin 1968 with a bunch of youngsters in the starting lineup. Sal Bando, Joe Rudi, Bert Campaneris, Rick Monday, Dave Duncan, Blue Moon Odom, Catfish Hunter, Chuck Dobson and Jackson were all aged 26 or younger in 1968. At age 22, Jackson showed both talent and immaturity in big measures. He bashed 29 homers, but struck out 171 times in 553 at bats. He showed off his strong arm with 14 outfield assists, but made 12 errors. Overall, Jackson's '68 season established him as the most major league-ready of the A's youngsters. The A's were hopeful that Jackson would iron out the rough spots in his game in 1969, while unleashing more power.

In 1969, the height of the pitcher's mound was lowered to increase offense, in response to dominance by pitchers in 1968, and offense was further helped in 1969 by expansion which diluted pitching. The overall AL batting average increased from .230 to .246, while the league ERA rose from 2.98 to 3.62.

In the first half of the 1969 season, the baseball world buzzed about Reggie Jackson. By the end of July, Jackson had already crushed an improbable 40 home runs, and was two weeks ahead of Roger Maris' record pace. The league caught up with Jackson in a big way, however, limiting him to seven homers in the season's last two months. The A's were competitive in the newly formed AL West throughout the season, finishing in second place, nine games behind the Minnesota Twins.

Jackson led the league in runs scored, slugging percentage and relative production. His homer total ranked third in the AL (Harmon Killebrew led with 49, while Frank Howard had 48). Jackson was also third in RBI (Killebrew had 140, Boog Powell 121). Reggie also finished second in doubles (Tony Oliva had 39), and walks (Killebrew had 145), and third in OBP (Killebrew led at .430 with Frank Robinson next at .417). For his efforts, Jackson could only manage a fifth place finish in the MVP voting, won by Killebrew.

The A's finished second again in 1970, with their fifth manager in four seasons, John McNamara. Owner Charlie Finley spun the wheel again in 1971, and came up with a winner in Dick Williams. Williams allowed his young free spirits to be themselves, and they quickly realized their potential. They won their first division title in 1971, with Jackson launching his first two postseason homers as the A's were swept by the Orioles in the playoffs.

Jackson was not yet Mr. October. In fact, when the A's won their first of three consecutive World Series in 1972, Jackson missed the entire series with a pulled hamstring. Jackson would more than make up for it in the ensuing years. After an MVP season in 1973, he led the A's past the Mets with four hits in Game 2, two doubles and the only two RBI of Game 6, and a homer and two great catches in the clinching Game 7. In 1974, he homered in Game 1 of the series against the Dodgers, laced a key double in Game 2, and made a pivotal outfield assist in Game 5. He reached his postseason zenith after moving on to the Yankees in 1977. He hit single homers in Games 4 and 5 against the Dodgers, then outdid himself with the three consecutive homers in the clinching Game 6, against Burt Hooton, Elias Sosa and Charlie Hough, all on the first pitch of those three at bats.

Jackson ranks high on the all-time lists in many power categories. He finished his career with 563 homers (6th), 1702 RBI (17th), 1375 walks (23rd) - and is the all-time strikeout leader (2597) by a whopping margin of 661! His career on base percentage is a relatively low .358, due to his modest .262 career batting average, but he posted a career slugging percentage of .490. He led the AL four times in homers (1973, 1975, 1980, 1982), and relative production (1969, 1973-74, 1976), three times in slugging (1969, 1973, 1976), twice in runs scored (1969, 1973), and once in RBI (1973). Surprisingly he never led the league in walks or strikeouts. He is the only player to ever hit 100 homers for three different clubs (169 for the A's, 144 for the Yanks, 123 for the Angels). His flair for the dramatic also extended to the midsummer classic; his prodigious 1971 blast off of the transformer atop Tiger Stadium is one of the most enduring images in All Star Game history.

Reggie's flamboyant personality was not appreciated by many of his contemporaries such as Jim Palmer,

Bill Lee, and Don Sutton were just a few of those who voiced concerns about the gap between Jackson's ability and his boasting.

After his big 1969 season, Jackson held out during the following spring training, beginning a sequence of squabbles with owner Finley. In 1974, he fought teammate Bill North in the clubhouse, separating his shoulder in the process. He held out for the first month of the 1976 season, and was then traded to the Orioles. He was suspended in 1977 for a June 18 fight with his new manager, Billy Martin. After failing to bunt as ordered in one game in 1978, Jackson was suspended for five games, but then led the Yanks to an improbable comeback from fifteen games down to overtake the Red Sox in the AL East.

Even when he was relatively well-behaved, Jackson drew negative attention with his public statements. For example, with the Yankees he claimed to be "the straw that stirs the drink," and sometimes boasted of his allegedly high IQ. He owned a fleet of flashy antique cars and even had a candy bar named after him. When all was said and done, he was an easy first ballot Hall of Fame selection in 1993.

It was impossible for any fan of the time to be lukewarm about Reggie Jackson. He was both a truly dangerous slugger, often delivering in the clutch, and also a too-easy strikeout victim, delighting the opposition pitcher and frustrating his own team whenever he whiffed with a runner on third and less than two outs.

Both confident and cocky, a winner and a whiner, Jackson surely had a knack for finding a way to keep playing baseball late into October year after year. Jackson's favorite quote, borrowed from the legendary Dizzy Dean, sums up his baseball career: "If you can do it, it ain't bragging."

In 1969, as a green 23-year-old, Jackson proved, for the first time, that he surely could "do it."

Johnny Bench - 1970
by Greg Gajus

G	AB	R	H	2B	3B	HR	RBI	BB	SO	AVG	OBP	SLG	SB
158	605	97	177	35	4	45	148	54	102	.293	.351	.587	5

You had to be there. It is hard to imagine the impact that Johnny Bench made when he arrived in the majors as a 19-year-old rookie in 1967. The Reds, who had been a poor to mediocre team since 1964, traded Frank Robinson after the 1965 season. Except for Pete Rose, their starting lineup had no exciting personnel, and their franchise had an overall lackluster roster. This changed with the arrival of the new young catcher from Oklahoma in September 1967. Everything Bench did on the field was very different from the other catchers of his time. Catchers of the time were typically slow and lumbering, and the backstop profession was going through a period of offensive drought, with no hitting stars anywhere close to the Berra-Campanella era; even Del Crandall and Gus Triandos had recently retired.

Bench demonstrated immediately that he was extraordinarily agile behind the plate, and he got into double-digit home runs in his rookie year of 1968. Bench had a rifle arm, a unique one-handed style of catching, and a field presence unlike anyone seen in Cincinnati for a very long time. Bench became the first catcher to ever win the Rookie of the Year award, and by 1970 he was one of the best hitters in the majors.

Bench's breakthrough season in 1970 (at age 22) is one of the best offensive seasons ever by a catcher, nearly identical to Campanella's 1953 season (.312 average, 41 homers and 142 RBI). In terms of power, those two seasons (and I suppose Bench's equally fine 1972 season) stand out from the other great catchers in history: Berra, Gary Carter, Carlton Fisk, Gabby Hartnett, Bill Dickey, and Mike Piazza frequently posted 30 homer, 100 RBI years, but no one reached the peaks that Bench and Campanella did in their best years. The competition for the best year ever by a catcher comes down to Campy in 1953 and Bench in 1970.

Bench posted career highs in homers, RBI, hits, average, and slugging percentage. The strange thing is the season could have been even better. The Reds moved from cozy Crosley Field in midseason. Had they stayed at Crosley for the full season, Bench could have made a run at the NL record for homers. He played in 158 games (140 as a catcher) and led the league in homers and RBI. In 14 fewer games, Campanella fell just short of Bench's power totals but had better on base, slugging, and batting averages. Both catchers won the MVP award and led their team to league titles (Bench, Tony Perez, and Lee May spent the 1970 World Series lining rockets at Baltimore's Brooks Robinson). Based on the averages, runs created, the fact that Ebbets Field did not particularly help Campanella in 1953 (22 homers at home, 19 on the road), I can see a narrow edge for Campanella's '53 season over Bench's '70, but it is very close.

If Campy's 1953 season is the best season ever for a catcher, and Bench's 1970 is second, the third best season is Bench's 1972 season. Following an off year in 1971, Bench bounced back with a .270 average, 40 home runs and 125 RBI, again leading the league in

homers, RBI, and winning the MVP award for the second time. In 1972, Bench also posted his career best on base average, thanks to a career high in walks (100). In '72 he also capped game five of the playoffs with a ninth inning game tying home run as the Reds rallied to beat the Pirates. Bench posted these numbers while knowing for the last six weeks of the season that he had a spot on his lung that would require surgery at the end of the season, and that his career might possibly be over.

Like most catchers, Bench had to fight off injuries that frequently would damage his season totals. In 1975, he was troubled by a shoulder problem all season after a collision with Gary Matthews in an April game (Bench still hit 28 homers and had 110 RBI). His last great season was 1977 (.275-31-109), as the years of catching 140 games a year took their toll. As the Big Red Machine disappeared, Bench became the only link to the team's past until his retirement in 1983.

In addition to posting the best seasons ever by a catcher, Campanella and Bench are remarkably similar in other ways. Both mixed great seasons with seasons where they clearly played hurt (Bench in 1971 and Campanella in 1954, for example) and if Campy had the slightly higher peak, he also had the lower valleys in his off years. Both anchored great teams and both, through no fault of their own, should have posted better career numbers. The main factor that cut Campanella's career short was not his tragic auto accident (he was 36 at the time and already in a serious decline) but by the color line -- Campy was age 26 when he finally made his debut in 1948. And while not as tragic as Campanella's case, I believe Bench's career totals were impaired by front office malpractice.

The Reds traded Tony Perez after the 1976 season to make room for Danny Driessen, who was considered a hot hitting prospect at the time. The trade failed to work on so many levels that it is considered one of the worst in team history. Players uniformly cited the loss of Perez for ruining the clubhouse chemistry. Driessen never developed. And worst of all, Dick Wagner felt committed to Driessen at first base, while Bench needed a place to play after the strain of catching 1600 games in 12 years. In short, you have one of the greatest players in team history, who still has plenty of power (Bench hit 25 home runs with 92 RBI in his last two years in part time play) and who wouldn't move a mediocre player to play the Hall of Famer? Wagner had a "better" idea, making Bench into a third baseman, where he embarrassed himself and the team, hastening his retirement. Bench retired at age 35, but as a first baseman could have played until he was 40, pushing his home run total well over 400. It was a sad end to a brilliant career, and all too typical of the Wagner years in Cincinnati.

Although Campanella may have had the best year ever for a catcher, no catcher was as brilliant at a such a young age as Johnny Bench. Piazza is the best young catcher now, but at age 22 he was playing at class A Bakersfield while Bench at 22 was winning his first MVP award, and doing it very impressively.

Dick Allen - 1972

by Tony Blengino

G	AB	R	H	2B	3B	HR	RBI	BB	SO	AVG	OBP	SLG	SB
148	506	90	156	28	5	37	113	99	126	.308	.422	.603	19

1972 was not one of the most memorable years in baseball history. Among the prominent occurrences in '72 were the first in-season strike in baseball history, and the famed Bert Campaneris bat-throwing incident during the ALCS. On the flip side, Steve Carlton won 27 games for a hopeless Phils' squad, and Roberto Clemente cracked his 3000th hit on the last day of the season. Sadly, it would be both his last hit and season.

One noteworthy event was the most awesome offensive display of the season (and the decade), by Dick Allen of the White Sox. His hitting dominance at least matched, and probably exceeded, Carlton's dominance on the mound. The raw numbers don't do his season justice. Allen batted .308 with 37 home runs, 113 RBI. When put into the context of the American League in 1972, those not-so-glamorous stats can be appreciated as truly overpowering.

First, it was a strike year, and each club lost about eight games. More importantly, it was an awesome year for American League pitchers. The AL batted only .239 in 1972, with a .308 on base percentage and anemic .343 slugging. The league ERA was 3.06, the mark of a star pitcher in the mid-1990's. Allen led the league in homers and RBI by wide margins; only one other AL hitter banged more than 26 homers (Bobby Murcer had 33), while only one other hitter had more than 96 RBI (John Mayberry with 100).

Throw 19 stolen bases into the mix, and you have one of the most dominant all-around seasons ever.

In 1970, the Chicago White Sox went 56-106 and drew less than 500,000 fans. Though they were marginally better in 1971, the attendance was still well under a million. The White Sox needed a star box office attraction. Thus, they were not worried about Allen's problem child reputation, and dealt Tommy John and Steve Huntz to the Dodgers for Allen following the 1971 season.

Allen developed a unique relationship with Manager Chuck Tanner, who treated him as the franchise from the beginning. One day, when Allen was late boarding the team bus after a game, players implored Tanner to let the bus leave. "He can catch a cab. He makes enough money," they said. "You can take the cab; I'm waiting for Dick Allen," replied Tanner. The Sox kept pace with the soon-to-be-three-time-champion A's until late in the season, eventually finishing five and a half games back.

The White Sox outscored their opponents by a margin of only 566-538; using Bill James' Pythagorean method of projecting won-lost records, the Sox should have lost by 18 games to the A's. Allen was the only reason they were in the hunt. The team batted .238: Allen .308. The team had an on base percentage of .311: Allen .422. The team slugged .346: Allen .603. He led the club in homers with 37: Carlos May was next with 12. He led the club with his 113 RBI: May was next with 68. Allen led the AL with 99 walks, and the timing of those walks illustrates the best way to approach the Sox in 1972. He drew 53 walks in the 65 losses in which he played, and only

46 in the 83 wins. Pitch around Allen, beat the '72 Sox. And possibly most important to Allen, he was a hero for the first time in his career. He revitalized the franchise for the city of Chicago. The team surged to over one million in attendance in each of Allen's three years in Chicago, only to fall back under after his departure in 1975. Allen came within ten points in batting average of winning the Triple Crown. He led all three categories as late as September 9th. The White Sox' franchise had been so devoid of sluggers that the fans instantly embraced him after seeing a few of his tape measure shots. He rewarded them with many more blasts and even by hitting two inside-the-parkers in a game against the Twins in 1972. Heck, the White Sox radio contract more than doubled between the 1972 and 1973 seasons.

Dick Allen's story, sadly, includes much unrealized potential. While part of the blame for this must be laid at Allen's feet, one cannot help but empathize with some of the bad luck he endured. "Richie" Allen (as he was then called) was a runaway Rookie-of-the-Year in 1964 for the Phillies. Then a third baseman, he led the league with 125 runs and 13 triples, and batted .318 with 29 homers, 91 RBI, 201 hits, a .383 on base percentage and .557 slugging percentage. He might have been a hero in pennant-starved Philadelphia; but the Phils, who led by six games with only 12 to play, promptly lost 10 in a row, and choked away the pennant, forever obscuring Allen's exploits.

Beyond that, Allen was the first African American star athlete in Philadelphia, one of the last U.S. cities to successfully integrate its sports franchises. In the mid-1960's Allen faced much of what Jackie Robinson endured in the late-1940's; but he didn't have Robinson's strength of character to pull him through. Over the next three seasons (1965-'67), Allen put up double figures in doubles, triples, homers and steals, with on base percentages ranging from .378 to .404 and slugging percentages from .494 to .632 in one of the most pitcher-dominated eras of all time. The feats attracted little appreciation from Philadelphia fans.

Allen was one of the first players to publicly admit that he liked to have a little fun off the field. Many fans took that as lack of dedication. When he was injured,

the razzing intensified. Before long, he withdrew, became adversarial with the media, and truly did become a problem child. It all came to a head in 1969, when Allen didn't show for a doubleheader with the Mets. He was suspended for a month, and the Phils quickly swapped him at season's end, ironically for Curt Flood, who would never play for the Phillies. Was that story a 1960's version of Charles Barkley's tenure in Philadelphia, or what? Like Barkley, Allen continued to produce after his exit from Philadelphia. He ripped 34 homers for the Cards in 1970, but was traded to the Dodgers for reigning Rookie of the Year Ted Sizemore. Allen hit 23 homers in 1971 for the Dodgers, but was then swapped to the Sox. His reputation preceded him at this point.

After his big 1972 season, Allen started 1973 very well, batting .316 with a .398 on base percentage, .612 slugging percentage, and 16 home runs in 72 games, before breaking his leg. In 1974, he was at it again, in more ways than one. In only 128 games, he led the league in homers with 32, and hit .301 (.379 on base percentage, .563 slugging percentage). However, Allen abruptly quit on September 12, to go back to Pennsylvania. Even Chuck Tanner had had enough at this point, and Allen was moved to the Braves, and then again to the Phils, before ever playing a game in Atlanta. His skills then rapidly declined amid nagging hand and wrist injuries. Allen faded out of baseball in 1977 at age 35.

Dick Allen finished his career with 351 homers, 1119 RBI, a .292 career average, .381 on base percentage and .534 slugging percentage, while playing in an era noted mostly for pitcher dominance. Allen's career relative production index is an outstanding 156, the same as Hank Aaron's, and just behind Willie Mays' 157. Allen's natural gifts simply didn't last as long or produce anywhere near the same kind of results as these great Hall-of-Famers achieved. Allen will never get in the Hall, of course, but if Allen had come of age in a different era in a different city, he might have performed near the Mantle/Mays/Aaron level. Unfortunately for him, Allen was a player of the 1990's living in the 1960's, when a black man with money and a public zest for life, in a blue collar northeastern city, was not accepted easily.

Steve Carlton - 1972

by Tony Blengino

W	L	PCT	G	GS	CG	SV	IP	SO	BB	B/I	ERA
27	10	.730	41	41	30	0	346	310	87	1.00	1.97

Steve Carlton is widely regarded as the fourth greatest lefthanded starting pitcher in history. Sandy Koufax and Warren Spahn in the National League, and Lefty Grove in the AL, are the only southpaws with better career accomplishments.

Putting statistics aside, the most enduring images of Carlton are his devastating slider, his ability to strike out anyone at any time, and his long silence toward the media (before he voiced his highly unconventional opinions about society following his retirement).

Carlton posted a career 329-244 (.574) mark with a 3.22 ERA. Both were impaired by the struggles to hang on late in his career (from 1985 through 1988 he was 12-34 with a 5.47 ERA). Counting all seasons when he pitched enough to qualify for the ERA title, Carlton's career winning percentage was 37 points higher than the teams he pitched for. This figure is well behind that posted by arch rival Tom Seaver (88 points) but comparable to such luminaries as Robin Roberts, Gaylord Perry, and Rube Waddell. Carlton's park-adjusted ERA index (115, based on a league average defined as 100) places him behind Seaver (127), better than Roberts, Nolan Ryan, and Don Sutton, and equal to Fergie Jenkins. Carlton led the NL in wins four times, winning percentage once, complete games three times, innings pitched five times, strikeouts five times, and ERA once. He led the NL in relative control/power factor three times, making him 10th on the all time list.

In 1983, Carlton broke Walter Johnson's long standing career strikeout mark (3508), and alternated with Nolan Ryan atop the all time list for the rest of that season, before Ryan pulled ahead. Carlton finished his career second on the all time whiff list with 4136.

1972 was the crown jewel of this long, illustrious career. Carlton, then 27, had been obtained by the Phils from the Cards following the 1971 season, in exchange for Rick Wise. The trade was unpopular with Phillies' fans, who had watched Wise develop from an 18-year old hurler for the ill-fated 1964 Phils, into a pitcher who won 17 games (including a no-hitter) with a 2.88 ERA in 1971.

The Phils, it must be noted, were a truly pathetic ballclub. In 1971, they had finished dead last in the NL East, behind the third-year expansion Expos. Philadelphia looked even worse going into 1972. Carlton was of little help in the early going, getting off to a 5-6 start despite pitching well. I was nine years old then and just getting into baseball, attending as many home Phillies games as my uncle allowed. The summer of '72, from that point on, became unforgettable. I witnessed every home start of Carlton's 15-game winning streak, as well as the loss that ended it.

The most memorable win occurred in the first game of a Sunday doubleheader against the Expos. Carlton had a fifty-something scoreless inning streak snapped by a Bob Bailey homer, but won the game nonetheless. After the second game, I met Carlton, who would be on speaking terms with the media for approximately one more month. He looked somewhat aloof, in dark sunglasses and a cowboy hat, but he politely gave me an autograph, and chatted for a while. Another memorable outing, the loss that ended the streak, was a complete game, extra-inning defeat at the hands of Phil Niekro and the Braves.

The numbers Carlton posted in 1972 are truly difficult to comprehend, because of the context of the bad team for which he pitched. Carlton was 17 games over .500 for a team that was 38 games under. Without Carlton's decisions, they would have been 55 games under .500! The Phillies were 32-87 (.278) in games in which Carlton didn't receive a decision.

How bad were the Phillies that year? Well, no regular player batted above .281, none hit more than 18 homers, or drove in more than 68 runs. The team leader in all three categories was 21-year-old Greg Luzinski, and he received little help from the rest of the offense which produced a pathetic total of 503 runs. The pitching staff was also a disaster, outside of Carlton. No other pitcher on the staff had a winning record, not even a 1-0 or 2-1 record. In fact, the other five starters with 10 or more starts (Wayne Twitchell, Woody Fryman, Billy Champion, Dick Selma and Ken Reynolds) combined for a poor 17-57 record. Carlton's record is all the more amazing because he lost two starts due to the labor problems which wiped out the first week of games.

After the season ended, Carlton was rewarded with the first of his four Cy Young Awards. He finished only fifth in the MVP voting, which was won by Johnny Bench. An even greater reward was his 1973 salary, a then-record $167,000.

Known mainly for his silent demeanor, Carlton was an extremely disciplined and cerebral player, a wine connoisseur and a classical music aficionado. During the 1980 World Championship season, rookies Marty Bystrom and Dickie Noles were summoned to the majors for the stretch run. Not knowing of Carlton's musical tastes or of the respect he was accorded in the clubhouse (especially before games when he was going to start) they started playing the likes of Led Zeppelin at high volume. To state the result mildly, no loud music incident like this ever happened again.

Carlton credits the Phillies' conditioning coach Gus Hoefling for his physical and mental development during his long tenure in Philadelphia. Hoefling introduced Carlton to the martial arts, to which Carlton credits his lengthy career. Carlton insists he never paid attention to the opposing hitter; it was just Lefty and the catcher's glove.

Alas, Carlton did hang around too long, staging numerous comeback attempts with the Phillies, Giants, White Sox, Indians and Twins. There were reports that Carlton needed the money, but to the end he kept making earnest assertions that he could regain his dominant form. Carlton was elected to the Hall of Fame in 1994, but unfortunately had his speech professionally written, denying the public possibly its last chance for some insight into the psyche of this fascinating man. To Phils' fans, however, he will always remain a hero, the pitcher who won the clinching game of their only World Championship, in 1980. His status as one of the very best starting pitchers of the last quarter-century is unquestioned.

Gaylord Perry - 1972

by Fred Matos

W	L	PCT	G	GS	CG	SV	IP	SO	BB	B/I	ERA
24	16	.600	41	40	29	1	342	234	82	1.01	1.93

"I had 40 decisions," Gaylord Perry quickly recalled when I asked about his outstanding 1972 season. "...and I also had a save," he pointed out, lest I overlook the statistic.

Of course, the 40 decisions don't make for an exceptional year, but it takes an exceptional pitcher to participate in 40 decisions. Forty decisions have been achieved only five times in the post-World War II era. The five reaching 40, plus others almost reaching the 40 level are:

Wilbur Wood (1973)
44 decisions, 24-20 record

Bob Feller (1946)
41 decisions, 26-15 record

Wilbur Wood (1972)
41 decisions, 24-17 record

Phil Niekro (1979)
41 decisions, 21-20 record

Gaylord Perry (1972)
40 decisions, 24-16 record

Johnny Sain (1948)
39 decisions, 24-15 record

Robin Roberts (1953)
39 decisions, 23-16 record

Mickey Lolich (1971)
39 decisions, 25-14 record

Stan Bahnsen (1973)
39 decisions, 18-21 record

Wilbur Wood (1974)
39 decisions, 20-19 record

Warren Spahn (1950)
38 decisions, 21-17 record

Robin Roberts (1954)
38 decisions, 23-15 record

Jim Kaat (1966)
38 decisions, 25-13 record

Ferguson Jenkins (1970)
38 decisions, 22-16 record

Gaylord Perry (1973)
38 decisions, 19-19 record

Joe Coleman (1973)
38 decisions, 23-15 record

Jim Bibby (1974)
38 decisions, 19-19 record

Nolan Ryan (1974)
38 decisions, 22-16 record

Dennis Leonard (1978)
38 decisions, 21-17 record

Wilbur Wood and Phil Niekro were both soft-tossing knuckleballers who could pitch forever as there isn't much arm strain in throwing the knuckler. The list is notable because of the many big names who aren't included. Tom Seaver, Don Drysdale, Steve Carlton, Early Wynn, Bob Lemon, and Catfish Hunter never reached the 38 level, and Hall-of-Famers such as Bob Gibson, Sandy Koufax and Whitey Ford never came close.

Achieving 40 decisions requires three things:

1) a good and healthy pitcher who can pitch a lot of innings, and who can be expected to win a lot of games, because managers are not going to let some turkey go 10-30, for example.

2) a team with only one or two good starters, forcing the manager to start the ace or aces at nearly every possible time. The 1972 Indians had rookie Dick Tidrow and Milt Wilcox as the other top pitchers in the rotation, both of whom can be charitably described as mediocre pitchers.

3) a poor bullpen, with relievers usually much worse than the tired ace starter, so the starter usually stays in the game unless it really gets lopsided. Cleveland closer Steve Mingori was demoted to the minors at mid-year, but finished the season with an 0-6 record and 10 saves.

The 1972 Indians had a 72-84 record finishing fifth in a six-team East Division. It was a dead ball year, and the Indians team batting average was .234, tenth in the American League, but still 17 points better than the Texas Rangers with a woeful .217. To provide an even better perspective on the lack of offense, Graig Nettles led the Indians with 17 homers and 70 RBI, and Chris Chambliss was second with 44 RBI. Chambliss was Rookie of the Year in 1971, but he was still not a hitting force, although he would eventually go on to have some good years with the Yankees, as would Nettles.

The 1972 Indians were a far cry from the Big Red Machine, and Perry knew that if he was to win, he had to pitch a good game every time out. The truly great pitchers like Bob Feller, Steve Carlton and Perry will win even with poor teams, a fact of which today's "baby-arm" whiners should take note.

Perry did indeed step it up a notch in 1972, coming through with a 24-16 record, 29 complete games, a sharp 1.92 ERA in 343 innings, 24 wins tying for the league lead, and the 29 complete games leading the league. His 1.92 ERA was within a hair of Luis Tiant's league leading 1.91. But the overall American League ERA was 3.06, just a tad worse than the 2.98 of 1968, which forced a lowering of the pitcher's mound to get more offense. The composite league batting average was .239, and Rod Carew's .318 won the batting championship, providing yet more evidence that it was a dead-ball year.

Regarding the 29 complete games, Perry said "I was trained in the Giants organization to finish games." With the emergence of bullpen specialists of various kinds, and an effort to protect pitchers' arms, complete games have declined substantially in the 1980's and 1990's. The mid-1970's are the last time 30 complete games were achieved, but the truly great pitchers finished many of their games.

Bob Feller - 1946
36 CG

Robin Roberts - 1953
33 CG

Robin Roberts - 1952
30 CG

Juan Marichal - 1968
30 CG

Fergie Jenkins - 1971
30 CG

Catfish Hunter - 1975
30 CG

Steve Carlton - 1972
30 CG

Hal Newhouser - 1946
29 CG

Robin Roberts - 1954
29 CG

Fergie Jenkins - 1974
29 CG

Mickey Lolich - 1971
29 CG

Gaylord Perry - 1972
29 CG

Gaylord Perry - 1973
29 CG

Perry's major league career began in 1962 with the San Francisco Giants, and by 1972, his career record was 134-109. It was Perry's first year in the American League, but he didn't let differences in hitters, strike zones, or anything else stand in the way of winning. He had won 20 games twice before with the Giants, and was known as a very durable pitcher having twice pitched over 300 innings in a season and over 280 in three other years. But he had slipped to 16-12 in 1971, down from 23-13 in 1970, and the Giants swapped him and a rookie infielder for fireballer Sam McDowell. It was a very unpopular trade with the Cleveland fans as "Sudden Sam" was a local hero. As it turned out, it was one of the best trades in Cleveland history, as McDowell soon developed arm problems severely curtailing his career.

As expected when a great pitcher is on a poor team, he will have a number of tough losses where he pitched well but received very little run support. Perry did indeed have a number of tough losses, where a few more runs here and there would have put him in the victory column. With a few more runs, and a break or two, he could have won 30.

Among Perry's tough losses were:

1) a 2-1 complete game loss to the Tigers on May 19, holding them to five hits.

2) a ten-inning effort against the A's on June 5, a 3-2 loss as Reggie Jackson and Bert Campaneris homered.

3) a ten-plus inning effort, a 3-2 loss to the Angels on June 13 as he held them to six hits. The winning run scored on an error.

4) a 1-0 loss to the Yankees on June 30, whom he held to four hits in the complete game.

5) an 11-inning 4-3 loss to the Tigers on August 5th.

6) losing two games by 3-2, and a 4-2 game.

Perry threw a fastball, slider and a changeup forkball. He was always around the plate, walking very few men. Being consistently in or around the strike zone, Perry gave up a few gopher balls, much like Robin Roberts.

Perry pitched a lot of innings every year and finished a lot of games, a throwback to the ironman days of yesteryear. But he didn't walk very many, and consequently, in 1972 he pitched two amazing complete games in which he used only 80 and 88 pitches, both superbly low numbers when compared to today's pitchers. Perry was a very efficient pitcher.

As expected, Perry's outstanding 1972 year had many highlights. Among them were:

1) a 12-0 shutout of the White Sox on May 6, pitching a three-hitter.

2) going 10 innings and beating Texas 4-3 on May 14, holding them to six hits.

3) winning his sixth in a row with a four-hit shutout of the Yankees, on May 23.

4) going 13 innings on July 14, beating Texas 2-0,

scattering nine hits.

5) going 10 innings on July 28, beating the tough Orioles 4-1, scattering six hits.

6) holding the Orioles to two hits on August 1, beating them 2-0.

Perry said he used various hand movements on the mound, touching the front and back of his cap, rubbing his elbow, shoulder and belt, and so on, as a psychological ploy leading the hitter to believe a spitter was coming.

In June, Tigers Manager Billy Martin was so upset about umpires not prohibiting Perry's alleged greaseball that he threatened to teach all of his pitchers how to throw spitters.

On July 10th, following a 2-1 loss to Perry, White Sox manager Chuck Tanner filed a protest with the American League accusing Perry of using grease balls, but nothing came of it.

On July 23, Tanner used psychology against Perry by asking, on three different occasions, umpires to search Perry for foreign substances. Nothing was found, but Perry was bothered by this, and gave up a home run to Dick Allen. Tanner requested an inspection in the ninth inning, and Perry gave up two hits and walked two, to lose the game 2-1 for another tough loss. Coincidence? Maybe.

On August 30th, umpire Nester Chylak ordered Perry to change his shirt at the request of Oakland Manager Dick Williams. Perry soon gave up a home run. Another coincidence? Only Perry knows.

After several games interrupted for inspections of Perry and his uniform, Indians General Manager Gabe Paul complained to American League President Joe Cronin. Paul made a strong case that inspections should not be mandatory at the discretion of opposing managers, but instead left up to the umpires. Cronin agreed, and managers could no longer request a shakedown of Perry.

For his outstanding 1972 season, Perry received the Cy Young award. He went on to have many more good years, proving that he was a winning pitcher in dead ball years, lively ball years, and in years somewhere in between. He was given the ultimate recognition: enshrinement into the Hall of Fame. The best description of Gaylord Perry is ''WINNER.''

Willie Stargell - 1973
by Bill Gray

G	AB	R	H	2B	3B	HR	RBI	BB	SO	AVG	OBP	SLG	SB
148	522	106	156	43	3	44	119	80	129	.299	.395	.646	0

"Here's Stargell," Pirate announcer Bob Prince would proclaim, as Willie stood in at the plate. "Willie can hit a baseball out of any park in America.... including Yellowstone."

It was appropriate that Stargell would hit the first home run at Three Rivers Stadium right after it opened on July 16, 1970; Stargell christened the park properly. This was the start of a golden age of baseball in Pittsburgh. From 1970 to 1979 the Pirates were National League champions six times, winning two National League championships and two World Series. Willie Stargell by this time was reaching his peak as a hitter. Long recognized as one of the most devastating power hitters in the game, Stargell crushed monumental home runs in every National League park. He remains the only man to hit a ball completely out of Dodger Stadium, a feat he accomplished twice. Before Three Rivers Stadium became Stargell's home, Forbes Field undoubtedly cost him 10 to 15 home runs a year from 1963 to mid 1970. Stargell did however smash seven "long taters" (as he called his more impressive blasts) over the 86-foot high right field roof at Old Forbes. Only 18 baseballs were ever hit over that roof in 61 years, and no other player did it more than once.

After winning the NL East in 1970, the Pirates met the Reds in the NLCS. For all the firepower on both teams, it was a pitchers' series, and the Reds prevailed in three tight games. Stargell was the lone bright spot for the Pirates, hitting an even .500.

In 1971, the 31-year-old Stargell reached a new level as a hitter. To kick off the season he hit 11 home runs in April, and had 28 before June was over. He would remain at a high level for three years, blasting 125 homers and driving in 356 runs from '71 to '73.

Had Stargell not injured his knee midway through the 1971 season, it could have been more. In July, his knee condition rapidly deteriorated, and surgery was recommended, but Stargell played on. Reflecting on the 1971 season, Stargell said: "I still feel that if I hadn't hurt my knee in 1971, I could have hit more than 61 home runs." Despite the severe pain, he led the league in home runs with 48, but struggled throughout the second half. "I probably struck out 100 times in the second half of the season," he recalled. "I couldn't put any pressure on it (the knee) at all." The Pirates easily blew away the NL East, but Stargell literally limped through the NLCS and the World Series. In the LCS and Series games, Stargell managed only five hits and one RBI, but the Pirates depth carried them in the playoffs. Then, everyone simply watched in the Series as Roberto Clemente took over and led the Pirates to their come-from-behind win over Baltimore.

1972 proved to be a pivotal year for Stargell and the Pirates. If anything, they were a stronger team. The young hitters were a year better, Clemente was still rolling along, and the supposed weak link, pitching, was much better than expected.

Midway through the 1972 season the Pirates as a

team were hitting over .290. *Sports Illustrated*, in a July 3, 1972 feature on the Pirates, named the middle of the batting order (Clemente, Stargell, Al Oliver and Manny Sanguillen) ''Four Murderers in a Row.'' Stargell led the Bucs in home runs with 33, and they won their third straight division title. Pittsburgh again faced the Reds in the NLCS, and the defending World's Champions appeared to be headed back to the World Series. With the series tied two games apiece, the Pirates led the deciding fifth game 3-2 going into the bottom of the ninth. Dave Giusti, their reliable closer, took the mound for the ninth inning but promptly gave up a game tying home run to Johnny Bench. After yielding two more singles, Giusti was replaced by Bob Moose. Moose easily retired the first two batters, then threw a pitch in the dirt which got past Manny Sanguillen. George Foster scored from third. The Pirates headed to the locker room in shock.

In their silent locker room, Clemente would not allow them to hang their heads. Pittsburgh author Bob Smizik reported the scene as Clemente spoke. ''Can you help it? Don't worry about it. There is nothing we can do about it! Pick up your head!'' Clemente screamed. ''We don't quit now! We go home and come back in February.'' Clemente stopped at every locker. ''He was giving us his own personal message,'' Steve Blass said. ''Never lose your dignity. Never lose your dignity!'' That moment had a profound effect on Stargell. He would soon need to reach deep within himself to rally his teammates from unbelievable tragedy.

On New Years Eve, Stargell was hosting a party at his home. The phone rang. The caller didn't bother to identify himself, but told Stargell that Clemente had been in a plane crash in Puerto Rico. Stargell snapped ''This is a helluva joke.'' The caller cut him off and said it was all over the radio. Stargell called Clemente's home and was told it was true, that his plane had gone down in the ocean. In an interview with George Plimpton years later, Stargell was still shaken. ''It was the damnedest shock of my life,'' he said. ''It was a real empty feeling knowing we would never see him again.'' Stargell also said: ''To this day, I have no idea who that caller was.''

The impact of Clemente's death was devastating to the team, and his loss is still felt in Pittsburgh. In 1973, somehow, Stargell had to come through for the team and the fans, to numb the pain. The dream to win it for Clemente was pervasive. The team needed someone to take Clemente's place. Manny Sanguillen, who for days following the crash resolutely dove into the waters near the wreckage searching for his friend's body, was given the honor. Seeing Sanguillen, number 35, run to right field on Opening Day was a surreal moment for players and fans alike. The reality of it all finally sank in. Clemente was gone.

The swaggering Bucs still talked a good game, but it rang hollow. Pitcher Jim Rooker, acquired by the Pirates in the off season noted the Pirates were still a cocky, confident team. He recalled the team's mantra, ''We'll get it going'' but he added, ''they never did.''

Stargell, a man whose pride, decency and character overshadowed his considerable gifts as a baseball player, remained publicly upbeat. He went to work to bring home a championship. Playing in a career high 148 games, he led the league in homers, RBI, and slugging (with a career-high .646). Amazingly, 90 of Stargell's 156 hits went for extra bases! At age 33, Stargell had the finest season of his career, but he was the Pirates' only consistent hitting threat. Then the pitching deteriorated, and the team never mounted a serious winning streak. The NL East had become a weak division, and 1973 was called ''the season nobody wanted to win.'' The Pirates fell to 80-82, but because of Stargell's heroic play, stayed in the race until the very last day.

The next two years the Pirates won the NL East, and Stargell's presence and determination became the foundation for another Pirate resurgence in 1979. During the '79 season the 39-year-old Stargell was the National League MVP and Championship Series MVP. Stargell led another come-from-behind Series victory over the Orioles and was named World Series MVP. After the series, Stargell was asked about a parallel to Clemente's heroic 1971 series performance. He summed up his triumph with a final tribute to Clemente: ''Whatever contribution I've made has been merely an extension of what Roberto started.''

Fred Lynn - 1975

by Tony Blengino

G	AB	R	H	2B	3B	HR	RBI	BB	SO	AVG	OBP	SLG	SB
145	528	103	175	47	7	21	105	62	90	.331	.405	.566	10

More than 55 years had elapsed since the sale of Babe Ruth from the Red Sox to the Yankees, when Fred Lynn showed up in center field for the Sox. The club was in the midst of a streak of .500+ seasons which would eventually extend to seventeen (so much for "long-suffering" fans). Since their near-miss in the 1967 World Series against the Cardinals, the Sox had been perennial contenders, but were always seemingly a player or two short. Enter Lynn and Jim Rice, two outfielders who would combine to make the most noise of any rookie teammates in baseball history.

Lynn could hit for average and power, and in his heyday was one of baseball's most graceful defensive center fielders. He was made for Fenway Park, offensively and defensively. He regularly took aim on the short porch in right, and he was more than crafty enough to decipher the intricacies of playing the bizarre angles in center field. All of his skills were prominently on display in his rookie season of 1975, when he became the only player in baseball history to win the Rookie of the Year and MVP awards in the same season. Along with Rice, Lynn led the Red Sox to the AL pennant and a date with the Big Red Machine in the World Series, in what would go down as an all-time classic battle. It seemed certain that Lynn and Rice would eventually, if not in 1975, help to break the spell of the "Curse of the Bambino." Alas, 1975 turned out to be a big tease, as Lynn was plagued by injuries throughout the rest of his career, and would only show flashes of the ability he consistently displayed that season.

The Boston Red Sox had been a pretty good ballclub in 1974, posting an 84-78 record and finishing third in AL East, seven games behind the Orioles. Their strength was offense, as they led the AL in runs scored with 696. They possessed a 22-year-old sophomore right fielder named Dwight Evans who was in the process of establishing himself as one of the best young players in the AL. In left and center field, the starters were the young - but limited - Bernie Carbo, 26, and Juan Beniquez, 24.

In September, with their standing in third place secure, the Sox auditioned a pair of kids for Carbo's and Beniquez' jobs. Lynn, 22, was an immediate sensation, batting .419, slugging .698, and driving in 10 runs in 43 at bats. Rice, 21, was only slightly less impressive, batting .269 and driving in 13 runs in 67 at bats. Both secured full-time jobs for 1975 with their impressive play, and the transformation of Beniquez and Carbo into bench players greatly fortified the club's depth.

The 1975 version of the Red Sox scored a full 100 runs more than their 1974 counterparts, and also led the league in batting average, on base percentage, and slugging percentage, a lethal combination. It was a balanced offense with a youthful nucleus. Rice, 22, batted .309 with 22 home runs, 102 RBI; Evans, 23, batted .274 with 13 homers, 56 RBI; C Carlton Fisk, 27, hit .332 with 10 homers, 52 RBI (despite being limited to 79 games by a broken arm); first baseman and DH Cecil Cooper, 25, hit .311 with 14 homers, 44 RBI, and Carbo, 27, hit .257 with 15 homers, 50

RBI. Old pro Carl Yastrzemski, now 35, chipped in with a .269 average and 14 home runs, 60 RBI. The big story, however, was Lynn.

At age 23, Lynn led the AL in runs scored (103), doubles (47), and slugging percentage (.566). He finished second in batting average (.331, behind Rod Carew's .359), third in RBI, (105, behind George Scott's 109), fifth in on base percentage (.405, behind Carew's .428), and tied for second in relative production (on base percentage plus slugging percentage, relative to the league and adjusted for park factor, with league average defined as 100) with 158 (behind John Mayberry's 167). His 21 homers were one behind Rice for the team lead. His seasonal highlight was a three-homer, 10-RBI onslaught against the Tigers on June 18. Lynn also played a breathtaking, acrobatic brand of center field defense. His feat of being named Rookie of the Year and MVP in the same year was unprecedented.

The Sox needed good hitting, because their pitching was thin. The team ERA of 3.98 was only good enough for ninth in a 12-team league. Veterans Rick Wise, Luis Tiant and Bill Lee won 19, 18 and 17 games, respectively, but all posted ERA's ranging between 3.95 and 4.02. Lefty Roger Moret was a lifesaver, going 14-3 as a spot starter and middle reliever. The rest of the bullpen was borderline hideous - the best ERA among the group was Jim Willoughby's 3.56. Closer Dick Drago had 15 saves, with a 3.82 ERA.

The Sox won the AL East by 4 1/2 games over the Orioles, and headed to the playoffs to meet the three-time defending World Champion Oakland A's. However, a late-season broken wrist would cost the Sox the postseason services of Jim Rice. It didn't matter much in the ALCS, as the Red Sox mauled the A's in a three-game sweep. Lynn batted .364 (4-for-11) with three RBI, including a key RBI single in game two. In this series, a .364 ranked Lynn only fifth among Sox' starters; Yastrzemski (.455), shortstop Rick Burleson (.444), Fisk (.417) and Cooper (.400) all posted higher averages. Next up were the Cincinnati Reds. A World Series for the ages was about to unfold.

The Red Sox won game one 6-0 on a Luis Tiant shutout. Tiant had previously pitched a three-hitter in the playoff opener against Oakland, and was now clearly in a groove. The Red Sox' Achilles Heel - their bullpen - bit them in game two, as two runs against Dick Drago in the ninth inning gave the Reds a 3-2 win. Game three was a thriller won by the Reds, 6-5 in 10 innings. Evans homered in the ninth to tie the game, and Joe Morgan singled in the game winner for the Reds in the bottom of the 10th. It was Tiant time in game four, and Looie came through again with a 5-4 complete game win, evening the series at two. Tony Perez bashed two homers in game five, pacing the Reds to a 6-2 win, bringing them to within a win of the World Championship as the series returned to Boston. And it rained.

And rained. Three days of rainouts ensued between games five and six. This seemed to work in favor of the Sox, as it enabled them to bring back Tiant. Lynn opened the scoring with a three-run, first inning homer. Tiant's hot streak had finally run its course, however, and the Reds built a 6-3 lead by the eighth inning. In the meantime, Lynn had appeared to be seriously injured attempting to catch a fly ball by Ken Griffey, which fell for a triple. Lynn crashed into the wall and lay motionless for several minutes, arguably the most eerily quiet moment in recent World Series history. Lynn not only remained in the game, but he singled to lead off the eighth, and scored on Bernie Carbo's game-tying homer. You know the rest: the 12th inning, Carlton Fisk, the foul pole, the body English, the jumping and dancing, utter joy throughout New England. Of course, the next night the Reds roared back from a 3-0 deficit to win on a Morgan bloop single in the ninth, 4-3. The Curse lived on. Lynn finished with a .280 average (7-for-25), one homer and five RBI. After the long winter's hangover wore off, Sox fans thought : no problem; Rice is back, Lynn is the man; we're the team to beat for a long time.

Not so fast - Lynn came back to earth with an ordinary 1976. He batted a solid .314, but managed only 10 home runs and 65 RBI as the Red Sox slumped to third place. Lynn would not recapture his rookie year form until 1979, when - on paper - he exceeded it. Lynn won his only batting title that year (.333), and finished tied for second in homers (39), and fourth in RBI (122). He was second in on base percentage (.426), and led in slugging percentage (.637) and relative production (173). He used his home park advantage to maximum benefit - he hit .386 with 28 home runs, 83 RBI at home, and accumulated only 11 home runs with 39 RBI on the road. However, at age 27, he had already played his one and only season in which he participated in more than 150 games. He would accumulate enough plate appearances to qualify for the batting title in only seven seasons. Most of the injuries were relatively minor - only a 1980 broken toe and a 1988 ankle injury were of greater severity. Many considered Lynn a malingerer for this reason. A true superstar would have played through the pain, they argued.

Fans continued to hold Lynn in high regard through his travails. He appeared in the All-Star game in each of his first nine major league seasons. In his ninth and final appearance, he cracked the first grand slam in All Star history, against Atlee Hammaker, staking the AL to a 9-1, third inning lead. After losing 19 of the previous 20 matchups, the AL romped to a 13-3 win, and hasn't looked back since. He also had a knack for coming through on the postseason stage. In addition to his fine 1975 performance, Lynn was a monster in the 1982 playoffs as a California Angel. Lynn batted an amazing .611 (11 for 18) with 1 homer, 5 RBI - only to see his Angels blow a 2-0 series lead, losing three straight to the Milwaukee Brewers.

Lynn ended his career with a .283 average, .364 on base percentage, a .484 slugging percentage, 306 home runs, 1111 RBI, 1063 runs, 1960 hits, and a 129 relative production index. When he was healthy, he was solid, based on his relative production figures, he was 20% more productive than the average AL player on a per-at-bat basis in 11 of his 15 seasons as a starter. However, he managed to cram virtually all of his brilliance into two regular seasons and two post-seasons. Lynn became a journeyman (Angels in 1981, Orioles in 1985, Tigers in 1988, Padres in 1990) whose arrival on a new team seemed to coincide with the team's imminent steep decline.

No, Fred Lynn did not become the next Willie Mays. He reached his peak level for only two seasons, as injuries prevented him from having a material impact on a significant number of seasons. However, when Fred Lynn was at his best, as he was in 1975, he combined line drives and power blasts with scintillating defense, as only a very few players have ever done. All of his efforts, however, were not quite enough to purge the Curse of the Bambino during that magical season in Beantown.

Joe Morgan - 1976

by Greg Gajus

G	AB	R	H	2B	3B	HR	RBI	BB	SO	AVG	OBP	SLG	SB
141	472	113	151	30	5	27	111	114	41	.320	.453	.576	60

Personally, I'm happy for baseball that I won. What I mean is that kids should strive to be complete players. With the DH in the American League, I hear some kids saying 'Well, I can hit, so I guess I can be a designated hitter.' But, there's more to baseball than doing this one thing.

That was Joe Morgan's quote after being named the National League MVP in 1975, and it sums up his talent. He did everything well. In 1976 he put together what could be considered one of the best seasons ever by a middle infielder.

The two most important statistics for evaluating offensive performance are on base percentage and slugging average, and in 1976 Joe Morgan led the league in both categories by wide margins (38 points in on base percentage and 46 points in slugging). While being the league leader in both categories is not very rare in itself (it had been done as recently as 1972 by Dick Allen) it is a rare feat for a middle infielder. Honus Wagner, Nap Lajoie, Rogers Hornsby, and Arky Vaughan, who have been league leaders in both on base percentage and slugging averages, are good exclusive company indeed.

The breadth of Morgan's accomplishments in 1976 are what make this season more than just another great offensive year. Morgan was among the league leaders in runs (second), home runs (fifth), RBI (second), walks (second), batting average (fifth), and steals (second). As a bonus, he led the league in stolen base average, sacrifice flies, and fewest grounded-into double plays (despite batting third behind Pete Rose and Ken Griffey, who both had .400+ on base percentage in 1976, giving Morgan about as many opportunities as anyone ever had to ground into double plays). As a fielder, he won the fourth of five consecutive Gold Gloves at a key defensive position. His team won 102 games in the regular season and did not lose a postseason game. In the postseason, Morgan was hitless in the playoffs, but homered in Game 1 of the World Series and hit .333 (with .733 slugging) overall. He easily won the league MVP (by 90 points over teammate George Foster, who had led the league in RBI). What else is there?

The problem with picking 1976 as Joe Morgan's best season is, it was almost indistinguishable from his 1975 season (which Morgan cited as his best in his autobiography). Choosing between 1975 and 1976 is like choosing between Cindy Crawford and Elle McPherson. I chose 1976 because of his league leading slugging average (a career high .576) and power difference (27 homers in 1976 versus 17 in 1975) but the difference is small. In 1975, Morgan had 18 more walks (a career high 132), seven more steals (tied his career high of 67) and an on base percentage of .471 (the best in thirteen years). His defensive stats were slightly better and he drove in the run that won the memorable 1975 World Series. The 1975 team won six more games and the MVP vote was also more impressive, as he beat Greg Luzinski by 168 points. But the rarity of a sweep of the on base and slugging crowns and the relative value of 10 more home runs versus the value of a few walks and steals make the 1976 season Morgan's best, and possibly the best all around year until Barry Bonds remarkable 1993 season.

Despite winning back-to-back MVP's, Morgan did not receive the credit his performance deserved, and if it is possible for a first ballot Hall of Famer to be underrated, he is. For Morgan, it started in his rookie year (1965) when he hit .271 with 14 homers, 40 RBI, 97 walks, and had 20 steals for Houston. Jim Lefebvre got the Rookie of the Year award by hitting .250 with 12 homers, 69 RBI, and three steals (of course Lefebvre was helped by being with the Dodgers). In 1972, his first season with the Reds, Morgan led the league in runs scored, walks, on base percentage, and was fourth in the MVP vote. In 1973, Joe had one of his best power years (26 homers and 82 RBI batting second) and he was again fourth in the MVP, which was won by teammate Pete Rose, surprising many observers.

In 1974 Morgan raised his on base percentage and slugging percentage, but dropped to ninth in the voting. Craig Wright suggests that the only reason Morgan won the 1975 MVP was his move to third in the lineup, which gave him the RBI count to merit serious MVP consideration. In his "off year" in 1977 (22 homers, 78 RBI, 113 runs, 117 walks, 49 steals) he did not receive a single MVP vote. Bill James considered Morgan to be the best player in the National League from 1972-1977, and even in his decline Morgan was rated in the *Baseball Abstracts* as one of the top three second basemen in the majors through 1983, when he was 39. After he left the Reds, he contributed to a Houston division title in 1980, an improbable 87 win season with San Francisco in 1982 and a league title for Philadelphia in 1983.

Another problem for Morgan was that his accomplishments got lost in the greatness that was the Big Red Machine. Pete Rose got the most attention, as both the hometown hero and a flashy player. Johnny Bench was the best catcher of his generation, and Tony Perez was the most loved player ever to wear the Reds uniform.

It is important to recognize Morgan's dominance at his position relative to his contribution to his team. While there were other players in the National League who were about as good as each of the Reds at the time (compare Tony Perez to Willie Stargell, Steve Garvey, and Bob Watson; Pete Rose with Mike Schmidt, Bill Madlock, Ron Cey, and Darrell Evans; and Bench with Ted Simmons), there was no one even close to Morgan in the league among second basemen (Rennie Stennett and Dave Cash were his "closest" competition). American Leaguers Bobby Grich and Rod Carew were his best contemporaries, and Morgan was clearly better than both of them.

There are some great young second basemen in the majors now, and all you have to do to get an idea of Joe Morgan's superiority is compare them to him:

> Roberto Alomar: add 10 homers and 40 walks a year, and you've got Joe Morgan.
> Carlos Baerga: add 90 walks and 50 steals.
> Craig Biggio: add 50 walks and 20 steals.
> Delino DeShields (when healthy): add 25 homers and you have Joe Morgan.

You get the idea. There was a lot of talk about Ryne Sandberg as one of the greatest second basemen ever when he retired, but if you take into account the effect Wrigley had on his stats, no one should consider him close to Morgan. Ryno may be a Hall of Famer, but he's no Joe Morgan.

The recent increase in offense makes Joe Morgan's performance in the 1970's appear less impressive than it was in the context of the time (and the value of 130 walks a year has always been ignored by the public). Morgan's heroes were Nellie Fox, Jackie Robinson and Ted Williams, and as a player he was an almost perfect blend of them, with Nellie's defense, Robinson's intensity and will to win, and Williams' strike zone judgement and study of the game. Morgan is one of the 25 greatest players ever, but you rarely hear anyone but statisticians consider him as such. Only a handful of players were as complete, and very few of them played second base.

Nolan Ryan - 1977

by John Benson

W	L	PCT	G	GS	CG	SV	IP	SO	BB	B/I	ERA
19	16	.543	37	37	22	0	299	341	204	1.37	2.77

Nolan Ryan is noted both for longevity, as reflected in his career strikeout total of 5714 (so far ahead of second-best Steve Carlton that it's proportionately equivalent to someone topping Hank Aaron's 755 home runs with a career mark of 1,043) and for high moments, including his seven career no-hitters -- another mark that looks eternally beyond the reach of others.

For all his brilliant accomplishments and unique staying power in the game of baseball, Ryan got meager recognition through most of his career. Conventional thinkers moaned about his mediocre winning percentages and streams of walks that accompanied the many strikeouts, while sabermetric writers tended to focus on the same win/loss marks (while many of the same writers, in other places, were saying that win/loss marks are a very poor measure of effectiveness, because there are so many contributing factors outside the pitcher's control) and also pointed to the walks as evidence of weakness. Ryan's career may be the best case where baseball people (scouts, players, coaches, managers, front office types, fans, journalists, etc.) and sabermetric analysts tended to think alike, with both camps missing the point for a very long time.

It was only during Ryan's final years, when he continued to dominate at an age long past the point when all the other ''great'' pitchers had faded and retired, that observers both subjective and quantitative began to see that Nolan Ryan was a unique physical specimen. In this new light, many of his past accomplishments began to take on added luster. Ryan himself became an inspiration for not-so-young-anymore fans, especially those from the baby-boom generation of which Ryan himself was a part. He also became an icon for believers of mind over matter in the field of physical strain, and added considerably to the sales of a pain relief medication that he endorsed. In personal interviews which filled his schedule with increasing frequency as his career wound down, Ryan exuded a quiet fortitude from which many listeners inferred that great pitchers of the past might have extended their careers if they had simply been able to stand the pain for a few more years.

Choosing one individual greatest season for Ryan is a challenge. After some years of unfulfilled promise and personal unhappiness with the Mets in 1966-1971, he asked for a trade and got it, blossoming rather suddenly after moving on to California. Angels pitching coach Tom Morgan and catcher Jeff Torborg, a master of pitcher-handling, helped Ryan win 19 games in 1972, when he held the league's hitters to a .171 average, the second best (!) of all time, after Luis Tiant's high-mound effort yielding a .168 average in 1968. That was of course Ryan's career best. In 1973 Ryan posted his career high in strikeouts with 383 while winning 21 games for the sub-.500 California team, and then he achieved two more career highs with 332 innings (leading the league) and 22 wins, while the Angels fell to last place (68-94) in 1974. Ryan's last outing that year was a no-hitter, the third of his career. His best ERA was 1.69 in the strike-shortened season of 1981.

★ ★ ★ ★ ★ ★ ★ ★ ★ ★ ★ ★ MOST GAMES,
10-OR-MORE STRIKEOUTS, LIFETIME

'77 RECORD BREAKER

★ ★ ★ ★ ★ ★ ★ ★ ★ ★ ★ NOLAN RYAN

Why 1977? Ryan led the league in strikeouts (of course) and in complete games with 22. He held the opposition to a .193 batting average, not even one of his five best seasons by this measure, but good enough to lead the league in that category. His 19 wins lifted a team that won only 74 in total. What's hidden in this picture is that the American League expanded in 1977. The league batting average jumped 10 points, total home runs soared from 1,122 to 2,013 (yes, there were two additional teams made up part of the increase, but home runs shot up for the old teams as well; the ratio of home runs per at bat went up 52%). The AL's composite ERA went from 3.52 to 4.06. If you take 54 points off of Ryan's 2.77 ERA, you get a rough idea just how good he was within a 1976 context, say about a 2.23.

Breaking the all-time record for total games with ten or more strikeouts, while still just age 30, was a landmark accomplishment. The back of the Topps(r) card illustrated here says it all:

"At Anaheim Stadium, July 16, 1977, Nolan Ryan fanned 12 Seattle Mariners as Angels copped 5-4 decision. The game marked the 98th time that Nolan has reached 10 K's in a contest. Nolan had 6 additional 10-or-more K games later in the season giving him 104 such outings lifetime. Sandy Koufax had 97 with the Dodgers."

Ryan cruised through 1977 as if the American League was the same as it had always been. While other pitchers were finding it more difficult to last nine innings, with diluted talent putting a strain on each rotation and pressing each bullpen to work harder then ever (and thus remain tired all year), Ryan got one more complete game in 1977 than he had in '76, and reached 20 or more complete games for the fifth time in six years.

The complete games are a critical issue when assessing Ryan's value. The long-standing criticism of his tendency to issue a walk is negated by the complete games, for the following reason: any pitching coach will tell you that the problem with bases on balls (and even with strikeouts) is that they consume too many pitches. The high pitch counts then bring on fatigue early in the game. The tired starter must then give way to a relief pitcher (read in: strain on the bullpen cuts

into the manager's options for the next day). And if the reliever uses too many pitches, then the poor manager is even more messed up. So managers and coaches drum it in: throw strikes! But that model is based on normal, human pitchers, not Nolan Ryan. Ryan could throw all the pitches he wanted, never tiring, and in fact giving the bullpen a day of total rest on many occasions when he took the mound, by pitching a complete game. For Ryan pitch counts were nearly meaningless, and so were the walks.

A similar argument, based on that obvious fact that Ryan was extremely unusual, can be used to dismiss the sabermetric expected value of a walk for the offense. Standard values for offensive events are based on huge data samples built with a cross section of *all* pitchers. The value of a walk with Ryan on the mound was less than the value of a walk with the average pitcher on the mound, because Ryan was much more likely to get a strikeout or a popup from the next batter, meaning the runner could not advance. The extremely low opponents' batting averages prove that, as do the low ERA's. And the conventional wisdom, that it's a bad inning if you walk the bases full and then strike out the side (to use the most extreme case as an example) because it uses so many pitches and tires the pitcher prematurely, is thinking that gets turned upside down when you see all the complete games that Ryan produced. He was unique, defying both conventional wisdom in the dugout and statistical probability models in computers.

When Ryan got done, he had 215 games with ten or more strikeouts in his career. But in 1977, the total of 98 was the best ever, enough to pass the immortal Koufax. Ryan deservedly attracted increased national attention in '77. He was named *The Sporting News* American League Pitcher of the Year, the only time he would be so honored with a major seasonal award.

In the late 1990's we can look back and say that Ryan might have been stiffed when he came in second in the Cy Young voting of 1973, for example, and find several other similar cases in his career, but in 1977 he got that one notable prize. It was a heck of a season from a unique athlete.

Ron Guidry - 1978

by Tony Blengino

W	L	PCT	G	GS	CG	SV	IP	SO	BB	B/I	ERA
25	3	.893	35	35	16	0	273	248	72	0.96	1.74

Not since Lefty Grove, in the early 1930's, has a pitcher dominated the American League as Ron Guidry did in 1978. The Yankees were two different squads in the season's two halves: they had different managers and different results. But Guidry was the constant that kept the team on the fringes of the race throughout their miserable first half, and who led them to eventual victory down the stretch.

1978 was only Ron Guidry's second full season in the major leagues, despite the fact that he was already 27 years old. Guidry was excellent in his rookie year, going 16-7, 2.82, with 176 strikeouts and only 65 walks in 211 innings, and helping the Yanks to the World Championship. This was only a prelude to his 1978 tour de force. The Yanks struggled mightily through the first half, with Manager Billy Martin experimenting wildly, actually trying Thurman Munson in right field, and shuffling marginal pitchers like Larry McCall and Dave Rajsich in place of injured stars Don Gullett and Catfish Hunter. By July 17, the Yankees had fallen 14 games behind the surging Boston Red Sox. They stayed that close because Guidry was in the midst of a 13-game winning streak. At this point, Manager Martin suspended Reggie Jackson for five games. After one more week of verbal assaults on Jackson and owner George Steinbrenner, even while producing a string of victories, Martin resigned under pressure on July 24. Enter laid-back Bob Lemon, just canned by the White Sox, with the Yanks 10 1/2 games behind the Red Sox.

Lemon's first words to his troops were: "Today's the first day of your season. Go out and have some fun". Some fun, indeed. The relaxed Yanks calmly, methodically began to cut into the Sox' comfortable lead. Suddenly, the Sox were the team with the injury woes; second baseman Jerry Remy broke his wrist, catcher Carlton Fisk continued to play despite cracked ribs, outfielder Dwight Evans suffered from dizzy spells; and, worst of all, their pitching staff faltered. Meanwhile, in the Yankee camp, Hunter regained his health for the Yankees, and Guidry kept right on rolling.

The Yanks entered Fenway Park on September 7 for a four-game series, trailing the Red Sox by four games. After winning the first two games the Yanks sent Guidry (20-2) to the hill to face Sox' ace Dennis Eckersley (16-6). The Sox got two on with one out in the first, but Guidry wriggled free. The Red Sox best moment of the series had passed; their only chance was gone. Eckersley appeared to be cruising, with two out, nobody on in the fourth. After two runners reached base, Lou Piniella hit a weak fly just between Rick Burleson and Fred Lynn. After another flare by Bucky Dent, the floodgates were open. By inning's end, it was 7-0 Yankees, and that's the way it ended. Guidry finished with a two-hit complete game shutout (only the 2nd complete game by a lefty in Fenway that year) and the first shutout by a lefty in Fenway in four years. The Yanks completed the sweep the next day, and were tied for first. The Yanks took two out of three from the Sox the following weekend in New York, but a last gasp comeback in the season's final week brought Boston into a tie for the division title, necessitating a one-game playoff.

Whichever team mustered its 100th win of the season would be the division champ. And, though he would be pitching with only three days rest, Guidry was the Yanks' obvious choice to start the playoff game.

Guidry clearly didn't have his best stuff in the big game. He fell behind 2-0 on a solo homer by Carl Yastrzemski and an RBI single by Jim Rice. In the top of the seventh, immediately after replacing a broken bat, shortstop Bucky Dent stuck a dagger into the hearts of Red Sox' fans by depositing a three-run homer into the left field screen. The Yanks tacked on two more in the seventh, giving Guidry a three-run lead. Guidry didn't survive the 7th, but he got the win as Rich Gossage notched a shaky save, giving up two runs in 2 2/3 innings.

In the ALCS, Guidry wasn't used until Game 4, but he responded with eight brilliant innings, allowing seven hits and one run, striking out seven while walking only one in a 2-1 win. In Game 3 of the World Series, Guidry pitched a complete game, with the Yanks winning 5-1, despite an uncharacteristically high seven walks by their ace lefty.

Guidry's regular season numbers were phenomenal. He held the American League's hitters to a .193 average and .250 on base percentage. For his efforts, he was a runaway Cy Young Award winner, and finished second to Jim Rice of the Red Sox in the MVP voting. Including the postseason, Guidry was an awesome 27-3.

Although his 1978 season is universally admired by fans and analysts, Guidry has received little appreciation for his career accomplishments. He finished in 1988 with a 170-91 record (.651) and a 3.29 ERA. Though he pitched for some solid clubs, his winning percentage of .651 exceeded his clubs' (.573) by .078, a very healthy margin when compared to some of the game's greats. He ranks 13th in all-time career relative control/power factor (and 11th in peak value). Despite all of this, Guidry has been virtually ignored in his first few years of Hall of Fame eligibility, and is on the verge of dropping off the ballot, despite the fact that he was a Yankee (this factor a supposed boon to close-call Hall candidates).

For the big picture, compare Guidry's career stats to those of Sandy Koufax:

	GUIDRY	KOUFAX
WINS-LOSSES	170-91	165-87
WINNING PCT.	.651	.655
TEAM W-L PCT.	.573	.561
DIFFERENTIAL	.078	.094
ERA	3.29	2.76
ERA INDEX*	119	131
IP	2392	2324
BB	633	817
K	1778	2396

* (league average equal to 100)

Koufax is the better pitcher, but the two are clearly similar. Nowhere is there a gap big enough to justify the common perception that Koufax is the second greatest lefty of all time (behind Lefty Grove) while Guidry is merely an above average pitcher who had one great year. Ron Guidry, quite arguably, belongs in the Hall of Fame. Guidry's career won-lost record was undermined by subpar performances in his last three seasons. Koufax, by contrast, retired after a 27-9 season, still just age 30. Guidry took a long time to reach the majors but then pitched until he was 38. At age 35 his won/lost mark was 154-68, for a .694 winning percentage. If he had retired at that point, he would look better than Koufax; if he had gone just 11-19 after that point, Guidry would have finished his career with exactly the same record as Koufax.

With a slender frame and crackling fastball, Guidry was nicknamed Louisiana Lightning by the media and Gator by his teammates. Guidry's whip-like motion allowed him to throw a blazing fastball with remarkable precision throughout most of his career. When age took a toll on his velocity, Guidry adjusted brilliantly, and in 1985 posted a 22-6 record and 3.27 ERA. After that, he was never effective with any consistency.

Guidry's best years coincided with the era of Billy Martin, George Steinbrenner, Reggie Jackson, and many others who attracted more attention. In the Bronx Zoo, Ron Guidry was the quiet constant, and he was at his best in 1978.

Jim Rice - 1978

by John Benson

G	AB	R	H	2B	3B	HR	RBI	BB	SO	AVG	OBP	SLG	SB
163	677	121	213	25	15	46	139	58	126	.315	.373	.600	7

Jim Rice literally followed in the footsteps of Ted Williams and Carl Yastrzemski, when he began patrolling the left field grass in front of Fenway's Green Monster. Rice didn't enjoy quite the career longevity of his predecessors, but he did reach a comparable peak in offensive performance and lasted long enough to trail only those two luminaries on Boston's all time career leader lists for home runs, RBI, hits, and total bases. Rice's 1978 season was clearly the best of his career, and just as clearly above all other hitters that year.

Rice rose quickly through the Red Sox farm system. In 1973 at age 20 he paced the Double-A Eastern League in batting average. The next year he won the triple crown of the Class AAA International League, producing a .337 average, 25 home runs, and 93 RBI while playing in the tough hitters' park at Pawtucket. Rice and teammate Fred Lynn both won major league starting jobs in 1975 and helped carry Boston to the World Series. Rice had a very strong rookie season, hitting .309 with 22 homers and 102 RBI, but Lynn was the one who captured honors as Rookie of the Year and MVP in '75, and Rice became a spectator in the excitement of the 1975 World Series, after suffering a broken hand when hit by a pitch from Detroit hurler Vern Ruhle during the final week of the season.

After a mild sophomore dip in 1976, Rice arose to lead the American League in home runs in 1977, the first of three homer crowns in his career, and in slugging percentage. The Red Sox made a run at another championship, but the '77 Yankees were too tough in the stretch, holding on despite an 11-game winning streak by Boston in August. The Bosox finished two and a half games out.

In 1978 Boston fielded one of the strongest teams in their franchise history, featuring a lineup that soared to a 14-game lead over the defending champion Yankees and 10 games over the upstart Brewers by mid July. The Red Sox' irrepressible offensive, and their amazing ability to come from behind, was reflected in reliever Bob Stanley's overall 15-2 record. The heart of the order, literally and figuratively, was Jim Rice, reaching full blossom at age 25. Rice was the strong, quiet type of hitter, letting his thunderous bat do the talking year after year. In 1978 his .315 batting average was third in the league, and Rice was first in home runs, RBI, hits, triples, slugging percentage, and total bases. He produced more total bases than any American Leaguer since Joe DiMaggio in 1937.

The only plausible candidates for MVP in 1978 were Rice and Yankee pitcher Ron Guidry. The New York southpaw had tamed the league's hitters and carried his team to the pennant, with a 25-3 mark and a 1.74 ERA, but when the votes were counted it was Rice who was elected as most valuable in the American League. Debate still smolders, especially around Boston and New York, about that outcome. Guidry supporters argue that without him, the Yankees would have finished in the middle of their division -- no playoff game featuring Bucky Dent, no LCS, and no World Series, while the Red Sox without Rice would have finished ... second, the same as they actually did. Rice supporters simply observe that no other hitter of the late 1970's came anywhere close to Rice's accomplishments.

1978 was the center of a remarkable three-year run by Rice. In 1979 he hit .325 with 39 home runs and 130 RBI, and became the only player in major league history to produce three consecutive seasons with 35 home runs and 200 hits each year. The lines for the three years tell the story of a classic all-around hitter at his peak. 1977: 206 hits, 39 home runs, 114 RBI, .320 average. 1978: 213 hits, 46 home runs, 139 RBI, .315 average. 1979: 201 hits, 39 home runs, 130 RBI, .325 average.

For carving a place in history, Rice has context working both for and against him. Critics like to discount Rice's accomplishments because he played half his games in hitter-friendly Fenway Park, and because he was a left fielder and designated hitter, and all LF/DH types are expected to hit well. And Rice was never much of a defensive force; he learned to play the bounce off the Green Monster and threw out lots of runners at second base, especially later in his career (21 assists in 1983, for example). Finally, Rice in his prime was only a fair baserunner, especially prone to hit into the groundball double play.

The biggest positive in my mind is that, with the passing of time, Rice is gradually and finally coming out of the shadow of his predecessors Williams and Yastrzemski. The longer Rice's 16-year career lines sit in the record books, the longer his career seems to grow. Taking nothing away from the oft-injured Mike Greenwell and his career .300+ batting average, it's still fair to say that Jim Rice was the last of the three great left fielders to play in Boston. And 1978 was his best season, by far.

Bruce Sutter - 1979

by Bill Gray

W	L	PCT	G	GS	CG	SV	IP	SO	BB	B/I	ERA
6	6	.500	62	0	0	37	101	110	32	0.98	2.22

Bruce Sutter was the greatest money pitcher in baseball. Before you begin using your encyclopedia as a statistical ax to hack that comment apart, let me put it into proper context.

Certainly, Sutter was an extremely effective closer for the Cubs and Cardinals, though less so for his last team, the Braves. He perfected an absolute killer pitch in the split fingered fastball; but he was also an All-Star closer of some tremendous financial transactions, for himself and for all baseball players. Sutter was and is as financially astute as any baseball player since Ty Cobb, and the impact Sutter had on the money end of baseball reverberates from Coogan's Bluff to the halls of Congress even today.

Let's look at Sutter, the pitcher. His gift to the game, for pitchers to be sure, was the split-fingered fastball, a pitch he developed in the minor league. The splitter was one mother of an invention, and yes, it was born of necessity. Sutter injured his arm in the minors and did not want his parent club, the Chicago Cubs, to find out about it. He decided to have the elbow surgery and pay for it out of his own pocket. In spring training, Sutter was reluctant to throw a curve ball, fearing his elbow was still not stable enough to handle the stress. A pitching coach suggested that he try throwing a forkball, a pitch that had been successfully used by Joe Page and Elroy Face, relief aces of the 1950's and 1960's. Sutter began to work with the pitch, but because of his exceptionally big hands and long fingers, was able to grip the ball more between the spread fingers and less in the palm, and yet throw the pitch hard, at fastball velocity and with excellent location.

When perfected, the pitch left Sutter's hand and looked like a decent fastball. It came toward the batter with a velocity in the mid eighties and had a lot more spin than the rather lazy action of the forkball. Lots of spin and velocity usually means fastball. Hitters thought: "If it looks like a fastball and acts like a fastball, it must be a fastball!" Just as the pitch reached the plate, it would suddenly drop as if rolling off a table. The batter, swinging at the "fastball" suddenly saw nothing and could miss by a foot or more. Sutter began to dominate in the minors and was called up to the Cubs in 1976.

Sutter recorded 10 saves in 1976 to go along with a 6 and 3 record and a 2.70 ERA. By season's end, he had earned the Cubs full time closer job. He tore through the league in the first half of 1977, recording 26 saves by the All-Star break. Just before the All-Star break, Sutter pulled a muscle, causing him to miss the All-Star game, and struggle in the second half. He managed only five more saves all year. Looking at the complete season, it was possibly Sutter's finest. He had been on a pace for a 50-save year, but the muscle pull caused a big reduction in his opportunities.

Throughout his career, Sutter suffered a variety of physical problems, and had surgery eleven times. The splitter was suspected as a cause for some of Sutter's injuries; still despite the injuries, Sutter was probably the best closer in the game until about 1985. A nine-year run of excellence for a closer is outstanding longevity for that profession.

After recording 27 saves in 1978, Sutter turned it up a notch in 1979. He saved 37 games and was honored as the National League's best pitcher, earning the Cy Young Award, only the second relief pitcher in history to be so honored. Sutter decided to cash in on his well deserved status. He filed for salary arbitration, asking the Cubs to pay him $700,000. The Cubs countered with an offer of $350,000.

Salary arbitration at the time was a still a relatively new and untested concept. The Players Association, led by Marvin Miller, had negotiated and won the right to use a third party arbitrator to settle a salary dispute, but few players had tried this new process. Players were not used to negotiating in any way, and the arbitration process involved not only tough negotiating, but also "going against the team" by dragging the general manager in front of an independent authority. Most players just didn't feel comfortable with the whole idea.

Sutter had been cited as the National League's best pitcher. With million-dollar salaries beginning to appear in the free agent market, it seemed reasonable to Sutter that he must be worth about $700,000 and he was willing to argue the point with an arbitrator. He did, and he won.

Sutter had another fine season in 1980, but the Cubs, in a ''cut off nose to save face'' move, decided to trade him. The Cardinals sent the Cubs three players, and the deal was done. Despite Sutter's brilliance as a closer, the Cubs never registered any better than third in the standings in the NL East. But to the Cardinals, Sutter was the 17th jewel in their watch. With him they were easily the best team in the National League.

Unfortunately, the 1981 season was shortened by the strike. Then-commissioner Bowie Kuhn's infamous split-season format, with convoluted playoff rules, made this travesty of a season even worse. The Cardinals held the best overall record in the NL East,

but because of the split season, finished second. So the Cardinals were excluded from this bizarre season's championship playoffs. Despite losing seven weeks of games, Sutter still recorded 25 saves.

In 1982, the Cardinals won it all. Sutter was perfect in the National League Championship Series, allowing the Braves no runs or hits in 4 1/3 innings. He saved one game and won another in the three-game Cardinal sweep. Then, in a surprisingly competitive World Series with the Milwaukee Brewers, the Cardinals had to struggle to win in seven games. Sutter picked up two saves and a win.

1982 was Sutter's only World Series, but he was still at the top of his game; maybe not quite as dominant as in his Chicago days, but still as good as any closer in baseball despite suffering more injuries and having more medical operations. In 1983 he had only 21 saves, his lowest total since his rookie year. He was involved in an unusually high number of decisions (19) winning nine, and losing ten. But any thoughts that Sutter was fading were put to rest in 1984 as he led the majors with a league record-tying 45 saves. Following his huge season, the 32-year-old Sutter, with his eye on his financial future as always, declared himself a free agent and began to field offers.

Sutter had impeccable timing in pitching and business. The Braves entered the bidding and got out their checkbook, without much return. From 1985 to 1988, while the Braves were 261-383, Sutter saved exactly forty of those games for a team going nowhere. He pitched fairly well with 23 saves in 1985 but was injured and appeared in only 16 games for the Braves in 1986 and missed all of 1987. He tried to come back in 1988, and he did pitch, but by the end of the year, he knew he was through, and retired. The fourteen saves he recorded in 1988 left him with an even 300 for his fine career.

The business deals he pulled off? In his final contract with Atlanta, he had the foresight to structure the deal so that an investment option will pay him $1 million a year through the year 2020.

A money pitcher. And a closer for the ages.

Mike Schmidt - 1980

by Tony Blengino

G	AB	R	H	2B	3B	HR	RBI	BB	SO	AVG	OBP	SLG	SB
150	548	104	157	25	8	48	121	89	119	.286	.388	.624	12

Let's cut the suspense and get to the point: Mike Schmidt is clearly the greatest third baseman of all time. In addition to being the greatest offensive third sacker in history, his defensive record outshines them all, even Brooks Robinson. Where does one begin? Schmidt won three MVP Awards, eight home run titles, and four RBI titles. He led the league in on base percentage three times, slugging percentage five times, walks four times, and runs scored once. He won eight Gold Gloves, and still holds the two highest single season assist marks (1974 and 1977) among NL third basemen. He had a 30/30 season erased in 1974, when a rainout eliminated a stolen base. Schmidt's career relative production rating was 147 -- the highest of all time among third basemen. He finished with 548 homers (seventh all time), 1595 RBI (22nd), a .384 on base percentage and .527 slugging average. That kind of production (especially the high OBP number) makes any criticism of his career .267 batting average pointless.

For many years, fielding percentage was widely regarded as the best available measure of defensive ability. In recent years more fans and media have come to appreciate total chances as a meaningful overall measure of defensive performance. Such measurements as range factor, defensive winning percentage, and fielding runs have deepened the serious fan's understanding of defense.

Take fielding runs as an example. This invention, featured in *Total Baseball*, calculates the number of runs saved (or allowed) by an individual fielding performance, compared to the league average of all players at the same position in the same year. A below-average defensive player gets a negative number for fielding runs. For his career, Schmidt led all third baseman in fielding runs, with 265. Brooks Robinson is sixth on the all-time list, behind Clete Boyer, Buddy Bell, Aurelio Rodriguez and Terry Pendleton. Just based on this measure, the case can be made that Schmidt was better defensively than Robinson. Offensively, there is no comparison. Robinson's relative production figure is barely above average at 105. Schmidt's 147 is on top, followed by Eddie Mathews (145), George Brett (137) and Ron Santo (123).

Schmidt was remarkably consistent over the 14-year period from 1974-87, averaging 37 homers and 106 RBI per season over that span. His career reached its apex in 1980 and 1981, both MVP seasons. In the '81 strike season, Schmidt batted a career high .316, while leading the league in runs (78), walks (73), on base percentage (.439), slugging percentage (.644), homers (31) and RBI (91). That put him on pace for 47 home runs, and 138 RBI in a full season. However, 1980 must be singled out as Schmidt's signature season. It was also the only year in history that the Phillies won the World Championship.

In 1980, Schmidt's huge performance was necessary for the Phils, because Greg Luzinski was injured most of the season and Pete Rose was beginning to decline. Schmidt was quite often the sole force in the Phils' offense, and was pitched around often. The

Phils had been a juggernaut from 1976-78, but had fallen apart in their playoffs. Many regarded 1980 as this veteran club's last shot at the big prize. They struggled for much of the season, then seemed to be shaken to life by a late-summer clubhouse tantrum from Manager Dallas Green. An unbelievable run of relief pitching by Tug McGraw, and Schmidt's massive hitting campaign, sent the Phils to Montreal for the last series of the season. Philadelphia was in position to clinch the NL East. In the second game of the three-game set, the Phils found themselves down a run in the late innings, with the Expos aiming for a division lead with a game to play. A ninth-inning single by Bob Boone tied it up, and sent the game to extra innings.

What happened in the 11th inning will always be remembered, with anguish, by Expos' fans. With Stan Bahnsen on the mound for Montreal, the Phils had the lead run on base with Schmidt coming to bat. Rookie catcher Don McCormack, who had never batted in the majors, and who was the Phils' only remaining catcher, waited on deck. Inexplicably, Expos' Manager Dick Williams allowed Bahnsen to pitch to Schmidt, rather than leave it to McCormack. Schmidt hit one that went about nine miles, and the NL East belonged to the Phils.

Schmidt struggled through the playoffs, batting .208 without a homer as the Phillies outlasted the Astros in their epic playoff series. He rebounded with an MVP effort in the World Series, batting .381 with two homers and seven RBI, and smoking a key two-run shot in the pivotal Game 5 win in Kansas City which enabled the Phils to return home with a 3-2 Series lead. Steve Carlton won the sixth game, with McGraw finishing.

Mike Schmidt was the Phils' second-round pick in 1971, out of Ohio University. Many clubs had shied away from him because of his arthritic knees, damaged while playing football. Schmidt debuted in 1972, and in 1973 he struggled mightily, batting .196 with 136 whiffs in 367 at bats. He showed promising power,

however, nailing 18 homers. Phase I of his stardom began in 1974, featuring tape measure homers and loads of strikeouts. From 1974-76, he led the NL in homers each year, averaging 36 homers, 105 RBI, and 156 whiffs per season. The Phils began their streak of three consecutive playoff series defeats in 1976, and Schmidt's 1-for-16 showing in the 1977 NLCS moved fans to label him as a poor clutch hitter, a tag which some in Philadelphia fans still apply, without good reason.

The arrival of Pete Rose in Philadelphia pushed Schmidt's stardom into its second phase. Rose convinced Schmidt that he had the ability to be the greatest player in the game, and to lead the Phils all the way to a world title. Schmidt's trademark perfectionism, combined with his newfound high confidence, led him to reach a still-higher level in 1980-81. Following the 1983 season, Schmidt made a conscious effort to cut down his swing and eliminate his uppercut. The distance of his homers decreased, but their frequency did not. His batting average bounced back up, and his strikeouts went down. He made these necessary adjustments relatively late in his career, and thus prolonged it (Dale Murphy, for contrast, did not).

A memorable Mike Schmidt moment was homer number 500. Contrary to the label of poor clutch hitter, Schmidt cracked a game-winning ninth-inning homer against the Pirates' Don Robinson in April 1987 to reach the milestone. With a normal decline, Schmidt could have reached 600 homers, but he announced his retirement abruptly in May, 1989. He had begun the season with a brief home run binge, but didn't want to finish it, feeling that he could no longer play up to his own lofty standards.

Mike Schmidt entered the Hall of Fame in the summer of 1995 as the greatest third baseman ever. Some may sneer at his .267 career batting average, but consider that Schmidt's *lowest* on base percentage between 1974 and 1987 was .367. Brooks Robinson exceeded that mark only once in his entire career.

J.R. Richard - 1980

by Bill Gilbert

W	L	PCT	G	GS	CG	SV	IP	SO	BB	B/I	ERA
10	4	.714	17	17	4	0	113	119	40	0.92	1.90

J.R. Richard did not have one of the top 100 seasons of all time. However, he was well on his way in 1980 with the Houston Astros when he was tragically felled by a stroke which ended his unique career at the age of 30.

Richard was the first pick by Houston in the 1969 draft. A graduate of Lincoln High School in Ruston, Louisiana, he had an ERA of 0.00 in his senior year and once hit four consecutive home runs in a game. At 6'8", he also excelled in basketball and reportedly passed up over 200 basketball scholarship offers to sign with the Astros.

Richard first brought his blazing fast ball to the major leagues in September, 1971 when he fanned 15 San Francisco Giants to tie Karl Spooner's major league record for strikeouts in a major league debut. However, lack of consistency and control problems kept him shuttling between the majors and the minors for the next three years. He arrived in the majors to stay in 1975 and the following year he was a 20 game winner and finished second in the National League in strikeouts behind Tom Seaver.

Richard won 18 games in each of the next three seasons as the Astros started to build a contending team. Richard developed a devastating hard slider which complemented his fast ball and, in 1978, he became the first National League righthander to record 300 strikeouts in a season with 303. He surpassed this in 1979 with 313 strikeouts, and more importantly, he achieved greater command of his slider which allowed him to reduce his bases on balls from 4.6 per 9 innings in 1978 to 3.0 per 9 innings in 1979. At last, he was a complete pitcher and a dominating one, leading the league in ERA (2.71), opponents batting average (.196 in 1978 and .209 in 1979) and strikeouts in 1978 and 1979. In 1979, his 313 strikeouts were 100 higher than runner-up Steve Carlton.

In 1979, the Astros surprisingly built a 10 game lead over Cincinnati in July, but fell short at the end by 1 1/2 games. During the off-season, Houston made free agent Nolan Ryan the first $1 million player and the team, despite a glaring lack of power, was regarded as a strong contender in 1980 with a starting rotation of Richard, Joe Niekro, Ryan and Ken Forsch. Opposing teams were confronted with the frightening prospect of facing the heat of Richard and Ryan sandwiched around the fluttering knuckleballs of Joe Niekro.

Richard began the 1980 season as if he were going to record one of the top seasons of all time. In his first start, he pitched 6 1/3 perfect innings against the Dodgers in a 3-2 win. In his next start, he did not receive a decision while working 5 innings against Atlanta. He left the game with shoulder stiffness, possibly the first sign of problems to come. He came back five days later, allowing only an infield hit by Reggie Smith in beating the Dodgers for the 13th straight time. He picked up his 100th major league win in his next start, but once more left with shoulder stiffness. Again, he came back strong with a 5-1 win over Cincinnati, becoming the first NL pitcher with a 4-0 record.

Richard then hit a dry spell as he gave up four runs in 1/3 inning in a rain delayed game in Montreal. Next came a nine-inning, no-decision start in Atlanta when he was bothered by back stiffness, followed by losses to Philadelphia and New York. He beat San Diego 4-1 on May 26th, but again experienced back problems. He then began a streak which gave new meaning to the word "unhittable" and brought forth frequent comparisons with Sandy Koufax in his prime. He threw two consecutive three hit shutouts against the Giants and followed that with a six hit shutout against Chicago. Next came a 7-1 win over the Cubs when he left the game after 5 innings with a "dead arm," the first real sign of trouble.

After skipping a start, Richard had a bad outing against Cincinnati, losing 8-5, before beating Atlanta in his last start before the All-Star break. He was selected to start the All-Star game and worked two innings, allowing one hit and two walks while striking out three. After being examined by Dr. Frank Jobe in Los Angeles, Richard told the media that he was advised to take 30 days off, a statement he later retracted. He started a game against Atlanta three days later but left in the fourth inning with an upset stomach. Although no one could know it at the time, it was to be J.R.'s last appearance in a major league game. He threw in the bullpen two days later, experienced fatigue and was placed on the 21-day disabled list.

Richard was admitted to a hospital, where a diagnostic study revealed a blockage in two arteries in his right arm. He was discharged and allowed to undergo supervised workouts on July 26. He was re-examined on July 29. On July 30, he collapsed in the Astrodome during a light workout and was rushed to nearby Methodist Hospital, where doctors determined that he had suffered a stroke. He underwent emergency surgery to remove clots from arteries in his neck, restoring circulation to his brain. The stroke weakened his left side severely. He remained in the hospital for six weeks undergoing therapy. Later he underwent additional surgery to remove a blockage in an artery in his shoulder.

When Richard went down, he had a 10-4 record with 119 strikeouts in 113 2/3 innings and an ERA of 1.90. For a full season, he was on target to lead the league in wins, strikeouts and ERA. Vern Ruhle replaced Richard in the Astro rotation and compiled a 12-4 record, helping the Astros to the best season in their 19 year history. Entering the final weekend of the season in Los Angeles with a three game lead over the Dodgers, the Astros were swept in a three game series. In a one-game playoff the following day, Houston finally won 7-1 behind the pitching of Niekro and the hitting of Art Howe.

The ensuing five-game playoffs with the Phillies provided one of the most exciting series ever with the last four games going into extra innings. Amidst a thundering ovation in the Astrodome, Richard returned to throw out the first ball in game four. Philadelphia finally won the series taking game five in the tenth inning after Ryan failed to hold a 5-2 lead entering the eighth inning. The Phillies went on to win their first World Series in the twentieth century as Phillie batters heaved a sigh of relief that they didn't have to face Richard in the NL playoffs.

Richard made a valiant effort to resume his career. He pitched in the minors in 1982 and 1983, but his reflexes and coordination were severely diminished. He had difficulty adjusting to life outside baseball, suffering business and family setbacks. His well-known generosity and lack of self discipline ultimately resulted in financial problems. In 1994, it was discovered that Richard, for a time, had been homeless, living under a Houston freeway. With the help of former teammates, Bob Watson, Enos Cabell and Jimmy Wynn, among others, J.R. is back on his feet, grateful, ever optimistic and ready to begin what he hopes will be a new season of his life, even better than the one that might have been.

Robin Yount - 1982

by John Benson

G	AB	R	H	2B	3B	HR	RBI	BB	SO	AVG	OBP	SLG	SB
156	635	129	210	46	12	29	114	54	63	.331	.384	.578	14

At spring training 1995 (the real spring training, after the major leaguers returned) I went to the Brewers complex in Chandler, Arizona early one morning to scout the newest crop of baby-faced phenoms. The field at Chandler lies at the bottom of a hill, and comes into view immediately when you walk from the players' parking lot, past the home clubhouse and batting cages. On this particular morning, just as I got my first glimpse of the field, there was a shortstop working out with a coach hitting grounders and a first baseman taking throws. The shortstop caught my attention with a deft backhand snare and fired a rifle-shot to first. The graceful athlete took a few more grounders, showing decent range, extremely smooth hands, and a very accurate arm. Then he went to the outfield and shagged some flies, showing a prescient jump and ease of movement. He could have been a strong prospect worthy of underlines in my notebook; but this was no prospect. It was number 19, Robin Yount, retired. "He just loves to get back out there," said a younger player walking down to the field.

Loving the game is exactly what Yount did for 20 years in the majors, getting an early start as a full-time player at age 18. He made an extremely rare jump from The New York-Penn League directly to the bigs, and set marks for youth throughout his career. In 1976 he became the youngest ever to play 161 games in a season, and in 1980 became one of the youngest players ever to reach the 1,000 hit mark. At the next milestone, Yount was early again. Among all players who would eventually reach 3,000 hits, the youngest to reach the 2,000 mark along the way were Ty Cobb, Hank Aaron, and Yount third, followed by Rogers Hornsby and Mel Ott. Good company indeed.

In a career noted for a youthful start and remarkably consistent play year in and year out for two decades -- despite numerous injuries -- it is nonetheless easy to pick Yount's single best season, 1982. As a prelude, Yount had made a conscious effort to become more of a power hitter. He began a vigorous weight lifting program to build strength in 1979. After good results in 1980 and 1981, he reached his career high in home runs in 1982.

It was a magical season for the Brewers, who went to the World Series for the first time in franchise history and took it all the way to the seventh game. Yount carried his team, leading the majors in hits, doubles, total bases, and slugging. He was second in batting average, just .001 behind Willie Wilson, and second in runs scored behind teammate Paul Molitor.

Yount became the first shortstop ever to lead the American League in total bases and slugging, and the first AL shortstop ever to hit .300 with 20 homers and 100 RBI. He joined Chuck Klein and Billy Herman as the only three players ever to amass over 40 doubles, 10 triples, 20 homers and 20 steals in a single season. And that was just the hitting. On defense, Yount led the league's shortstops with 489 assists and won his first Gold Glove award. He was an easy and near-unanimous choice for MVP.

Yount remained strong in postseason play. In the 1982 ALCS, California's pitchers generally kept the ball away from him, letting Cecil Cooper, Paul Molitor and Gorman Thomas do most of the damage; still Yount collected four hits and five walks for a .429 on base percentage.

In the World Series, Yount batted .414 with a home run, six runs scored and six batted in. He became the first player in Series history ever to have two four-hit games (game one and game five, both of which the Brewers won) and finished with 12 hits in total. It was everything that could have been expected from Yount. In the end, Milwaukee simply didn't have enough pitching. Brewers' hurlers yielded a 4.80 ERA versus 3.84 for the Cardinal pitchers. The postseason heroics, in front of a national audience, helped Yount become the biggest vote-getter in fan balloting for the 1983 All-Star game.

After the 1984 season, Yount got a surgical overhaul of his damaged right shoulder, and moved to the outfield for 1985. At first he played in left, but as the shoulder healed more fully, he moved to center in July of that year. Eventually he became one of the league's best center fielders, and after an off year in 1985 he proceeded to hit over .300 in four consecutive years, 1986-1989.

Yount won his second MVP award in '89, on the strength of a .318 average, 21 home runs, and 103 RBI. But Yount never again returned to the heights of 1982. The Bill James *Historical Abstract* rated Yount third among all shortstops for peak value, behind only Honus Wagner and Ernie Banks.

Cal Ripken Jr. - 1983

By Lary Bump

G	AB	R	H	2B	3B	HR	RBI	BB	SO	AVG	OBP	SLG	SB
162	663	121	211	47	2	27	102	58	97	.318	.373	.517	0

Before including Ripken in this book, we had to answer a couple of questions:

(1) As a player best known for his career performance, does any one of his individual seasons stand out?

(2) In that best season, was he so much better than his contemporaries that he, and not someone else, should be represented here?

The answer to the first question is simple. Ripken has had two exceptional seasons (1983 and 1991) for which he received American League MVP awards. He was also a standout in 1984 based largely on superior defense. For a player noted for consistency, at least so far as being in the lineup every day, Ripken has been inconsistent. He has left a trail of slumps and hot streaks, and fluctuated considerably in his performance from year to year. In his first 13 full seasons, through 1994, he batted better than .300 four times: 1983, 1984, 1991, and 1994. In both 1985 and 1986, he finished at .282. In his seven other seasons before 1995 he batted from .250 to .264.

His power and production have been more consistent than his batting average. Going back to include minor league play, Ripken hit between 21 and 28 home runs every year from 1980 to 1990. He had three 100-RBI seasons, and has been below 80 only with 72 in 1992 and 75 in the strike-shortened 1994.

Based on total player ratings in *Total Baseball*, Ripken has varied from being the best player in the American League (1983, 1984, and 1991) to being downright below average (1990 and 1992). Overall, the peak seasons are certainly high enough to give Ripken a place in this book.

So the second question is: "If we include Ripken, what would be his best year?"

The second question creates a larger problem. In 1991, when Ripken had the best raw numbers of his career in the Triple Crown categories (.323-34-114), a number of other players also stood out offensively. Cecil Fielder led the league in RBI and tied Jose Canseco for the home run crown. Julio Franco had the highest batting average, and Danny Tartabull led in slugging percentage. And none of that includes Frank Thomas, who led in many of the esoteric sabermetric categories such as Runs Created and Total Average. Finally, in 1991, Ripken's second MVP season, he was the first American Leaguer to win the award while playing for a team with a losing record. So 1991 is questionable as Ripken's best year.

We can also raise questions about 1984 as Ripken's best year. The most obvious difficulty with that selection is that his offense (.304 average, 27 home runs, and 86 RBI, for example) pales in comparison to 1983 and 1991. What Ripken did that was so great in 1984 was play great defense. He didn't just lead the league in assists with 583; he got the sixth highest total of all time for a shortstop. Among all shortstops since the 1920's, only Ozzie Smith and Ivan DeJesus, once each, ever had more in a season. Honus Wagner peaked at 517 back in 1905 when slap hitters put almost every ball in play, and rarely struck out. We will give Ripken's 1984 season an honorable mention for the fine glovework (he also reached his career highs in putouts and range factor) but not labor over the methods used to measure and value defense, when there is yet another year to consider, one packed with offense as well.

In 1983 the biggest question in player ranking was whether Ripken or teammate Eddie Murray should be the American League's MVP. Murray finished at .306-33-111. Ripken topped him with his .318 batting average, and was close behind with 27 homers and 102 RBI. They were the only two players named on every writer's MVP ballot, and Ripken came out ahead, 322 points to 290. That year the Orioles won the AL East title, the Championship Series and their most recent World Series title.

Ripken acknowledged the effect of having Murray batting behind him in the cleanup spot in '83, in a way Babe Ruth never would have credited Lou Gehrig: "I don't think they're going to pick at the corners with Eddie behind me in a close game." Still, Junior won the prize and was the first player to be named Rookie of the Year and MVP in consecutive seasons.

The clinching argument was *The Sporting News*' explanation of why they named Ripken as their choice for American League Player of the Year (and later Major League Player of the Year): He played every game. He raised his batting average 54 points. He led the majors in doubles and hits, scored 121 runs, and had impressive Triple Crown stats. He did it while learning to play shortstop, one of the most demanding positions in the game.

We've included Ripken for one additional reason. *The Sporting News* didn't know then that Ripken would become famous beyond baseball for his relentless pursuit of Gehrig's record streak of 2,130 consecutive games.

The Orioles had come into the 1983 season on somewhat of a sour note. Under Earl Weaver, they'd spent the previous early fall chasing down and catching the Brewers. The winner of the season's final game, Milwaukee at Baltimore, would be the AL East champion. The Brewers pounded Jim Palmer, and went on to the World Series. They were the Baseball Writers Association of America's choice to repeat, with the Orioles rated third behind the Yankees.

Baltimore went into the season with a relatively untested shortstop. Ripken had played mostly third base in the minors, and only slightly more at short than third in his first season-plus in the big leagues. Then there was the issue of his size. At 6'-4" he would be one of the tallest regulars ever at his position, the Randy Johnson of shortstops. Weaver had retired, and new manager Joe Altobelli went with a set infield for the first month: Murray at first, Rich Dauer at second, Ripken at short, and Leo Hernandez at third -- until Dauer suffered a back injury May 15. Later, Hernandez struggled, so veteran Aurelio Rodriguez auditioned for a few games before Baltimore traded for Seattle shortstop Todd Cruz June 30. After some debate over whether Cruz or Ripken would move to third base, Altobelli said he'd prefer to keep Ripken (batting .283 with 12 homers and 45 RBI) at short. It seemed to be the right move. In *The Sporting News*, Jim Henneman wrote that Ripken was "dispelling the notion that he didn't have the range to play shortstop" and that his arm was "rapidly earning recognition as one of the best in the league at any position."

Ripken may or may not be a natural athlete, but he is surely a natural student of the game, and his father is one of its best teachers. Cal Ripken Sr. was a minor league manager during young Calvin's formative years, so Dad wasn't home much. But his son was at the ballpark, absorbing whatever he could from Baltimore farmhands such as Johnny Oates, Doug DeCinces and Al Bumbry, but mostly from Cal Sr. Later, Junior would say, "I watched him teach players the fundamentals. I didn't think there was any other way to play."

The younger Ripken made up for any lack of quickness by proper positioning. Careful study of all the league's hitters, and intense focus on each pitch and where it was likely to be hit, gave Ripken superior range, 4.98 compared to league average of 4.15 in 1983.

Through June of 1983, the Orioles had been up and down. After a 23-13 start, their best since their previous world championship year in 1979, they lost seven in a row through May 26, but still stood just a game behind Toronto and Boston on Memorial Day. The Birds still considered Milwaukee the team to beat, and delighted in winning the first five times the teams met in '83. On June 15, the Brewers took a 7-0 lead, but powered by Ripken's three-run homer, the Orioles battled back to send the game into extra innings. Again Ripken came through, with a two-run double in the 10th as Baltimore won 11-8.

"I'd be lying if I said that 1982 wasn't still ringing in our ears," Ripken admitted. "This year we don't want to be guilty of not getting our wins early. We want to beat the teams that have a chance to win."

On the Fourth of July, the traditional time to take stock of possible pennant-winning teams, Baltimore still trailed Toronto by one game. The Orioles were there despite injuries that had deprived them for a time of pitchers Palmer, Mike Flanagan and Tippy Martinez and outfielder Dan Ford. One constant in the lineup was Ripken. Another was Murray. During July, though, Murray had a 225 consecutive-game streak snapped when he strained a knee at second base. (On July 29, Steve Garvey's National League record streak of playing in 1,207 consecutive games came to an end.)

Meanwhile, Ripken was drawing attention for having played not just in every game since May 29 of the previous year, but also in every *inning* since June 5, 1982. Even after the pennant was clinched, through the playoffs and World Series, Ripken never once left a ballgame. "Once you've played all the games in a season," said Ripken, who did that for the first time in '83, "then half the battle is over. You're no longer questioning that you're capable."

Nevertheless, he started hearing criticism, as Gehrig did before him. Ruth suggested that Gehrig might be hurting his career by playing through injuries. Ripken's response has been matter-of-fact, but pointed: "I thought the idea was to come to the park and play, not sit in the dugout and watch. The criticism, it would

seem to me, ought to be directed at those who don't want to play."

Ripken wanted to play, and he played well. He hit a home run in a 7-3 win at Oakland, on July 23, that stretched a hitting streak to 11 games. Four days later, at California, he went 4-for-6 with three RBI in a 10-4 romp. By the end of July, his average was up to .294 despite a 3-for-32 dry spell.

Another seven-game losing streak dropped the Orioles to fourth in the tight AL East, but on August 13, Ripken's two-run homer in the eighth inning broke a 2-2 tie as Baltimore beat red-hot Chicago. Two days later, the Orioles led the division by the slimmest of margins, one percentage point over Detroit, half a game over the Yankees, one game over Milwaukee and just 1 1/2 ahead of fifth-place Toronto. A week later, the pack had begun to disperse. Milwaukee was in a virtual tie with Baltimore, but no one else was closer to the lead than 1 1/2 games.

Then came one of the most famous games in Orioles history, August 24, 1983, against the Blue Jays. Altobelli had been a notorious platoon manager, even in the minors when he had an opportunity. This year he had received maximum mileage from righthander Gary Roenicke and lefty-swinging John Lowenstein in left field. But this night, Altobelli reached the end of regulation play in a 3-3 tie with no position players on the bench. The Orioles took the field for the 10th with a patchwork lineup that included Roenicke at third base, Lowenstein at second and infielder Lenn Sakata behind the plate. They quickly fell behind 4-3, and they knew the Blue Jays couldn't wait to start stealing bases against Sakata. Instead, Martinez picked three consecutive runners off first base to end the inning. In the bottom of the 10th, Sakata won the game with a tie-breaking three-run homer. What's all but forgotten is that before Sakata's home run, Ripken had hit a solo homer to tie the game 4-4.

With that impetus, the Orioles rode a six-game winning streak into September. Ripken was at .300, but he was just getting started. At Minnesota on September 3, Ripken had one of the greatest games in the team's history. His five hits tied an Orioles record, as did his 37th and 38th doubles of the season. His 13 total bases also were a team record, and his 22nd and 23rd homers established a Baltimore record for shortstops. And the Orioles won 13-0. By Labor Day, they were at 80-53 and 4 1/2 games ahead of the Yankees and Tigers, with the Brewers five back. In effect, the race was over.

The division's last hope had been a stretch from August 29 to September 25 when 22 of the Orioles' 29 games were on the road. But the Birds won 16 of the 22 to finish the away portion of their schedule 48-33, an eight-game improvement over the previous year and the best road mark in the majors in 1983. That was a key factor in their eventual six-game winning margin over second-place Detroit. (Milwaukee was fifth, 11 games out.) The Orioles also were a hit at home. For the first time in 30 major-league seasons, more than two million fans visited Memorial Stadium, many of them to see the big kid playing shortstop. The pennant clincher, fittingly, came September 25 in Milwaukee. With Ripken going 2-for-4, Baltimore won 5-1. Ripken had a great stretch run, batting .393 (53-for-135) with six homers and 19 RBI during September.

That set the stage for an American League Championship Series against the White Sox. There had been bad blood between Altobelli and young Chicago manager Tony LaRussa, who thought Altobelli and the Orioles coaches had tried to show him up when they wore their caps backward in encouraging Sakata to get his first hit against a White Sox staff that had previously worn him out. Later, Altobelli protested a game when LaRussa remained in the dugout after being ejected. The postseason rivalry was short-lived. The Orioles won three games to one. Ripken batted .400 (6-for-15) with a run batted in.

Baltimore then dispatched Philadelphia in the World Series. This is the way the 1983 season ended, in the fifth game of the World Series: A line drive by Garry Maddox, caught by Cal Ripken, Jr. Ripken got three hits and three walks in the five games, and (of course) he played every game.

Ripken played most of that 1983 season at age 22. Normal growth would have meant bigger seasons to come in future years, with a normal peak occurring around age 27 or 28. With the possible exception of 1991, when he turned 31, Ripken hasn't had another season like it. Of course, he has been on a career path that could never be described as "normal." Altobelli put it well: ''You don't expect anybody to improve on that kind of year.''

George Brett - 1985

by Bill James

G	AB	R	H	2B	3B	HR	RBI	BB	SO	AVG	OBP	SLG	SB
155	550	108	184	38	5	30	112	103	49	.335	.442	.585	9

Make APBA or Strat-O-matic cards for every player's season in the history of baseball, spread them on the table, and pick an All-Star team. Yes, I know that would take one heck of a big table, but let's stay on the subject here. At first base you could have Jimmie Foxx, 1932, or Lou Gehrig, 1927, or George Sisler, the year he hit .420 and stole 51 bases, or--well, just look through the book. There's a whole bunch of first basemen who have had BIG numbers. At second base you've got Joe Morgan, or Rogers Hornsby, or Nap Lajoie, or Ryne Sandberg, or Bobby Doerr, and each of these guys had several seasons that you wouldn't kick out of the dugout for eating crackers.

And at third base, you've got George Brett, 1980. It might be the easiest position to pick. Maybe you'd argue for Al Rosen in '53 or Mike Schmidt in one of his umpteen MVP-type years, but let's put it this way: if two guys are picking teams, George Brett is going to get picked. He hit .390, the closest anyone has come to .400 in more than half a century. Almost 40% of his hits were for extra bases, accounting for a .664 slugging percentage, an all-time record for a third baseman. He ran well. His fielding was OK. He had more home runs than strikeouts, drove in more than a run per game, and his on base percentage was somewhere up around the temperature of the sun.

The funny thing is, it wasn't really his best year. George Brett was an awesome player in 1980, but in terms of value to his team, he was a great deal more significant in 1985.

The 1980 season, in a sense, pitched George Brett into a mid-career slump. It was well-known, among baseball men, that Brett was a better fastball hitter than breaking-ball hitter. Now, it happened in 1980 that Brett hit only .233 against the Oakland A's, as opposed to .406 against the rest of the league. It happened as well that the Oakland A's manager, Billy Martin, was the TV analyst for the network broadcast of the American League championship series. Billy Martin was as modest as he was mature, so he spent the entire series bragging about how his pitchers had been able to get Brett out, which was that they simply never threw him a fastball in the strike zone. He had a policy: an automatic $50 fine for any pitcher who threw George Brett a fastball in the strike zone. Brett was to see 100% off-speed stuff.

Well, as I said, everybody knew that George was a better fastball hitter than he was a breaking-ball hitter, but pitchers like to throw fastballs. Pitchers, by and large, are big strong guys who can throw hard, and they like to throw hard. This is what they do for a living. They are very well aware that a good fastball is the essential difference between a major league pitcher and a Triple-A pitcher.

Goose Gossage had the best fastball in the American League at that time, registering a consistent 97 MPH on the radar guns. The 1980 AL championship playoff, a best-of-five series, revolved around two players: George Brett and Goose Gossage. The point of the game, from the Yankees' standpoint, was to get a lead and get into a position where Goose

Gossage could nail it down. The point of the game, from the Royals' standpoint, was to give George Brett a chance to win the game.

The Yankees never got to Gossage in the first two games of the series, so when they had a 2-1 lead in the seventh inning of the third contest, Gossage rushed to the mound. There were two men on, two men out. Gossage threw a fastball.

Brett put it into orbit.

There was a somber moment in Yankee Stadium. As Brett crossed home plate the crowd grew eerily silent, then began to titter nervously, like schoolboys leaving a funeral. The announcers sat in stunned silence. ''That was not a 97 mile-an-hour fastball,'' said the lead broadcaster. He was following the broadcaster's rule: a pitch that gets hit is, by definition, a bad pitch. If Brett hit it that far, it must not have been a good fastball.

''It was 98,'' said the third man in the booth, who had seen the radar gun.

Billy Martin closed the sale. Martin had been saying for three days that Brett could hit any fastball. You couldn't throw a fastball so hard that Brett couldn't hit it. When Gossage threw Brett the best fastball he had to offer and Brett hit it halfway to Connecticut, everybody finally believed Martin.

And for four years after that, George Brett never saw a fastball.

That is an over-statement, of course, but Brett from 1981 through 1984 must have seen more changeups, slurves, slow curves and bullpen knuckleballs than any hitter since the heyday of the Pacific Coast League. He had to fundamentally re-adjust his approach at the plate, from hitting the first good fastball he saw to sorting them out, fighting them off, trying to get ahead in the count, forcing the pitcher to give him something to hit. He became a sadder but wiser hitter.

By 1985 George Brett was a different hitter, and the

Royals were a different team. The Royals of 1980 were a tremendous team, facing almost no competition from within their division. It might be an over-statement to say that the Royals could have won the American League West in 1980 with no third baseman, but they could certainly have marched in easily if Brett had hit .290. The other 100 points were just for show.

By 1985 Amos Otis was gone, Darrell Porter was in St. Louis, and all four members of the starting rotation had been replaced. Frank White, a good player in 1980, was a better player by 1985. But Willie Wilson, an MVP candidate in 1980 (he was fourth in the voting behind Brett, Reggie and Gossage) and a batting champion in 1982, was never an effective player after he got out of jail. The Royals in 1980 hit .286 as a team, highest in the majors, and scored 809 runs. In 1985 they finished 13th in a 14-team league in runs scored. In 1985 the Royals needed every hit that George Brett could give them.

What he gave them was amazing. I think most of us would agree that the three most useful offensive stats are batting average, on base percentage, and slugging percentage. Brett's percentages in 1985 were .335, .442 and .585. Although those numbers are not as good as Brett's figures in 1980 (.390, .461 and .664), they remain among the best figures ever for a major league third baseman. Mike Schmidt, Brett's contemporary and rival for consideration as the greatest third baseman of all time, had a .585 slugging percentage in a full season only once in his great career, and never approached Brett's 1985 batting average or on base percentage. Eddie Mathews topped the .585 slugging percentage four times, but never hit .335 or had a .432 slugging percentage, while Pie Traynor topped the .335 average five times, but never matched the on base percentage or slugging average. Brooks Robinson, Ron Santo and Ken Boyer never matched any of those percentages, while Al Rosen's 1953 season came close to matching all three figures (.336, .422 and .613).

So Brett's 1985 season, looked at as an APBA card, is

(a) nowhere near as good as his 1980 season, but
(b) still among the five best-hitting seasons ever for a third baseman.

In the context of a pitching-and-defense team that didn't score many runs, the impact of that one great hitter was enormous. But why was Brett's 1985 season, when he hit .335, actually better than the year he hit .390? Five reasons:

1. Durability. Brett in 1980 was great -- for 117 games. In 1985 he played 155 games.

2. Defense. Brett in 1980 was an underrated defensive player, showing good range but fielding .955. In 1985 he won, and richly deserved, the Gold Glove. His .967 fielding percentage just missed leading the league (a platoon player fielded .971), while he did lead the league with 339 assists and 33 double plays.

3. Control of the strike zone. Brett in 1980 walked 58 times, an above-average number. In 1985 he walked 103 times.

Of course, many of those were intentional (Brett threatened the league record for intentional walks), and many more were semi-intentional. But that's the point: by 1985 he had learned to lay off those pitches. He scored 108 runs in 1985, although nobody who hit behind him, fifth through ninth, hit as high as .250.

4. Baserunning. Brett was never fast, but in 1980 he was aggressive. By 1985 he was aggressive and smart. He was 9-for-10 as a base stealer, and many of his 38 doubles were taken out of an outfielder's hide.

5. Impact on the pennant race. The 1980 Royals were going to win their division anyway. Without Brett, the 1985 Royals wouldn't have been in the race.

You can add in clutch statistics if you want--Brett in 1985 hit .367 with men on base, .388 with men on base and two out, .396 with runners in scoring position and two out. With men on base in late-inning pressure situations, he hit .440.

Outweighing all of those things, though, is the string of astonishing performances that Brett delivered in the closing days of the 1985 season. On September 28, 1985, the Royals were tied for first place with eight games to go.

On Sunday, September 29, Brett drove in two runs with two doubles, but the Royals lost to Minnesota, 6-3, dropping them a game behind. California came to town for a four-game series, beginning Monday.

On Monday, Brett homered and drove in a run with a sacrifice fly, as the Royals won 3-1, pulling the race into a tie. Brett had four RBI in two games.

On Tuesday he had an RBI single, but the Royals lost, 4-2, dropping a game behind.

On Wednesday he singled, doubled and homered, driving in three runs in a 4-0 victory that re-tied the race.

Eight RBI in four games.

On Thursday he hit another home run, also walked and scored, leading a 4-1 victory. The Royals were a game ahead with three to play.

Nine RBI in five games. Three homers. The Athletics came to town.

On Friday, Brett singled and homered, driving in two. The Royals won, 4-2.

Eleven RBI in six games. Four homers. California lost; they were two back with two to play.

California, playing Texas, won that Saturday, cutting the margin to a game and a half. The Royals trailed, 4-0, going to the bottom of the sixth. A loss would leave the pennant to be decided on the last day of the season.

Brett walked and scored in the sixth, cutting Oakland's lead to 4-1.

He hit a two-run homer in the seventh, tying the game.

The Royals won in the tenth.

Five homers, 13 RBI in seven games.

Should Brett have won the MVP Award in 1985?

Well, let's start with Willie Stargell's MVP. Willie Stargell won the MVP Award in 1979 when he hit .281 with 32 homers, 82 RBI. He won the Award because he had some big hits, several game-winning hits, in September.

That's all well and good, but Willie Stargell drove in only 18 runs in September, 1979. George Brett in 1985 drove in thirteen runs in a week. Not in A week; in THE week in which the pennant race WAS decided.

Stargell won the MVP award because he had several big hits in highly visible games, in New York City and/or on National TV. Somebody focused attention on him, early in the month, by arguing that despite his so-so statistics Willie Stargell was the heart and soul of the Pittsburgh Pirates, and Stargell confirmed that with several game-breaking hits.

What Brett did in his week slipped beneath the view of the nation's sportswriters--but on it's own merits, it is much, much more impressive. Kansas City, in those seven games that were their whole season, scored only 25 runs--3, 3, 2, 4, 4, 4, and 5. Brett drove in 13 of those 25 runs. The Pirates in September, 1979, scored exactly 150 runs in 30 games; Stargell drove in 18 of them, or 12%. If Willie Stargell deserved the MVP Award in 1979, Brett certainly deserved it in 1985.

This, of course, is false logic, but stay with me; I'll bring it together in a moment. It is false logic because:

a) It assumes as true that Willie Stargell deserved the MVP award in 1979, which is very questionable, and

b) George Brett in 1985 was not competing with Willie Stargell, he was competing with Don Mattingly.

Mattingly had a hell of a year, drove in 145 runs, and I'm glad he's got an MVP Award in his cabinet. Brett had a better batting average, a better on base percentage and a better slugging percentage. Both players won Gold Gloves, but Brett did so at a position which puts more emphasis on defense.

Compare Mattingly to the other first basemen in the

American League that year--Darrell Evans, who hit 40 homers and drove in 94 runs, Eddie Murray, who hit 31 homers and drove in 124 runs, Bill Buckner, who drove in 110 runs, Cecil Cooper, who drove in 99, Steve Balboni, who hit 36 homers and drove in 88 runs. Kent Hrbek, Pete O'Brien and Greg Walker all had about the same numbers--31 to 38 doubles, 21 to 24 homers, 92 or 93 RBI. The top ten first basemen in the American League that year averaged 35 doubles, 26 homers and 102 RBI. Granted, Mattingly was better than a typical first baseman, but how much better?

Now compare Brett to the other 13 third basemen. One of them was an MVP candidate, too (Boggs), but whereas nine American League first basemen drove in 88 or more runs, no American League third baseman, other than Brett, drove in 88 runs.

Why did Mattingly win the MVP award? Playing in New York wasn't a factor. Surprisingly, studies show very convincingly that playing in New York does NOT help a player win an MVP award, and probably hurts him. Mattingly won the Award because:

a) He batted third behind the greatest leadoff man in the history of baseball, Rickey Henderson, having a tremendous season. Mattingly batted 315 times with men on base, as opposed to 221 for Brett, which gave Mattingly a huge advantage in terms of driving in runs.

b) Many sportswriters still focus on the wrong offensive numbers. There is still a huge (and inappropriate) focus on ''payoff'' statistics like RBI.

I'm not knocking sportswriters, and I'm certainly not knocking Don Mattingly. Here's my argument:

1) George Brett's 1985 batting statistics, on their own merit, are as good as Don Mattingly's. Mattingly's bonus for driving in 145 runs is inappropriate, because that wasn't a function of ability, but of opportunity.

2) When you remember that Brett was not only a third baseman, but a gold glove third baseman, he

ranks clearly ahead of Mattingly. Brett compared to a typical third baseman is a lot more valuable than Mattingly compared to a typical first baseman.

3) If Brett had been given a bonus for carrying the team down the stretch, as Willie Stargell was or as other players have been, he would have finished far ahead of Mattingly.

Well, enough about that. Most people reading this book probably don't expect the MVP vote to be the last word on a player's season, anyway. After closing the season with his homer-a-day program, Brett carried on into the post-season. In the third game of the American League playoff, Brett had the best game that I ever saw any baseball player have.

In the first inning he swung gently at a pitch near his ankles, and deposited it 30 to 40 feet behind the right field fence.

In the top of the third he made a spectacular three-element defensive play. With Damaso Garcia on third, the batter ripped a hard one-hopper right at the bag. Garcia broke for the plate, probably thinking the smash was through, but Brett lunged for it, and came up with the ball, element one. He had a fortieth of a second to choose between the play at first and trying to get Garcia at the plate, element two. He decided to make the play at the plate--but he was standing right on the line, directly behind Garcia. He had to loop the throw around Garcia, over Garcia's right shoulder and into the catcher's glove. Somehow he did it, and Garcia was out at the plate.

In the fourth, with the wind now howling in from right field, Brett ripped the ball off the top of the fence in right-center. He eventually scored, giving the Royals a 2-0 lead.

The Blue Jays exploded for five in the fifth, however, and it was 5-3 when Brett batted in the sixth. There was a man on first. Brett lofted a high fly to right, just over the fence at the 385 sign, tying the score at 5-5.

It was still 5-5 when he batted in the eighth. He singled, and eventually scored the game-winning run. He was 4 4 4 3--four at bats, four runs scored, four hits, three RBI. If one of his homers had been a triple, he'd have hit for the cycle. Throw in the defensive gem and the fact that the Royals' season was over if they didn't win that game, and you might have the best one-game performance in the history of baseball.

In the 14 post-season games Brett hit .360 with a .600 slugging percentage, and the Royals survived two hard-fought seven-game struggles for their only World Championship. Brett didn't homer in the seventh game of the World Series, but then, he didn't need to; it was 11-0. It must have been the only time that year the Royals blew anybody out.

One of the greatest 100 seasons of all time?

Unquestionably. What didn't he do that year? He hit over .330 with 30 homers and 100-plus runs scored and RBI; how many people do that? He won a Gold Glove, and his team won the World Championship. Who else ever did all of those things in one season-- hit .330, hit 30 homers, drive in and score 100 runs, win a Gold Glove, and win a World Championship ring? Nobody else ever did all of that in one year, although I imagine Willie Mays might have won the Gold Glove in 1954 if the award had been around then. More than all that, George Brett carried to the World Championship a team that was absolutely going to lose unless he did something remarkable.

Rickey Henderson - 1985

by John Benson

G	AB	R	H	2B	3B	HR	RBI	BB	SO	AVG	OBP	SLG	SB
143	547	146	172	28	5	24	72	99	65	.314	.422	.526	80

In his sophomore year, 1980, Rickey Henderson stole a hundred bases, set a new American League record and began a seven-year run as the league's leading base stealer. In 1982 he reached 130 steals, breaking Lou Brock's all-time single season record of 118. Henderson at the time remarked that he could have stolen 150 bases, if it hadn't been for lucky throws by catchers and bad calls by umpires. The ability may indeed have been there, but Henderson got over 100 steals just once more (108 in 1983) and never again talked about the 150 mark.

The braggadocio, combined with contract hassles, intangible injuries, unnecessarily flashy catches on easy fly balls, and frequent difficulties communicating with and through writers helped Henderson alienate a broad spectrum of fans, management, teammates and media. For all his accomplishments, Henderson was perhaps the least appreciated star of his generation.

On the field and on paper, forgetting the sideshow antics, Henderson looked in every way like what he was: the best leadoff hitter in the history of the game. He scored over 100 runs 11 times, and also led the AL with 89 runs in the short 1981 season. He drew over 100 walks five times, and maintained a career on base percentage over .400. And he became the all-time leader in stolen bases with several good years left in his career. His record now looks unapproachable.

Among Henderson's many glittering seasons, 1985 and 1990 stand out the most. In 1990 he led the majors with 119 runs and a career-high .441 on base percentage. Amazingly, in the same year he produced his career high slugging percentage of .577. But avoiding the obvious temptation to add OBP and SLG (two fractions that don't have the same denominator, anyway) I would still pick 1985 as the best season of Henderson's career.

The 1985 performance was most remarkable for several reasons. He missed the first 15 games of the season with an ankle sprain, yet came back to score 146 runs, the most in the majors since Ted Williams in 1949. And his rate of 1.02 runs per game was the highest since Jimmie Foxx in 1939. Since 1920, the only players to reach that level have been Henderson, Foxx, Babe Ruth, Al Simmons, and Lou Gehrig.

Other feats in 1985: becoming the first American Leaguer ever to hit 20 home runs and steal 50 bases in the same year. (Henderson did it again in 1986, 1990, and 1993.) In 1985, MVP Don Mattingly drove in 145 Yankees, and 56 of them were Henderson crossing the plate.

Both critics and admirers point to the fact that Rickey became a power hitter only after his 1984 arbitration hearing, in which the A's argued, successfully, that Henderson was not a complete ballplayer; he didn't produce home runs. By 1989 Henderson had passed Bobby Bonds' all-time record for career homers by a leadoff man. Henderson's career marks and single season peaks will linger long after fans have forgotten the sore "hammies" and salary complaints. Many will recall watching him as a pleasure and an education.

Dwight Gooden - 1985

by John Benson

W	L	PCT	G	GS	CG	SV	IP	SO	BB	B/I	ERA
24	4	.857	35	35	16	0	276	268	69	0.98	1.53

The 1983 Mets' starting rotation featured Ed Lynch, Walt Terrell, a 36-year-old Mike Torrez, and 38-year-old Tom Seaver. The fifth starter, Craig Swan, finished 2-8 with a 5.51 ERA. They won only 68 games and finished last, of course. Three years later the Mets swaggered to a world championship, having crushed the NL East with a 21 1/2 game bulge. The turnaround was founded on new pitching, and the heart of the rebuilt staff was young Dwight Gooden. Doctor K. The Good Doctor.

Pitchers who dominate, like Dwight Gooden did beginning in 1984, are natural box office attractions. On a strong, winning team, they become genuine bigger-than-life folk heroes. Mets fans hanging their big red "K" signs in the stands, to count the strikeouts, became a fixture at Shea Stadium. Rarely in the history of baseball has it been so easy to know who's pitching, by simply glancing around the seats.

From the beginning, Gooden was a rare talent with performance matching his skills. At the age of 18, he led the Class A Carolina League in wins, ERA, shutouts, and strikeouts. His 300 K's broke a league record of 275 that had stood since 1947. From May 30 to August 23 he was 15-0. Today, with major league teams visibly strapped for pitching, and when minor league performances get taken more seriously than they did in decades gone by, such a pitcher wouldn't be allowed to spend all year at one level, but in 1983 Gooden stayed put through the summer. He nonetheless became *Baseball America* Player of the Year, chosen over all those who had performed at

Double-A and Triple-A in 1983. Although he didn't pitch a regular-season game above A-ball, Gooden joined the Tidewater team for the Triple-A World Series, and helped them win the title. The very young righty made quite an impression on Tides manager Davey Johnson, who said of Gooden, simply, "Wherever I manage in 1984, I will have him."

In 1984, when Johnson got promoted to manage the big league Mets, he brought Gooden with him. While a few skeptics openly wondered about jumping a 19-year-old from Class A to the majors, fans and critics alike climbed all over the Gooden rookie bandwagon when they saw the way he dominated hitters in the National League.

If you ask a dozen of the NL's best veteran hitters to name the toughest pitcher of the 1980's, Gooden's name invariably surfaces, at or near the top of everyone's list. What made him so tough, from the beginning, was his ability to get the most out of a basic two-pitch repertoire, a fastball and a curve. He could hit spots with his 95 MPH fastball, and worked hard to fine-tune his control even while achieving amazing success in 1984 and 1985. With the craft of a finesse pitcher who succeeds by moving the ball around, Gooden drove hitters mad by using the same intelligent style, but with a fastball that always arrived with blow-'em-away velocity.

Gooden's "other" pitch, the curve, was already among the best in the majors when he arrived. Players at the time commonly called a tough curveball "Uncle

Charlie," but when they saw Gooden's break, they nicknamed it "Lord Charles" because it was, indeed, something special. With an extra-sharp late break that hitters described as falling off the table, Gooden quickly developed the confidence to throw his big hook any time in the count, and he showed the ability to spot the curve, too. With either the breaking pitch or the big heater, Gooden could take something off to keep hitters off balance. He commonly cut through a batting order with 95 MPH heat the first time, a mixture of many curves and 90 MPH fastballs the second time through, and then more mid-90's stuff until the game was over.

Gooden's rookie season in 1984, when he was 19, featured all kinds of "youngest-ever" achievements, not the least of which was being the youngest ever to win the Rookie of the Year award. He not only won the ROY; he dominated it, getting 23 of 24 first place votes and beating runner-up Juan Samuel (.272, 105 runs scored, 15 home runs, 72 stolen bases, and a league-leading 19 triples) by a total point count of 118 to 67.

Dwight's major league career began April 7, 1984 in the Astrodome. He beat Houston 3-2 while yielding only three hits and one earned run. Quickly he rose from credible rookie to all-around star, with performances such as a no-hitter going into the eighth inning against Pittsburgh on June 6 (Doug Frobel broke it up with a single).

Gooden became the youngest All-Star in history in 1984, and didn't disappoint anyone except the batters he faced in the midsummer classic. In Gooden's first inning, he struck out the side: Lance Parrish, Chet Lemon, and Alvin Davis; in two innings of work he allowed just one hit, no walks, and no runs to the American League's best hitters.

On August 27, Gooden beat Los Angeles 5-1 at Shea with a five-hitter, fanning a dozen Dodgers and, for the 11th time in 1984, delivered a game with ten or more strikeouts; in that game he beat Gary Nolan's record for most strikeouts by a rookie under age 20. And Gooden's rookie season was hardly over. On September 7 he fanned 11 Cubs in a one-hit shutout (Keith Moreland singled) and blew past Pete Alexander's all-time National League rookie record of 227 strikeouts, set in 1911. In his next outing September 12, The Doctor amassed 16 whiffs in another shutout, this time blanking the Pirates, and shattered the major league rookie record of 245 strikeouts set by Herb Score in 1955. Gooden was on a roll. September 17 he recorded 16 more K's (despite a loss in which he balked home the winning run). Those back-to-back games with 32 strikeouts broke the NL two-game record held by Sandy Koufax and tied the major league mark set by Luis Tiant and Nolan Ryan in the American League. The three-game streak September 7th, 12th, and 17th gave Gooden 43 strikeouts in 26 innings; Ryan once had 47 strikeouts in three games with 27 1/3 innings for the all-time high.

When the season was over, Gooden had produced 15 games with 10 or more strikeouts, one of many Mets records he would take away from Tom Seaver (13 games with 10+ K's in 1971). Gooden averaged 11.39 strikeouts per nine innings to set an all-time major league record, leaving Sam McDowell's 1965 record of 10.71 far behind.

Gooden was not just the best rookie in 1984; he was arguably the best pitcher in the majors, rivaling Lamar Hoyt, Mike Boddicker, and Jack Morris from the American League and Al Pena, Joaquin Andujar, and Mario Soto in the National. Gooden finished first in strikeouts in the NL, had the lowest opponents' batting average, stood second in ERA behind Pena (2.60 to 2.48) among all major leaguers, and he was third in victories in the NL.

What makes the 1984 season so remarkable, in retrospect, is that it all became prelude to his mythic performance in 1985. Gooden at his best, as when he carried a 1.05 ERA over seven consecutive starts from August 11 to September 12, 1984, was the same prime Gooden that the baseball world would see throughout 1985.

To begin his sophomore year in 1985, Dwight set another record just by throwing his first pitch on April 9; he became the youngest pitcher to start an Opening

Day game, beating Fernando Valenzuela by 15 days (OK, so we're not counting John Montgomery Ward of the Providence Grays in 1889; this book starts in 1901). Gooden took a no-decision in the Mets' victory, getting six K's in six innings.

On May 30, 1985, Gooden started his 14-game winning streak which lasted until August 25. During the streak, which included 10 complete games and four shutouts, he made 18 starts with four no-decision games, and had a 1.72 ERA. The streak included the third 16-strikeout game of Gooden's young career, shutting out the Giants at Shea on August 20. His 20th victory was also the 14th and final game of that winning streak, a six inning effort with two earned runs, beating the Padres in New York. In his next start, against the Giants at Candlestick, Gooden delivered another six inning effort with two earned runs, but this time the Mets fell, 3-2. The winning pitcher for San Francisco was Jim Gott.

Gooden was always proud of his hitting, which he took seriously as part of the game of baseball. One of his lesser-known records of the 1985 season was the highest total of base hits ever by a Mets pitcher, 21. In one classic game he showed the best way for pitchers to overcome a lack of run support, filling the role of offensive star. On September 21, Gooden went three-for-four at the plate, drove in four runs, and smashed his first career home run, taking Rick Rhoden deep in the first inning. The Pirates were defeated 12-1, while Gooden was on yet another pitching streak.

From August 31 to October 2, 1985, Gooden went 49 innings without allowing a single earned run, giving him a September ERA of 0.00. He also hurled 31 consecutive scoreless innings from August 31 to September 16. His "worst" month had been August, with a 2.45 ERA.

After the '85 season, Gooden became the youngest pitcher ever to win a Cy Young award, taking another distinction away from Valenzuela (who had won the Cy at age 21 in the shortened season of 1981). Among his many "youngest" achievements, Dwight won 20 games in a season at the earliest age of any modern-era pitcher, notching his 20th victory of 1985 on August 25, at age 20 years and nine months, a month younger than Bob Feller in 1939 and four months younger than Christy Mathewson (the previous NL youngest) in 1901. Gooden and Herb Score are the only two pitchers ever to get 200 or more strikeouts in both of their first two seasons.

Gooden was the seventh pitcher in history to get the Cy Young award by unanimous vote. The other six were Sandy Koufax, Denny McLain, Bob Gibson, Steve Carlton, Ron Guidry, and Rick Sutcliffe. Comparing Gooden to his 1985 peers hardly offers enough context to appreciate what he did. Gooden's 1.53 ERA was the lowest in the majors since Gibson in 1968. He led the majors in wins, strikeouts, and ERA, the first major league pitchers' Triple Crown since Steve Carlton in 1972. Gooden was only the eighth pitcher in history to so dominate the majors. The others: Koufax, Walter Johnson, Pete Alexander, Dazzy Vance, Lefty Grove (all in the Hall of Fame) and Hal Newhouser.

For many players in this book, the editors had some difficulty in choosing a single best year. In Gooden's case, there is no such problem. His rookie 1984 season was a great story: the dramatic arrival of a teenager who dominated the best adult professionals in his game. But then Gooden did even better -- much better -- in his second year in 1985. After 1985, despite many more victories and milestones on the field, Gooden was never the same again.

New York fans spent the winter of 1985-1986 fantasizing about 15 or 20 more years from Gooden, like the one he gave them in 1985. After all, with his fluid pitching motion, simple repertoire, modest demeanor, and incredible composure, why shouldn't he remain effective until age 39 or 40 or even longer? Even if the fastball slowed a little after 10 or 15 years, wouldn't Gooden easily learn a slider and a changeup? Maybe he would actually get better for a few years, before any decline would set in after age 30? The Hall of Fame was regarded as a given. Numbers like 400 wins and 5,000 strikeouts were tossed around in conversation with a naivete that now appears silly

There was, of course, no way Gooden could improve over his 1985 performance. He wasn't Superman. In real life, he faced a mighty challenge just to maintain a similar level of excellence. Hitters and their coaches had spent the winter studying videotape and pitch charts, searching for predictable patterns and looking for adjustments that might produce more success against Gooden in 1986. Laying off the high fastball was one idea that had become popular before the '86 season even opened. Looking for more curveballs in the middle innings was another. The list goes on. Baseball is a game founded on adjustments, pitch by pitch, game by game, year to year. The National League made some adjustments to Dwight Gooden.

When the first batter he faced in 1986, Pittsburgh outfielder R.J. Reynolds, hit a home run off him, fans immediately began asking The Question that would never go away: "What's wrong with Dwight Gooden?" It's still a good question, if stated without the gratuitous implication that there must be something wrong. What's wrong with a pitcher who goes 4-0 in April and 17-6 for the year, with a 2.84 ERA and 200 strikeouts, while his team wins the World series? Answer: nothing. But in New York, the tabloids don't sell well when filled with such routine questions and answers.

Newspaper sales are boosted by questions like these: Why didn't Gooden blow away American League hitters in the 1986 All-Star game, like he did in 1984? (Lou Whitaker touched him for a two-run homer and handed Gooden the loss.) Why didn't Gooden win any postseason games? (He held the Astros to one run in NLCS game one, and one run in ten innings in game five, then struggled in the World Series while working on three days' rest.) Why didn't he win 20 games? Why didn't he strike out a batter per inning. Why couldn't he be like 1985 forever?

After Gooden went through a scuffle with police in Florida during the winter, and then started the 1987 season in an upscale drug treatment program, his 15-7 record with a 3.21 ERA was regarded with disdain by fans and media. Where was the Championship? In 1988 Gooden was 18-9 with a 3.19 ERA and again led a very strong staff in strikeouts as the Mets won their division, but New York fans focused on his second All-Star game loss and the game-tying, ninth-inning, tide-turning home run shot yielded to Mike Scioscia in NLCS game four. Nevermind that Gooden had a 2.95 ERA in his three NLCS starts, and nevermind that he tied the NLCS record with 20 strikeouts. Doc just clearly didn't have the right medicine any more, the pseudo-pundits asserted.

In 1989 Gooden was shut down from July 2 to September 2 with a sore shoulder; he finished the year with 9-4 mark and a 2.89 ERA. In 1990 he staged a strong physical comeback, winning 19 games and collecting 223 strikeouts, his best in both categories after 1985. At age 25, when most pitchers are still toiling in the minors, Gooden was a comeback case.

At the end of the 1990 season, Gooden had a 119-46 career won-lost mark. His .721 career winning percentage placed higher than all-time leaders Whitey Ford (.690, major league best) and Christy Mathewson (.665, National League best). By going "only" 13-7 in 1991, the year in which he didn't pitch after August 24 because he was diagnosed as having a "tiny perforation" in his rotator cuff (that's a small tear, for those who like one-syllable words) Gooden slipped to .705 career winning percentage, and after his first losing season, 10-13 in 1992, he dropped even further, to .683. If Gooden had retired then, at age 28, he would have gone into the record books ahead of Mathewson among all pitchers with 200 or more career decisions. But Gooden was under .500 again in 1993, and after the 1994 season, involving another trip to the disabled list and a year-ending suspension starting June 28, he was down to .649 for his career -- right alongside Lefty Gomez and just above Mordecai Brown. For a pitcher with so many problems, and one who's had "something wrong" ever since 1985, that's very good company.

Roger Clemens - 1986

by John Benson

W	L	PCT	G	GS	CG	SV	IP	SO	BB	B/I	ERA
24	4	.857	33	33	10	0	254	238	67	0.97	2.48

Roger Clemens began the 1986 season as a physical question mark. He was penciled in as the Red Sox fifth starter, but manager John McNamara waited cautiously to give him his first start. In two major league seasons Clemens had dazzled fans and scouts alike with his mighty fastball and gritty determination, but Clemens had twice succumbed to injuries -- a torn forearm muscle in 1984 and shoulder surgery in 1985. Just when everyone was beginning to wonder if and when Clemens would ever stay healthy for a full season, everything came together. In 1986, he wasted no time in rising to dominance among American League pitchers.

In April Clemens was 4-0 with a 1.62 ERA. His victories included the 20-strikeout, zero-walk performance against Seattle on April 28, the game that kick-started the Red Sox. Before that game, Boston was just one game over .500 and barely in contention. The big strikeout game launched a 12-2 run that carried the team to first place. In three games April 29th and May 4th and 9th during the streak, Clemens collected 41 strikeouts to tie Nolan Ryan's record for three consecutive nine-inning games.

By the end of May, Clemens had improved his record to 8-0, including a victory May 25 against the Rangers in which he took a no-hitter two outs into the eighth inning, before Oddibe McDowell singled to center.

By the end of June Clemens was not only 14-0, but the team had 15 victories in his 15 starts. Finally on July 2 he suffered his first loss, 4-2 against Toronto. He lost once more before the All-Star break.

In the All-Star game Clemens returned to dominance, hurling three perfect innings. He needed only 25 pitches (21 were strikes) to get those nine outs. The All-Star MVP award was the first of many honors he would win in 1986.

Clemens lost for the last time on August 4, as one unearned run produced a score of 1-0. Win number 20 came on August 30th at Fenway, a four-hitter with 11 strikeouts and just one walk against Cleveland. His final seven decisions were all victories, and his two-month unbeaten streak included a nine-inning shutout effort against Toronto, on September 26, which the Red Sox lost 1-0 in the tenth inning.

Throughout the year, Clemens was both dominant and consistent. He did not have any particular isolated hot streak covering a long stretch of games; he just kept winning and dominating all year. Amazingly, he threw only one shutout in this brilliant season (compared to seven in 1987, eight in 1988, and an average of four per year from 1989 through 1992). Overall, Boston won 27 times in Clemens' 33 starts. He pitched into the seventh inning in 30 of those games, held the opposition to a .195 batting average for both righty and lefty hitters, struck out 10 or more batters eight times, and struck out the side 13 times.

Detractors have pointed to Clemens' immense run support in 1986, more than six runs per game. With just average run support, he would probably have had three or four fewer victories. On the other hand, his losses and no-decisions included enough brilliant outings to support claims that he could easily have won three or four more games and had a record like 28-2. The conjecture on both sides of this argument is neither necessary nor helpful; there is no need to add or detract from this great season.

Clemens joined Sandy Koufax and Denny McLain as the only pitchers ever to win the MVP, Cy Young, and *Sporting News* Player of the Year honors in the same year. Clemens stood alone as the only pitcher to be the MVP, Cy Young, and All-Star MVP in one year. He joined Cy Young (1903) and Smokey Joe Wood (1912) as the only Red Sox pitchers to lead the league in wins and winning percentage the same year.

In post-season competition, Clemens was both brilliant and overworked. He was indisputably the victim of bullpen failure, or he could have been the hero of both the ALCS and the World Series, with the same dominance that made him the hero of the regular season. He made three starts against the ill-fated 1986 Angels of Gene Mauch and Donnie Moore. In the fourth game Clemens pitched eight shutout innings and walked off the mound in the ninth with a 3-1 lead. In a gloomy foreshadow of things to come, however, Calvin Schiraldi couldn't close that game, and Boston eventually lost in extra innings. Clemens finally nailed down the victory and the pennant in game seven with a four-hit, one-run performance, even while pitching with a case of the flu.

In the World Series, Clemens started game two but left in the fifth inning. The Red Sox won anyway. In game six Clemens gave the Sox a 3-2 lead with seven highly effective innings (four hits, two runs including one unearned, two walks, and eight strikeouts). But then Schiraldi and Bob Stanley both became tragic figures when The Mookie Wilson Grounder went under Bill Buckner's glove. It was a sour end to a sweet season, as game seven became an anti-climax.

In 1987 Clemens won another Cy Young award, joining Jim Palmer and Sandy Koufax as the only pitchers ever to win back-to-back Cy's (Greg Maddux joined them in 1993). Clemens peaked again in 1990, when he posted his career best 1.93 ERA. Clemens' consistency over the years has been unique among American League starters of his era.

Clemens' great 1986 season might have been better remembered as a high point, if he hadn't remained so dominant for so long afterward. A decade after reaching the majors, he was still throwing 95 MPH and hitting spots. Over the years he made increasing use of his curve, slider, and high-velocity forkball, but it was the big heater that made him the league's top pitcher and kept him at that high level for so long.

In a city deeply supportive of its baseball franchise, Clemens emerged as a major cult hero in 1986. While attendance was consistently strong all year in Boston, an extra 65,000 fans packed themselves into Fenway Park for games pitched by Rajah, The Rocket.

Overall it was not a bad year ... for a fifth starter.

Jack Clark - 1987

by Tony Blengino

G	AB	R	H	2B	3B	HR	RBI	BB	SO	AVG	OBP	SLG	SB
131	419	93	120	23	1	35	106	136	139	.286	.461	.597	1

The St. Louis Cardinals teams of the mid-1980's are remembered mainly for their speed and defense. In fact, the Cards did lead the National League in steals for seven consecutive seasons (1982-88) on the swift feet of speed merchants like Vince Coleman, Willie McGee, and Lonnie and Ozzie Smith. With Ozzie, Keith Hernandez and others, the Cards won more than their share of Gold Gloves. However, this club would not have accomplished what they did, without the presence of one solitary power force in the heart of their order. That force was Jack Clark.

In his three year tenure (1985-87) with the Cards, Jack Clark was an overwhelming offensive power, when healthy. He suffered a serious injury in each of those three seasons. In 1987, his signature season, an injury and resulting missed time probably cost him an MVP Award and a World Series championship ring.

Clark posted awesome numbers in 1987, but they only tell part of the story. He notched career highs in home runs and RBI.. Of his 120 hits, 59 went for extra bases, and he drew a league-leading 136 walks. As a result, Clark won the real offensive Double Crown -- leading the league in both on base percentage and slugging. His relative production (OBP + SLG, relative to the league and adjusted for park factor, with league average defined as 100) was an excellent 174, ahead of some guys who won the Triple Crown in other years. For any player on any club, those numbers in and of themselves would make a player extremely valuable. On the 1987 Cards, they meant much, much more. It was the "Rabbit Ball" year; the National League as a whole, pitchers

included, batted .261 with a .331 OBP and .404 SLG. Though the Cards had a potent offense, with Terry Pendleton, McGee, the Smiths, Coleman and Tommy Herr all making big contributions, the home run fever spreading over the majors never reached St. Louis.

The Cards hit the fewest home runs in the major leagues. Their total of 94 homers were 19 behind the second least productive club, the 65-97 Padres. Five major league clubs in 1987 clouted more than 200 dingers. In St. Louis, Clark produced 37% of his team's homers, despite missing 31 games. The dominance of his contribution was most visible at mid-season. On July 3, the Cards had 48 homers, half by Clark. About that time, the pitchers collectively gave up and began to just pitch around Clark.

From July 18 to August 10, Clark walked in 16 consecutive games, a National League record. In one stretch, Clark batted 27 times with runners in scoring position -- and walked 17 times. As we say repeatedly in this book, walks are often overlooked as an offensive weapon. Clark had little protection in the lineup to make the opposition pay. The second biggest home run hitter on the club was Pendleton with 12. Pitchers were quite willing to take their chances with Pendleton and company rather than pitch to Clark.

The Cards, who appeared to be running away with the NL East in the early going, suddenly began to fade, with the Mets and Expos closing fast. Then the unthinkable happened; Clark suffered his annual serious injury, a badly sprained ankle in late August, which all but ended his season. To the Cardinals' credit, they re-grouped in the heat of the pennant race, beating back the Mets as Terry Pendleton lashed a key homer in the pivotal game.

In the postseason, the Cardinals were much affected by the loss of their power source. They outlasted the Giants in seven games, coming back from a 3-2 deficit in the NLCS, getting a shutout from John Tudor (with Todd Worrell and Ken Dayley) in Game Six and another shutout, from Danny Cox, in Game Seven. In the World Series, the home team won every time, with the Twins four games in the Metrodome. Clark could do nothing but sit restlessly on the bench as the Cards lost their second seven-game World Series in three seasons.

Despite his exploits during the regular season, Clark was denied the MVP Award, which instead went to Andre Dawson of the last place Cubs. Dawson hit 49 home runs and had 137 RBI, but Clark was clearly the more productive player. Compare Clark's OBP and SLG numbers to Dawson's .329 and .568. The fact overlooked in MVP balloting was that Dawson made 443 outs; Clark only 299. One of the amazing oddities of Clark's season was that he put the ball in play in barely half of his plate appearances (283 of 555); but he batted .424 when he did so. When Jack Clark hit the baseball in fair territory, it was usually unplayable.

Near the end of his 18-year career in 1992, Clark had become so noted for his frequent injuries and difficult personality, that many fans and media retained only faded memories (if any memories) of his great accomplishments, especially those from his ten-year stint with the San Francisco Giants. Clark made his major league debut with the Giants on September 12, 1975, at age 19. By Opening Day 1977 he was the Giants' full-time right fielder. He made the NL All-Star team in both 1978 and 1979. He was amazingly consistent in his next five seasons with the Giants, though he was not an All-Star in any of those seasons. He was red hot in early 1984, batting .320 with 11 homers and 44 RBI in 57 games, when he suffered his first serious injury, to his hip, forcing him to miss the rest of the year. In his absence, replacement Dan

Gladden starred, batting .351, prompting the Giants to trade Clark to the Cards in the off-season.

In each of his three seasons with the Cards, Clark was very productive, though often injured. In 1985, he batted .281 with 22 homers and 87 RBI, in only 126 games, missing time with an injured finger. He did have a career high moment in the final game of the '85 NLCS, when Dodger manager Tom Lasorda went to the mound to advise his relief ace, Tom Niedenfuer, how to pitch to Clark; it must have been bad advice, as Clark blasted the very next pitch for a long, deep, game-winning home run. The '85 Cards fell in Game Seven of the World Series with the Royals, marking Clark's last postseason appearance. His value to the team was underscored again in 1986; Clark was lost to a back injury after 65 games, and the Cards finished dead last in the National League in runs scored with 601, after the leading the league in 1985 with 747.

After Clark's definitive 1987 season, he became a free agent. Clark wanted to return to St. Louis, but packed his bags for the Big Apple to play for the Yankees. The loss of Clark sent the Cards into a downward spiral from which they have yet to recover. Though Clark was at this point a sub-.250 hitter, his enormous walk totals and extra-base potential kept him among baseball's most productive sluggers through 1991. In 1989 and 1990, with Padres, he topped the National League in walks drawn. However, during this period Clark had become even more one-dimensional than ever, and was a target of boo-birds even in his home parks. Off the field, he experienced major financial woes as he lived way beyond his means, buying a stable of classic automobiles and even briefly financing his own stock car racing team, the venture that finally forced him into bankruptcy.

Clark finished his career with 340 home runs and 1,180 RBI, with an excellent .383 OBP and .476 SLG. He amassed these numbers despite playing in pitchers' parks for most of his career. People often forget that Clark was once an excellent all-around player. If he had remained healthy; the 500 homer mark was clearly within reach. Easier for all to grasp is the fact that, in 1987, Clark was one of the most valuable players any pennant-winning club ever had.

Jose Canseco - 1988

by David Luciani

G	AB	R	H	2B	3B	HR	RBI	BB	SO	AVG	OBP	SLG	SB
158	610	120	187	34	0	42	124	78	128	.307	.394	.569	40

Let's take a look at an ideal batting order. Your speedy leadoff hitter steals 40 bases and gets caught just 16 times. Your number two hitter, chosen for his great eye, walks about 80 times and gets on base with a hit-by-pitch another 10 times. Your number three hitter bats .307. And your cleanup hitter, feared for his tremendous power, clubs over 40 home runs. If those represented the main features of the top four spots in my lineup, I'd be very content to use those players every day. Those wonderful, multidimensional stats, of course, are not from four players; they are from one player: Jose Canseco in 1988.

Canseco's achievement of 40 home runs and 40 steals in the same season did more than just call attention to his standing among baseball's superstars. For longtime fans, especially for those who enjoy statistics as a form of story-telling, Canseco established a new dimension for statistical comparison. Even among fans who paid little attention to the numbers aspect, there was widespread curiosity to see if Canseco could actually accomplish what no one else in history had ever done. The concept of "40/40" was simple enough for every fan to understand. Media attention was perhaps less than would have been paid to a chase of 60 home runs or a .400 batting average, but Canseco's stretch drive of 1988 was one of the most-watched personal campaigns in recent memory. Add to that the rising popularity at that time of both the Oakland A's and the brightest star of the "Bash Brothers," and you had a guaranteed formula for public interest. Oakland, in 1988, was giving birth to its mini-dynasty that would endure for most of the

next five years, officially ending when Canseco was shipped to Texas in 1992. Jose Canseco, in 1988, was by far the most celebrated member of the team.

To appreciate his accomplishments, it's important to consider what the rest of the baseball world was doing at that time. Canseco's league-leading 42 home runs were eight more than runner-up Fred McGriff (then with the Blue Jays) had. In fact, only four players in all of baseball hit more than 30 home runs that year. Also that year, Canseco was one of just four players in the American League to steal 40 or more bases. He was second in the major leagues in runs scored, led the majors in RBI and slugging percentage and was ninth in the AL in batting average. All this happened in a year Canseco played his home games in the vast Oakland Coliseum. He hit 26 of his home runs on the road.

It was, of course, a career year for the already-established superstar. Canseco's batting average was forty points higher than his lifetime average of .267 (going into 1995). He set personal career marks that still stand in hits, runs, RBI, hit by pitch, stolen bases, batting average, on base percentage and slugging percentage.

Where his 1988 season stands in historical perspective is more problematic. Many will argue convincingly that Mickey Mantle, for example, could have achieved forty home runs and forty stolen bases in the same season if he had thought such an accomplishment worth trying. Certainly, if you transport Mantle and his abilities, having him play under today's aggressive managers, he well could have nailed 40/40 or even 50/50. Bobby Bonds also was as close to being a 40/40 player. Check out the elder Bonds' 1973 season for example. Before the end of his career, the younger Bonds, Barry, might well match Canseco's best season.

When evaluated against some of the all-time great players and what they actually did (as opposed to what they might have done) Canseco's performance remains the standard of comparison for looking at power and speed in the same season. He was the first (and is still the only) player to put up that 40/40 mark. The accomplishment helped launch the media-PR fad, still in fashion, to compare players with multiple accomplishments: e.g. "one of only four players who have accomplished A, B, C *and* D."

The 1988 Athletics cruised to the American League West title that year. The closest the Minnesota Twins ever got, after Oakland's fast start, was three games behind, just after the All Star break. By the beginning of September, Oakland was coasting with a nine game lead and the focus was more on Canseco's individual accomplishments than the progress of the team. Like a walk in the park, Oakland went through Boston in the playoffs to advance to their first World Series since 1974. Canseco paced the team with a .313 average and three home runs in the four-game sweep.

The first game of the Series started as though it would be yet another stage for Canseco's act of domination over pitchers everywhere. Canseco, who had never hit a grand slam, belted his first ever off Dodgers' starter Tim Belcher in the top of the second inning. It would be Canseco's only hit in 19 World Series at bats. That game ended with Kirk Gibson limping around the bases with his famous ninth-inning shot off Dennis Eckersley and the Dodgers went on to upset the A's in just five games. Canseco would bat .053 for the Series, the grand slam his only offensive contribution. He did, however, pace the Athletics with five RBI, while backup Stan Javier got two and no one else had more than one. It just wasn't the A's

year. Mark McGwire also had just one hit in the series.

Canseco's season undoubtedly influenced the way certain players today think about their performance. There was a time when players simply played their best game and let someone else add up the numbers. Is a thirtieth stolen base really worth much more than the twenty-ninth? Today many fans and some players would say yes. The fact that Canseco reached the 40/40 mark has inspired other players to think more about similar milestones and achievements. No one knows for sure exactly when it happened (the proliferation of computers and publications filled with stats also helped) but Canseco's 40/40 season confirmed the trend in baseball to focus more on individuals, an emphasis different from what we saw in the 1970's and earlier. This isn't to say Canseco was selfish. The media attention, not Canseco, signaled the change. Canseco would very likely have been lauded as the MVP even if he had finished with a 39/39 season.

Critics say that Canseco has a big ego. If having a big ego means recognizing and discussing your own ability, then he is guilty of it. Unlike many others though, the Canseco of the late 1980's said what he would do and then did it. In '88 he created a situation that force him to perform or suffer. He performed. Since that 1988 season, the "Canseco method" has generally backfired. He did tie for the league lead in home runs in 1991 and he was able to steal 26 bases that year (his best total since 1988). But twice he has made preseason references to the magic 40/40 mark and twice he has failed to do it.

It hasn't been long enough for us to see how history will treat the Canseco of 1988. His injury problems of succeeding years make his place in history more precarious than it was six or seven years ago.

Whether he ends up in the Hall of Fame will dramatically influence whether fans remember 1988 as an all-time great season or if it gets grouped with the likes of Hal Trosky's 1936 effort (42 home runs, 162 RBI, .343 Average): a great year without a great career. We'll see.

Bret Saberhagen - 1989

by Marc Bowman

W	L	PCT	G	GS	CG	SV	IP	SO	BB	B/I	ERA
23	6	.793	36	35	12	0	262	193	43	0.97	2.16

Bret Saberhagen's on-again, off-again career has featured a number of fine seasons interspersed with more pedestrian efforts, often due to injury. In 1985, then in only his second major league season, the 21-year old Saberhagen won twenty games, helped pitch the Royals to their only World Series championship (winning the World Series Most Valuable Player award in the process) and won his first Cy Young award.

In 1987, Saberhagen went 18-10 and placed among league leaders in many pitching categories. He tossed a no-hitter in 1991 on his way to another good season. In 1994, Saberhagen's 2.74 ERA was second only to Greg Maddux's 1.56 mark among National League pitchers. That year he went 14-4 and walked just one batter per eleven strikeouts; he was again among the league leaders in most pitching categories.

But 1989 was Sabes' best year.

In that season his Kansas City Royals were primarily an aging conglomerate of stars on the downhill sides of their long careers mixed with otherwise marginally talented players. Future Hall-of-Famer George Brett led the offense, but the three-time batting champion had his lowest batting average since entering the league fifteen years earlier. Leadoff hitter Willie Wilson had his worst year out of more than thirteen full seasons in Kansas City. Long-time second base standout Frank White was now 38 years old and no longer the power hitting threat he had been for much of the previous decade. In short, the Royals' offense was below average, ranking 11th out of 14 American League teams in runs scored.

For the 1989 Royals to challenge the potent Oakland Athletics, they'd have to have great pitching. Fortunately, they had an experienced staff of hurlers including Saberhagen, Mark Gubicza, Charlie Leibrandt and Floyd Bannister. But, as often happens with pitchers, things didn't go as planned. Bannister only made 14 starts due to several injury problems. Leibrandt made 27 starts, but a shoulder injury made him far less effective than in previous seasons; his 5.14 ERA was nearly two runs per game higher than his 1988 mark. Except for Saberhagen, Gubicza and Leibrandt, no Royals pitcher made more than 16 starts in 1989. The strength of the team, starting pitching, wasn't nearly as dominant as expected. Without Saberhagen, the Royals had only average pitching in 1989.

Fortunately for the Royals, though, Saberhagen was in excellent form for much of the season and pitched particularly well during the pennant chase. From late-May until the end of the season, Saberhagen went 20-2, including two winning streaks of six games and one eight-game win streak. As the pennant race heated up, Saberhagen became almost unhittable. Over his final 14 starts, Saberhagen went 13-1 with a 1.25 ERA. In the middle of September, Saberhagen set a team record by pitching 31 straight innings without allowing an earned run, he finished the season on his best streak of all, allowing just eight earned runs in his final 80 innings pitched, a 0.90 ERA.

You want clutch performances? Consider that while Saberhagen beat every other American League team at least once, he was unbeaten against rival American League West teams, winning 12 of 16 starts. Against the team the Royals were chasing all summer, the Oakland A's, Saberhagen went 3-0 with a 0.38 ERA. He allowed just one earned run in 24 innings, fanning 27 while allowing only 13 hits.

As the Royals chased the A's through the summer, Saberhagen kept his team in the race. Whenever he pitched, the Royals won, or so it seemed. The most telling statement of his value to the Royals is that in the 35 games when he started they went 29-6 (including a 23-2 mark in his last 25 starts); in the other 127 games they were a mediocre 63-64. In fact, the Royals might have won those other six games had they been able to provide Saberhagen with slightly better run support. In his five losses as a starter, the offense scored a total of just two runs.

Entering September, the Royals stood at 79-55, just a game and a half in back of Oakland. Alas, Saberhagen's marvelous pitching wasn't enough. His 6-1 mark in the final month couldn't overcome the team's 7-14 record when he wasn't pitching. Meanwhile, the surging Athletics went 18-9 down the stretch to beat Kansas City by seven games, then went on to win the American League championship and World Series.

Saberhagen concluded the season with major league bests in victories, ERA, complete games (12), innings pitched (262.1), winning percentage (.793) and opposition on base percentage. His 23 wins remain a Royals club record.

Following the season Saberhagen was rewarded with his second Cy Young award, becoming the fourth American League pitcher to win the award more than once and the second youngest pitcher in baseball history to win a second award. Saberhagen also won a Gold Glove in 1989.

Saberhagen's phenomenal success can be attributed to spectacular control of a great live fastball. He controls the pitch with fingertip pressure which makes the ball hop in the strike zone. He also keeps hitters off-stride with a slider, curve and change-up, but his perfect fastball is the pitch which produced his 1989 performance. Because he can throw the fastball with different movement on it, he can throw it throughout a game without letting the hitters see the same pitch in the same location.

Obviously, Saberhagen's great pitching had a large impact on his team's fortunes and on the AL West pennant race in 1989, but his great season also stands up well in historical terms. Since the mound was lowered and the strike zone was shrunk following the 1968 season, Saberhagen's .252 opponent OBP ranks eighth best in the majors over the last 26 seasons and fourth best in the American League. His season also ranks among the best ever in winning percentage and walks per nine innings.

When Saberhagen is on a roll, he's untouchable. He got into one of those streaks late in May of 1989 and never let up. The result was the best year of his career and one of baseball's all-time top 100 seasons.

Ryne Sandberg - 1990

by Robert O. Wood

G	AB	R	H	2B	3B	HR	RBI	BB	SO	AVG	OBP	SLG	SB
155	615	116	188	30	3	40	100	50	84	.306	.359	.559	25

Ryne Sandberg's fabulous 1990 season earned him the honor of becoming baseball's first $7 million player. The recipe for earning such riches? Be a perennial All-Star and Gold Glove middle infielder, and then lead the league in numerous offensive categories including a milestone 40 home runs. After Ryno's 1990 season, Bill James wrote that "Sandberg has to be considered a serious candidate for the position as the greatest second baseman of all time."

Sandberg had a great offensive season, leading the league in home runs, runs scored, and total bases. He became the first second baseman to lead the NL in home runs since Rogers Hornsby in 1925. Sandberg fell just four hits shy of becoming the first NL player since Ducky Medwick in 1937 to lead the league in hits, runs scored, total bases, and home runs.

Belting 40 home runs in a season is a truly historical accomplishment, especially for a middle infielder. Sluggers who never had 40 home runs in a season include Stan Musial, Dave Winfield, Eddie Murray, Lee May, Boog Powell, Joe Adcock, Willie Horton, Don Baylor, Greg Luzinski, Dave Parker, Bobby Bonds, Jack Clark, Don Mattingly, and Darryl Strawberry, to name a few.

On top of his offensive achievements, Sandberg won his eighth consecutive Gold Glove, and deservedly received a great deal of publicity for his stellar defense. Overlapping the 1989-1990 seasons, Ryno strung together a record defensive streak of 123 consecutive games and 582 chances without an error.

The choice of Sandberg's best season was not easy. It came down to 1984 versus 1990. 1984 was the breakthrough season in which he overwhelmingly won the MVP award while leading the Cubs to their first title in 40 years. Sandberg had 200 hits and led the league with 114 runs scored and 19 triples.

By 1990 Sandberg was already a superstar with little left to prove, or so we thought. Yet he elevated his game to another level, making him not only one of the best players in his era, but one of the best players in any era. Sandberg had career highs in runs scored, home runs, RBI, and slugging percentage. This was undoubtedly a great player having his greatest season.

1990 placed Ryno in heady company. Sandberg became only the third player ever to have a .300 average, 40 home runs, 100 RBI, and 25 steals, following Hank Aaron in 1963 and Jose Canseco in 1988. In addition, he became the first second baseman ever to hit 30 home runs in consecutive seasons, and the only second baseman in history other than Rogers Hornsby to hit 30 home runs and bat over .300 in the same season.

Second basemen are typically banjo hitters better known for their glove work than their batting prowess. Only a few notable second sackers have combined solid defense with power hitting. Most experts consider the four greatest second basemen to be Hornsby, Eddie Collins, Nap Lajoie, and Joe Morgan. Sandberg ranks with Charlie Gehringer right behind this elite group. Like Gehringer, Sandberg was an

all-around great player, smooth and graceful, a leader by example, very popular with fans and players, and modest to a fault.

Sandberg came to prominence on June 23, 1984 in a nationally televised game at Wrigley Field versus St. Louis. He hit two dramatic game-tying home runs, including one off ace reliever Bruce Sutter. He went on to lead the Cubs to their first title in forty years and won the MVP award deservedly.

Sandberg followed his MVP season with another great season in 1985. After being merely great in 1986-1988, Ryno recaptured his superstar status in 1989 by belting 30 home runs and leading the Cubs to another division title.

Ryno entered the 1990 season as an established superstar, but people wondered whether he would begin a downward spiral now that he had turned 30. To make better use of his new-found power, Sandberg was moved from the number two spot to the middle of the Cub batting order. The stage was set for the crowning of a new Mr. Cub.

On opening day, Sandberg extended his consecutive errorless game streak, tying Joe Morgan's all-time record. The streak lasted until mid-May when he was charged with a throwing error (his first in three years). Sandberg made a valiant off-balance diving underhanded throw, on a grounder, that Mark Grace could not reach as he was scrambling back to first.

After his customarily slow offensive start (.250 with one homer in April), Sandberg heated up with the weather, blasting 23 home runs and batting .375 in May and June.

At the All-Star break, Sandberg led the league in home runs, runs scored, hits, extra base hits, total bases, and slugging percentage, and was second in batting and fourth in RBI. He suffered through a hitting and fielding slump in July, partially due to the death of his brother-in-law.

A sprained ankle in early September prevented Sandberg from stealing 30 bases (and thus having the

Cubs' first 30/30 season), but the sprain did not prevent him from having a good final month of the season. Sandberg got his 100th RBI on his last at bat of the season (a feat he duplicated the next season).

Had Sandberg never produced his great 1990 season, he would have been remembered as one of the greatest fielding second basemen in baseball history. Along with his nine Gold Gloves, Sandberg owns the highest all-time fielding average among major league second basemen (.990). Red Schoendienst, who has been in baseball since the 1940's, claimed that Sandberg was the best fielding second baseman he had ever seen.

Sandberg was a great fielder in every aspect. He kept his hands loose and out in front of him, so he could handle any hop. He had phenomenal range, especially early in his career. Very few balls ever got through the right side of Wrigley's infield. Sandberg was also a great pivot on the double play, possessing a quick release and a very accurate arm.

Watching Sandberg play the field was watching an artist at work. The single most characteristic play in Sandberg's arsenal was taking away a sure hit up the middle with a backhanded stab and off-balance one-hop throw from the outfield grass that just nips the frustrated batter.

After his power numbers increased, Sandberg was no longer thought of as merely a good hitter and great glove. His combination of power, speed, and defense elevated him to the top of his profession. Sandberg and Barry Bonds are the only players in history to have (separate) seasons with 40 home runs and 50 stolen bases.

If he hadn't retired (somewhat prematurely) in the middle of the 1994 season, Sandberg would have become the fourth player besides Willie Mays, Bobby Bonds, and Andre Dawson to hit 300 home runs and steal 300 bases. Bill James summed up the career this way: "Sandberg ranks with Willie Mays as the closest thing I have ever seen to a perfect player." Ryno was given seven million reasons to believe that in 1990 he was at his most perfect.

Rob Dibble - 1990

by Bill Gray

W	L	PCT	G	GS	CG	SV	IP	SO	BB	B/I	ERA
8	3	.727	68	0	0	11	98	136	34	0.99	1.74

The ball approached the plate at 92 MPH. The batter thinking "fastball" would swing just as the ball dived suddenly downward, to the corner of the plate, and the batter would miss by a foot. He would mutter, "what was that?" And then the fastball *would* come in, at about 102 MPH. The batter might lean in this time, but now the ball would explode by him, hissing and rising as the hitter froze, unable to adjust. The matchup was effectively over. One more pitch, either a slider or a fastball, would finish the formalities. Maybe some more heaters would buzz around the batter's head before the final slider put him away, but the results were consistently lethal. If you watched closely you would see on the batter's face simultaneous relief and bewilderment as he headed back to the dugout. On the bench of the Cincinnati Reds, players would be shaking their heads or covering a smirk.

For the 1990 world champion Reds, their knockout artist was Rob Dibble. Dibble's dominance was relatively brief. Reds manager Pete Rose watched Dibble throw in 1987 and doubted Dibble would have a very long career. Rose said Dibble's herky-jerky motion placed too much stress on both his shoulder and his elbow. Unfortunately for Dibble, Rose was right. Dibble was on the way down by 1993, had rotator cuff surgery in 1994, and by 1995 he had become a rehab case, bouncing between minor league tune-ups and major league "what the heck" chances for a comeback. Long after the glory days, Dibble still maintained he could blow away hitters. But the injuries stole the two key elements that made Rob Dibble so effective. The first element was the supercharged fastball, but the other was more important. He lost his confidence. Without his heater, Dibble faded from major league dominance as fast as he'd arrived.

At his best from 1988 to 1991, Dibble did things people will remember for years, such as the time he struck out the side against the Padres on nine pitches. On the other hand, he will also be remembered for the incidents, like wrestling with manager Lou Piniella in the Reds locker room, or, after a rare bad outing, heaving a ball from the infield into the center field stands and injuring a fan.

Despite Rose's reservations, it was evident that the Reds had something special. Dibble and was promoted to the majors in June 1988, and worked 59 1/3 innings of setup relief, striking out 59 batters and limiting the opposition to a .207 batting average. In 1989, the emergence was unmistakable. If you were discussing strikeout artists, Dibble's name came up more often than anybody north of Nolan Ryan. Dibble fanned 141 batters in just 99 innings and established a major league record for strikeouts per nine innings -- not that any reliever would ever pitch nine innings -- with a rate of 12.4. Dibble's composite stats for the 1988-'89-'90 seasons show that in a total of 256 innings pitched, roughly the equivalent of one season for a number one starter, he produced:

W	L	ERA	SV	SO	BB
19	9	1.90	13	336	94

Dibble was at his best as a setup man. In 1990 he shared the setup work with Norm Charlton, usually leaving the ninth inning for closer Randy Myers, to form the most devastating late inning pitching combination in modern era baseball. Arguably, the "Nasty Boys" were the best bullpen trio of all time.

The raw power in Dibble's velocity was not that of a typical flamethrowing wildman. Dibble's control was excellent. Look at Dibble's line in the 1990 National League Championship against the Pirates: four games, five innings and one save. He allowed no runs, no hits, just one walk, and he fanned ten.

The Reds and Dibble earned a World Series matchup against the defending champion Oakland A's, who featured a super-potent offense led by Rickey Henderson, Mark McGwire, Jose Canseco and Carney Lansford. They also had great pitching with starters Dave Stewart, Bob Welch, and Mike Moore. In the bullpen, and in his prime was Dennis Eckersley. The A's had won ten consecutive postseason games before the Series began. When it was over their current record had dropped to 10 and 4, as the underdog Reds swept the A's in four straight. When the mighty "Bash Brothers" got a look at the late-inning work of Dibble, Myers, and Charlton (as a group: 9 2/3 inning with six hits, one walk, and zero runs), they walked away muttering "what was that?"

"That" was the Nasty Boys. And Dibble was the nastiest of the bunch. After the season the Reds' dilemma was how to keep the bullpen together. Dibble obviously had the ability to be a top closer, but Myers was a top closer and he was more effective with Dibble and/or Charlton doing setup work. With such help, Dibble rarely needed to pitch more than one inning, and he never needed to hold anything back. Picture the three of them coming in to every game and just being free to empty the gas tank each time if necessary, keeping nothing in reserve. This was a luxury the Reds wanted to preserve. Dibble wanted to be a closer, and he made comments to that effect after the 1990 Series. Piniella acknowledged the reality of the situation and said he'd get Dibble into more save situations. This disclosure tweaked Myers ever so slightly, but the Reds opened the 1991 season with much the same look in their bullpen.

Dibble made his case on the field in 1991. In April and May of that season he was superb. Against the Astros in one April game, he fanned six straight batters, tying a National League record. He was capable of pitching two or even three innings, at full velocity, with little or no rest. When Dibble pitched the eighth inning with blow-'em-away dominance, he forced Piniella to leave him in and get the save. How could you have your "setup" guy start the eighth, strike out the side, and then sit him down, and bring in your stopper? To stop what? So Dibble continued to pitch, and pitch a lot. He made ten appearances in May and gave up just five hits and no runs for the entire month, picking up seven saves.

Dibble nailed down ten more saves in June, and his ERA for the season stood at 1.29. He tied another NL record for consecutive saves with 23 in a row. He made his second straight All-Star appearance and pitched a scoreless inning. But when the season resumed after the All-Star break he was not the same, and never would be so utterly dominant again. The difference was remarkable. Once unhittable, Dibble yielded a .371 average to opposing batters in July. He was 0-2 from September 1st until the end of the season, and his ERA for this period was 6.75. Largely on the strength of his fabulous first half, he notched 31 saves for the season and set another record for strikeouts per nine innings pitched with 13.8 (124 K's in 82 1/3 innings).

Doctors diagnosed muscle weakness in both shoulders in 1993. Dibble was shut down for the rest of the year. In 1994 he pitched poorly in spring training, lacking both control and velocity, and he tried a sidearm delivery. Finally, it was determined that Dibble would need rotator cuff surgery. After the operation, Dibble was desperate to return, but the Reds wanted no part of their former nasty boy. He went to Cincinnati's Indianapolis club to rehab. The results were poor. Dibble struggled on, with a fastball only in the mid 80's, a slider with less bite, and control problems growing worse. He had fallen a long way since powering his way to the top of the pitching profession.

Dennis Eckersley - 1990

by David Luciani

W	L	PCT	G	GS	CG	SV	IP	SO	BB	B/I	ERA
4	2	.667	63	0	0	48	73	73	4	0.61	0.61

The average strikeout/walk ratio is under two-to-one. The best pitchers may get three or four strikeouts for every walk. Imagine someone getting over 18 strikeouts per walk! That's exactly what Dennis Eckersley did in 1990.

Looking through Eckersley's career, it's not difficult to see that his best years have come as a reliever. As a starter, he had a couple of great years (20-8 with a 2.99 ERA in 1978, and 17-10 with a 2.99 ERA in 1979). But, as a reliever, Eckersley has redefined the role of the closer. From mid-1987 up until the last week of the 1992 season, he dominated the game unlike any pitcher in the current generation of players.

It's not easy to describe just how good Eckersley was in 1990, but let's try. He allowed only five earned runs in 73.1 innings. That's close to averaging fifteen innings per earned run allowed! I've already mentioned the strikeout/walk ratio, but consider also that he struck out a batter an inning. He allowed just two home runs, and 1990 was the second year of his three season streak without throwing a single wild pitch. He blew only two saves in fifty opportunities.

Eckersley's season attracted little notice at the time, not just because of his achievements of 1989 but also because of his place in the shadow of teammates Bob Welch and Dave Stewart, the Athletics top starters. Welch was on his way to a 27-win season (and the Cy Young Award) and Stewart wrapped up his fourth straight (and final) 20-win year. What went unnoticed was Eckersley's improvement from the year before.

Eck lowered his ERA by almost a full run from 1.56 to 0.61. He improved his save total by 15, from 33 to 48. He allowed only two home runs compared to five the year before.

No pitcher intimidated batters quite the same way. Nolan Ryan, in 1990, could still throw hard enough to scare off anyone. Roger Clemens was at the top of his game, and Randy Johnson had not yet harnessed the control he later commanded. Unlike these others, when Eckersley came to the mound, you just felt that the game was over. Past tense. Eckersley led an Oakland bullpen that was 89-2 when it took a lead into the ninth inning that year.

Every great year seems to have a blemish somewhere, and Eckersley's was no exception. After dominating the game the entire regular season (including a scoreless inning in the All-Star game of course), Eckersley looked ready to cut through the post-season without difficulty. Against Boston in the Championship Series, Eckersley pitched three times in four games, without allowing a walk or a run. That carried the A's into the World Series against the Cincinnati Reds, where the A's (winners of 306 games from 1988-1990) were heavily favored to win. After a scoreless inning in the first game, a game the A's lost, Eckersley allowed three hits in game two, retiring only one batter in the ninth. He would not appear again in the '90 World Series. The Reds swept Oakland in four straight games, shocking the defending champs and astounding many so-called experts. Eckersley's line for the series? 0-1 with a 6.75 ERA while retiring only four batters -- and no saves. But those negatives all came in a short four-game series.

Eckersley's 1990 season now looks better, in retrospect. Although he didn't help his team win the World Series, he certainly helped get them there. In the history of relief pitching, his 1990 season stands as the finest single-season ever. Guillermo ''Willie'' Hernandez in 1984 won both the MVP and Cy Young awards, with 140 innings, 96 hits, 36 walks, and a 1.92 ERA. He pitched more than Eckersley in 1990, but certainly not better. Eckersley was far more effective. Mark Eichhorn, in 1986, turned in a much-overlooked season; he wasn't a closer (157 innings, 105 hits, 45 walks, and a 1.72 ERA) but beyond those guys, you start to look at the best single seasons of the aces. Rollie Fingers was fantastic in the strike-shortened 1981 season (78 innings, 55 hits, 13 walks, and a 1.04 ERA). Goose Gossage in the late seventies had a couple of years worthy of comparison. But in every case, Eckersley's numbers stand out as the best, performance-wise, of the whole group. His only shortcoming is that he pitched in an era which gave him fewer innings to showcase his talent.

But even in 1990, Eckersley wasn't the highest ranking reliever in the Cy Young voting. That honor went to Bobby Thigpen, who established the mark that still stands for saves in one season (57). Thigpen's ERA was more than a full run higher. He walked almost thirty more batters than Eckersley did, and he pitched only fifteen more innings. In sixty-five save opportunities, Thigpen blew eight. Eckersley blew only two in fifty chances. Clearly, it was the all-time saves record that got Thigpen the Cy votes. In the same way that Bob Welch's season was essentially inferior to Dave Stewart's (as reflected by the difference in MVP voting and Cy Young voting -- Stew finished ahead of Welch), the voters felt they had to reward the unusual. Welch won 27 games, so they gave him the Cy Young award over Stewart.

Thigpen broke the saves record (shattered it, actually) so he finished higher in the voting than Eckersley. If there's any doubt who was better, compare the performances of Thigpen and Eckersley, asking yourself which you'd rather have on your team. In fact, find any relief pitcher in the history of baseball that, relative to their era, you'd rather have as your closer than the 1990 Eckersley. Don't worry if you can't find him, because he doesn't exist.

There was only one season ever like Eckersley's in 1990, and there will probably never be another.

Roberto Alomar - 1993

by David Luciani

G	AB	R	H	2B	3B	HR	RBI	BB	SO	AVG	OBP	SLG	SB
153	589	109	192	35	6	17	93	80	67	.326	.408	.492	55

It's easy to forget just how young Roberto Alomar is and how much he has already accomplished in his career. In 1991, at the age of 23, he became the first player since Ty Cobb to get 40 doubles and 50 steals in a season.

Alomar's 1993 season went somewhat unnoticed as he spent much time in the shadow of teammate and eventual batting champ John Olerud (who spent most of the year chasing .400). When the season was over, everyone was talking about Joe Carter's home run. However, when people talked about second basemen, Alomar by 1993 was the overwhelming favorite among both fans and the media. Alomar's Blue Jays were destined to become the first team since the 1977-78 Yankees to repeat as World Series champions. The Toronto market gave Alomar a key place in a mix of superstars who, in 1993, were the best in baseball. Alomar, Olerud and designated hitter Paul Molitor, became the first teammates of this century to finish 1-2-3 in the batting average race. That achievement was possible only because Alomar pulled ahead of Kenny Lofton for third place on the final day of the season.

Alomar's 1993 season was far superior to his previous seasons. He essentially doubled his home run output to 17 (he had never hit more than nine in any prior year), he posted a career-best batting average of .326 (his career average going into 1995 was .298), he topped his career-high in RBI by 17 (up from 76 in 1992). His 55 stolen bases and 109 runs scored were also career bests. He was voted to the All-Star team for the fourth straight year and won his third straight Gold Glove. Try to think of the best defensive infielders and then match them up against Alomar's 1993 offensive numbers. There is no comparison. More remarkable was that the big RBI total came while batting second for most of the year.

Alomar played a key role in the success of the Blue Jays of 1993. In late August, for example, Toronto had lost three straight games in Seattle, and the Jays were showing signs of sliding, with the Yankees, Orioles and Tigers all poised to take over first place. In the fourth game of the series against the Mariners, Alomar clubbed a grand slam off Erik Hanson, and the slump was temporarily cured. Then there was Alomar's tremendous postseason play. In game five of the American League Championship Series against the White Sox, Alomar reached base every time he came to the plate (two walks and three hits), leading the Jays to a 5-3 win and a 3-2 lead in the series.

The World Series was even better. Lost in shadows of Carter's memorable home run and Paul Molitor's MVP performance was Alomar, who hit .480 for the series with five runs scored, six RBI and four stolen bases. Without Alomar, the Blue Jays wouldn't have won the World Series in 1993 (or even have been in the Series, for that matter). To his benefit, the fact that they repeated as World Champions will ensure fans and future historians' attention to the whole Toronto roster and Alomar's many accomplishments.

In 1993, Alomar was not only known as the best

second baseman in the game, but also one of the best players at any position. He was elected as a starter on the All Star team (and hit a home run -- the first by any Blue Jay All-Star ever).

Alomar's presence, and his success in 1993, mark a shift of sorts in baseball. Second base had always been dominated by defensive specialists with few offensive stars. Alomar leads the pack of a new group that includes Carlos Baerga, Jeff Kent, Craig Biggio, Delino DeShields and Chuck Knoblauch. He has been one of the few players in the 1990's who has noticeably raised the standard of what teams expect offensively from a specific position in their lineup. Baerga, the most distinguished of Alomar's peers, summed it up well with his quote in Alomar's autobiography, *Second To None*. ''For me ... Robbie right now is one of the most complete players in the big leagues. I can compare him with Barry Bonds and Kirby Puckett and Ken Griffey Jr.'' If recognition by one's peers is testimony to value, then Alomar's value especially in 1993 did not go unnoticed.

Alomar has been described as self-absorbed, even quietly arrogant, like a Rickey Henderson who smiles but rarely talks. Like many of today's superstars he is more than a little aware of his numbers. This is a guy who went up against the Blue Jays and beat them in an arbitration case, the first time the negotiation-tough Jays management had lost in arbitration since 1983. He knows that he is regarded as one of the best players in baseball and keeps quiet about it most, but not all of the time.

With a career still ahead of him, it is improbable that Alomar's peak will always be his 1993 season. He is well past the 1,000 hit mark, having reached that milestone at age 25, and he just turned 27 in February, 1995. Likely there will be many more great seasons. In ten or twenty years, Alomar should be remembered as the best player on a star-studded, World Champion Blue Jays team and one of the best players of the 1990's.

Barry Bonds - 1993

by Bill Gray

G	AB	R	H	2B	3B	HR	RBI	BB	SO	AVG	OBP	SLG	SB
159	539	129	181	38	4	46	123	126	79	.336	.458	.677	29

Unlike Jeff Bagwell, Albert Belle, and Matt Williams, who had career peaks in 1994 with an implied asterisk for the shortened season, Barry Bonds had been to the top of the mountain before and will very likely return again. Bonds in 1994 might have had 50 home runs and 40 stolen bases; we will never know. What we do know is what Bonds did in 1993, with no asterisks and no speculation about what might have been.

Bonds is the latest member of the Greats of the Game club (if you want to take some friends or family to see one of the all-time greats in his prime, someone who will later be compared to Jimmie Foxx, Joe DiMaggio, Stan Musial, and company, go see Bonds). He plays with an overwhelming combination of speed, power and defense, the trademarks of today's star players.

Bonds has been so dominant, sometimes it seems as if he's won a dozen MVP awards. But it's "only" three. His gifts cover the spectrum; he is a major weapon in every way a player can be, producing near Triple Crown numbers year after year. If stolen bases were the fourth crown category in baseball, Bonds would be among the leaders in every Quadruple Crown race. Runs scored? Right there. Defense? There are some outfielders with stronger arms, and Bonds has been faulted at times for using unnecessary "style" in the field, but few if any of his fellow left fielders can track down a sure double or triple, or snatch a home run from the sky with a leap above the fence, as Bonds can. He simply does it all.

Position players are commonly rated in seven categories by scouts: hitting, hitting for power, baserunning skill, raw speed, defensive range, throwing, and fielding skill. Many players now holding full-time major league jobs are below average in most of these categories. Bonds is not just above average in every category. He is so far above average, some TEAMS don't have any player who can match up to Bonds in *any* of the seven categories.

Take a look at the current population of .300 hitters. Very few of them will ever hit 40 home runs. The few possessing good power will never steal 30 or 40 bases in a season. And the few .300 hitters with great speed do not hit for power or drive in runs. There is only one who does it all: Barry Bonds.

In other essays in this book, I've made a point of discussing players relative to their era and their peers. Since major league baseball's recent expansion, talent is inevitably diluted. Bonds began his career in a two division league and saw it grow to three divisions in 1994. Doubtless he will see another expansion if he plays into his mid 30's. And certainly a crop of "Not-Ready-For-Prime-Time-Pitchers" have served some cookies to Bonds. But there have also been many accomplishments against top competition. Even in a meaningless 1995 spring training game, seeing Bonds rocket a long home run off a stud like Randy Johnson, the only pitcher in Arizona who was throwing at high velocity after the longest winter ever, and the pitcher who has been pure King Cobra venom to lefthanded batters -- makes it difficult to imagine Bonds' productivity would diminish in any era.

Bonds won the National League MVP award in 1990,

1992 and 1993. He finished second to Atlanta's Terry Pendleton in 1991, and second again in 1994. That's the best five year run in the history of MVP voting. Pendleton had a career year in 1991 as he raised his batting average 89 points above his 1990 season. Bonds' 1991 season was not quite as strong as his 1990 campaign, but probably better than Pendleton's. Voting is often affected by subjective thinking and events off the field. Bonds has made some mistakes on the PR front, and the attitude issue probably cost him the opportunity to win four consecutive MVP awards. The 1994 MVP award went to Houston's Jeff Bagwell, and deservedly so, as Bagwell had a huge year. Still, there is room for speculation due to the premature end of the 1994 season. When the players struck on August 12th, Bonds was knocking home runs and stealing bases virtually at will. For students of long hot streaks, consider Bonds after June 10th of 1994: batting average of .335 with 24 home runs, 47 RBI, and 18 stolen bases. For those who enjoy pro-rated numbers, that's a pace of 70 home runs, 137 RBI, and 52 stolen bases in 600 at bats. Could Bonds have won another MVP award in 1994? You bet he could. Bagwell too, was red hot after the All Star break, but he broke his hand just days before the strike, ending his great year. Dick Groat missed some time late in 1960 and still won the MVP, so I suppose Bagwell could have done the same, but there was no player like Barry Bonds in 1960. So there's one more item for the great what-if list of 1994.

Back to unqualified reality: Bonds, from 1990 to 1994 earned three MVP awards, and finished a close second twice. There are few players who have earned three MVP awards: Jimmie Foxx, DiMaggio, Musial, Mantle, Berra, Mike Schmidt, and Bonds; and only Berra, who won in 1951, 1954, 1955, rivals Bonds' concentrated dominance within a five-year time frame.

What effect does Bonds have on a team? His first team, the Pittsburgh Pirates, had hit skid row in the mid eighties. When the 21-year-old Bonds joined the club on May 30, 1986, the Pirates had a foundation upon which to rebuild. Bonds would be the most significant player to arrive in Pittsburgh since Willie Stargell in 1963.

Bonds was one of the most highly regarded rookies in years, a product of the legendary Arizona State baseball program. After finishing his collegiate career, Bonds played briefly for the Pirates' Class A club in Hawaii, but was quickly jumped up to Pittsburgh. He was to be the cornerstone player around whom GM Syd Thrift would construct a contending team. Thrift made brilliant trades for Bobby Bonilla, Andy Van Slyke, Jay Bell, Mike Lavalliere and Doug Drabek. By 1990 the Pirates, under Jim Leyland, were again a contending team. Bonds had shown flashes of offensive genius in his first four seasons. In 1986 he appeared in 113 games and hit 16 homers.

The Pirates were expected to fade from contention in 1992 after losing Bonilla to the arch rival Mets. Without Bonilla in the lineup, many figured Bonds would struggle at the plate. Bonds responded to challenge. He cut his strikeouts to a career low 69 while walking 127 times. He hammered 34 homers, stole 39 bases, drove in 103 runs and scored 109 times in the "weakened" Pirate lineup. Worth noting is that Bonilla, who enjoyed some huge seasons in Pittsburgh, fell into the worst season of his career with the Mets. While New York failed to contend, Bonds led the Pirates to the NL East title for the third consecutive year, and became MVP for the second time.

When he became a free agent in 1993, Bonds was obviously too high-priced for Pittsburgh's budget. He was baseball's best player, and no one knew for sure what he could command on the market. He signed with the Giants for over seven million dollars a year. Despite the ongoing public outcry about overpaid baseball players, comparatively little was said about Bonds deserving such a huge salary. He did, however, place himself under a media microscope for the 1993 season. With such a huge paycheck, could Bonds possibly earn it? No problem! It was MVP time again, for yet another season, making number three.

The batting average of .336 was a career high, as were the 46 home runs and the 123 RBI. Runs scored: another career high. Slugging percentage: also a career high. On base percentage (you guessed it) yet another career high. Despite Bonds' efforts, the Giants did not win the pennant, falling a game short with a season ending loss to the Dodgers. But nobody blamed Bonds. Without him they would not have come close.

Barry Bonds is simply the best player the game has produced in many, many years.

Jeff Bagwell - 1994

by Bill Gilbert

G	AB	R	H	2B	3B	HR	RBI	BB	SO	AVG	OBP	SLG	SB
110	400	104	147	32	2	39	116	65	65	.368	.461	.750	15

In 1968, Bob Gibson crafted a 1.12 ERA, while Carl Yastrzemski led the American League in hitting by 11 points with a batting average of .301. The major league batting average that year was an all-time low of .237, prompting rules changes which included the lowering of the pitching mound.

However, hitters were not completely shut out in 1968, particularly on May 27. On that date, Frank Thomas was born in Columbus, Georgia and Jeff Bagwell was born in Boston. Twenty six years later, they would become the offensive leaders in a season that would be for hitters what 1968 was for pitchers. Bagwell and Thomas (along with Albert Belle) became the first batters to record slugging averages over .700 since Ted Williams in 1957. Bagwell's .750 slugging average was the highest since Babe Ruth (.772) and Lou Gehrig (.765) in 1927.

The success Thomas enjoyed in 1994 was not unexpected, as he had already established himself as one of the top players in the game in his first 3 1/2 seasons, winning the AL MVP award in 1993. Bagwell, the NL Rookie of the Year in 1991 with the Houston Astros, had improved in each of the next two seasons to rank in the upper tier of major league hitters. However, the magnitude of his success in 1994 was not expected, even by Bagwell. Signifying the unanticipated nature of Bagwell's season, he won an "Espy" award from ESPN as the "Break-through Athlete of the Year".

Bagwell virtually rewrote the Astros record book in 1994, even while the season was shortened by 47 games. His 39 home runs eclipsed Jimmy Wynn's club record of 37 and his 116 RBI topped the team record of 110, set by future GM Bob Watson. Bagwell's 300 total bases tied the mark held by Cesar Cedeno, and his .368 batting average easily surpassed Rusty Staub's record of .333, which had stood for 27 years. Staub's on base average record of .402 also went by the boards as Bagwell came in 49 points higher.

The most remarkable aspect of Bagwell's season was his .750 slugging average. It ranks second in NL history, behind only Rogers Hornsby's .756 in 1925. Bagwell was only the fourth NL slugger to reach the .700 mark, joining Hornsby (twice), Hack Wilson and Stan Musial. Think about it. Hank Aaron, Willie Mays, Mel Ott, Ernie Banks, Eddie Mathews, Frank Robinson, Willie McCovey and Mike Schmidt never came close to .700, much less .750.

Bagwell was first in runs scored, runs batted in, on base percentage, and slugging average and second in batting average and home runs. He became the first NL player to finish first or second in all of these categories since Chuck Klein in 1932. With 116 RBI in 110 games, he became the first major league player since George Brett (in 1980) to average more than one RBI per game. He was a unanimous choice as National League MVP, only the third player to be so honored, along with Orlando Cepeda (1967) and Mike Schmidt (1980).

A season like Bagwell's inevitably has some major

highlights. He was named NL player of the month in both June and July. On June 24 against the Dodgers, he hit two home runs in the sixth inning and homered again in his next at bat to join Wynn as the only players to hit three homers in one game in the Astrodome. He also set a single-season record with 23 home runs in the Astrodome. Bagwell played in his first All Star game and won his first Gold Glove for his defensive work at first base.

Bagwell's rise to prominence has mirrored that of the Astros. He was part of a rebuilding effort when he was a rookie in 1991, and the team finished with a league worst 65-97 record. As Bagwell improved the next two years, the team regained respectability with records of 81-81 and 85-77. When the 1994 season ended abruptly on August 12, the Astros were only one-half game behind Cincinnati in the NL Central and were on a pace to win 93 games.

The Astros had become a contender and Bagwell had clearly become a franchise player, a status for which he was rewarded with a long-term contract by the Astros after the season.

Bagwell's accomplishments in 1994 are just a little tainted by the shortened season. Two days before the strike started, Bagwell broke a bone in his left hand when hit by a pitch, an injury that would have sidelined him for three or four weeks. Consequently, his achievements would not have been as impressive, relative to the rest of the league, if the season had run it's course. His 1993 season ended in a similar manner, causing concerns about his aggressive batting style, crowding the plate to command the outside corner. Another injury of the same type in 1995 further deepened these concerns.

What is ahead for Bagwell? Can he finish a season without injury? Can he possibly improve? He is one of the hardest workers in the game, constantly building his strength and bat speed. And he has been able to make the necessary adjustments to stay ahead of the pitchers. Entering the 1996 season at age 27, his prime years should still be ahead of him. However, it is hard to imagine improving Bagwell on his 1994 achievements. If he does, he will be on his way to becoming one of the all-time greats.

Greg Maddux - 1994

by Marc Bowman

W	L	PCT	G	GS	CG	SV	IP	SO	BB	B/I	ERA
16	6	.727	25	25	10	0	202	156	31	0.93	1.56

Forget about any asterisks.

Despite losing the last seven weeks of the 1994 season due to the labor dispute, Greg Maddux turned in a performance that easily ranks among the very best ever by any pitcher any year. While batters were enjoying their most prolific hitting season of this generation, Maddux bucked the scoring trend by posting the third lowest ERA since the end of the dead ball era. His 1.56 ERA was an astounding 2.65 runs below the National League average. Bob Gibson's 1.12 in 1968, often cited as the ultimate reference point for ERA dominance, was only 1.87 better than the National League as a whole.

Of course, Maddux had been very good over previous seasons, winning the Cy Young award in 1992 and 1993. Throwing four different pitches with precision and timing made Maddux an increasingly difficult pitcher to hit. Described by Bill James as ''nature's perfect pitcher,'' Maddux uses a smooth delivery that prevents injury and allows him to be the most durable pitcher in the game. By working directly and throwing strikes consistently, Maddux gets large numbers of innings with small numbers of pitches. His workload is therefore lighter than his innings totals would suggest.

Maddux never missed a start due to injury in eight seasons, and led the National League four consecutive years (1991-1994) in innings pitched and batters faced. He was pursuing his fifth consecutive year leading the league in both innings and batters faced

(and ERA again) in August 1995 when this essay was being completed. In July 1995 the Braves media department proudly issued a report that Maddux had pitched for a three-year span with the biggest difference between individual ERA and league ERA in the history of the national pastime.

Still, it is the 1994 performance that stands out as his personal best. Maddux led the National League in almost every category while tying for the league lead with 16 wins and three shutouts. But his performance went beyond these individual accomplishments; Maddux was by far the single biggest factor keeping an otherwise unspectacular team in the race for a division title.

From 1991 to 1993, the Atlanta Braves were one of baseball's best offensive teams. They finished among the top three National League teams in runs scored each year, barely off the pace set by the league leaders and also led the league in home runs in 1992 and 1993. In 1994, however, the Braves were a far more pedestrian team at the plate, scoring 542 runs, barely above the league average of 530 per team.

In 1994 it wasn't as if Atlanta's scoring pace fell off from the 1992-1993 level; indeed, their 4.75 runs per game in 1994 was up from 4.52 in the previous three years. The difference was that over the same span National League team scoring averages rose from 4.12 in 1991-93 to 4.62 in 1994. The 1994 Braves thus became a merely average offensive team. They managed their 68-46 record, second best in the

National League - on the strength of the league's best pitching.

Before Maddux arrived, the Braves had a terrific trio of Tom Glavine, John Smoltz and Steve Avery. As a group they averaged 700 innings of 3.14 ERA each year from 1991 to 1993, but in 1994 their combined ERA jumped nearly a full run to 4.05. This mark is good, but not good enough to keep the Braves in contention had Maddux not cut his own ERA by almost a run.

Maddux's success depended not only on avoiding baserunners (he led the league in opponents' batting average with .207 and opponents' on base percentage .245) but also prevented extra-base hits. He led the league in opponents' slugging average (.259) and in home run rate - an incredible 0.18 homers per nine innings. Maddux allowed just four homers in 202 innings pitched.

Maddux gave the Braves a chance to win every time he took the mound. Perhaps the most telling statistic is that he made 24 quality starts out of 25 games started. His only bad start was against the Expos on June 27th when he left after surrendering five runs in 6 2/3 innings. Pitchers don't get any more consistent than 96% quality starts. Anyone around 65% to 70% is likely to be regarded as successful and reliable, and the 80% level roughly defines stardom.

Maddux managed to get even better down the stretch, posting a 0.93 ERA over his final eight starts, fanning more batters than he allowed to reach base. While he went 6-2 over that stretch, including five complete games, the Braves were only 16-17 without Maddux on the mound. Pitching carried the team and it was Maddux who carried the pitching staff. After the season he was rewarded with an unprecedented third consecutive Cy Young award.

Since Babe Ruth ushered in the home run era, only Bob Gibson in 1968 (1.12) and Dwight Gooden in 1985 (1.53) have posted a better ERA than Maddux had in 1994. Consider the context in which Maddux created this marvelous pitching performance: 1994 represented the blossoming of a long-term trend towards increased scoring. Indeed, the 1994 rate of 4.62 runs per game was the National League's highest in 41 years. In 1953, when the Braves were still in Milwaukee and there were only eight teams in the league, National League teams averaged 4.75 runs per game. Another Braves' pitcher, Warren Spahn, led the league that year with a 2.10 ERA.

Only three other National League starters managed an ERA below 3.00 in 1994: Bret Saberhagen at 2.74, Doug Drabek at 2.84 and Jeff Fassero at 2.99. Only three times in the previous 33 seasons had fewer than five pitchers posted sub-3.00 ERA's (1970, 1979 and 1987). While all were above average offensive years, none matched 1994 for scoring, and none boasted a singular pitching performance anywhere close to that which Maddux fashioned.

The difference of 2.65 between the Maddux ERA and the league average ERA is the largest margin in the history of the major leagues. The closest any other pitcher has come to Maddux's feat was in 1930 when Dazzy Vance posted a 2.61 ERA against the league average of 4.97, a difference of 2.36.

For additional historical perspective, consider that Maddux is one of only two National League ERA champs ever to lead the second-place finisher by more than a full run per game. Vance posted an ERA that was 1.26 better than Carl Hubbell's in 1930, another very big year for hitters at the expense of pitchers. 1994 was certainly another Year of the Hitter, but not when Greg Maddux pitched! Although it's unfortunate that labor unrest prevented Maddux from finishing such a superb season, missing the final seven weeks of 1994 cannot undo his spectacular accomplishment.

Fans wishing to see an all-time great can still catch the Greg Maddux show. While it's too late to watch Vance or Hubbell, there is one living legend you can see now and talk about in future decades. Bring the kids, too, and suggest they try counting how many pitches it takes Maddux to record each out; they can tell their grandchildren about it.

Frank Thomas - 1994

by Tony Blengino

G	AB	R	H	2B	3B	HR	RBI	BB	SO	AVG	OBP	SLG	SB
113	399	106	141	34	1	38	101	109	61	.353	.494	.729	2

How good is Frank Thomas? Well, in a strike-interrupted 1994 season, in which hitting exploits abounded, Thomas' star shone the brightest. Thomas is unquestionably at the head of the class of what arguably is the most accomplished group of twenty-something players in baseball's last half-century. Thomas possesses the rarest and most desired combination of offensive skills: he is the best in baseball at reaching base and at moving runners around the bases, and is certainly on his way to becoming one of baseball's all-time greats.

Inevitably, when runs increase throughout baseball, talk of a "rabbit ball" becomes rampant. Interestingly enough, a whole lot of these rabbit ball seasons immediately follow major league expansion. Or is it a coincidence that hitting bursts in 1961 and 1994 both closely followed major league expansion? In 1961, the American League expanded by 25%, and Roger Maris, Mickey Mantle and Norm Cash went bonkers. In 1993, the NL expanded by two teams, but drafted players from both leagues, further depleting the already-thin pitching corps. A year later, we witnessed the spectacle of the multi-player chase of Roger Maris' single-season home run record. Matt Williams and Ken Griffey, as the majors' home run leaders most of the way in 1994, got the bulk of the national attention. But just as in 1961, when Norm Cash's productivity closely rivaled the media-hyped years of Yankee teammates Maris and Mantle, the most productive major leaguer in 1994 was relatively ignored. Thomas racked up one of the most formidable stat lines in baseball history, and was robbed of

single-season immortality by the strike. Thomas led the American League in most key offensive categories, and ranked in the top three in virtually all of the non-speed statistical categories. He was third in batting average and in RBI and second in home runs, and he led the league in runs, walks, on base percentage, and slugging percentage.

Thomas had a relative production figure of 212, also pacing the league. Thomas actually had better numbers in the percentage categories until he slumped about a week before the strike, and just missed becoming the first major leaguer since Ted Williams in 1957 to record a .500 on base percentage. His .729 slugging percentage in 1994 was the highest in the majors since Williams' .731 in 1957 (although Jeff Bagwell did even better in 1994). When looking for players comparable to Thomas, names like Williams and Ruth inevitably pop up .

It is fun, though risky business, to extrapolate abbreviated 1994 stats to estimate individual full-season equivalents. Still, Thomas was on track to hit 54 homers, with 145 RBI, 152 runs scored and 156 walks. Hitters' season or not, Thomas and Albert Belle were robbed of legendary full-season accomplishments by the strike. No one -- not Babe Ruth, Ted Williams, Lou Gehrig, or Jimmie Foxx - has *ever* reached all of those levels in the same season. But 1994 is just one season, How does Thomas' career to date match up with the all-time greats?

In just four and a half major league seasons, Thomas

(at age 27) proved himself as clearly one of the foremost offensive players of any era. After 1994, Thomas had a career batting average of .326. Among active players, only singles hitters Wade Boggs (.335) and Tony Gwynn (.333) ranked higher. But it is in the production stats, the on base and slugging percentages, where Thomas' greatness reaches out and grabs you. After 1994, Thomas had a career on base percentage of .455 and slugging percentage of .590. Check out where Thomas ranks among the all-time career leaders in those categories. His career on base percentage trails only Williams (.483) and Ruth (.474) in the modern era. His slugging percentage ranks sixth, trailing only Ruth (.690), Williams (.634), Gehrig (.632), Foxx (.609) and Greenberg (.605). Most of those players enjoyed the bulk of their careers in hitter-dominated eras, making Thomas' career numbers look even better. He has been amazingly consistent. Thomas has never recorded an on base percentage below .434, a slugging percentage below .529, or a relative production figure below 176. A career relative production figure equal to his *worst* single season mark would rank him fourth on the all-time list, tied with Rogers Hornsby (Gehrig is third at 182).

Like Williams, Thomas tends to draw huge numbers of walks, and this skill will hold down his totals in the media's favorite categories, like hits and home runs. Using Bill James' career projection methods, Thomas has established only a 10.6% chance of reaching 3000 hits, and a 37.8% chance of reaching 500 home runs. However, his key traits, patience and power, both age well, so Thomas should perform at a very high level for a very long time, and post formidable raw career numbers in the Triple Crown categories, and Top Five (or maybe Top Three) numbers in career on base percentage and slugging percentage.

What makes Thomas so special? Well, put simply, he swings at strikes, takes balls, and hits the ball where it's pitched with extreme power. It sounds simple, but very few players can master all of these arts at the major league level. He led the American League in walks and on base percentage in three of his first four full major league seasons. This has enabled him to score between 104 and 108 runs in each of the last four seasons despite a lack of speed. Unlike most power hitters, Thomas makes good contact consistently. After whiffing 112 times in 1991, he averaged only 67 strikeouts per season over the next three years, including an amazing 54 in 661 plate appearances in 1993. Also, righty-hitting Thomas sends the majority of his homers to center field or right field. He's not one of those "turn your hips and crank" kinds of sluggers. There are absolutely no holes in Thomas' swing, and he isn't vulnerable to any particular type of pitch in any particular location. And if you're a lefty pitcher, forget it. Thomas batted .408, .376, .357, .311 and .385 against lefties in his first five seasons. On 1994's All-Star Game telecast, announcer Jim Kaat stated that Thomas draws too many walks -- that he hurts the White Sox by taking pitches instead of going out of the strike zone to try to drive the ball. Hogwash, I say. Thomas is not a .300 hitter because he sprays the ball around and puts it in play; he is a .300 hitter because he minimizes the denominator of the batting average ratio by *never* getting himself out. Which would you rather have: Thomas' awesome all-around numbers, with only 258 outs made, or "noted run producer" like Joe Carter's illusory 103 RBI, with a .326 on base percentage (.313 career) and 317 outs made? Next question.

How does one spot the next Frank Thomas? Well, keep your eyes peeled for hitters who are at or below their minor league's average age, and who have on base and slugging percentages far above their league's average. In 1990 at Double-A Birmingham, Thomas had a .472 on base percentage and .581 slugging percentage. Six teams passed on the young first baseman Thomas in the 1989 draft, for various reasons. Most ironically, the Phillies, drafting fourth, chose outfielder Jeff Jackson because they were supposedly "set" at first base, with Ricky Jordan who, soon after the draft, lost his starting job.

Thomas is already an all-time great offensive player, at or near his career peak and going strong. It is appropriate to end with his story, because there is obviously more to come!

Glossary of Selected Terms

Adjusted - adjective meaning a statistic has been normalized to league average and adjusted for home park factor, may also be described as "relative" to differentiate from raw official statistics.

Adjusted Batting Runs - The Linear Weights measure of Batting Runs, normalized to league average and adjusted for home park factor, where the league average is zero. Thus a positive number indicates an above-average performance, and a negative number indicates below average performance.

Adjusted Batting Wins - The number of runs needed by a batter to create an additional win, with offense adjusted for home park factor.

Adjusted ERA - an ERA index where the league average is defined as 100, and each individual ERA has been park-adjusted. Thus an Adjusted ERA index above 100 means better than average, one case where a higher number means a better ERA.

Adjusted Production - same as Relative Production. See also Production.

Batting Runs - The Linear Weights measure of runs contributed beyond those of a league average batter or team, such league average defines as zero. The formula depends upon the run values for each offensive event that results from Pete Palmer's computer simulation of all major league games played since 1901. See also the Introduction chapter.

Batting Wins - Adjusted batting runs divided by the number of runs required by a batter to create an additional win beyond average, where the average is .500. Thus, a translation of offensive effectiveness into expected resulting wins above that average.

Earned Run Average (ERA) - earned runs times nine, divided by innings pitched.

Fielding Runs - the Linear Weights measure of runs saved by a fielder, compared to the average performance of other players at the same position in the same league.

Games Behind - Standings, figured by adding the difference in wins between a trailing team and the leader to the difference in losses, and dividing by two. Thus a team that is three games behind may trail by three in the win column and three in the loss column, or four and two, or any combination of wins and losses totaling six.

Home Run Percentage - home runs per 100 at-bats.

Linear Weights - A system created by Pete Palmer to measure all the events on a ballfield in terms of their average impact on runs scored. At the root of this system, as with other sabermetric figures such as Runs Created, is the knowledge that wins and losses are what the game of baseball is about, that wins and loses are proportional to runs scored and runs allowed, and that runs in turn are proportional to the events that go into their making. See also the Introduction chapter of this book.

On Base Percentage - hits plus walks plus hit by pitch, divided by at bats plus walks, plus hit by pitch.

Opponents Batting Average - the batting average of all hitters who faced a particular pitcher or pitching staff, i.e. hits allowed divided by the at bats of opposing batters. The measure allows more perspective on pitcher effectiveness, e.g. a pitcher yielding a .300 Opponents Batting Average may be said to have had a bad year, unless the year was 1930.

Opponents On Base Percentage - same concept as Opponents Batting Average, but using OBP.

Pitching Runs - the Linear Weights measure of runs saved beyond what an average pitcher would achieve, the average being defined as zero.

Production - On Base Percentage plus Slugging Percentage: a simple but useful measure of overall batting prowess, in that the weaknesses on one-half of the formula, On Base Percentage, may be countered by the strengths of the other, Slugging Percentage, and vice versa. When PRO, as it is abbreviated, is adjusted for home park and normalized to league average to become PRO+ or Relative Production, the calculation is modified to create a baseline reference point of 100 for a league-average performance. For PRO+, the calculation is

[(Player On Base Pct.) / (League On Base Pct.)] + [(Player Slugging Avg.) / (League Slugging Avg.)] - 1

This produces a figure with a decimal point - an above-average figure, like 1.46, or a below-average figure, like 0.82. For ease of display, in this book we drop the decimal and express these as 146 and 82, meaning the league average is 100.

Quality Start - a game in which the starting pitcher lasts for six innings or more and allows three runs or less.

Range Factor - the number of chances (putouts plus assists) times nine divided by the number of defensive innings played. A high range factor may indicate good movement by the fielder, or pitching and ballpark conditions that cause many balls to be hit into that fielder's designated area.

Ratio - baserunners per inning, calculated as hits plus walks, divided by innings pitched. Some authorities including *Total Baseball* include hit batsmen as baserunners. Abbreviated as B/I in this book. Many sources use the figure baserunners per nine innings, which would be Ratio times nine.

Real Slugging Average (RSA) - a creation of Larry Thompson, RSA is a lengthy, but simple, calculation to measure batting efficiency in a manner similar to slugging average but taking into account walks and stolen bases as well. For more information about this measure, see *The Perfect Game* edited by Mark Alvarez and published by Taylor Publishing.

Relative Control/Power - see the essay beginning on page 307.

Relative ERA - Earned run average adjusted for the home ballpark factor and compared to the league average, where the league average is 100. See Adjusted ERA.

Relative Production - a convenient index showing how much offense a player brings to the plate by adding on-base percentage and slugging percentage and adjusting for ballpark factor and comparing to the league average defined as 100. A number over 100 would be better than average production, while under 100 would be lower than average.

Runs Created - Bill James' formulation for run contribution from a variety of batting and baserunning events. Many different formulas are used, depending upon data available. In general, an estimate of the number of runs that could be expected to result from a player's overall offensive statistics in many other categories.

Sabermetrics - phrase coined by Bill James, in honor of the Society for American Baseball Research (SABR) as "the search for objective knowledge about baseball" or, earlier, "the mathematical and statistical analysis of baseball records." James now explicitly includes any objective information, not just baseball statistics, as the evidence to be considered in sabermetrics.

SABR - Pronounced "saber", this is the acronym for the Society for American Baseball Research, the organization that has, since its founding by Bob Davis in 1971, steadily advanced the state of baseball knowledge.

Slugging Average - total bases divided by at bats; combines nicely with On Base Percentage to create "production."

Slugging Percentage - same as slugging average.

Total Average - Tom Boswell's formulation for offensive contribution from a variety of batting and baserunning events; as with Runs Created, we have calculated Total Average to make use of the maximum available data in a given year. The concept of the numerator is bases gained, that of the denominator is outs made:

(Total Bases + Steals + Walks + Hit-by-pitch - Caught Stealing) / (At Bats - Hits + Caught Stealing + Grounded-into-double-play)

Total Pitcher Index - the sum of a pitchers Pitching Runs, Batting Runs, and Fielding Runs, all divided by the Runs Per Win factor for that year.

Total Player Rating - The sum of a player's Adjusted Batting Runs, Fielding Runs, and Base Stealing Runs, minus his positional adjustment, all divided by the Runs Per Win factor for that year.

Triple Crown - long defined as leadership in batting average, home runs, and RBI all in the same league in the same year. In the early years of this century, some journalists wrote of Ty Cobb shooting for the "triple crown" of batting average, runs, and hits.

Win-loss Percentage - wins, divided by total decisions: [(wins) / (wins plus losses)] with the average of .500 resulting when wins and losses are equal.

John Benson's All-Time 40 Man Roster
For Single Season Greatness

Catcher:
Yogi Berra 1956, Roy Campanella 1953, Johnny Bench 1970

First Base:
Lou Gehrig 1927, Jimmie Foxx 1932, Orlando Cepeda 1967

Second Base:
Joe Morgan 1976, Frankie Frisch 1930, Rogers Hornsby 1925

Third Base:
George Brett 1985, Mike Schmidt 1980

Shortstop:
Honus Wagner 1908, Ernie Banks 1958, Cal Ripken 1983

Left Field:
Carl Yastrzemski 1967, Ted Williams 1941, Stan Musial 1948, Joe Jackson 1911

Center Field:
Joe DiMaggio 1939, Ty Cobb 1911, Mickey Mantle 1956, Willie Mays 1954

Right Field:
Babe Ruth 1920, Frank Robinson 1966, Roberto Clemente 1966

Starting Pitcher:
Dizzy Dean 1934, Joe Wood 1912, Walter Johnson 1913, Greg Maddux 1994, Lefty Grove 1931, Christy Mathewson 1908, Sandy Koufax 1965, Ron Guidry 1978, Bob Gibson 1968, Roger Clemens 1986, Tom Seaver 1969, Dazzy Vance 1924

Relief Pitcher:
Dennis Eckersley 1990, Bryan Harvey 1991, Bruce Sutter 1979

MY PERSONAL TOP 100

By Tony Blengino

Following is my personal Top 100 individual seasons list. Again, I have not indicated the season for each player who appears on the ''Pittsburgh Consensus'' list - the season which I consider those players' best may or may not be the one covered in this book. Unlike the ''Pittsburgh Consensus'' list, I have not made any attempt to balance this list by position. 87 players are on both lists - the 13 who are on my personal list only are in ALL CAPS, with their peak season indicated. I guess you could say that my list begins and ends with the greatest player in baseball history.

1- OF Babe Ruth	37- OF Reggie Jackson	73- C Johnny Bench
2- OF Ted Williams	38- OF Carl Yastrzemski	74- RP Dennis Eckersley
3- SP Walter Johnson	39- SP Three-Finger Brown	75- SP Rube Waddell
4- 1B Lou Gehrig	40- OF Hank Aaron	76- RP Bruce Sutter
5- OF Mickey Mantle	41- SP Roger Clemens	77- 1B Hank Greenberg
6- 2B Rogers Hornsby	42- SP Warren Spahn	78- OF Roberto Clemente
7- SP Christy Mathewson	43- 1B Willie Stargell	79- SP Harry Brecheen
8- 1B Jeff Bagwell	44- 2B Joe Morgan	80- SP Bret Saberhagen
9- 1B Willie McCovey	45- SS Arky Vaughan	81- OF Duke Snider
10- SP Lefty Grove	46- OF Tris Speaker	82- SS Lou Boudreau
11- SP Smokey Joe Wood	47- OF Willie Mays	83- OF Chuck Klein
12- SP Pete Alexander	48- OF Joe DiMaggio	84- SP Sandy Koufax
13- 1B Frank Thomas	49- OF Ed Delahanty	85- 1B Orlando Cepeda
14- OF Ty Cobb	50- SP Tom Seaver	86- SS Cal Ripken
15- OF Barry Bonds	51- SP BUCKY WALTERS (1939)	87- 3B RON SANTO (1966)
16- 2B Nap Lajoie	52- SP ED WALSH (1908)	88- OF TIM RAINES (1985)
17- SP Cy Young	53- OF Ralph Kiner	89- OF TONY GWYNN (1987)
18- SS Honus Wagner	54- 1B George Sisler	90- 1B PEDRO GUERRERO (1985)
19- 3B George Brett	55- 3B Al Rosen	91- RP JOHN HILLER (1973)
20- 1B Jimmie Foxx	56- OF Rocky Colavito	92- 1B ROD CAREW (1977)
21- OF Frank Robinson	57- 2B Eddie Collins	93- OF JOE MEDWICK (1937)
22- SP Carl Hubbell	58- OF Mel Ott	94- 2B Jackie Robinson
23- SP Steve Carlton	59- SP Hal Newhouser	95- RP JIM KERN (1979)
24- SP Bob Gibson	60- SP Lefty Gomez	96- SS Ernie Banks
25- SP Dwight Gooden	61- SP Dizzy Dean	97- C Roy Campanella
26- 1B Norm Cash	62- 3B Eddie Mathews	98- 1B JOHN OLERUD (1993)
27- 1B Dick Allen	63- OF Hack Wilson	99- RP RICH GOSSAGE (1977)
28- SP Greg Maddux	64- SP Ron Guidry	100-SP BABE RUTH (1916)
29- SP Dazzy Vance	65- SP Bob Feller	
30- SP Gaylord Perry	66- SP Juan Marichal	
31- 3B Mike Schmidt	67- 3B Harmon Killebrew	
32- OF Stan Musial	68- OF Fred Lynn	
33- OF Kevin Mitchell	69- OF Al Simmons	
34- OF Harry Heilmann	70- 1B Jack Clark	
35- OF Rickey Henderson	71- OF Jose Canseco	
36- OF Joe Jackson	72- SS Robin Yount	

The Pittsburgh Concensus

By Tony Blengino

The process of deciding which players to include in this book and then subsequently rank them took a year. It began at The Ballpark in Arlington in June 1994, the same night O.J. Simpson's infamous white Bronco ''chase'' captivated the nation, and ended at the SABR convention in Pittsburgh almost exactly one year later. When it got started, the Rangers' new stadium offered a fine visual setting for talking baseball, while the teams on the field were playing a less-than-captivating game that offered sharp illustrations of expansion's impact on pitching and the overall need for players to work more on fundamentals. Those two topics were hardly enough to fill nine innings with chatter. The conversation soon meandered.

John Benson, his son James and myself were discussing the greatest individual seasons of all time, as the Bensons were choosing their all-time greatest teams for a father-versus-son computer-simulated season using dream-team rosters. Rogers Hornsby 1924, Babe Ruth 1927, Lou Gehrig 1936 and the like were quickly drafted. Soon the greatest Hall of Famers were being joined by some of the greatest one-year wonders such as Smoky Joe Wood. In one of those amazing moments of group telepathy when two or more people get the same idea at the same time, it dawned upon us that this same topic could make for quite an interesting book.

Several of this book's writers submitted players' names and their best individual seasons for consideration. Before long, we had a working list of close to 150 players, with sixty or so ''must have'' essays heading the list. The authors then picked the essays they most desired to write. These included some of the players who were not on the ''must have'' list, meaning that some of the players included in this book might not make my personal Top 100 list,

but were included because a particular author wished to cover that player. In hardly any cases were any writers actually assigned an individual essay; the vast majority sprung the writer's own desire to tell the story. By the spring of 1995, about 75 essays had been written, and some hard decisions had to be made about the remaining 25.

Then came the SABR (Society for American Baseball Research) convention in Pittsburgh in mid-June. Several of the authors: myself, John Benson, Bill Gray, Bill Gilbert, Lary Bump and Fred Matos, to name a few, were all in attendance. Several skull sessions among small groups of us finally determined the final population of players, which was largely based upon performance relative to the league. Now came the hard part - ranking them.

Our list actually includes 101 players - 12 first basemen, 8 second basemen, 7 shortstops, 5 third basemen, 4 catchers, 30 outfielders, 31 starting pitchers and 4 relief pitchers. We all piled into John Benson's hotel room following a horrible Padres-Pirates game on the second night of the convention, to begin the process. Thankfully, Fred Matos brought beer -- lots of it. We decided that the best method of beginning this process was to rank the players within their positions first, where it would less problematic to compare one player to another, and then intersperse the positional rankings to create the final list. We started at first base, and had all pertinent relative statistical information for what we considered each player's best single season (even if the essay in this book is about another, more dramatic story, as in the case of Jackie Robinson for example).

It was not a purely statistical exercise by any means. That would have been too easy, given the reference materials that we had at the ready. We debated extensively about unmeasured defensive values, intangibles such as leadership, and team performance. It took about ten minutes to realize that we could argue forever, and never come up with a list. So we developed a method to help move the process along. The writers sat in a circle. Going clockwise in turn, each writer nominated a player (I went first, and nominated Gehrig at first base, if I remember correctly), and the other writers in turn either agreed or nominated/voted for someone else. I was dubbed the tie-breaking vote. The person to my left would then nominated the second best first baseman, and so on. Personally, I was surprised at how low Dizzy Dean was ranked among pitchers, and how high Kevin Mitchell was ranked among outfielders, to name a couple. But hey, this is what democracy's all about, right?

The next night, after the SABR banquet speaker Chuck Tanner got done telling us what a great manager he was, we went back upstairs to compile the final rankings (and drink more beer). We tried to intersperse players from all positions as we went along, though we were not nearly as strict about the concept of filling out a complete "team" (with a player at every position including a righty pitcher and a lefty pitcher) as was Bill James when he did his Peak Value ranking in the Historical Abstract. We did strictly adhere to the prior evening's positional rankings, not allowing time to re-debate what we had decided the night before.

The list that follows is sure to provoke lots of discussion and argument; in fact, that is its primary purpose. You won't find too many singles hitters here; nor will you find many finesse pitchers. You will find players who contributed much more than stats -- players who changed the way the game is played, who crossed the color barrier, who managed ballclubs at age 24. Check out the listings below, and feel free to gasp when you see Kevin Mitchell ranked ahead of Joe DiMaggio. Remember, this list ranks players' performance in their ONE best season. Players like DiMaggio, Mays and Aaron, who had incredible careers without any exaggerated peaks, are not worse players for being consistent. This ranking is only about individual seasons, not whole players' careers. And there is more at work here than just writers' opinions voiced in a very informal setting (heck, John was fueled exclusively by non-alcoholic Coors Cutter, so you know he was 100% serious). We all took the job seriously, and those who felt the most discomfort about Mitchell nosing out DiMaggio were the most consoled to see that Total Baseball had the same finding in its total player ratings, with defense and baserunning and league context and ballpark effects etc. all taken into consideration: DiMaggio 1941 was a 6.4 while Mitchell in 1989 was a 7.0. Career-wise, of course, The Yankee Clipper dwarfed the oft-injured outfielder ("a stocky version of Eric Davis" as he has been described in another of Benson's books) who went to Japan after playing for five major league teams in ten years. Anyway, you could look it up.

1- OF Babe Ruth
2- OF Ted Williams
3- SP Walter Johnson
4- 1B Lou Gehrig
5- 2B Rogers Hornsby
6- OF Mickey Mantle
7- 1B Jimmie Foxx
8- SS Honus Wagner
9- 1B Jeff Bagwell
10- 1B Willie McCovey
11- SP Bob Gibson
12- OF Frank Robinson
13- SP Christy Mathewson
14- OF Ty Cobb
15- SP Lefty Grove
16- 2B Nap Lajoie

35- OF Joe DiMaggio
36- SP Mordecai "Three-Finger" Brown
37- OF Joe Jackson
38- SS Arky Vaughn
39- SP Steve Carlton
40- OF Hank Aaron
41- OF Tris Speaker
42- SP Carl Hubbell
43- OF Willie Mays
44- SP Dazzy Vance
45- SP Roger Clemens
46- 1B Willie Stargell
47- 2B Eddie Collins
48- 3B Al Rosen
49- C Roy Campanella

68- 2B Jackie Robinson
69- SP Lefty Gomez
70- 1B Orlando Cepeda
71- 1B Hank Greenberg
72- OF Al Simmons
73- SP Gaylord Perry
74- OF Rocky Colavito
75- SP Nolan Ryan
76- SP Bob Feller
77- 1B Jack Clark
78- SS Robin Yount
79- SS Cal Ripken
80- C Mickey Cochrane
81- RP Dennis Eckersley
82- OF Jose Canseco
83- OF Chuck Klein

THE "PITTSBURGH CONSENSUS"

17- 1B Frank Thomas
18- OF Barry Bonds
19- 3B George Brett
20- SP Greg Maddux
21- 3B Mike Schmidt
22- OF Stan Musial
23- 2B Joe Morgan
24- 1B Dick Allen
25- SP Pete Alexander
26- SP Dwight Gooden
27- OF Carl Yastrzemski
28- 1B George Sisler
29- C Johnny Bench
30- SP Cy Young
31- OF Rickey Henderson
32- 1B Norm Cash
33- SP Smoky Joe Wood
34- OF Kevin Mitchell

50- 3B Eddie Mathews
51- SS Lou Boudreau
52- SP Hal Newhouser
53- SP Tom Seaver
54- SP Sandy Koufax
55- SP Ron Guidry
56- OF Roberto Clemente
57- OF Harry Heilmann
58- OF Ralph Kiner
59- SS Ernie Banks
60- 3B Harmon Killebrew
61- OF Mel Ott
62- SP Warren Spahn
63- OF Duke Snider
64- OF Roger Maris
65- OF Hack Wilson
66- C Yogi Berra
67- OF Reggie Jackson

84- OF Fred Lynn
85- OF Ed Delahanty
86- RP Bruce Sutter
87- SP Harry Brecheen
88- SP Rube Waddell
89- SP Juan Marichal
90- SP Whitey Ford
91- SP Dizzy Dean
92- OF Jim Rice
93- 2B Ryne Sandberg
94- SP Bret Saberhagen
95- SP Herb Score
96- SP Denny McLain
97- 2B Roberto Alomar
98- RP Rob Dibble
99- RP Roy Face
100 (tie) -2B Frankie Frisch
100 (tie) -SS Maury Wills

Hitter # 101's Stats

NAME	YEAR	G	AB	R	H	2B	3B	HR	RBI	BB	SO	AVG	OBP	SLG	SB
Appling, Luke	1935	138	526	111	204	31	7	6	128	85	25	.388	.474	.508	10
Ashburn, Richie	1958	152	615	98	215	24	13	2	33	97	48	.350	.441	.441	30
Baker, Home Run	1912	149	577	116	200	40	21	10	130	50	NA	.347	.404	.541	40
Belle, Albert	1994	106	412	90	147	35	2	36	101	58	71	.357	.442	.714	9
Boggs, Wade	1987	147	551	108	200	40	6	24	89	105	48	.363	.467	.588	1
Brock, Lou	1974	153	635	105	194	25	7	3	48	61	88	.306	.368	.381	118
Burkett, Jesse	1901	142	601	142	226	20	15	10	75	59	NA	.376	.440	.509	27
Canseco, Jose	1988	158	610	120	187	34	0	42	124	78	128	.307	.394	.569	40
Carew, Rod	1977	155	616	128	239	38	16	14	100	69	55	.388	.452	.570	23
Carty, Rico	1970	136	478	84	175	23	3	25	101	77	46	.366	.456	.584	1
Chapman, Ray	1917	156	563	98	170	28	13	2	36	61	65	.302	.370	.409	52
Clift, Harlond	1937	155	571	103	175	36	7	29	118	98	80	.306	.413	.546	8
Collins, Jimmy	1902	108	429	71	138	21	10	6	61	24	NA	.322	.360	.459	28
Cravath, Gavvy	1915	150	522	89	149	31	7	24	115	86	77	.285	.393	.510	11
Crawford, Sam	1911	146	574	109	217	36	14	7	115	61	NA	.378	.438	.526	37
Cronin, Joe	1930	154	587	127	203	41	9	13	126	72	36	.346	.422	.513	17
Davis, Eric	1987	129	474	120	139	23	4	37	100	84	134	.293	.401	.593	50
Dawson, Andre	1987	153	621	90	178	24	2	49	137	32	103	.287	.329	.568	11
Dickey, Bill	1936	112	423	99	153	26	8	22	107	46	16	.362	.428	.617	0
Doby, Larry	1952	140	519	104	143	26	8	32	104	90	111	.276	.383	.541	5
Doyle, LArry	1915	150	591	86	189	40	10	4	70	32	28	.320	.358	.442	22
Evers, Johnny	1912	143	478	73	163	23	11	1	63	74	18	.341	.431	.441	18
Fielder, Cecil	1990	159	573	104	159	25	2	51	132	90	182	.277	.380	.592	0
Foster, George	1977	158	615	124	197	31	2	52	149	61	107	.320	.386	.631	6
Galarraga, Andres	1993	120	470	71	174	35	4	22	98	24	73	.370	.408	.602	2
Garvey, Steve	1979	162	648	92	204	32	1	28	110	37	59	.315	.354	.497	3
Gehringer,Charlie	1936	154	641	144	227	60	12	15	116	83	13	.354	.431	.555	4
Gentile, Jim	1961	148	486	96	147	25	2	46	141	96	106	.302	.428	.646	1
Gibson, Kirk	1988	150	542	106	157	28	1	25	76	73	120	.290	.381	.483	31
Gonzales, Juan	1993	140	536	105	166	33	1	46	118	37	99	.310	.369	.632	4
Gordon, Joe	1942	147	538	88	173	29	4	18	103	79	95	.322	.409	.491	12
Goslin, Goose	1928	135	456	80	173	36	10	17	102	48	19	.379	.442	.614	16
Griffey, Ken	1993	156	582	113	180	38	3	45	109	96	91	.309	.412	.617	17
Guerrero, Pedro	1985	137	487	99	156	22	2	33	87	83	68	.320	.425	.577	12
Gwynn, Tony	1994	110	419	79	165	35	1	12	64	48	19	.394	.458	.568	5
Gwynn, Tony	1987	157	589	119	218	36	13	7	54	82	35	.370	.450	.511	56
Hafey, Chick	1931	122	450	94	157	35	8	16	95	39	43	.349	.404	.569	11
Hartnett, Gabby	1935	116	413	67	142	32	6	13	91	41	46	.344	.404	.545	1
Herman, Babe	1930	153	614	143	241	48	11	35	35	66	56	.393	.455	.678	18
Howard, Frank	1970	161	566	90	160	15	1	44	126	132	125	.283	.420	.546	1
Kaline, Al	1955	152	588	121	200	24	8	27	102	82	57	.340	.425	.546	6
Keller, Charlie	1941	140	507	102	151	24	10	33	122	102	65	.298	.416	.580	6
Kluszewski, Ted	1954	149	573	104	187	28	3	49	141	78	35	.326	.410	.642	0
Marion, Marty	1943	129	418	36	117	15	3	1	52	32	37	.280	.334	.337	1
Mattingly, Don	1986	162	677	117	238	53	2	31	113	53	35	.352	.399	.573	0
McGwire, Mark	1987	151	557	97	161	28	4	49	118	71	131	.289	.374	.618	1
Medwick, Joe	1937	156	633	111	237	56	10	31	154	41	50	.374	.414	.641	4
Minoso, Minnie	1954	153	568	119	182	29	18	19	116	77	46	.320	.416	.535	18
Mize, Johnny	1947	154	586	137	177	26	2	51	138	74	42	.302	.384	.614	2
Munson, Thurman	1973	147	519	80	156	29	4	20	74	48	64	.301	.364	.487	4

NAME	YEAR	G	AB	R	H	2B	3B	HR	RBI	BB	SO	AVG	OBP	SLG	SB
Murcer, Bobby	1971	146	529	94	175	25	6	25	94	91	60	.331	.429	.543	14
Murphy, Dale	1987	159	566	115	167	27	1	44	105	115	136	.295	.420	.580	16
Murray, Eddie	1984	162	588	97	180	26	3	29	110	107	87	.306	.415	.509	10
Olerud, John	1993	158	551	109	200	54	2	24	107	114	65	.363	.478	.599	0
O'Doul, Lefty	1929	154	638	152	254	35	6	32	122	76	19	.398	.465	.622	2
Piazza, Mike	1993	149	547	81	174	24	2	35	112	46	86	.318	.374	.561	3
Raines, Tim	1985	150	575	115	184	30	13	11	41	81	60	.320	.407	.475	70
Reiser, Pete	1941	137	536	117	184	39	17	14	76	46	71	.343	.406	.558	4
Robinson, Brooks	1964	163	612	82	194	35	3	28	118	51	64	.317	.373	.521	1
Rose, Pete	1969	156	627	120	218	33	11	16	82	88	65	.348	.432	.512	7
Santo, Ron	1966	155	561	93	175	21	8	30	94	95	78	.312	.417	.538	4
Seymour, Cy	1905	149	581	95	219	40	21	8	121	51	NA	.377	.429	.559	21
Sheffield, Gary	1992	146	557	87	184	34	3	33	100	48	40	.330	.390	.580	5
Stone, George	1906	154	581	91	208	25	20	6	71	52	NA	.358	.417	.501	35
Strawberry, Darryl	1988	153	543	101	146	27	3	39	101	85	127	.269	.371	.545	29
Terry, Bill	1930	154	633	139	254	39	15	23	129	57	33	.401	.452	.619	8
Torre, Joe	1971	161	634	97	230	34	8	24	137	63	70	.363	.424	.555	4
Traynor, Pie	1923	153	616	108	208	19	19	12	101	34	19	.338	.377	.489	28
Walker, Dixie	1944	147	535	77	191	37	8	13	91	72	27	.357	.434	.529	6
Waner, Paul	1934	146	599	122	217	32	16	14	90	68	24	.362	.429	.539	8
Williams, Billy	1970	161	636	137	205	24	4	42	129	72	65	.322	.393	.586	7
Winfield, Dave	1979	159	597	97	184	27	10	34	118	85	71	.308	.396	.558	15
Zimmerman, Heinie	1912	145	557	95	207	41	14	14	99	38	60	.372	.418	.571	23

Pitcher # 101's Stats

NAME	YEAR	W	L	PCT	G	GS	CG	SV	IP	SO	BB	B/I	ERA
Adams, Babe	1913	21	10	.677	43	37	24	0	313	144	49	1.02	2.15
Arroyo, Luis	1961	15	5	.750	65	0	0	29	119	87	49	1.13	2.19
Blue, Vida	1971	24	8	.750	39	39	24	0	312	301	88	0.97	1.82
Bunning, Jim	1966	19	14	.576	43	41	16	1	314	252	55	1.07	2.41
Chance, Dean	1964	20	9	.690	46	35	15	4	278	207	86	1.01	1.65
Chandler, Spud	1943	20	4	.833	30	30	20	0	253	134	54	1.01	1.64
Chesbro, Jack	1904	41	12	.774	55	51	48	0	454	239	88	0.96	1.82
Cicotte, Eddie	1917	28	12	.700	49	35	29	4	346	150	70	0.92	1.53
Cone, David	1994	16	5	.762	23	23	4	0	171	132	54	1.11	2.94
Coombs, Jack	1910	31	9	.775	45	38	35	1	353	224	115	1.04	1.30
Cooper, Mort	1942	22	7	.759	37	35	22	0	278	152	68	1.00	1.78
Crowder, General	1932	26	13	.667	50	39	21	1	327	103	77	1.21	3.33
Drysdale, Don	1964	18	16	.529	40	40	21	0	321	237	68	1.00	2.18
Duren, Ryne	1958	6	4	.600	44	1	0	20	75	87	43	1.19	2.02
Eichhorn, Mark	1986	14	6	.700	69	0	0	10	157	166	45	1.00	1.72
Fingers, Rollie	1981	6	3	.667	47	0	0	28	78	61	13	0.89	1.04
Gossage, Rich	1977	11	9	.550	72	0	0	26	133	151	49	0.97	1.62
Gossage, Rich	1981	3	2	.600	32	0	0	20	46	48	14	0.79	0.77
Harvey, Bryan	1991	2	4	.333	67	0	0	46	78	101	17	0.88	1.60
Hernandez, Willie	1984	9	3	.750	80	0	0	32	140	112	36	0.97	1.92
Hershiser, Orel	1988	23	8	.742	35	34	15	1	267	178	73	1.07	2.26
Hunter, Catfish	1974	25	12	.676	41	41	23	0	318	143	46	1.00	2.49
Jenkins, Fergie	1971	24	13	.649	39	39	30	0	325	263	37	1.07	2.77
Johnson, Randy	1993	19	8	.704	35	34	10	1	255	308	99	1.18	3.24
Joss, Addie	1908	24	11	.686	42	35	29	2	325	130	30	0.81	1.16
Kaat, Jim	1966	25	13	.658	41	41	19	0	304	205	55	1.08	2.75
Kern, Jim	1979	13	5	.722	71	0	0	29	143	136	62	1.14	1.57
Konstanty, Jim	1950	16	7	.696	74	0	0	22	152	56	50	1.04	2.66
Lemon, Bob	1948	20	14	.588	43	37	20	2	293	147	129	1.23	2.82
Leonard, Dutch	1914	19	5	.792	36	25	17	3	224	176	60	0.92	0.96
Lolich, Mickey	1971	25	14	.641	45	45	29	0	376	308	92	1.16	2.92
Lopat, Ed	1953	16	4	.800	25	24	9	0	178	50	32	1.14	2.42
Lyle, Sparky	1977	13	5	.722	72	0	0	26	137	68	33	1.21	2.17
Maloney, Jim	1965	20	9	.690	33	33	14	0	255	244	110	1.19	2.54
Marquard, Rube	1911	24	7	.774	45	33	22	3	277	237	106	1.19	2.50
Marshall, Mike	1979	10	15	.400	90	1	0	32	142	81	48	1.29	2.65
McDowell, Sam	1965	17	11	.607	42	35	14	4	273	325	132	1.16	2.18
McNally, Dave	1968	22	10	.688	35	35	18	0	273	202	55	0.88	1.95
Niekro, Phil	1969	23	13	.639	40	35	21	1	284	193	57	1.04	2.56
Palmer, Jim	1975	23	11	.676	39	38	25	1	323	193	80	1.03	2.09
Pfiester, Jack	1907	14	9	.609	30	22	13	0	195	90	48	1.00	1.15
Quisenberry, Dan	1983	5	3	.625	69	0	0	45	139	48	11	0.93	1.94
Radatz, Dick	1964	16	9	.640	79	0	0	29	157	181	58	1.07	2.29
Reulbach, Ed	1905	18	14	.563	34	29	28	1	291	152	73	1.02	1.42
Reynolds, Allie	1952	20	8	.714	35	29	24	6	244	160	97	2.06	1.22
Richard, J.R.	1979	18	13	.581	38	38	9	0	292	313	98	1.10	2.71
Richard, J.R.	1980	10	4	.714	17	17	4	0	113	119	40	0.92	1.90
Roberts, Robin	1952	28	7	.800	39	37	30	2	330	148	45	1.03	2.59
Ruffing, Red	1939	21	7	.750	28	28	22	0	233	95	75	1.23	2.93
Scott, Mike	1986	18	10	.643	37	37	7	0	275	306	72	0.93	2.22

NAME	YEAR	W	L	PCT	G	GS	CG	SV	IP	SO	BB	B/I	ERA
Shantz, Bobby	1952	24	7	.774	33	33	27	0	279	152	63	1.07	2.48
Sutton, Don	1972	19	9	.679	33	33	18	0	272	207	63	0.93	2.08
Thigpen, Bobby	1990	4	6	.400	77	0	0	57	88	70	32	1.04	1.83
Tiant, Luis	1968	21	9	.700	34	32	19	0	258	264	73	0.89	1.60
Trout, Dizzy	1944	27	14	.659	49	40	33	0	352	144	83	1.13	2.12
Walsh, Ed	1908	40	15	.727	66	49	42	6	464	269	56	0.88	1.42
Walters, Bucky	1939	27	11	.711	39	36	31	0	319	137	109	1.14	2.29
Wetteland, John	1993	9	3	.750	70	0	0	43	85	113	28	1.03	1.37
Wilhelm, Hoyt	1965	7	7	.500	66	0	0	20	144	106	32	0.84	1.81
Wilhelm, Hoyt	1959	15	11	.577	32	27	13	0	226	139	77	1.18	2.19

19th Century Hitters Statistics

NAME	YEAR	G	AB	R	H	2B	3B	HR	RBI	BB	SO	AVG	OBP	SLG	SB
Anson, Cap	1881	84	343	67	137	21	7	1	82	26	4	.399	.442	.442	NA
Barnes, Ross	1876	66	322	126	138	21	14	1	59	20	8	.429	.462	.590	NA
Brouthers, Dan	1883	98	425	85	159	41	17	3	97	16	17	.374	.397	.572	NA
Browning, Pete	1882	69	288	67	109	17	3	5	NA	26	NA	.378	.430	.510	NA
Burkett, Jesse	1896	133	586	160	240	27	16	6	72	49	19	.410	.461	.541	34
Childs, Cupid	1890	126	493	109	170	33	14	2	NA	72	NA	.345	.434	.481	56
Clarke, Fred	1897	128	518	120	202	30	13	6	67	45	NA	.390	.462	.533	57
Connor, Roger	1885	110	455	102	169	23	15	1	65	51	8	.371	.435	.495	NA
Duffy, Hugh	1894	125	539	160	237	51	16	18	145	66	15	.440	.502	.694	48
Dunlap, Fred	1884	101	449	160	185	39	8	13	NA	29	NA	.412	.448	.621	NA
Ewing, Buck	1889	99	407	91	133	23	13	4	87	37	32	.327	.383	.477	34
Glasscock, Jack	1889	134	582	128	205	40	3	7	85	31	10	.352	.390	.466	57
Hamilton, Billy	1894	129	544	192	220	25	15	4	87	126	17	.404	.523	.528	98
Jennings, Hughie	1896	130	521	125	209	27	9	0	121	19	11	.401	.472	.488	70
Keeler. Willie	1897	129	564	145	239	27	19	0	74	35	NA	.424	.464	.539	64
Kelley, King	1886	118	451	155	175	32	11	4	79	83	33	.388	.483	.534	53
McGraw, John	1899	117	399	140	156	13	3	1	33	124	NA	.391	.547	.446	73
O'Niell, Tip	1887	124	517	167	225	52	19	14	NA	50	NA	.435	.490	.691	30
Thompson, Sam	1895	119	538	131	211	45	21	18	165	31	11	.392	.654	.654	27
White, Deacon	1877	59	266	51	103	14	11	2	49	8	3	.387	.405	.545	NA
Williamson, Fred	1884	107	417	84	116	18	8	27	84	42	56	.278	.344	.554	NA

19th Century Pitchers Statistics

NAME	YEAR	W	L	PCT	G	GS	CG	SV	IP	SO	BB	B/I	ERA
Bond, Tommy	1879	43	19	.694	64	64	59	0	555	155	24	1.02	1.96
Bradley, George	1876	45	19	.703	64	64	63	0	573	103	38	0.89	1.23
Caruthers, Bob	1885	40	13	.755	53	53	53	0	482	190	57	1.04	2.07
Clarkson, John	1885	53	16	.768	70	70	68	0	623	308	97	0.96	1.85
Hecker, Guy	1884	52	20	.722	75	73	72	0	670	385	56	0.89	1.80
Hecker, Guy	1882	6	6	.500	13	11	10	0	104	33	5	0.77	1.30
Keefe, Tim	1880	6	6	.500	12	12	12	0	105	43	17	0.83	0.86
Kilroy, Matt	1886	29	24	.460	68	68	66	0	583	513	182	1.17	3.37
King, Silver	1888	45	21	.682	66	65	64	0	585	258	76	0.92	1.64
McCormick, Jim	1883	28	12	.700	43	41	36	1	342	145	65	1.11	1.84
Nichols, Kid	1898	31	12	.721	50	42	40	4	388	138	85	1.07	2.13
Radbourn, Old Hoss	1884	59	12	.831	75	73	73	1	678	441	98	0.92	1.38
Rusie, Amos	1894	36	13	.735	54	50	45	1	444	195	200	1.42	2.78
Spalding, Al	1875	55	5	.917	72	63	52	8	575	NA	14	1.02	1.52
Stratton, Scott	1890	34	14	.708	50	49	44	0	431	207	61	1.10	2.36
Sweeney, Charlie	1884	17	8	.680	27	24	22	1	221	145	29	0.82	1.55
Ward, John	1879	47	19	.712	70	60	58	1	587	239	36	1.03	2.15
White, Will	1882	40	12	.769	54	54	52	0	480	122	71	1.00	1.54

The Negro Leagues

by John Benson and Lary Bump

Where in this book is Josh Gibson? Surely he was as great a catcher as the four who made it into our top 100 seasons. And what about Satchel Paige? Surely he had better seasons that some of the pitchers who got an essay here. And what of all the others who were barred from ''organized'' baseball in the first half of this century?

When this book was being conceived, the authors were thrilled by the possibility of including some of the great Negro League players, who indeed had seasons that make great stories and include accomplishments well worthy of comparison to the other players here.

Try as we might, however, we were unable to find any good method for giving the Negro Leagues a presence in this book. The essential problem was the book's inclination toward rankings and comparisons; there just wasn't any clear way to approach that issue fairly and with intellectual honesty. There were two possible methods considered for including Negro Leaguers in this book. One was to include them on the basis of their reputations, as passed down through oral history or the story telling of sports writers with vastly differing styles and levels of documentation and attribution. The other was to go on the basis of the partial statistical evidence contained in the scant records that were made and preserved successfully. In too many cases records were not kept, or were incomplete. Some games were official league contests, but many more were barnstorming exhibitions against varying levels of competition. The statistical problem has been clearly stated in ''The Negro Leagues Book'' published in 1994 by SABR:

''A complete statistical Negro Leagues encyclopedia is impossible at present, and won't become possible for years. In fact, many of the statistical lines in the 'record' are dubious and subject to change.''

Official league stats were published for just a handful of years, and even those were not balanced for accuracy. Thus far, despite serious efforts, it has not been possible to recreate statistics from newspaper box scores; in many cases game stories appeared without any box scores in black-audience newspapers, and many of those papers were published only once a week. Another problem with reporting was that so many games were played at neutral sites not the home city of either team. Finally, among the box scores that do exist, many are fragmentary or include conflicting data.

The Negro league schedules were not only flexible; they were also short. Josh Gibson's .517 average in 1943 was compiled in the Homestead Grays' 40 games. As good a player as this Hall of Famer was, including that season would be akin to including Hurricane Hazle's .403 season based on 41 games with the 1957 Milwaukee Braves. Pitching performances presented another problem. When Slim Jones won 22 games in 1934, his Philadelphia Stars played just 36 league games. Does his season compare with Doc Gooden's 24-4 in 1985, or is it more like a 19th-century pitcher, taking the mound almost every day? We just don't know, and don't know how to find out.

Even with players as great as Gibson and Pop Lloyd, and all the others whose careers were relatively well documented, the evidence is both incomplete and inconsistent. In his preface to ''The Biographical Encyclopedia of the Negro Baseball Leagues,'' James A. Riley referred to ''the parallel world of black baseball'' and to its players as ''forgotten specters from the shadows of the past.'' Like SABR's initial effort and like Riley's, the writers of this book, initially, tried to shed light onto the shadows of that parallel world. After some effort, we concluded that we just can't see the black game anywhere near as clearly as way we can see major league baseball over the past hundred years.

There are many great and wonderful stories of the superbly talented and deeply committed athletes who were deprived of their right to play in the major leagues. Every fan should have, just once, the privilege of looking into the spirit-illuminated face of Negro League star like Buck O'Neil, and listen to him talk about baseball and the lifestyle and culture of his league-mates. Or briefly enjoy the company of Monte Irvin, who unlike O'Neil at least was able to get in eight major league seasons and play in two World Series. Hall of Famer Irvin, who also served in the commissioner's office, provided a poignant foreword to Riley's "Biographical Encyclopedia." Irvin wrote that he learned to use his wrists and pull the ball by watching Joe DiMaggio, but "the team that impressed me after I got to know baseball was the Homestead Grays. They had a great club, with Josh Gibson and Buck Leonard. Also they had Raymond Brown, Roy Partlow, Howard Easterling, Jerry Benjamin, Lick Carlisle, Jelly Jackson, Boojum Wilson, Blue Perez, Big Tom Parker, and all the rest. They had a perfect team."

But until Irvin was 28 years old, it was impossible even for that perfect team to cross over into the parallel world of the majors. Irvin himself had to wait until he was 30 to cross: "As you got older, you got to the point where you thought: All I need is chance to make the majors. These guys can't play any better than we can ..." If Jackie [Robinson] had not made it, it would only have delayed the process, because there was Roy Campanella and Don Newcombe who would have stepped in and filled the role of being first. There is no question that the greatest black players of the first half of this century, if they been allowed to play in the major leagues, would have produced numerous seasons allowing -- even demanding -- their inclusion in this book. Certainly the number of essays here covering black players (no, we haven't counted them, and never even thought of that until the time of writing this apology) beginning with Robinson in 1947 will prove the point that blacks were ready and competent all along.

We ended up with a choice of doing some sketchy profiles, weak on accuracy, or leaving the Negro Leagues in the shadows where they have been. The first choice, we knew in our hearts, would have been tokenism (we could probably have made the essays look scholarly and accurate, adding a dose of illusion to mix with the tokenism). That method probably would have helped us sell more books, but it was the worse of the two evils that we had to choose from, and the one that would have left us with more lingering discomfort than the alternative. The other choice, leaving the Negro League players aside, where they all stood before 1947, perpetuates the sin of exclusion. We are not happy with it, but it was the only intellectually honest choice.

We leave this subject with regret, but not shame. The shame was that so many deserving players were excluded for so long from the game that we are describing here. The shame is that there was no equivalent of The Sporting News Register for Negro Leagues, no baseball cards with stat lines that youngsters could commit to memory for future arguments, none of those accouterments that gave permanence to major league play. The other world was separate, all right, and certainly not equal in any aspect except, perhaps, the skill of the players. We have all missed something of value, and must continue to miss it.

Some of that fragmentary evidence that we examined, in coming to that difficult conclusion, is offered for your consideration. We wish we had more.

Leading Negro Leagues individual season performances appear in the following format.
Player
Year Team
League
Stats

Brown, Willard
1948 Kansas City
Neg. AL
18 HR

Charleston, Oscar
1925 Homestead
East. Colored
20 HR

Gibson, Josh
1939 Homestead
Neg.NL
17 HR

Gibson, Josh
1943 Homestead
Neg.NL
.517 AVG

Hairston, Sam
1950 Indianapolis
Neg.AL
.424 AVG

Lloyd, Pop
1928 New York
East.Colored
.564 AVG

Moore, Dobie
1924 Kansas City
Neg.NL
.453 AVG

Smith, Chino
1929 New York
Am.Neg.Lg.
20 HR, .454 AVG

Suttles, Mule
1926 St. Louis
Neg.NL
27 HR

Watrous, Sherman
1952 Memphis
Neg.AL
20 HR

Wells, Willie
1929 St. Louis
Neg.NL
27 HR

Pitchers:
Foster, Willie
1927 Chicago
Neg.NL
21-3

Foster, Willie
1932 Chicago
Neg.So.
15-8

Heard, Jehosie
1951 New Orleans
Neg.AL
17-6

Jessup, Gentry
1945 Chicago
Neg.AL
15-10

Jones, Slim
1934 Philadelphia
Neg.NL
22-3

LaMarque, James
1948 Kansas City
Neg.AL
15-5

Rector, Connie
1929 New York
Am.Neg.Lg.
20-2

Trent, Ted
1928 St. Louis
Neg.NL
21-2

Winters, Jesse
1925 Philadelphia
East.Colored
21-10

In his 42-year career, Satchel Page won over 2,000 games and pitched over 100 no-hitters. There must have been great seasons in there somewhere!

The Most Dominant
Starting Pitchers Of All Time:
The Relative Control Power Factor

By Tony Blengino

The two most common yardsticks of starting pitchers' performance can be very misleading. Won-Lost records are heavily influenced by the strength of the pitcher's team offense, and ERA's are influenced by the pitcher's home ballpark, among other factors.

Two pitching statistics which are relatively unaffected by external stimuli are strikeout and walk totals. The relative control/power factor is a statistic which measures a pitcher's precision and dominance relative to his peers. The relative c/p factor is actually the sum of two sub-factors. The control factor measures a pitcher's strikeout/walk ratio compared to the average of other ERA title qualifiers in his league, while the power factor measures a strikeouts/9 innings ratio to the average of the other ERA title qualifiers in his league. I am purposely using K/W ratio rather than W/9 ratio to measure control. Both measure precision, but K/W ratio measures precision as it relates to dominance, which is more the focus of this study. Both factors are calculated by comparing the aforementioned ratios for all ERA title qualifiers in a given league to the average ratios for those qualifiers. The two sub-factors are equal to the number of standard deviations above or below the average ratio. After the control and power factors have been calculated, they are simply added together, resulting in the relative c/p factor.

In 1994, for example, NL qualifiers had a cumulative K/W ratio of 2.56 (with a standard deviation of 1.60), and a cumulative K/9 IP ratio of 6.31 (with a standard deviation of 1.42). Bret Saberhagen had a K/W ratio of 11.00 (+5.27 standard deviations), and a K/9 IP ratio of 7.26 (+0.66 standard deviations). His relative c/p factor of 5.93 led the NL in 1994. Randy Johnson led the AL with a +4.92 relative c/p factor (c=+1.78; p=+3.14). I have calculated relative c/p factors for all qualifying starting pitchers since 1901.

The benefits of this method are numerous. First, by comparing relative performance, pitchers from different eras may be readily compared. A 2.00 K/W ratio is below the 1994 NL qualifiers' average of 2.56, but way above the 1926 AL average of 0.91. This method would award a 1926 AL starter with a 2.00 K/W ratio a high positive control factor, but a 1994 NL pitcher with the same ratio a negative control factor. Since it is a relative statistic, the sum of all individual control, power, and c/p factors in a given league in a given season will be zero. This principle of relativity should be applied to virtually every baseball statistic - it would adjust for "lively" or "dead" ball eras.

An annual list of relative c/p factor leaders compares quite favorably to similar lists of league leaders in wins and ERA - there are very few flukes (like Ron Bryant, Buzz Capra, Jim Turner, Dave Koslo - a sampling of wins and ERA leaders) on the relative c/p list. An analysis of W-L records of all qualifiers at various relative c/p factor levels shows a direct correlation between c/p factor and winning percentage. An analysis of relative c/p factors by pitchers' age shows that a pitcher's control develops as a pitcher matures, while his power deteriorates. A pitcher's relative c/p factor tends to peak around age 29. The c factor also peaks around that age, while the p factor gradually decreases after age 23. Using the database of pitchers' factors dating back to 1901, one can match a current pitcher to the most similar pitcher of a similar age in any era. This type of analysis is quite useful when trying to determine which modern pitchers' careers will endure.

Obviously, it was easy to predict greatness for Saberhagen and Roger Clemens in their early years - but this method predicted long-term success for pitchers like Frank Viola and Bruce Hurst, despite mediocre W-L records and ERA's in their early years. This method currently predicts long-term success for such pitchers as Pedro Martinez, Kevin Appier, Andy Benes, Alex Fernandez and Jason Bere - but not so much for such pitchers as Ricky Bones, Jim Abbott or Bobby Jones. When projecting future success, a pitcher's age must be taken into consideration. The components of the c/p factor say as much about the pitcher as the factor itself. A young pitcher with a high p factor tends to be a better prospect than one with a high c factor, since control develops while power deteriorates over time.

THE MOST DOMINANT PITCHERS OF ALL TIME

From my database of starting pitchers' relative c/p factors since 1901, I have compiled a list of the most dominant major league pitchers. Well, actually, two lists. Following the terminology of Bill James, I have ranked the pitchers both in order of "Career Value" and "Peak Value". The Career Value list includes the 40 pitchers possessing the highest cumulative career c/p factors. These are derived by simply adding all of a pitcher's c/p factors from ERA title-qualifying seasons. Obviously, the Career Value list includes the pitchers who sustained their dominance over the longest period of time. In contrast, the Peak Value list includes the 40 pitchers possessing the highest cumulative c/p factors over a consecutive three-year period. This list includes many of the pitchers on the Career Value list, but also many other pitchers who dominated for a relatively short period of time, but couldn't sustain the dominance for

various reasons. Following is a thumbnail sketch of all the pitchers on either list in alphabetical order. Tables listing more detailed career and peak c/p factor and other statistical information are also presented.

BABE ADAMS - Adams was an extreme control pitcher who ranks #31 on the Peak Value list, and is unranked on the Career Value list. In an era when batters walked nearly as much as they whiffed, Adams possessed impeccable control. Adams peaked from ages 37 to 39, and his peak c factor of 11.38 ranks third all-time behind Cy Young and Christy Mathewson. Had 194-140 career record; very similar to Dazzy Vance (197-140), who is in the Hall, and Virgil Trucks (177-135), who is not.

PETE ALEXANDER - Alexander ranks #14 on the Career Value list, and #21 on the Peak Value list. Another extreme control pitcher; only three others on Career Value list had lower career p factor (C.Young, Roberts, Derringer). His career winning percentage (.642) exceeded his teams' (.535) by .107 - the largest margin of any pitcher in the study. In his peak period (1915-17) he went an amazing 94-35, 1.54. His relative ERA during his peak period was 182 (league average= 100), the 2nd best in the study (behind Walter Johnson).

JOHNNY ALLEN - Allen ranks #36 on the Peak Value list, and is unranked on the Career Value list. Following his peak seasons of 1935-37, Allen had a cumulative career record of 85-20! During his peak period, his winning percentage (48-17; .738) exceeded his teams' by .187, the 2nd best differential in the study (behind Dazzy Vance). Finished up at 142-75, with a 3.75 ERA (113 relative).

FLOYD BANNISTER - That's right - Floyd Bannister. He checks in at #40 on the Peak Value list, and is nowhere to be found on the Career Value list. He split his peak period between Seattle and Chicago (AL). He's living proof that every system of talent evaluation has flaws. Gave up an amazing 291 HR in 2388 innings, or 1.1 every nine innings. In his defense, he pitched for some truly rancid teams. He had a solid, workmanlike career (134-143), but never fulfilled his immense potential.

CHIEF BENDER - Bender checks in at #20 on the Career Value list, and is unranked on the Peak Value list. Bender had the good fortune of playing for some awesome A's teams in the first fifth of the century. His .625 winning percentage (212-127) appears impressive, but is only .041 above his teams' winning percentage. This is a solid but unspectacular figure in this company, ranking only 21st among the career top 40. His 112 relative ERA also finishes back in the pack. He's in the Hall, and deserves to be.

BERT BLYLEVEN - #6 on the Career Value list, and #20 on the Peak Value list. Amazingly, you don't hear his name mentioned very much when future Hall of Famers are discussed. He should be a first ballot selection. Has the 8th highest c factor ever, and is one of only five pitchers with c and p factors above 20 (also Johnson, Vance, Grove, Seaver). His career relative ERA (117) is better than Hall of Famers Jenkins, Carlton, Roberts and Bender, among others. However, his career winning percentage exceeded his teams' by only .023 - way down in Nolan Ryan territory (.022). To underscore Floyd Bannister's vulnerability to the gopher ball, Home Run Bert gave up only .78 HR/9 IP, well below Floyd's figure.

TOMMY BRIDGES - #19 on the Career Value list, and unranked on the Peak Value list. This guy was truly a victim of his era; on the surface, he appears to be wild (1672/1192 career K/BB ratio), but in the context of his times, he had very good control. In the 1930's and early 1940's, it was common for AL hitters to walk more than they struck out. Also, his 3.57 ERA appears only OK on the surface, but he had a very high relative ERA of 126 - 15th among the Career Value Top 40. The fourteen ahead of him are all either in the Hall of Fame or are named Roger Clemens - Bridges (194-138) is a slightly watered down version of Dazzy Vance, and belongs in the Hall.

JIM BUNNING - #14 on the Career Value list, #30 on the Peak Value list. If Bunning had pitched for better teams in his career, or had his career started about five years later, causing him to peak in the pitcher-dominated late 60's rather than the hitting-dominated early 60's, he would have been in the Hall a long time ago. Both his relative ERA (114) and his W-L pct. relative to his teams' (+.030) are somewhat low in this company. However, the best pitcher of any era merits Hall consideration - in Bunning's peak period (1959-61) he was arguably the best in baseball - a claim Nolan Ryan could never make.

STEVE CARLTON - #10 on the Career Value list, and #17 on the Peak Value list. Lefty made the Hall of Fame on the first ballot in 1994, and deservedly so. No pitcher on these lists from the second half of the century won more games than his 329, and he was second to Ryan in whiffs (4136). Like Ryan, Carlton peaked very late in his career. His peak period (1980-82) occurred between ages 35 and 37, and was truly awesome - 60-24 for a .714 W-L pct. .159 higher than his teams', with a relative ERA of 143. He ruined his raw career numbers by hanging around about four years too long, during which he went an abysmal 16-37.

ROGER CLEMENS - With his career still in full bloom, he already ranks #17 on the Career Value list, and stands at #12 on the Peak Value list. His stats through 1994 are remarkably similar to Sandy Koufax' career numbers. Clemens is 172-93 (.649), 2.93, with 2201 strikeouts in 2394 innings. Koufax was 165-87 (.655), 2.76, with 2396 strikeouts in 2324 innings. However, there are three strong arguments in favor of Clemens when comparing the two. Though Koufax' career ERA is lower, Clemens' relative ERA of 146 is far better than Koufax' 131, and ranks behind only Lefty Grove and Walter Johnson among the Career Top 40. This is underscored by the second argument - Clemens has comparable career stats to Koufax despite the fact that he has never faced an opposing pitcher in regular season play. Lastly, Clemens' Red Sox teams have a cumulative W-L pct. of .512, giving him a .137 advantage - the best of all time. Koufax' W-L pct. exceeded that of his Dodger clubs by .094. If Clemens ages gracefully, as he should, a very strong argument will be able to be made that he was the greatest pitcher of the second half of the 20th century - and maybe the greatest of all time.

DAVID CONE - Ranks #15 on the Peak Value list, and should break into the Career Value list with a strong 1995 season. Unfortunately for Cone, he hit his peak just as the Mets were beginning to slip from theirs. During his peak seasons (1990-92) he went 41-31 for a .569 winning percentage, .074 better than the Mets, and recorded a 3.14 ERA (116 relative). His peak stats are actually quite unspectacular relative to this group. Predictably, Cone bounced back to win the 1994 AL Cy Young Award, as his power declined but his control improved, right in line with relative c/p theory. He will likely fall short of Hall of Fame numbers - 111 wins is a little low for a world-class 31-year old.

DIZZY DEAN - Ranks #28 on the Career Value list (despite only six qualifying seasons) and #18 on the Peak Value list. In a hitters' era, Dean was phenomenal before being felled by injury. His .644 winning percentage (150-83) exceeded his teams' by .088, tied for eighth among those on the career list. His relative ERA of 130 is tied for 10th among those on the peak list. Dean was equal parts power and control, and as on his way to becoming an all time great when injured. A deserving Hall of Famer.

PAUL DERRINGER - Ranks #35 on the Career Value list, and is unranked on the Peak Value list. He was an extreme control pitcher; his 4.10 career p factor ranks ahead of only Robin Roberts among those on the career list. His other numbers are also relatively mediocre; his .513 career winning percentage (223-212) exceeded his teams' by a meager .003, and his 3.46 ERA was only 108 relative to the league. He is not in the Hall of Fame, and does not deserve to be.

BOB FELLER - Ranks #22 on the Career Value list, and #13 on the Peak Value list. Would rank much higher if the guts of his career weren't ripped out by his World War II military service. His career winning percentage of .621 (266-162) exceeded his teams' by .057, and he had a 3.25 career ERA (Relative= 122). Neither figure is in the extreme top echelon, but both are in Hall of Fame territory. He went 76-33 (.697) during his peak period (1939-41), .154 better than the Indians. This differential ranks him 9th among the

Peak Value Top 40. Then he went off to war - probably preventing him from crashing the Top 10 on both lists.

BOB GIBSON - Ranks #38 on the Career Value list, and is unranked on the Peak Value list despite his incredible 1968 numbers. This was due to the general pitching dominance in this era - the raw numbers posted by Gibson that year (1.12 ERA) are spectacular in any era - but weren't as overwhelming relative to the league as most think. Gibson's relative ERA was an outstanding 127 - all 12 higher relative ERA's on the Career List belong to Hall of Famers or to Roger Clemens. His career winning percentage of .591 (251-174) was .055 higher than his teams', and is also above average at this level of competition. A deserving Hall of Famer.

LEFTY GOMEZ - Ranks #23 on the Career Value List, and #29 on the Peak Value list. He is living proof of the value of comparing a pitcher's winning percentage to his teams'. His .649 winning percentage (189-102) appears phenomenal on the surface - but is only .003 better than the remarkable .646 mark recorded by the Yankees during his career. His 3.34 ERA (Relative= 125) in a hitters' era is quite impressive, however. Also, though his career strikeout/walk ratio (1468/1095) appears quite unimpressive by today's standards, it was very good for his era. A deserving Hall of Famer.

DWIGHT GOODEN - At age 30, he is already ranked on both the Career (#39) and Peak (#38) Value lists. However, his drug and injury problems over the past few seasons will likely keep from advancing much further up the career list. At the end of 1994, Sandy Koufax, Roger Clemens and Gooden all had winning percentages between .649 and .655. Gooden's relative ERA (117) isn't quite in their league, but his winning percentage of .649 exceeded those of his teams by .108 - second to only Clemens. (Obviously, neither has endured a decline phase, unlike most of the others on the list.) Gooden's peak seasons were his first three, and were truly awesome. He went 58-19 (.753; .144 better than three very strong Mets' clubs) with a 2.28 ERA (165 relative - 6th highest on the peak list). And he has apparently ruined it all by virtue of his drug abuse.

LEFTY GROVE - Ranks #4 on the Career Value list, and #3 on the Peak Value list. What a pitcher. His amazing .680 career winning percentage (300-141) was the highest of anyone on the career list, and was .091 better than his teams' excellent .589 percentage. This is the fifth best overall differential, the third best among retired players (behind Alexander and Johnson). His career ERA of 3.06 took place within the context of the greatest hitters' era ever - his 148 relative ERA is the best of all time. During his peak period (1928-30), he went an amazing 72-19 (.791) with a 2.64 ERA - 164 relative, the 7th best such mark ever. The greatest lefty ever, and probably just a shade behind Walter Johnson for the title of "Greatest Pitcher Ever".

RON GUIDRY - Ranks #13 on the Career Value list, and #11 on the Peak Value list. In light of his relatively short career, such high rankings might seem surprising. His absence from most discussions of Hall of Fame candidates truly amazes me. OK, he only won 170 games (losing only 91, for a .651 winning percentage), but relative to his league, he was awesome in every respect. His career relative ERA of 119 is better than those of Steve Carlton, Fergie Jenkins and Gaylord Perry, among others. His career winning percentage exceeded his teams' by .078, 12th among the career top 40. His 6.61 c/p factor in 1981 was the highest since 1928. Write your congressman - Ron Guidry deserves to be in the Hall of Fame.

HARVEY HADDIX - Ranks #29 on the Career Value list, and #39 on the Peak Value list. Next to Floyd Bannister, Haddix is the single greatest anomaly on either list. His 136 wins are the fewest among all pitchers on the career list, and his relative ERA of 108 (actual= 3.63) was tied for third worst, ahead of Marquard and Lolich. However, his .546 winning percentage exceeded those of his teams by a respectable .045 over his career. Haddix is also the only pitcher to record a losing record (35-37, .486) and a sub-100 relative ERA (96) during his peak period, which extended from 1955-57. Had the stuff to be a big winner.

CARL HUBBELL - Ranks #11 on the Career Value list, and #19 on the Peak Value list. Recorded the 11th highest career c factor. His career winning percentage of .622 (253-154) exceeded his teams' by a solid .067, 14th highest on the career list. His 130 career relative ERA (actual= 2.98) ranks 10th among those on the career list. Individual season factors would have been much higher if not for the existence of Dazzy Vance in his prime. A clear Hall of Famer, and one of the greatest lefties ever.

FERGIE JENKINS - Ranks #7 on the Career Value list, and #9 on the Peak Value list. Had the 5th highest career c factor of all time, and the best one since Lefty Grove. Only pitcher in history of baseball to have over 3000 strikeouts and less than 1000 walks (997) for his career. Had a career ERA of 3.34, for a less than glittering relative ERA of 115. This was particularly due to his vulnerability to the gopher ball (.97 per nine innings), made even more remarkable by the relative scarcity of homers in the mid-to-late sixties. His .557 career winning percentage exceeded his teams' by a respectable .051. An amazingly consistent craftsman who missed only a handful of starts in his 18 consecutive seasons as an ERA qualifier (1966-83).

RANDY JOHNSON - Ranks #16 on the Peak Value list, and is 1-2 solid seasons away from appearing on the Career Value list. His 1992-94 cumulative p factor of 9.90 is the third highest peak p factor of all time (behind Vance and Waddell) - he could challenge them with a big year in 1995. Johnson never gets to face an opposing pitcher, making his ungodly whiff totals even more amazing. His teams' winning percentage during his peak period was only .447, the worst on the list. His winning percentage over that span was .611, making him an excellent +.164 over time, 6th highest on the peak list. Could move even higher up the peak chart with a big 1995.

WALTER JOHNSON - Ranks #1 on the Career Value List, and #5 on the Peak Value list. The best pitcher of all time. Period. Has the highest career c factor, and the third highest career p factor (behind Ryan and Vance). He recorded a .599 career winning percentage (417-279) despite pitching for mediocre clubs most of the time. His teams recorded a cumulative .501 winning percentage; his +.098 advantage ranks second among retired players, behind Alexander. His career ERA is an amazing 2.16; 147 relative to the league, second all time, behind Lefty Grove (148). He won 97 games in his peak period, and had a .724 winning percentage, .154 higher than his clubs'. He had an unbelievable 1.42 ERA in his peak period; an earth-shattering 219 relative to the league! By comparison, the next best relative ERA over a peak period was 182, by Alexander. His dominance may never be matched.

SANDY KOUFAX - Ranks #18 on the Career Value list (despite only eight qualifying seasons) and #7 on the Peak Value list. Only Lefty Grove and Christy Mathewson have better winning percentages among those on the career list. Of course, Koufax got out of town before his decline phase, but to the voters' credit, he was an easy Hall selection despite only 165 career wins. Unfortunately, the same standard has not been applied to Ron Guidry, a slightly watered down version of Koufax. See the Clemens comment for discussion of the similarities between Koufax and the Rocket. His last six seasons were one extended peak period, with the last couple of seasons magnified by the increasing pitching dominance throughout baseball. The highest peak value of any pitcher since Grove, but could eventually be surpassed by Clemens as the best all-around pitcher in the second half of the 20th century.

DUTCH LEONARD - Ranks #40 on the Career Value list, and is unranked on the Peak Value list. His 139 wins are the second lowest number (ahead of Harvey Haddix) on the career list, and his .554 winning percentage only equaled that of his clubs. His 115 adjusted ERA (actual= 2.76) is also unspectacular in this elite group. Had an unbelievable season in 1914, going 19-5 with the most recent sub-1.00 ERA by an ERA title qualifier (0.96). Not nearly a Hall of Fame pitcher.

MICKEY LOLICH - Ranks #21 on the Career Value list, and is unranked on the Peak Value list. He very quietly exhibited well above average power and control from the mid-60's to mid-70's. However, his

adjusted ERA (104) and winning percentage relative to his teams (+.006) rank him 39th and 34th, respectively, among the Career Top 40. His vulnerability to the longball (.86 homers per nine innings) held him back. Clearly not a Hall of Famer.

RUBE MARQUARD - Ranks #31 on the Career Value list, and is unranked on the Peak Value list. Possibly the most controversial Hall of Fame selection on the career list. His career winning percentage of .532 (201-177) exceeded his clubs' by only .002, ranking 37th among the Top 40. His 103 adjusted ERA (actual= 3.08, in a pitchers' era) ranks dead last among the Top 40. Jim Bunning, Tommy Bridges and Billy Pierce are three examples of more deserving Hall of Famers who will likely never join Marquard in Cooperstown.

CHRISTY MATHEWSON - Ranks #5 on the Career Value list, and #4 on the Peak Value list. Is at the front of the second tier of all time greats, just behind the Johnson-Grove level. Mathewson was the consummate control pitcher; his career 40.89 c factor is the second highest ever, behind Walter Johnson, who had three more qualifying seasons. His .665 career winning percentage (373-188) is second to Grove among those on the career list, and was .082 better than his clubs'. His 2.13 career ERA was below both Johnson and Grove's, but his adjusted ERA was "only" 136, 6th best ever. He was 86-29 (.748) in his peak period (1907-09), and his peak period c factor of 12.32 is second only to Cy Young. Certainly one of the top five pitchers ever, and quite likely #3.

HAL NEWHOUSER - Ranks #32 on the Career Value list, and #25 on the Peak Value list. OK, OK - so he had his best seasons during wartime, and that could be responsible for landing him on both lists. However, he did win 20 games twice after the war, and both his career winning percentage differential over his clubs' (+.055) and his adjusted ERA (130) are quite solid. His 1944-46 peak period was massive by any standard - he went 80-27 (.748), .167 better than his clubs (5th on the peak list), and his 181 adjusted peak period ERA (actual= 1.99) ranks third on the peak list. The incredible numbers posted during the war were the difference that catapulted him into the Hall of Fame.

GAYLORD PERRY - Ranks #27 on the Career Value list, and is unranked on the Peak Value list. A late bloomer, he didn't qualify for an ERA title until age 25 in 1964, but then qualified 20 straight seasons, tying Nolan Ryan for second in that category behind Don Sutton among those on the career list. An amazingly consistent hurler, he repeatedly racked up moderate c and p factors, never leading the league, and not even coming close to making the Peak Value list. His .542 winning percentage (.036 better than his clubs') and 117 adjusted ERA (actual= 3.11) only rank him in the middle of the pack in this company. He was never the best pitcher in his league, but his longevity and consistency made him a 314-game winner and deserving Hall of Famer.

DEACON PHILLIPPE - Ranks #27 on the Peak Value list, and is unranked on the Career Value list. Phillippe was an extreme control pitcher who pitched for the Pirates at the turn of the century, posting a 189-109 career record. His peak period extended from 1902-04, during which he went 55-28 (.663), exceeding his clubs' mark by only .013. He had the 8th highest c factor, but third lowest p factor, among the peak Top 40. Not in the Hall, but he is clearly a better pitcher than say, Hall of Famer Rube Marquard.

BILLY PIERCE - Ranks #30 on the Career Value list, and #33 on the Peak Value list. Very quietly assembled a long, consistent 219-win career during a hitters' era. However, his .555 winning percentage exceeded his clubs' by only .010, only 33rd on the career list. His 119 adjusted ERA matched Ron Guidry and bettered Fergie Jenkins and Steve Carlton, among others. Interestingly, his winning percentage during his 1953-55 peak period was .025 LOWER than his clubs', by far the worst on the peak list. Very similar to Jim Bunning - both are on the outside of the Hall looking in, mainly because of the hitters' eras in which they played.

EDDIE PLANK - Ranks #33 on the Career Value list, and is unranked on the Peak Value list. 326-game winner Plank never led the league in c/p factor, but

was always near the top in his 16 qualifying seasons. His .627 career winning percentage appears impressive, but is less so when compared to his clubs' .586 mark - the +.041 differential places him in the middle of the Top 40 pack. His 122 adjusted ERA (actual= 2.35) matches that of Bob Feller, and is 18th among the career Top 40. He is in the Hall of Fame more so for his longevity and consistency than for his dominance, much like Gaylord Perry.

J.R. RICHARD - Ranks #26 on the Peak Value list, and is unranked on the Career Value list. Was about halfway into what could have been one of the greatest single seasons in baseball history in 1980 when he was felled by a stroke, ending his career. In 17 starts, he had allowed 65 hits in 114 innings, with 119 whiffs and a 1.90 ERA (173 adjusted). Completion of that season would have moved substantially higher on the peak list. Unfortunately, we were only able to witness the spectacle of teams having to face knuckleballer Joe Niekro sandwiched between by Richard and Nolan Ryan for one half of a season, as Ryan joined the Astros in 1980.

ROBIN ROBERTS - Ranks #24 on the Career Value list, and #37 on the Peak Value list. Roberts fits the strictest definition of a control pitcher. He actually posted a negative career p factor, the only pitcher in the career Top 40 to do so. His c factor (29.08) ranks 8th, however. As with most extreme control pitchers, his performance tailed off sharply around age 30, so his career winning percentage relative to his team (+.039) and adjusted ERA (113) are relatively unspectacular. He was extremely durable - he was one of only four on the peak list to pitch 1000 innings during his peak period, during which he won 74 games.

CHARLIE ROOT - Ranks #36 on the Career Value list, and is unranked on the Peak Value list. Quite possibly the least ballyhooed 200-game winner of the modern era - and for good reason. His .557 career winning percentage was .025 below his clubs', and his 110 adjusted ERA (actual= 110) ranks near the bottom of the career list. He is probably best known for allowing the so-called ''called shot'' homer by Babe Ruth in the 1932 World Series. Not in the Hall, and for good reason.

SCHOOLBOY ROWE - Ranks #35 on the Peak Value list, and is unranked on the Career Value list. Rowe's peak period occurred in his first three qualifying seasons (1934-36), in what was clearly a hitters' ERA, as evidenced by his 3.86 ERA, 117 relative to the league. He won 62 games in those three seasons - but only 87 in the next thirteen. He is yet another example of a young control pitcher who fizzled as his relatively meager power deteriorated - he never again struck out 100 batters in a season after his last peak season.

RED RUFFING - Ranks #26 on the Career Value list, and is unranked on the Peak Value list. After five full major league seasons, it sure didn't look like this guy was headed to the Hall of Fame. He was an amazing 39-93 pitching for some woeful Red Sox teams. Getting traded to the Yanks just in time for the '30's worked wonders. He was clearly overrated because of his presence on the Yanks - his career winning percentage (273-225, .548) lagged his clubs' by .005, while his adjusted ERA of 109 (actual= 3.80) was relatively mediocre. He's in the Hall because of his presence on the Yankees and his longevity - if Bert Blyleven, Don Sutton, Phil Niekro, Tommy John, etc. don't get in the Hall, it's a crime.

NOLAN RYAN - Ranks #2 on the Career Value list, and #14 on the Peak Value list. Anyone with 5714 career K's has to be near the top of the career list. What is surprising is his subpar relative ERA (112), by far the lowest among the career Top 10, and relative winning percentage (only .022 above his teams, also lowest among the career Top 10). Amazingly, his peak period occurred from ages 42-44! This sums up his career - he has done some incredible things which will never be equaled, but in no way does that make him one of the top 10 pitchers in history. At no time in his career could he unequivocally have been called the best pitcher in baseball.

MIKE SCOTT - Ranks #24 on the Peak Value list, and is unranked on the Career Value list. Was a pretty rotten pitcher (29-44) with the Mets before going to

the Astros and being introduced to the split-fingered fastball. In the words of Darrell Strawberry, Mike Scott was "kicking some high butt out there" in the 1986 NLCS. Scott went 48-31 (.608; .085 better than the Astros) with a 2.76 (134 adjusted) ERA from 1986-88. Added one more decent season in 1989, then flamed out. Guys with trick out pitches (except knuckleballers) have a limited period of excellence before their arms blow out or the league adjusts.

TOM SEAVER - Ranks #8 on the Career Value list, and #10 on the Peak Value list. Ranks in the very top echelon of pitchers from the second half of the century, along with Koufax and Clemens. He had a career ERA of 2.86 (127 adjusted), and his career winning percentage of .603 (311-205) was .088 better than his teams', seventh among the career Top 40. His peak period extended from 1971-73, and his 162 adjusted ERA (2.23 actual) over that span ranks eighth among the peak Top 40. A deserving first ballot Hall of Famer.

URBAN SHOCKER - Ranks #28 on the Peak Value list, and is unranked on the Career Value list. He thrived in a great hitters' era, posting a 3.17 career ERA (124 adjusted). His 346/158 peak K/BB ratio, and 983/657 career K/BB ratio aren't eye-catching, but they were fantastic when placed in the context of the 1920's in the AL. His 9.28 peak c factor ranks 11th among the peak Top 40. He won 187 games in his career despite not establishing himself until age 29, and then dying at age 38. Clearly a better pitcher than Marquard and others who are in the Hall of Fame, but is on the outside looking in. He won 20 games four straight years for generally mediocre St. Louis Browns clubs.

MARIO SOTO - Ranks #32 on the Peak Value list, and is unranked on the Career Value list. Was overpowering, but unlucky, during his peak period, going only 36-30 (.545) from 1980-82. Over that span he had a 3.02 ERA (120 adjusted), on the low end among ranked pitchers. After his peak period he had three more good seasons for generally weak Reds' clubs, but was then derailed by shoulder troubles at age 29. Stripped of his power, he was a mere shell of his former self in parts of three seasons thereafter.

DON SUTTON - Ranks #12 on the Career Value list, and is unranked on the Peak Value list. Qualified for more ERA titles (22) than any pitcher on either list. Had 11th best c factor on career list, third best in last forty years. Only won 20 games once, and was never recognized as one of top two or three pitchers in baseball, even in his prime. Had a career 3.26 ERA - only 108 adjusted, well below all of the pitchers ranked ahead of him on the career list. His winning percentage (324-256; .559) only exceeded his clubs' by .026, also subpar. He is most comparable to Gaylord Perry, and like him, deserves to be in the Hall of Fame based on his consistency over a very long period of time. You can't argue with 324 wins.

FRANK TANANA - Ranks #8 on the Peak Value list, and is unranked on the Career value list. No one seems to remember what an incredible pitcher he was as a youngster, routinely outpitching teammate Nolan Ryan. Between 1975-77, Tanana went 50-28 (.641) for teams that had a cumulative winning percentage of .458. This differential of .183 ranked him 3rd among those on the peak list. His power dropped way off in 1978, and the reason became evident in 1979 - major shoulder problems. What was shaping up as a surefire hall of Fame career became simply a very good one. A 240-game winner, but certainly not a Hall of Famer, with his .506 career winning percentage and 105 adjusted ERA (actual= 3.67).

VIRGIL TRUCKS - Ranks #37 on the Career Value list, and is unranked on the Peak Value list. Quietly put together a 177-win career despite losing two seasons to wartime early in his career. Trucks .567 winning percentage was better than his teams' by .036, and he had a 117 adjusted ERA (actual= 3.39) - all very good but unspectacular marks. Was probably never the best pitcher on his staff - he was in the shadow of Hal Newhouser in Detroit and Billy Pierce in Chicago, who both were in their prime when Trucks was their teammate. Not a Hall of Famer, on merit.

DAZZY VANCE - Ranks #3 on the Career value list, and #1 on the Peak Value list. Surprised? Consider this ..... Dazzy Vance had the 1st, 2nd and 5th highest single-season c/p factors in 1924, 1925 and 1928. Only two NL pitchers had greater than 100 strikeouts in 1924 when Vance set the all-time c/p record (9.18) - and Vance struck out 262! (Burleigh Grimes whiffed 135.) And get this.... Vance didn't crack a big league rotation until age 31! His career mark of 197-140 seems relatively tame at first glance, but his .585 winning percentage exceeded that of his clubs by .086 - Vance's teams had a .499 cumulative winning percentage; he is the only pitcher on the career list to pitch on teams with a cumulative losing record. His .702 peak period winning percentage exceeded his clubs' by .200, easily the highest mark of anyone on the peak list. Dazzy Vance utterly dominated hitters in an era when hitters utterly dominated pitchers. He is deservedly in the Hall of Fame, and had he either made the majors 8-10 earlier, or pitched for better clubs, he would be right there with the all-time greats.

JOHNNY VANDERMEER - Ranks #34 on the Peak Value list, and is unranked on the Career value list. And you thought that all he was good for was consecutive no-hitters? Vandermeer's peak period (1941-43) occurred predominantly during wartime, somewhat inflating his impact. He led the league in strikeouts all three years, and his peak p factor (8.95) ranks 7th among the peak Top 40. He went off to war for the next two seasons, and was never the same afterwards. He finished up with a losing career record (119-121).

RUBE WADDELL - Ranks #9 on the Career Value list (despite losing a qualifying season to the 1901 cutoff), and #2 on the Peak Value list. Waddell was borderline psychotic, according to many, but he was the first great power pitcher. He recorded the 3rd highest c/p factor ever, way back in 1902. Both his winning percentage (.574) and his teams' (.537) are exactly equal to Steve Carlton's corresponding figures. His 135 adjusted ERA (2.16 actual) ranks 7th among those on the career list. He was the chief competitor to Cy Young in the early 1900's, going 70-42 with a 155 adjusted ERA (2.01 actual) in his 1902-04 peak period. Like Dazzy Vance, he didn't win 200 games (193-143), but deservedly made the Hall of Fame because of sheer dominance.

ED WALSH - Ranks #34 on the Career Value list (despite only seven qualifying seasons), and #22 on the Peak Value list. Oh, what could have been......Ed Walsh finished his career with an unbelievable 1.82 ERA (145 adjusted - 4th behind Grove, Johnson, Clemens), and a .607 winning percentage (195-126), .072 better than his clubs' cumulative winning percentage. Virtually all of this was accomplished by age 31 - in 1913, Walsh was shut down with a sore arm, after pitching between 369 and 464 innings in five of the six seasons between 1907-12. In his 1910-12 peak period, he had a 161 adjusted ERA (1.89 actual). Walsh's peak period covered the exact span as that of Smokey Joe Wood - who pitched in the same league, and who suffered a similar demise, as you shall see in the next section.

SMOKY JOE WOOD - Ranks #23 on the Peak Value list (right behind his twin, Walsh), and is unranked on the Career Value list. Smokey Joe was 69-35 (.663) - .087 better than his Red Sox teams over that span. His 1.89 ERA over that period exactly matched Walsh's over the exact same period. In the ultimate irony, both Walsh and Wood were injured the following spring, effectively ending their days of dominance. Sadly, Wood was only 23 years old at the time. He finished his career 116-57, 1.89 - his 146 adjusted ERA is right behind Grove and Johnson, the all-time leaders. Smoky Joe Wood was on his way to becoming perhaps the game's greatest pitcher, but instead settled in for the better part of another decade as an outfielder.

CY YOUNG - Ranks #16 on the Career Value list (despite losing 10 qualifying seasons to the 1901 cutoff), and #6 on the Peak Value list. Well, now I know why they named an award after this guy. His astronomical wins and losses totals (511-316) were largely a product of three-man rotations, but there is no denying his longevity (20 qualifying seasons) or his effectiveness. His .618 winning percentage exceeded his clubs' by .090, 7th all-time. His 138 career adjusted ERA ranks 5th behind Grove, Johnson, Clemens and Walsh among those on the career list. By a quirk, his "peak" period included his 1906 season, in which he went 13-21, 3.19, but had a 140/25 K/BB ratio, rendering his peak period stats somewhat meaningless. If his full career were included, he would likely move into the #4 spot on the career list. Relative to his peers, I doubt that he was as dominant as Johnson or Grove, but he is certainly in the next group, with Christy Mathewson.

RETROSHEET

Organizational Description

Modern baseball analysis has grown increasingly sophisticated in the past decade and a number of new statistical categories have come into common usage among announcers and writers. All of these new methods require detailed play by play data for current games and several statistical organizations actively collect this information. Many fans would like to compare modern player performances to those from earlier this century but have been unable to do so, since play by play accounts have never been collected or organized in a systematic way. Therefore, a new organization, called Retrosheet, was founded in 1989 for the purpose of computerizing play by play accounts of as many pre-1984 major league games as possible (data for games since 1984 are available through the Project Scoresheet-Baseball Workshop data base).

Retrosheet's work has three distinct aspects. First is the collection of the game accounts, which have been obtained from several sources. The bulk of the collection has come from major league teams (24 to date) which have allowed us to make copies of their play by play accounts. Several sportswriters (most of them retired) have allowed copies to be made of their daily scorebooks. In addition, individual fans have donated copies of programs they scored at the park or on their own scoresheets at home. The second activity is the translation of these accounts to a unified, modern system, which is essential since there is an extraordinary variety of scoring systems which have been used. The final activity is the entry of the translated accounts into the computer. Retrosheet

has been very successful in the collection of game accounts with more than 100,000 currently in hand. A group of some 100 volunteers is actively involved in the translation work and the computer entry. However, the task ahead is enormous and we are always looking for more volunteers; any offers of help are greatly appreciated. Baseball fans interested in this historical effort are invited to volunteer their assistance in the translation and inputting efforts as well as to make available copies of game accounts they might have.

The ultimate objective of Retrosheet is to make this basic play by play information publicly available for all interested researchers. Several methods for data distribution will be followed, including depositing the final material in the Hall of Fame Library in Cooperstown. Additionally, electronic posting of some form is under serious consideration.

In order to volunteer or to obtain more information, contact David Smith at:
Retrosheet 6 Penncross Circle Newark, DE 19702